ON UGLINESS

ALSO BY UMBERTO ECO

ON UGLINESS

EDITED BY

UMBERTO ECO

TRANSLATED FROM THE ITALIAN
BY ALASTAIR McEWEN

Harvill *Secker*
LONDON

Published by Harvill Secker 2007

2 4 6 8 10 9 7 5 3

English translation copyright © Alastair McEwen 2007

First published with the title Storia della brutezza in 2007
by Bompiani, Milan

First published in Great Britain in 2007 by
HARVILL SECKER, Random House
20 Vauxhall Bridge Road
London SW1V 2SA

www.rbooks.co.uk

Addresses for companies within The Random House Group Limited
can be found at: www.randomhouse.co.uk/offices.htm

The Random House Group Limited Reg. No. 954009

A CIP catalogue record for this book is available from the British Library

ISBN 9781846551222

The Random House Group Limited makes every effort to ensure that
the papers used in its books are made from trees that have been
legally sourced from well-managed and credibly certified forests.
Our paper procurement policy can be found:
www.randomhouse.co.uk/paper.htm

Printed by G. Canale Borgaro Torinese (TO)

Editorial Director
Elisabetta Sgarbi

Editorial Coordination
Anna Maria Lorusso

Graphic Design
Polystudio

Typesetting
Paola Bertozzi

Picture Research
Silvia Borghesi

Production
Sergio Daniotti

© 2007 RCS Libri S.p.A., Bompiani

CONTENTS

ON UGLINESS

Introduction

In every century, philosophers and artists have supplied definitions of beauty, and thanks to their works it is possible to reconstruct a history of aesthetic ideas over time. But this did not happen with ugliness. Most of the time it was defined as the opposite of beauty but almost no one ever devoted a treatise of any length to ugliness, which was relegated to passing mentions in marginal works. Hence, while a history of beauty can draw on a wide range of theoretical sources (from which we can deduce the tastes of a given epoch), for the most part a history of ugliness must seek out its own documents in the visual or verbal portrayals of things or people that are in some way seen as 'ugly'. Nonetheless, a history of ugliness shares some common characteristics with a history of beauty. First, we can only *assume* that the tastes of ordinary people corresponded in some way with the tastes of the artists of their day. If a visitor from space went into a gallery of contemporary art, and if he saw women's faces painted by Picasso and heard onlookers describing them as 'beautiful', he might get the mistaken idea that in everyday life the men of our time find female creatures with faces like those painted by Picasso beautiful and desirable.

But our visitor from space might modify his opinion on watching a fashion show or the Miss Universe contest, in which he would witness the celebration of other models of beauty. Unfortunately, when revisiting times long past, this is what we cannot do – either in relation to beauty or ugliness – because all that is left to us of those periods are works of art.

Another characteristic common to both the history of ugliness and that of beauty is that we are restricted to discussing the story of these two values in Western civilisation. For archaic civilisations and for the

called primitive peoples we have artistic finds but we have no theoretical texts to tell us if these were intended to cause aesthetic delight, holy fear, or hilarity.

To a Westerner an African ritual mask might seem hair-raising – while for a native it might represent a benevolent divinity. Conversely, believers in some non-European religion might be disgusted by the image of Christ scourged, bleeding and humiliated, while this apparent corporeal ugliness might arouse sympathy and emotion in a Christian.

In the case of other cultures, with a wealth of poetic and philosophical texts (such as Indian, Chinese, or Japanese culture), we see images and forms but, on translating their works of literature and philosophy, it is almost always difficult to establish to what extent certain concepts can be identified with our own, although tradition has induced us to translate them into Western terms such as 'beautiful' or 'ugly'. Even if the translations were reliable, it would not be enough to know that in a certain culture something that possesses, for example, proportion and harmony, was seen as beautiful. Proportion and harmony. What do we mean by these terms? Even in the course of Western history their meaning has changed. It is only by comparing theoretical statements with a picture or an architectonic structure from the period that we notice that what was considered proportionate in one century was no longer seen as such in another; on the subject of proportion, for example, a medieval philosopher would think of the dimensions and the form of a Gothic cathedral, while a Renaissance theoretician would think of a sixteenth century temple, whose parts were governed by the golden section – and Renaissance man saw the proportions of cathedrals as barbarous, as the term 'Gothic' amply suggests.

Dance mask,
Ekoi (Eastern Nigeria),
New York,
Tishman Collection

Concepts of beauty and ugliness are relative to various historical periods or various cultures and, to quote Xenophanes of Colophon (according to Clement of Alexandria, *Stromata*, V, 110), 'But had the oxen or the lions hands, or could with hands depict a work like men, were beasts to draw the semblance of the gods, the horses would them like to horses sketch, to oxen, oxen, and their bodies make of such a shape as to themselves belongs.'

In the Middle Ages, James of Vitry (*Libri duo, quorum prior Orientalis, sive Hjyerosolimitanae, alter Occidentalis istoria*), in praising the Beauty of all the divine works, admitted that 'probably the Cyclops, who have only one eye, are amazed by those who have two of them, just as we marvel both at them and at creatures with three eyes ... We find black Ethiopians to be ugly, but among them it is the blackest who is considered the most beautiful.' Centuries later, this was echoed by Voltaire (in his *Philosophical Dictionary*): 'Ask a toad what beauty is, true beauty, the *tokalòn*. He will tell you that it consists of his mate, with her two fine round eyes protruding from her small head, her broad flat throat, her yellow belly and brown back. Ask a Negro from Guinea: for him beauty is a black oily skin, deep-sunk eyes, and a flat nose.

'Ask the devil: he will tell you that beauty is a pair of horns, four claws, and a tail.'

In his *Aesthetics*, Hegel notes: 'It may happen that whereas not every husband may find his wife beautiful, at least every young swain finds his sweetheart beautiful, indeed to the exclusion of all others; and if the subjective taste for this Beauty has no fixed rules, then we may consider this a good thing for both parties ... We often hear it said that a European Beauty would not please a Chinese, or even a Hottentot, insofar as the Chinese have a completely different concept of Beauty from the Negroes ... In fact, if we contemplate the works of art of these non-European peoples, the images of their deities, for example, images that have sprung from their fancy as sublime and worthy of veneration, they may strike us as the most hideous of idols. In the same way, just as the music of such peoples may strike us as a detestable racket, so in their turn will they consider our sculptures, pictures, and music as meaningless or ugly.'

Attributions of beauty or ugliness are often due not to aesthetic but to socio-political criteria. There is a passage in Marx (*Economic and philosophical Manuscripts*, 1844) in which he points out how the possession of money may compensate for ugliness: 'As money has the property of being able to buy anything, to take possession of all objects, it is therefore the pre-eminent object worth having ... The extent of my power is as great as the power of the money I possess ... What I am and what I can do is therefore not determined by my individuality in the slightest. I am ugly, but I can buy myself the most beautiful of women. Hence I am not ugly, since the effect of ugliness, its discouraging power, is annulled by money. As an individual I am lame, but money gives me twenty-four legs: hence I am not lame ... Does my money not transform all my defects into their opposite?'

Now, if we extend these observations on money to power in general we can understand certain portraits of monarchs of centuries past, devotedly immortalised by fawning painters who certainly had no intention of over-emphasising their defects, and who perhaps even did their utmost to refine their features. There is no doubt that such personages strike us as being very ugly (and probably they were thought to be so even in their own day) but their omnipotence lent them such charisma and glamour that their subjects saw them through adoring eyes.

Finally, if we read Fredric Brown's 'Sentinel', one of the finest short stories produced by contemporary science fiction, we see how the relationship between normal and monstrous, acceptable and horrific, may be turned

on its head depending on the point of view: whether it is we who are looking at the space monster or whether it is the monster who is looking at us: 'I was soaked to the skin and up to the eyes in mud and I was hungry and cold and I was fifty thousand light-years far from home.

'A foreign sun emitted an icy bluish light and the gravity, double what I was used to, made the slightest movement weary and painful ... It was very easy for the air force, with brilliant spacecrafts and superweapons, but when one arrived there, it fell to the infantryman to take and hold

from left to right
Anonymous,
*John the Fearless,
Duke of Burgundy*,
first quarter
of the fifteenth century,
Paris, Louvre

Diego Velázquez,
*Portrait of Philip IV
of Spain*,
1655,
Madrid, Prado Museum

The French School,
Portrait of Louis XI,
seventeenth century,
Paris

Luca Giordano (attr.),
*Portrait of Charles II
of Spain*,
1692,
Madrid, Prado Museum

*Portrait of Henry IV,
King of France
and Navarre*,
seventeenth century,
Versailles,
Musée National
du Château de Pau

Henri Lehmann,
*Portrait of Charles VII,
known as the Victorious,
King of France*,
nineteenth century,
Versailles, Chateaux de
Versailles et de Trianon

the position, with blood, inch by inch. Like this bloody planet of a star we had not heard of until we landed on it. And now it was holy ground because the enemy had come. The enemy, the only other intelligent race in the galaxy … cruel, repulsive, hideous creatures, horrible monsters … I was soaked to the skin and up to the eyes in mud and I was hungry and cold; the day was livid, the wind was blowing so hard that it hurt my eyes. But the enemies were trying to infiltrate and all the positions were vital. I was alert, the gun ready … Then I saw one of them creeping towards me. I aimed my weapon and opened fire on it. The enemy gave that strange horrible cry that all of them used to utter. Then a deathly silence. It was dead. The cry and the sight of the dead body made me shudder. In the course of time, many of us had become accustomed, took no notice of that; but not me. They were horrible disgusting creatures, with only two legs, two arms, two eyes, that sickening white skin and without scales …'

Saying that beauty and ugliness are relative to different times and cultures (or even to different planets) doesn't mean that people haven't always tried to see them as defined with respect to a stable model.

Agnolo Bronzino,
*The Dwarf Morgante
from the Back with
an Owl on his Shoulder,*
sixteenth century,
Florence, Galleria
Palatina

One might even suggest, as Nietzsche did in his *Twilight of the Idols* that 'when it comes to beauty, man posits himself as the norm of perfection' and 'he worships himself in this … At bottom man mirrors himself in things and sees as beautiful all things that reflect his image …Ugliness is seen as a sign and a symptom of degeneration … Every suggestion of exhaustion, heaviness, senility, fatigue, any sort of lack of freedom, like convulsions or paralysis, especially the smell, the colour, the form of dissolution, of decomposition … all this provokes an identical reaction, the value judgement "ugly" … What does man hate? There is no doubt about this: he hates *the twilight of his own type.*'

Nietzsche's argument is narcissistically anthropomorphous, but it does tell us that beauty and ugliness are defined with reference to a 'specific' model – and the notion of species can be extended from men to all things, as Plato does in the *Republic*, by agreeing to define as beautiful a pot made according to the correct rules of the art, or as Thomas Aquinas (*Summa Teologica*, I, 39, 8) does by stating that beauty is the result not only of due proportion, brightness or clarity but also of *integrity* – hence an object (be it a human body, a tree, or a vase) must have all the characteristics that its *form* has imposed upon the material. In this sense, not only was the term ugly applied to anything that was out of proportion, like a human being with an enormous head and very short legs, it was also used to describe the beings that Aquinas defined as 'shameful' inasmuch as they were 'diminished', or – as William of Auvergne was to put it (in his *Treatise on Good and Evil*) – those who lacked a limb or had only one eye (or even three, because you can be lacking in integrity by excess too). Consequently, the label 'ugly' was ruthlessly applied to freaks of nature, often mercilessly portrayed by artists. The same held for those hybrids of the animal kingdom whose appearance was an infelicitous blend of the formal aspects of two different species.

Can ugliness therefore continue to be simply defined as the opposite of beauty, albeit an opposite that changes along with modifications in the idea of its opposite? Can a history of ugliness be seen as the symmetrical foil of a history of beauty?

The first and most complete *Aesthetic of Ugliness*, written in 1853 by Karl Rosenkrantz, draws an analogy between ugliness and moral evil. Just as evil and sin are the opposites of good, whose hell they represent, so is ugliness the 'hell of beauty'. Rosenkrantz reverts to the traditional notion that ugliness is the opposite of beauty, a kind of possible error that beauty holds within itself, so that any aesthetic or science of beauty is also obliged to tackle the concept of ugliness. But it is precisely when he moves on from abstract definitions to a phenomenology of the various incarnations of ugliness that he gives us a glimpse of a kind of 'autonomy of ugliness', which makes it far richer and more complex than a series of simple negations of the various forms of beauty.

Rosenkrantz performs a meticulous analysis of ugliness in nature, spiritual ugliness, ugliness in art (and the various forms of artistic incorrectness), the absence of form, asymmetry, disharmony, disfigurement and deformation (the wretched, the vile, the banal, the fortuitous and the arbitrary, the gross), the various forms of the repugnant (the ungainly, death and the void, the horrendous, the vacuous, the sickening, the felonious, the spectral, the demoniac, the witchlike and the satanic). Too much to allow us to carry on saying that ugliness is merely the opposite of beauty understood as harmony, proportion, or integrity.

Mathias Grünewald,
*The Temptations
of St Anthony,*
a detail from the altar at
Isenheim,
1515,
Colmar,
Musée Unterlinden

If we examine the synonyms of *beautiful* and *ugly*, we see that while what is considered *beautiful* is: pretty, cute, pleasing, attractive, agreeable, lovely, delightful, fascinating, harmonious, marvellous, delicate, graceful, enchanting, magnificent, stupendous, sublime, exceptional, fabulous, wonderful, fantastic, magical, admirable, exquisite, spectacular, splendid and superb; what is *ugly* is: repellent, horrible, horrendous, disgusting, disagreeable, grotesque, abominable, repulsive, odious, indecent, foul, dirty, obscene, repugnant, frightening, abject, monstrous, horrid, horrifying, unpleasant, terrible, terrifying, frightful, nightmarish, revolting, sickening, foetid, fearsome, ignoble, ungainly, displeasing, tiresome, offensive, deformed and disfigured (not to mention how horror can also manifest itself in areas traditionally assigned to the beautiful, such as the fabulous, the fantastic, the magical and the sublime).

The sensibility of the common speaker reveals that, whereas all the synonyms for *beautiful* could be conceived as a reaction of disinterested appreciation, almost all the synonyms for *ugly* contain a reaction of disgust, if not of violent repulsion, horror, or fear.

In his essay *The Expression of the Emotions in Man and Animals*, Darwin pointed out that what arouses disgust in a given culture does not arouse it in another, and vice versa, but he concluded that nonetheless 'it appears that the various movements, which have now been described as expressing contempt and disgust, prevail throughout a large part of the world'.

We have certainly seen ostentatious manifestations of approval for something that strikes us as beautiful because it is physically desirable. Just think of the vulgar remarks made when a beautiful woman passes by or the glutton's unseemly expressions of joy at the sight of his favourite food. But in these cases we are not dealing with expressions of aesthetic pleasure so much as something similar to the grunts of satisfaction or even the belches emitted in certain cultures in order to express appreciation of a food (even though in such cases it is a form of etiquette). In general, in any case, it seems that the experience of beauty arouses what Kant (in his *Critique of Judgement*) defined as *disinterested pleasure*: whereas we would like *to have* all that seems agreeable to us or *to take part in* all that seems good, the judgement of taste at the sight of a flower procures a pleasure that excludes any desire for possession or consumption.

Hence certain philosophers have wondered whether it is possible to make an aesthetic judgement of ugliness, given that it arouses emotional reactions such as the disgust described by Darwin.

In truth, in the course of our history, we ought to distinguish between manifestations of ugliness in itself (excrement, decomposing carrion, or someone covered with sores who gives off a nauseating stench) from those of *formal ugliness*, understood as a lack of equilibrium in the organic relationship between the parts of a whole.

Domenico Ghirlandaio, *Portrait of an Old Man with his Grandson,* c.1490 Paris, Louvre

Let's imagine we see an almost toothless person in the street: what disturbs us is not the form of the lips or the few remaining teeth, but the fact that the few survivors are not accompanied by the others that *should be* in that mouth. We do not know this person, whose ugliness does not involve us emotionally, yet – faced with the inconsistency or incompleteness of that whole – we feel entitled to say dispassionately that that face is ugly.

This is why it is one thing to react emotionally to the disgust aroused in us by a slimy insect or a rotten piece of fruit, while it is another to describe a person as disproportioned or to say that a portrait is ugly in the sense that it is badly made (artistic ugliness and formal ugliness).

And, talking of artistic ugliness, let us remember that in almost all aesthetic theories, at least from ancient Greece to modern times, it has been recognised that any form of ugliness can be redeemed by a faithful and efficacious artistic portrayal. Aristotle (*Poetics* 1448 b) talks of the possibility of creating beauty through a masterful imitation of that which is repulsive and in Plutarch (*De audiendis poetis*) we read that, in artistic portrayals, imitated ugliness remains such but receives a kind of echo of beauty thanks to the mastery of the artist.

Thus we have identified three different phenomena: *ugliness in itself, formal ugliness* and *the artistic portrayal of both.* What should be borne in mind while leafing through this book is that in a given culture we can almost always infer what the first two types of ugliness were solely on the basis of evidence of the third type.

In doing this we run the risk of many misunderstandings. In the Middle Ages Bonaventure of Bagnoregio wrote that the image of the devil becomes beautiful if it is a good portrayal of his ugliness: but did the faithful who saw scenes of atrocious infernal torments on church doors or frescoes really believe this? Did they not perhaps react with terror and distress, as if they had seen ugliness of the first type, bloodcurdling and repugnant as the sight of a menacing reptile might be for us?

Theoreticians often fail to consider countless personal variables, idiosyncrasies and deviant behaviour. While it is true that the experience of beauty implies disinterested contemplation, nonetheless a disturbed adolescent might have an emotional reaction even on looking at the Venus de Milo. The same holds for ugliness: a child can have a nightmare about the witch he saw in a book of fairy tales, an image that may have been merely amusing for his peers. Probably many contemporaries of Rembrandt, rather than appreciating the mastery with which he depicted a dissected cadaver on a mortuary slab, might have had horrified reactions as if the corpse were real – just as someone who has lived through an air raid may not be able to look at Picasso's *Guernica* in an aesthetically disinterested way, and may be able only to relive the terror of his past experience.

Hence the caution we ought to use in following this history of ugliness, ugliness in all its varieties and multiple forms, the diverse reactions that those various forms arouse, and the nuances of behaviour with which we react to them. We should also consider, each time, how right the witches were – if indeed they were right – when, in the first act of Macbeth, they cry: 'Fair is foul and foul is fair ...'

Heinrich Füssli,
*Macbeth Consults
the Apparition
of a Helmeted Head,*
1783,
Washington DC,
Folger Shakespeare
Library

*Names or words printed **in bold** characters in the various chapters refer to the corresponding anthological quotations*

Chapter I

Ugliness in the Classical World

1. A World Dominated by Beauty?

Of the Greek world we usually have a stereotyped image, which springs from idealisations of that world produced during the neoclassical period. In our museums we see statues of Aphrodite or Apollo that, thanks to the whiteness of the marble, portray an idealised beauty. In the fourth century BC, Policlitus created a statue that was to become known as the *Canon* because it embodies all the rules of ideal proportion, while Vitruvius was later to express correct bodily proportions as fractions of the entire figure: the face was to be one tenth of the total length, the head one eighth, the length of the torso one quarter, and so on.

So, in the light of this idea of beauty, it's natural that all beings who did not embody such proportions were thought of as ugly. The ancients had idealised beauty, but neoclassicism idealised the ancients, forgetting that they (often influenced by Oriental traditions) also bequeathed the Western tradition images of beings who were the very embodiment of disproportion, and the negation of all canons.

The Greek ideal of perfection was represented by the *kalokagathia*, a term deriving from the union of *kalos* (generically translated as 'beautiful') and *agathos* (which is usually translated as 'good' but covers a whole series of positive values). It has been pointed out that being *kalos* and *agathos* generically defines what the English world would later describe as a *gentleman*, a person with a dignified air possessed of courage, style, ability, and proven sporting, military, and moral virtues. In view of this ideal, Greek culture produced a vast literature on the relationship between physical ugliness and moral ugliness.

Bronze statue of a satyr, Second half of the fourth century BC, Munich, Staatsliche Antikensammlungen und Glyptothek

Nonetheless it is still not clear whether by 'beautiful' the ancients meant everything that pleases, arouses admiration, draws the eye, and gratifies the senses thanks to its form, or a 'spiritual' beauty, a quality of the soul, which sometimes may not coincide with the beauty of the body. At bottom, the expedition to Troy was motivated by Helen's extraordinary beauty and paradoxically Gorgias had written an encomium on Helen. Yet Helen, the unfaithful wife of Menelaus, certainly could not be considered a model of virtue.

While **Plato** believed that the only reality was that of the world of Ideas, of which our material world is a shadow and imitation, then ugliness ought to have been identified with non-being, given that in the *Parmenides* he rejects the existence of ideas of foul or base things such as stains, mud or hairs. Ugliness exists, therefore, only in the sensible order, as an aspect of the imperfection of the physical universe compared to the ideal world. Later,

Plotinus, who more radically defined matter as evil and an error, was to identify ugliness clearly with the material world.

For example, if we reread the *Symposium* and the Platonic dialogue dedicated to Eros (as love) and to beauty, we may identify many other nuances. In this dialogue, as in the others for that matter, and–generally speaking–in almost all philosophical disquisitions on beauty and ugliness, these values are named but never clarified through examples (hence the necessity, as I said in the Introduction, to compare philosophical discourses with the concrete creations of artists). It's hard to describe the beautiful things that arouse our desire. As for the concept of good, in many respects the dialogue hinges on a celebration of *pederasty*, in the etymological sense of love of the beauty of young boys on the part of a wise, mature man. This behaviour was generally accepted in Greek society, but the dialogue itself reveals that the pederasty praised by Pausanias (carnal desire for the beauty

Ideas about Ugly Things
Plato (fifth – fourth century BC)
Parmenides, 130

Parmenides proceeded: And would you also make absolute ideas of the just and the beautiful and the good, and of all that class?

Yes, said Socrates, I should.

And would you make an idea of man apart from us and from all other human creatures, or of fire and water?

I am often undecided, Parmenides, as to whether I ought to include them or not.

And would you feel equally undecided, Socrates, about things of which the mention may provoke a smile? I mean such things as hair, mud, dirt, or anything else which is vile and paltry; would you suppose that each of these has an idea distinct from the actual objects with which we come into contact, or not?

Certainly not, said Socrates; visible things like these are such as they appear to us, and I am afraid that there would be an absurdity in assuming any idea of them
[. . .]

Moral Ugliness
Plotinus (third century AD)
The Enneads, 1, 6

Let us consider an ugly soul, intemperate and unjust. It is full of a great number of desires and the most profound anxieties. Fearful out of cowardice, envious out of meanness of spirit [. . .] it lives the life of the passions of the body and finds pleasure only in ugliness. Would we not say that the ugliness of this soul has come upon it from the outside like an illness that harms it, makes it impure and turns it into a confused tangle of ills? [. . .] The soul lives a life in the shadow of the impurity of evil, a life contaminated by the germs of death. It is no longer able to see what a soul must see: it can no longer repose within its own being because it is constantly drawn to external things, which are inferior and darker than the night. Impure, overwhelmed on all sides by the attraction of sensible things, it has blended with many characteristics of the body. Since the soul has accepted the form of matter, which is different from it, it has been contaminated by it, and its very nature has been polluted by that which is inferior to it [. . .]

of young men) and the sublimated (today we would say 'platonic') pederasty of Socrates are two different things.

Pausanias distinguishes the Eros of Aphrodite Pandemia, typical of men of little consequence for whom loving women and young men is all the same, and who love bodies more than souls, from the Eros of Aphrodite Urania, which is love solely for young men. Not with inexperienced little boys but with mature adolescents 'whose beards have begun to grow'. But Pausanias himself admits that among young men one should love the noblest and most virtuous ('even if they are uglier than the others'), and so a lover who loves the body more than the soul is wicked. In this sense, while pederasty does not exclude a physical relationship, it is also a form of erotico-philosophical alliance established between the beloved (the young man who accepts the company of an older man who initiates him into both wisdom and adult life, and to whom in exchange he offers his favours) and the lover, the wise man enamoured of the good looks and virtues of the young man.

After Pausanias, Aristophanes steps in to tell us how in the beginning there were three genders, male, female and androgyne, and only after Zeus had divided each into two, did there come along men who 'love to embrace other men', women 'with a propensity for other women' (and these two

Centaurs at the Court of King Pirithous, wall painting from Pompeii, first century AD, Naples, Museo Archaeologico Nazionale

categories 'are uninterested in nuptials and the procreation of children, but are obliged to take an interest by law'), and those whom—today we would call heterosexuals. At this point Agathon comes into the dialogue. Agathon represented Eros as eternally young and handsome (thus returning to a recurrent theme in the Greek world, from Pindar onwards, whereby beauty is accompanied by youth and ugliness by old age).

But then Socrates (who expresses his own ideas by attributing them to a fictional priestess called Diotima) showed that, if each of us desires what he does not have, Eros will be neither beautiful nor good, but a kind of ambiguous 'daimon', a striving towards ideal values that he forever fails to attain. Eros is the son of Penia (Lack, Poverty) and Poros (Expediency) and as such he has inherited his mother's wretched look (he is shaggy, barefoot and homeless), while from his father he has inherited the ability to 'stalk' and 'hunt for' that which is good. In this sense, the desire to procreate, to satisfy the human desire for immortality, is typical of Eros. Nonetheless, apart from physical procreation there is the procreation of spiritual values, from poetry to philosophy, through which we obtain the immortality of glory. One might say that ordinary folk produce children while those who cultivate the aristocracy of the spirit produce beauty and wisdom.

In the light of this not only is the man who is *kalos* and *agathos* one who

from left to right
Terracotta bust
of a Silen,
third–first century BC,
Munich,
Antikesammlungen

Portrait of Socrates,
sixth century BC,
Selcuk (Turkey),
Ephesos Museum

facing page
Antony Van Dyck,
Drunken Satyr,
*c.*1620,
Dresden, Gemälde
Galerie, Alte Meister
Staatliche
Kunstsammlungen

believes that 'the beauty of the soul is worth more than that of the body' and can look after a young man who has many qualities even though his body is not very beautiful, he is also one who will not stop at the beauty of one body. Through the experience of various beauties he will try to attain an understanding of Beauty-in-Itself, 'hyperuranian' Beauty, Beauty as Idea.

This is the love for young men to which Socrates devoted himself, and we understand this when the handsome Alcibiades, drunk, bursts into the banquet and says how, in his desire to share in the wisdom of Socrates, he had offered him his body several times, but Socrates had never wished to yield to carnal desire and had merely lain chastely at his side.

It is in this context that Alcibiades makes his famous eulogy of the apparent ugliness of Socrates, whose outer aspect was that of a Silen but whose features concealed a profound inner beauty.

And so, in a single dialogue, different ideas of beauty and ugliness are contrasted, thus making the simplistic notion that ugliness is merely the opposite of *kalokagathia* rather more complex. Further, Greek culture had always been aware of this complexity, as is proven by a later eulogy to another ugly man but one of noble soul and great wisdom, **Aesop**.

Portrait of Aesop,
engraving,
1490,
Basel

Thersites
Homer (ninth century BC)
The Iliad, II, 282
Thersites [. . .] was the ugliest man that
stood before Ilium: bandy-legs and lame
in one foot, he had round shoulders
hunched over his chest. He had a pointed
head and sparse, thin hair. Achilles and
Ulysses hated him the most, for he often
insulted them.

Aesop's Ugliness
Anonymous (first–second century AD)
The Aesop Romance, I
Aesop the great benefactor of humanity,
the fabulist, was a slave by condition, but
a Phrygian of Amorium by birth:
repugnant to the sight [. . .] disgusting, fat
belly, bulging head, pug-nose, gibbous,
swarthy and short, with flat feet, short
arms, bandy-legs, thick lips [. . .] Moreover
– a disability even worse than deformity –
he had not the gift of the word,
stammered, and was quite unable to
express himself.

Socrates as a Silen
Plato (fifth–fourth century BC)
Symposium, 203 c–d
I say therefore that he [Socrates] looks
very much like those Silens put on show
in sculptors' workshops. They fashion
these satyrs holding pipes and flutes and,
when the images are opened up, they
have images of the gods inside them.

The Greek world was shot through with other contradictions. In the *Republic*,
Plato maintained that ugliness (understood as a lack of harmony) was the
opposite of the goodness of the soul, and recommended that youngsters be
spared the portrayal of ugly things. But he did admit that, at bottom, there exists a
degree of beauty proper to all things, as long as they are suited to the
corresponding idea. Consequently you could say that a girl or a mare or a pot was
beautiful, but that each of these was ugly with respect to the preceding one.

In the *Poetics*, **Aristotle** sanctioned a principle that was to remain universally
accepted over the centuries, namely that it is possible to make beautiful
imitations of ugly things–and right from earliest times people admired the way
Homer made a fine portrayal of the physical and moral unattractiveness of
Thersites.

Finally we shall see, in Stoic circles, how Marcus Aurelius recognised that
even ugliness, even imperfections such as the cracks in a loaf of bread,
contribute to the agreeability of the whole. As we shall discover in the next
chapter, this principle was to dominate the patristic and scholastic view in
which ugliness is redeemed by context and contributes to the harmony of the
universe.

Diego Velázquez,
Aesop,
1639–42,
Madrid,
Prado Museum

On the Difficulty of Defining Beauty and Ugliness
Plato (fifth–fourth century BC)
Hippias Major, IX–XI
Socrates: A man put me in difficulty by asking me more or less this question with great arrogance: 'Tell me, Socrates, how do you know which things are beautiful and which are ugly?' [. . .]

Hippias: Socrates, to tell the truth, a beautiful girl is a beautiful thing [. . .]

Socrates: 'You are delightful,' he will say, 'my dear Socrates. But is not a fine mare also beautiful, one that the god has praised in the oracle?' [. . .]

Hippias: That's true, Socrates; for the god spoke truly. And in our land there are some most beautiful mares.

Socrates: 'Good,' he will say. 'And a beautiful lyre? Is that not a beautiful thing? [. . .] And a fine pot?' [. . .] If the pot was made by a good potter, it will be smooth, round, and well fired, as are certain truly fine two-handled pots that hold almost six litres. If he asked the nature of such a pot, we would have to admit that it was beautiful [. . .]

Hippias: I think, Socrates, that this object too is beautiful, if it is well made, but it is not right to judge it beautiful compared to a mare, a girl and anything else that is beautiful.

Socrates: I see, Hippias, that we must make objections of this kind to he who says things like: 'Man, you do not seem to know the truth of Heraclitus's saying, that the most beautiful of monkeys is ugly compared to humankind and the most beautiful pot is ugly compared to the female gender [. . .] If we compare the female gender to that of the gods, will it not be the same as comparing pots to girls? Will not the most beautiful girl seem ugly compared to the gods?'

Avoid Portraying Ugliness
Plato (fifth–fourth century BC)
Republic, III, 401
Ugliness and discord and disharmony go hand in hand with bad words and bad nature, while the opposite qualities are the sisters of good, virtuous characters, and resemble them [. . .]

So must we supervise only the poets, obliging them to imbue their works with good character, on pain of their being forbidden to make poetry in our lands? Or should we supervise the other artists, preventing them from portraying what is morally bad, unbridled, ignoble and ugly,

both in images of animate beings, buildings, and any other manufactured product? And are those incapable of doing this to be forbidden to work among us for fear that our citizens, raised amid corrupted images as in a bad pasture, by dint of feeding daily upon such fare, gradually and unwittingly accumulate a single great evil in their souls?

Imitate Beautifully
Aristotle (fourth century BC)
Poetics, 1448 b
The art of poetry seems to have arisen from two general causes, each of which is natural. In the first place, imitation comes naturally from childhood and this is what makes men different from other animals, for of all creatures they have the most marked tendency to imitate. In the second place it is through imitation that we learn our earliest lessons, while all take pleasure in the things imitated. Proof of this lies in practical experience. Things that we normally view with disgust we instead view with pleasure when images of them are portrayed with accuracy: such as repugnant beasts and dead bodies. The reason for this is that learning gives great pleasure, not only to philosophers but also to others, no matter how little they may get out of the process. Hence men enjoy seeing likenesses for, on contemplating them, they learn and reason about them.

There is no Ugliness in Nature
Marcus Aurelius (second century AD)
The Meditations, III, 2
When bread is baked some parts split here and there, but the parts that thus open, while contrary to the baker's art, are in a certain sense very fine and above all they whet the appetite wonderfully. In the same way, ripe figs also split open. Consider olives when they are fully ripe: it is precisely that almost rotten look that lends a particular beauty to the fruit. Things like ears of corn bent towards the ground, the proud looks of the lion, the slobber running from the jaws of wild boars, and countless other examples, considered separately, are far from beauty. But because they follow nature's order they help to adorn that order and give pleasure. And so it happens that, if someone has a liking for and an understanding of the phenomena of nature, he will find that any thing, even if it be the accidental consequence of other events, has its own rhythm and grace.

Perseus slitting Medusa's throat, a detail from the metope of the Temple of Selinunte, 540 BC, Palermo, Museo Nazionale

2. The Greek World and Horror

The Greek world was obsessed by many kinds of ugliness and wickedness. There is no need to fall back on the opposition between Apollonian and Dionysian: even though drunken and comically repugnant satyrs make their appearance at Bacchus' court, and in the *Symposium* Socrates' resistance to even the most abundant libations is hailed as a prodigious feat. At best there lingers a hint of ambiguity regarding the role of music, which arouses the passions; but Pythagorean aesthetics saw music as the realisation of ideal laws, the mathematical rules of proportion and harmony.

Nonetheless Greek culture had its subterranean zones where the Mysteries were practised and heroes (like Ulysses and Aeneas) ventured into the forlorn mists of Hades, whose horrors had already been recounted by **Hesiod**.

Classical mythology is a catalogue of indescribable cruelty: Saturn devoured his own children; Medea slaughtered them to revenge herself on her faithless husband; Tantalus cooked his son Pelops and served him up to the gods to test their perspicacity; Agamemnon didn't hesitate to sacrifice his daughter Iphigenia in order to propitiate the gods; Atreus offered his brother Thyestes the flesh of the latter's own sons; Aegisthus killed Agamemnon in order to steal his wife Clytemnestra, who was later killed by her son Orestes; Oedipus, albeit unwittingly, committed both parricide and incest ... It is a world dominated by evil, where even the most beautiful beings carry out 'ugly' atrocities. Through this universe wander terrifying creatures, foul because they are hybrids that violate the laws of natural forms: consider the Sirens in **Homer**, who were not the attractive women with the tail of a fish as described by a later tradition, but nasty, rapacious birds. Then there are Scylla and Charybdis, Polyphemus, and the Chimaera. In **Virgil** we find Cerberus and the Harpies; the Gorgons (whose heads were full of writhing snakes and who had the hoofs of a wild boar), the Sphinx with a human face and the body of a lion, the Furies, the Centaurs, thought to be bad because of their duplicity, the Minotaur with a bull's head and a human body, Medusa ... While posterity has fantasised about the age of *kalokagathia*, it was also influenced by these manifestations of the horrible, from **Dante** to our own day. And in fact the Christian world (which, as we shall see in the next chapter, worked out its own terrifying idea of ugliness), for example in the works of **Clement of Alexandria** or **Isidore of Seville**, used the monstrosities described by the ancients as a pretext for demonstrating the falsity of pagan mythology.

Ulysses and the Sirens,
detail from
a decorated vase,
third century BC,
Berlin, Staatliche
Museen

The Sirens

Homer (ninth century BC)
The Odyssey, XII, 52–82
First you will come to the Sirens who enchant all who come near them. If any one unwarily draws in too close and hears the singing of the Sirens, his wife and children will never welcome him home again, for they sit in a green field and warble him to death with the sweetness of their song. There is a great heap of dead men's bones lying all around, with the flesh still rotting off them. Therefore pass these Sirens by, and stop your men's ears with wax that none of them may hear; but if you like you can listen yourself, for you may get the men to bind you as you stand upright on a cross-piece halfway up the mast, and they must lash the rope's ends to the mast itself, that you may have the pleasure of listening. If you beg and pray the men to unloose you, then they must bind you faster.

When your crew have taken you past these Sirens, I cannot give you coherent directions as to which of two courses you are to take; I will lay the two alternatives before you, and you must consider them for yourself. On the one hand there are some overhanging rocks against which the deep blue waves of Amphitrite beat with terrific fury; the blessed gods call these rocks the Wanderers [. . .]

The Harpies

Virgil (first century BC)
The Aeneid, III, 354–358, 361–368
Saved from the sea, the Strophades we gain,
So called in Greece, where dwells, with Harpies,
Heavenly ire
Ne'er sent a pest more loathsome; ne'er were seen
Worse plagues to issue from the Stygian mire
Birds maiden-faced, but trailing filth obscene,
With taloned hands and looks for ever pale and lean.

Scylla and Charybdis

Homer (ninth century BC)
The Odyssey, XII, 112–141
Inside it Scylla sits and yelps with a voice that you might take to be that of a young hound, but in truth she is a dreadful monster and no one – not even a god – could face her without being terror-struck. She has twelve mis-shapen feet, and six necks of the most prodigious length; and at the end of each neck she has a frightful head with three rows of teeth in each, all set very close together, so that they would crunch any one to death in a moment [. . .]

Polyphemus

Homer (ninth century BC)
The Odyssey, IX, 235–244, 364–382, 474–479, 484–491, 498–502
This was the abode of a huge monster who was then away from home shepherding his flocks. He would have nothing to do with other people [. . .]

With a sudden clutch he gripped up two of my men at once and dashed them down upon the ground as though they had been puppies. Their brains were shed upon the ground, and the earth was wet with their blood. Then he tore them limb from limb and supped upon them. He gobbled them up like a lion in the wilderness, flesh, bones, marrow, and entrails, without leaving anything uneaten. As for us, we wept and lifted up our hands to heaven on seeing such a horrid sight, for we did not know what else to do; but when the Cyclops had filled his huge paunch, and had washed down his meal of human flesh with a drink of fresh milk, he stretched himself full length upon the ground [. . .]

His great neck hung heavily backwards and a deep sleep took hold upon him. Presently he turned sick, and, with much horrendous belching, threw up both wine and the gobbets of human flesh on which he had been gorging [. . .]

When the wood, green though it was, was about to blaze, I drew it out of the fire glowing with heat, and my men gathered round me, for heaven had filled their hearts with courage. We drove the sharp end of the beam into the monster's eye, and bearing upon it with all my weight I kept turning it round and round [. . .]

Even thus did we bore the red hot beam into his eye, till the boiling blood bubbled all over it as we worked it round and round, so that the steam from the burning eyeball scalded his eyelids and eyebrows, and the roots of the eye sputtered in the fire [. . .]

Cerberus

Virgil (first century BC)
The Aeneid, VI, 612–629
Crouched in a fronting cave, huge Cerberus wakes
These kingdoms with his three-mouthed bark. His head
The priestess marked, all bristling now with snakes,
And flung a sop of honied drugs and bread.
He, famine-stung, with triple jaws dispread,
The morsel snaps, then prone along the cave
Lies stretched on earth, with loosened limbs, as dead.

Gustave Moreau,
The Chimaera,
1867,
Cambridge,
Massachusetts,
Fogg Art Museum

following pages
John William Waterhouse,
Ulysses and the Sirens,
1891,
Melbourne,
National Gallery
of Victoria

The Underworld
Hesiod (seventh century BC)
Theogony, 736–73
This is a gloomy, squalid place, which
even the gods detest. Once you step
over the threshold of this immense
gulf, you would not reach the bottom
in the space of a whole year, for
violent storms would blow you this
way and that without granting you any
respite [. . .] Here stands the frightful
abode of shadowy Night, enveloped in
leaden clouds. Before it, planted firmly
on his legs, the son of Iapetus holds
up the heavens with his head and
tireless hands. In that point Night and
Day meet and greet one another as
they pass through the great bronze
threshold, the one on the point of
leaving and the other of coming back
in, or vice versa. They are never inside
the house together; but one is always
outside moving over the earth while
the other stays at home waiting until it
is time to leave. One brings the light
that makes all clear for the peoples of
earth; the other, dark Night cloaked in
a dense mist, bears in her arms Sleep,
the brother of Death. This is the abode
of Sleep and Death, sons of dark Night
and frightful gods. The bright Sun
never casts his rays upon them, neither
as he rises in the heavens, nor as he
sets. Of these two gods the first
wanders peacefully over the earth and
the vast sea, but the other has a heart
of iron, and a spirit within his breast
as ruthless as bronze: when he seizes
men he never lets go, and he is hateful
even to the immortal gods.
There, farther on, lies the echoing
abode of the god of the underworld,
mighty Hades and the frightful
Persephone.

37

The Arezzo Chimaera,
Etruscan bronze,
fifth century BC,
Florence,
Archaeological Museum

The Chimaera
Homer (ninth century BC)
The Iliad, VI, 222–26
[. . .] the Chimaera, who was not a human
being, but a goddess, for she had the head
of a lion and the tail of a serpent, while her
body was that of a goat, and she breathed
forth flames of fire; but Bellerophon slew
her, for he was guided by signs from heaven
[. . .]

The Ugliness of Pagan Divinities
Clement of Alexandria (150–215)
Protrepticus, 61
These are the teachings of your gods
that prostitute themselves together with

you! [. . .]

And what of your other images?! Certain
statuettes of Pan, certain naked female
figures, drunken satyrs and swollen
phalluses, painted without any clothing and
put to shame by their own immoderation!

These days, however, when you see –
openly and in public – paintings depicting
all kinds of unbridled licence, you feel no
shame. Indeed you keep these things and
hang them on your walls, just like the
images of your gods, and in your homes
you worship as sacred what are merely
shameless steles, and you care not if the
matter portrayed is the obscene poses of
Philenides or the labours of Hercules!

Painter of the Pygmy,
Kelebe with Trumpeter
(Volterra),
Late fourth to early
third century BC,
Colle Val d'Elsa,
Archaeological
Museum

Pieter Paul Rubens
*Saturn Devouring
his children*
1636–37
Madrid,
The Prado Museum

Pagan Monsters Reassessed by Christians

St Isidore of Seville (570–636)
Etymologies, XI, 3

There is also talk of other fabulous human portents, which are not real, but invented: they are symbols of a set reality. This is the case with Geryon, king of Spain, of whom it is said he was born with three bodies: in reality, there were three brothers who got on so well that it was almost as if the three bodies shared one soul. This is also the case with the Gorgons, prostitutes with snakes for hair, who with one look turned men into stone. They were said to have only one eye, which they took turns in using. In reality, they were three sisters all equally beautiful, almost as one to the eye, the sight of whom stunned men so much they fancied that the sisters had turned them into stone. The Sirens are thought to be three, part virgin and part bird, with wings and talons: one sang, the other played the reed-pipe, and the last the lyre. They used their song to lure sailors onto the rocks, shipwrecked. In truth, the sirens were whores: since they dragged passers-by into wretchedness, it was thought they had brought them to shipwreck [. . .] They say that the Hydra was a serpent with nine heads, called in Latin *excetra*, because on the *caedere*, or *cutting*, of a head three new ones were created. Nonetheless Hydra was a place that vomited up waters that devastated a nearby city: on the stopping up of one of the mouths, many others opened up. On seeing this, Hercules drained this place, hence closing the mouths from which the water gushed forth. Indeed the *Hydra* took its name from water [. . .] Some think that the Chimaera was a beast with the head of a lion, the tail of a dragon and the body of a goat. Certain experts on physical phenomena say that the Chimaera was no animal, but a mountain in Cilicia that in certain places offered nourishment to lions and goats, while in other parts it burned and in others again it was infested with serpents. Bellerophon made it inhabitable and this is why it is said that he slew the Chimaera. The *Centaurs*, half human and half horse, got their name from their appearance: some say that they were Thessalian horsemen who, since they galloped all over the battlefield in war, gave the impression of being one body made up of horses and human beings.

Chapter II

Passion,
Death, Martyrdom

1. The 'Pancalistic' View of the Universe

Greek culture did not hold that the world was necessarily wholly beautiful. Its mythology tells of monstrosities and errors, and Plato thought that sensible reality was merely a poor imitation of the perfection of the world of ideas. On the other hand in the gods artists saw the model of supreme beauty and this perfection was the aim of the statuary that represented the inhabitants of Olympus.

Paradoxically, with the advent of the Christian world this relationship – at least certain aspects of it – was inverted: from a theologico-metaphysical standpoint the entire universe is beautiful because it is a divine work and thanks to this total beauty even ugliness and evil are in some way redeemed.

By way of compensation, Christ, the human expression of divinity who suffered for us, is portrayed in the moment of his greatest humiliation.

From the earliest centuries the Fathers of the Church talked constantly about the beauty of all being. From *Genesis* they learned that, at the end of the sixth day, God saw that all he had made was good (1,31), and the *Book of Wisdom* said that the world was created by God according to *number, weight,* and *measure*, in other words according to criteria of mathematical perfection.

Alongside the biblical tradition, classical philosophy contributed to reinforcing this aesthetic view of the universe. The beauty of the world as a reflection and an image of ideal beauty was a concept of Platonic origin; and in his Commentary to the *Timaeus* Calcidius (between the third and fourth century AD) spoke of the 'splendid world of beings . . . of peerless beauty'.

Mathias Grünewald,
Crucifixion,
a detail from the altar
at Isenheim,
1515,
Colmar,
Musée Unterlinden

The medieval period was influenced by a work of a Neoplatonic stamp (fifth century AD), *On The Divine Names* by Pseudo-Dionysus the Areopagite. Here the universe appears as an inexhaustible source of splendour that radiates out to form a grandiose manifestation of the diffuse nature of primary beauty, a dazzling cascade of light: 'The Super-Essential beautiful is called Beauty because of the fairness that it dispenses to all beings each to his own measure, and because it is the cause of the harmony and splendour of all things. In the guise of light it showers all things with the outpourings of its natural rays, which make them beautiful, and calls to itself all things that we call Beauty – and within itself it contains all things' (*On The Divine Names*, IV, 7, 135).

Following the Areopagite, John Scotus Eriugena (ninth century) worked out a concept of the cosmos as the revelation of God and of his ineffable beauty through ideal and corporeal beauties and he expatiated on the beauty of all creation, on similar and dissimilar things, on the harmony of species and forms, and of the different orders of substantial and accidental causes culminating in marvellous unity (*The Four Divisions of Nature*, 3). All medieval authors returned to this theme of the *pancalia* or beauty of the entire universe.

For a traditional identification of the Beautiful and Good, saying that the entire universe was beautiful was tantamount to saying that it was also good – and vice versa. How to reconcile this pancalistic persuasion with the evident fact that Evil and deformity exist in that same universe?

The solution had been anticipated by St Augustine, who had made the justification of Evil in a world created by God one of his fundamental themes. In *De ordine* Augustine argued that, true, there seemed to be disharmony and 'an insult to the sight' when the parts of a building were erroneously arranged, but he pointed out that error too is a part of the general order. In the *Confessions* (VII) he tells us that evil and ugliness do not exist in the divine plan.

Corruption is a loss, but we talk of loss when a previous good has been diminished. If all that becomes corrupted is subjected to a loss of value, then it means that there was a positive value before corruption set in. If the loss of value is total, a thing would cease to exist.

Hence evil and ugliness in themselves could not exist, because they would be 'an absolute nothing'. In his polemic against the Manichaeans titled *De natura boni contra Manicheos* (XVII) Augustine says that not even what the ancients called *hyle*, in other words matter that is wholly unformed and devoid of quality, was an evil. Even timber that has yet to be worked lends itself those who work it, so that something may be got from it. If it could not accept the shape imposed upon it by a craftsman, it certainly could not be called matter.

Hildegard of Bingen, *The Universe in the Shape of an Egg*, the earth with the four elements around it, from *Scivias, Codex Rupertsberg*, twelfth century.

Monsters of Notre Dame, nineteenth-century reconstruction, Paris

So if a shape is a good, which is why all the things that draw some superiority from shape are called shapely, then there is no doubt that the capacity to be formed is also a good to some extent. If even formless matter is beautiful, then the same must hold even for beasts that some see as monstrous, like monkeys, because the proportion between their various members is correct. Augustine's reasoning crops up again in Scholastic philosophy, in which we find various examples of a justification of Ugliness within the framework of the overall beauty of the universe, where even deformity and evil acquire a value comparable to that of chiaroscuro, of the proportion between light and shadow in an image. In other words their presence reveals the harmony of the whole. Some said that even monsters are beautiful because they are *beings* and as such contribute to the harmony of the whole and that, while sin certainly destroys the order of things, this order is re-established by punishment and hence the damned in hell are examples of a law of harmony. Others tried to attribute the impression of ugliness to flaws in our perceptions, and hence some may find something ugly because of poor light, because it was too close or too far away, because they saw it from an oblique angle, or because of the misty air that deforms the contours of things.

The Beauty Dispensed by God
Pseudo Dionysus the Areopagite
(fifth century AD)
On the Divine Names, IV, 7
The Super-Essential Beautiful is called
beauty on account of the beauty it
dispenses to all things in accordance with
their nature. It is the cause of the
harmony and splendour of all things and,
in the form of the most resplendent light,
it showers them with its originating
beams. It is the cause of beauty, and calls
all things unto itself (. . .) drawing them
together and absorbing them into itself.

Les heures du Croy,
sixteenth century,
Vienna,
Osterreichische
Nationalbibliothek

The Ugly Being Contributes to Order
St Augustine (fourth–fifth century AD)
On Order, IV, 12–13
What is grimmer than an executioner?
What is more baleful and cruel than such
a soul? But he fulfils a necessary position
among the laws and is inserted in the
order of a well-governed state. [. . .] What
could be defined as more foul, devoid of
dignity and obscene than prostitutes,
pimps, and the other plagues of this kind?
Take away prostitutes from a society and
all will be overturned as a consequence of
disordered passions. Put them in the place
of honest women, and you will dishonour
every single thing with guilt and
shamelessness [. . .] Is it not true that if
you stare at certain members of the bodies
of animals, then you cannot look at them?
Nevertheless, the order of nature, given
that they are necessary, wanted them to
be present and, since they are indecent,
does not allow them to be easily visible.
And those deformed parts, occupying
their place, have left the better place for
better parts [. . .] The poets have utilised
what are called solecisms and barbarisms;
they have preferred, by changing the
names, to call them figures and
transformations, rather than avoid them as
evident errors. Well, take them out of
poetry, and we would miss the most
melodious sweetness. Gather many
together in a single composition, and it
will vex me because all will be mawkish,
pedantic, affected [. . .] The order that
governs and moderates such things would
not tolerate their being too many, nor too
few. A humble and almost disregarded
discourse highlights elevated expressions
and elegant movements, alternating
between one and the other.

47

Crucifixion,
c.420–30,
London,
British Museum

Evil and Ugly do not Exist on the Divine Plane

St Augustine (fourth–fifth century AD)
The Confessions, VII

And to Thee is nothing whatsoever evil: yea, not only to Thee, but also to Thy creation as a whole, because there is nothing without, which may break in, and corrupt that order which Thou hast appointed it. But in the parts thereof some things, because unharmonising with other some, are accounted evil: whereas those very things harmonise with others, and are good; and in themselves are good. And all these things which harmonise not together, do yet with the inferior part, which we call Earth, having its own cloudy and windy sky harmonising with it. Far be it then that I should say, 'These things should not be': for should I see nought but these, I should indeed long for the better; but still must even for these alone praise Thee; for that Thou art to be praised, do show from the earth, dragons, and all deeps, fire, hail, snow, ice, and stormy wind, which fulfil Thy word [. . .]

The Beauty of the Cosmos

St Augustine (fourth–fifth century AD)
On the Nature of Good, 3, 14, 15, 16, 17

The more things are according to measure, form and order, the more they are surely good; but the less they are according to measure, form and order, the less good they are. Therefore, let us consider these three aspects: measure, form and order, not to mention countless others that can be traced back to these three; well, it is precisely these three aspects – measure, form and order – that are like a general good in God's reality, both in the spirit and in the body [. . .].

Nevertheless, among all these good things, those that are small, when compared with those that are largest, are named by opposites: for example, compared with the human form, whose beauty is greater, the beauty of a monkey is called deformity. In this manner, careless people are deceived, as if that thing were good and this thing were evil; they do not recognise in the body of the monkey its proper measure, the symmetrical harmony of its limbs, the cohesion of its parts, the protection of its safety, and other aspects that it would take too long to address. Even a monkey possesses the gift of beauty, though to a lesser degree [. . .] In this manner, we speak of light and darkness as two opposites: and yet even that which is dark has some light; if it has none whatsoever, then there is darkness insofar as there is absence of light, just as silence is the absence of sound [. . .] Yet even this privation of things re-enters at that point in nature's general order, to take its own, not unsuitable position in the meditations of the wise. God, in fact, by not illuminating certain places and times, has created darkness in a way that is as convenient as the days. For that matter, if we, holding back sound, punctuate our discourse with a convenient silence, how much more will He, as the perfect artifice of all things, produce in a convenient manner privations in some of these things? [. . .] Therefore no nature is evil, insofar as it is nature [. . .]

Beauty and Ugliness

Alexander of Hales (thirteenth century AD)
Summa Teologica, II

Just as a dark colour is appropriate in a painting when it is placed in the right location, so is totality of things beautiful even with sinners.

Vincent of Beauvais
(twelfth–thirteenth century AD)
Speculum Majus, 27

The deformity of evil does not diminish the beauty of the universe.

Robert Grosseteste
(twelfth–thirteenth century AD)
De Divisione

If beauty and health, which are considered good, are a proportion of the parts and members with the beauty of colour [. . .] in ugly and diseased bodies this proportion does not entirely dissolve, but is only transformed, and therefore ugliness and disease can be called lesser goods rather than true, real evils.

2. The Suffering of Christ

When art has to deal with the Passion of Christ, we realise what Hegel pointed out in his *Aesthetics*, 'you cannot use the forms of Greek beauty to portray Christ scourged, crowned with thorns, dying on the cross'. This acceptance of the 'ugliness' of Christ was not immediate, however. True, there was a page in **Isaiah** in which the Messiah is portrayed as disfigured by suffering, and this mention had not escaped certain Fathers of the Church, but then **Augustine** reabsorbed this scandalous evidence into his pancalistic vision, stating that Jesus certainly appeared deformed when he was hanging on the cross, but through that superficial deformity He expressed the inner beauty of his sacrifice and the glory it promised us.

Paleo-Christian art had restricted itself to the fairly idealised image of the Good Shepherd. The crucifixion was not seen as a suitable iconographic subject and at most it was evoked through the abstract symbol of the cross. Some have suggested that this reluctance to portray Christ's sufferings was due to theological controversies and to the battle against the heretics who wanted to affirm his human nature and deny his divinity.

It is only in the late Middle Ages that the man on the cross begins to be seen as a real man, beaten, bloodied, disfigured by pain, while the portrayal both of the crucifixion and of the various phases of the Passion becomes dramatically realistic as it celebrates the humanity of Christ through his sufferings. In *The Mourning of Christ* painted by Giotto for the Scrovegni Chapel in Padua all the characters shown are weeping (including the angels) thus suggesting to the faithful feelings of compassion for someone with whom they are supposed to identify. In this way the image of a suffering Christ was handed down to Renaissance and Baroque culture in a crescendo of the eroticism of suffering, where the insistence on the divine face and body tormented by pain became a play verging on complacency and ambiguity, as is the case with the Christ who doesn't so much bleed as drip with gore in Mel Gibson's movie version of the Passion.

But **Hegel** had also observed that with the advent of Christianity the ugly appears in a polemical form in the portrayal of the persecutors of Christ.

Master Theodoric,
Imago pietatis,
c.1360,
Karl štejn Castle

The Annunciation of the Messiah

Isaiah, 53:2–7

For he shall grow up before him as a tender plant, and as a root out of a dry ground: he hath no form nor comeliness; and when we shall see him, there is no beauty that we should desire him.

He is despised and rejected of men; a man of sorrows, and acquainted with grief: and we hid as it were our faces from him; he was despised, and we esteemed him not. Surely he hath borne our griefs, and carried our sorrows: yet we did esteem him stricken, smitten of God, and afflicted.

But he was wounded for our transgressions, he was bruised for our iniquities: the chastisement of our peace was upon him; and with his stripes we are healed.

All we like sheep have gone astray; we have turned every one to his own way; and the LORD hath laid on him the iniquity of us all.

He was oppressed, and he was afflicted, yet he opened not his mouth: he is brought as a lamb to the slaughter, and as a sheep before her shearers is dumb, so he openeth not his mouth.

Giotto,
Deposition,
1304–6
Padua,
Scrovegni Chapel

The Deformity of Christ

St Augustine (fourth–fifth century AD)
'Sermon 27', 6

In order to maintain your faith Christ deformed himself, while He remains eternally beautiful [. . .] *And we saw Him and He possessed neither beauty nor attractiveness, rather His face was repellent and His position deformed. This is His power: He was reviled and His position was deformed; a man covered with sores, one who has experienced every weakness.* Christ's deformity renders you shapely. If, in fact, He had not wished to be deformed, you would have never reacquired the divine form that you had lost. Therefore, He was deformed when He hung on the cross, but His deformity constituted our beauty. Therefore in our present life we cling to the deformed Christ. What does 'deformed Christ' mean? Far be it from me to take glory in anything but the cross of our Lord Jesus Christ, by whom the world is crucified for me, as I am for the world. This is Christ's deformity [. . .] We bear the sign of His deformity on our foreheads. We are not embarrassed by Christ's deformity! We walk this path, and we will see the light; and when we have seen the light, we will see His equality with God.

Aelbrecht Bouts,
Christ Suffering, detail,
*c.*1490,
Cambridge,
Massachusetts,
Fogg Art Museum

He was referring to the north German painters (and he might have added the Flemish school) but note how even a delicate artist like Fra Angelico shows us a persecutor whose looks are not only coarse, but who vulgarly spits in Jesus' face. None of this excludes the countless idealised and reconciled images of Christ, all the way down to the popular holy figurines that show him as tall and handsome, with delicate, often almost maudlin features. But the introduction of ugliness and suffering to the celebration of the divine encouraged other types of ugliness, which were taken to extreme limits for moralistic and devotional purposes: from images of death, hell, the devil, and sin, to those showing the sufferings of the martyrs.

from left to right
Hans Memling,
Christ at the Pillar,
1485–90,
Barcelona, Mateu
Collection

Hispanic-Flemish
Master,
The Burial of Christ
(The seventh sorrow
of the Virgin Mary),
c.1488–90,
Madrid, Prado Museum

Mel Gibson (director),
The Passion of the Christ,
2003

The Representation of Pain

Georg Wilhelm Friedrich Hegel
(1770–1831)
Aesthetics: Lectures on Fine Art, II, 1
The real turning-point in this life of God
is the termination of his individual
existence as *this* man, the story of the
Passion, suffering on the cross, the
Golgotha of the Spirit, the pain of death.
This sphere of portrayal is separated *toto
caelo* from the classical plastic ideal
because here the subject-matter itself
implies that the external bodily
appearance, immediate existence as an
individual, is revealed in the grief of his
negativity as the negative, and that
therefore it is by sacrificing subjective
individuality and the sensuous sphere that
the Spirit attains its truth and its Heaven
[. . .]

Christ scourged, with the crown of
thorns, carrying his cross to the place of
execution, nailed to the cross, passing
away in the agony of a torturing and slow
death – this cannot be portrayed in the
forms of Greek beauty [. . .]

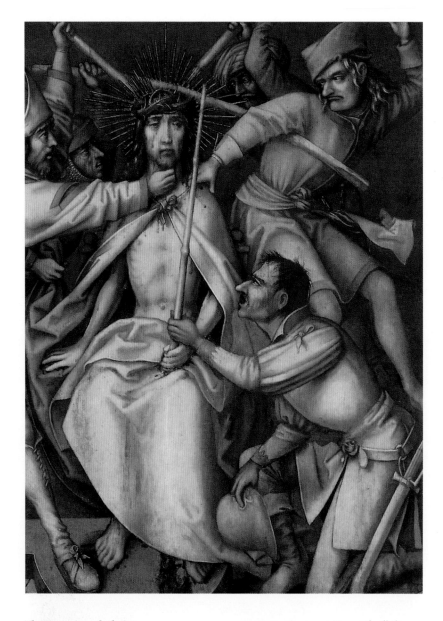

Hans Holbein,
Christ Mocked,
*c.*1495,
Stuttgart, Staatsgalerie

facing page
Hieronymus Bosch
(copied from),
The Arrest of Christ,
*c.*1500,
San Diego,
Museum of Art

Beato Angelico,
Christ Mocked, detail,
1440–41,
Florence,
Convent of St Mark

The Enemies of Christ

Georg Wilhelm Friedrich Hegel
(1770–1831)
Aesthetics: Lectures on Fine Art, II, 1
But the enemies are presented to us as
inwardly evil because they place
themselves in opposition to God,
condemn him, mock him, torture him,
crucify him, and the idea of inner evil
and enmity to God brings with it on the
external side, ugliness, crudity, barbarity,
rage, and distortion of their outward

appearance. In connection with all these
there enters here as a necessary feature
what is unbeautiful in comparison with
the beauty of Greek art [. . .]

In this field the North German masters
in particular distinguished themselves
when, in scenes from the Passion, they
highlighted with great energy the
coarseness of the undisciplined soldiery,
the wickedness of their mockery, and the
barbarousness of the hatred of Christ
during His Passion and Death.

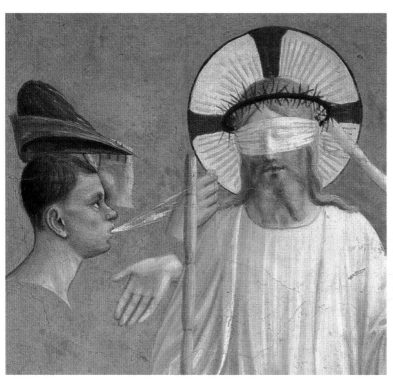

3. Martyrs, Hermits, Penitents

In the Christian world sanctity is none other than the imitation of Christ. Suffering, atrocious suffering at that, was the lot of those who gave their lives to bear witness to their faith, and these were the people addressed by **Tertullian** (second–third century AD) in his *Exhortation to Martyrdom*, inviting men and women to bear the unmentionable sufferings (described with ill-concealed sadism) they were doomed to face.

In medieval art the martyr is seldom shown as deformed by his torments, as some had dared to do with Christ. When portraying Christ, artists emphasised the incomparable immensity of his sacrifice, whereas martyrs (to exhort people to imitate them) are depicted with the seraphic serenity with which they went to their respective fates. And so decapitations, roasting on the gridiron, and the removal of breasts can give rise to graceful compositions, almost balletic in form. As we shall see, enjoyment of the cruelty of such tortures came along a little later with the art of the seventeenth century.

During and after the Renaissance, in a climate marked by the re-evaluation of the human body and its beauty, there was a tendency to an excessive 'beautification' of some extremely distressing events, so much so that – more than the torture – what counted was the virile strength or feminine sweetness with which the saints faced their torment. This led to images that were quite often homoerotic, proof of this being the various representations of the martyrdom of St Sebastian.

The area where concessions were no longer made to gentility was often the portrayal of the hermit, who by tradition and definition was made ugly by long sojourns in the desert. Baroque spirituality used these models to celebrate the penitences of the saints and their disdain for the body, weakened by fasting, flagellation, and other forms of discipline (see, for example the text by Father **Segneri**).

Among the hermits of the early centuries the ugliest were the stylites, who isolated themselves atop a column, bearing the inclemencies of the weather, not to mention the insects and worms that crawled all over them as they struggled with hauntingly seductive visions or diabolical nightmares (for a modern treatment of this theme, see **Tennyson**).

Master of the
St Ursula Legend,
*The Massacre
of the Vandals*, detail,
1474–75,
Bruges, Groeninge
Museum

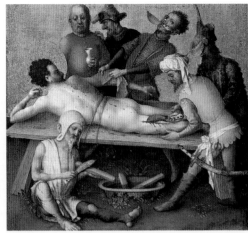

Stefan Lochner,
*Panels Showing
the Martyrdom of the
Apostles,*
fifteenth century,
Frankfurt,
Städelches Museum

facing page
Beato Angelico,
*Triptych of Saint Peter
Martyr,* detail,
c.1425,
Florence, St Mark's
Museum

Exhortation to Martyrdom
Tertullian (second–third century AD)
'To the Martyrs', 4
But fear of death is not as great as the fear of torture. An Athenian woman succumbed to the executioner, when, subjected to torture by the tyrant for having taken part in a conspiracy, and still making no betrayal of her confederates, she ultimately bit off her tongue and spat it in the tyrant's face, so that he would know that his torture would prove useless, no matter how long it might last. And that which the Spartans consider a rite of the utmost importance is also well known: flagellation. In this sacred ceremony the noblest youths are scourged before the altar, whipped while their parents and kinsmen stand by and encourage them to bear it out bravely.

For it will be always counted even more honourable and glorious should the body perish on account of these sufferings yet the youth give no cry of pain. Therefore, if it is legitimate, for love of earthly glory, to require a similar test of strength and soul and senses, so that they can demonstrate their indifference to the wounds of weapons, the agony of flames, the torments of the cross, the fury of wild beasts, the refinements of torture, and all for nothing but the mirage of human praise, then I can firmly state that your sufferings are but trifles when compared with celestial glory and divine reward. If glass is so precious to us, what must a true pearl be worth? And who would not be willing to give for truth as much as others have willingly offered for falsehood?

St Simeon Stylites

Alfred, Lord Tennyson (1809–92)
'St Simeon Stylites'

Although I be the basest of mankind,
From scalp to sole one slough and crust of
sin,
Unfit for earth, unfit for heaven, scarce meet
For troops of devils, mad with blasphemy,
I will not cease to grasp the hope I hold
Of saintdom, and to clamour, mourn and sob,
Battering the gates of heaven with storms of
prayer,
Have mercy, Lord, and take away my sin.

Let this avail, just, dreadful, mighty God,
This not be all in vain, that thrice ten years,
Thrice multiplied by superhuman pangs,
In hungers and in thirsts, fevers and cold,
In coughs, aches, stitches, ulcerous throes
and cramps,
A sign betwixt the meadow and the cloud,
Patient on this tall pillar I have borne
Rain, wind, frost, heat, hail, damp, and sleet,
and snow;
And I had hoped that ere this period closed
Thou wouldst have caught me up into thy
rest,
Denying not these weather-beaten limbs
The meed of saints, the white robe and the
palm.

O Lord, Lord,
Thou knowest I bore this better at the first,

For I was strong and hale of body then;
And though my teeth, which now are
dropped away,
Would chatter with the cold, and all my
beard
Was tagged with icy fringes in the moon,
I drowned the whoopings of the owl with
sound
Of pious hymns and psalms, and sometimes
saw
An angel stand and watch me, as I sang.
Now am I feeble grown; my end draws nigh;
I hope my end draws nigh: half deaf I am,
So that I scarce can hear the people hum
About the column's base, and almost blind,
And scarce can recognise the fields I know;
And both my thighs are rotted with the dew;
Yet cease I not to clamour and to cry,
While my stiff spine can hold my weary head
. . .

The Penitence of Saint Ignatius

Paolo Segneri (1624–94)
'Panegyric on St Ignatius of Loyola'

Having sacrificed to God the higher part of
himself, which was his spirit, with humble
abjection, all that remained was to sacrifice to
Him the lower portion, which was the flesh,
with the most painful torments; and by so
doing perhaps train himself, in an almost
familiar battle, against those two tremendous
enemies that he would have to encounter as
the greater divine glory spread throughout
the universe: trials of the soul, torments of
the body. How do you think he tortured his
body? Listen to what I have to say, and then,
if you can, give yourselves over to horror.
He wore a rough sack over a barbed chain:
wrapping his bare flanks with stinging nettles,
or thorny weeds, or sharp iron; fasting on
bread and water every day, excepting
Sunday, when he could add some bitter herb
flavoured with ash or earth; passing three,
six, or even eight entire days without food;
flagellating himself five times between day
and night, always with a chain and always
until bloody; and beating his bare chest
furiously with flint. He had no bed upon
which to lay his body except for the hard
earth, and no pillow upon which to rest his
head except for cold rock. Seven hours a day
he would spend on his knees in deep
contemplation, never weeping, never ceasing
to torture himself. This was the kind of life he
led in the grotto of Manresa, never alleviating
his sufferings despite the long and
extremely tormented infirmity that he soon
contracted, with listlessness, tremors,
spasms, fainting and fevers until finally, by
the grace of God, he passed on.

4. The Triumph of Death

While saints awaited death with joy, the same cannot be said of the great mass of sinners; in this case, it wasn't so much a matter of inviting them to serenely accept the moment of their passing as of reminding them of the imminence of that crossing so that they might repent in time. Hence both verbal preaching and the images that appeared in holy places were intended to serve as reminders of the imminence of death and to cultivate the terrors of the torments of hell.

That this was a particularly deeply felt theme in the Middle Ages (but also later) was due to the fact, in a period when life expectancy was shorter than our own and it was easy to fall victim to plagues and famine, and at a time when war was an almost permanent state, that death was a presence almost impossible to ignore – far more so than in our own day, when, surrounded by models of youth and fitness, we try to forget death, to hide it, to relegate it to the cemeteries, while we beat about the bush to avoid mentioning it directly, or exorcise it by reducing it to a simple element of spectacle, thanks to which we forget our own death by having fun watching someone else's. In literature, the subject of the triumph of death appears in the twelfth century, with the *Verses on Death* by **Hélinand of Froidmont** and was continued in variations on the poetic theme of *ubi sunt* (where are the beautiful women, the splendid cities of long ago? All has vanished).

Sometimes, in the Middle Ages, death appears like something painful but familiar, a sort of fixed character (at times almost puppet-like) in the theatre of life. In many pictorial cycles (such as the one in the Camposanto in Pisa) the triumph of death is celebrated.

In Rome, during the triumphs held for victorious leaders, a servant sitting alongside the illustrious one constantly repeated the words 'remember that you are a man', a kind of *memento mori*.

This model led to a literature of Triumphs (see, for example, **Petrarch**) in which there is always a Triumph of Death, which overcomes all human vanity, time, and fame.

The Triumph of Death is accompanied by the vision of the Last Judgement, another form of warning for the faithful that inspired theatrical works and carnival floats (see **Vasari**).

The Dance of Death, detail from *Heures à l'usage de Rome,* c.1515, Paris, Gillet Haroduin

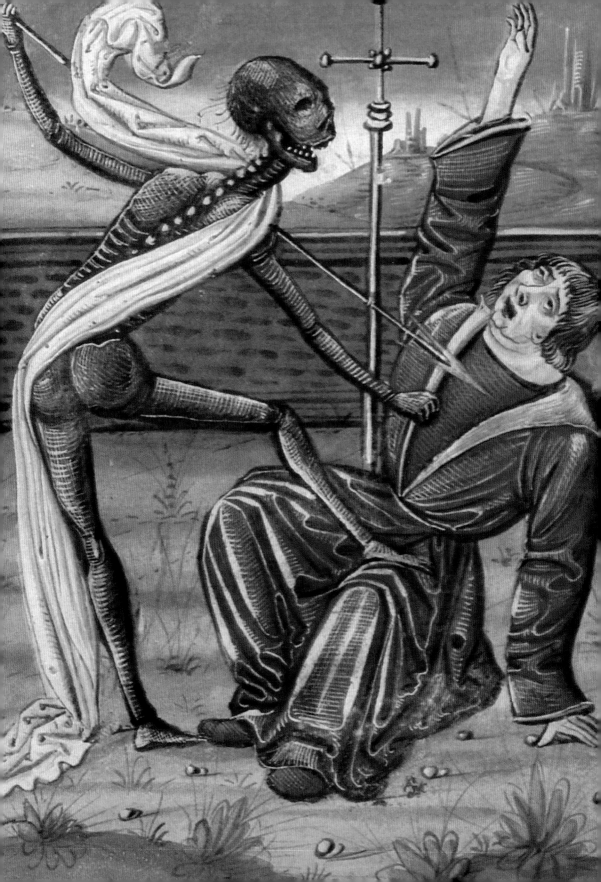

The Triumph of Death,
1485,
Clusone, Oratorio
dei Disciplini

Death in One Hour
Hélinand de Froidmont
Verses on Death (1197)
In one hour Death undoes all.
What price beauty, what price riches?
What price honours, what price nobility?

The Triumph of Death
Petrarch (1304–74)
The Triumph of Death, I, 73–90
And here from afar we see an army
Of the dead strewn o'er the plain,
No prose nor verse can comprehend
Their number, from India, from China,
From Morocco and from Spain
From all the corners of the earth they came,
Men said to be happy,
Popes, kings and emperors;
Now they lie naked, wretched, beggars.
Where are their riches now? Where their
honours
Their gems, sceptres, crowns,
Their mitres and their purple?
Wretched is he who hopes in worldly things
(But who does not do so?), and if, in the
end,
They are deceived, then this is just.
O ye blind, wherefore all your toil?

Carnival 1511
Giorgio Vasari (1511–74)
Lives of the Artists: 'The Life of Piero di
Cosimo', III
It was a procession, an enormous wagon
drawn by black oxen, decorated with
pictures of dead men's bones, and white
crosses, and on the wagon sat a huge effigy
of death holding a scythe in one hand.
There were many covered sepulchres
around the wagon, and wherever the
procession stopped to sing these tombs
opened up and out came figures dressed in
black cloth, upon which skeletons were
painted, the bones of the arms, chest, back
and legs, white on black. And in the
distance there appeared several figures
carrying torches and wearing death masks
with skulls front and back, stretching down
to the throat. Apart from seeming extremely
realistic it was horrible and frightening to
see. And at the sound of certain muffled
trumpets that made a rough and dull sound,
these dead men emerged from the tombs,
and sitting down on top of them sang . . .
'Dead we are as you can see
And dead we'll see you one day be.'

As Soon as this Body . . .
Sebastian Pauli (1684–51)
Lenten Sermons

As soon as this body, all things considered well put together and well organised, is closed up in its tomb it changes colour, becoming yellow and pale, but with a certain nauseating pallor and wanness that makes one afraid. Then it will blacken from head to toe; and a grim and gloomy heat, like that of banked coals, will cover it entirely. Then the face, chest, and stomach will begin to swell strangely: upon the stomach's swelling a foetid, greasy mould will grow, the foul product of approaching corruption. Not long thereafter, that yellow and swollen stomach will begin to split and burst here and there: thence will issue forth a slow lava of putrefaction and revolting things in which pieces and chunks of black and rotten flesh float and swim. Here you see a worm-ridden half an eye, there a strip of putrid and rotten lip; and further on a bunch of lacerated, bluish intestines. In this greasy muck a number of small flies will generate, as well as worms and other disgusting little creatures that swarm and wind around one another in that corrupt blood, and latching on to that rotten flesh, they eat and devour it. Some of these worms issue forth from the chest, others with I don't know what filth and mucus dangle from the nostrils; others, intermixed with that putridness, enter and exit from the mouth, and the most satiated come and go, gurgling and bubbling down the throat.

from left to right
Mummified body,
c.1599,
Palermo, Capuchin
Catacombs

Mummified bodies,
c.1599,
Palermo, Capuchin
Catacombs

Skull from the coffin
of Emperor Charles VI,
c.1618,
Vienna, crypt of the
Capuchin church

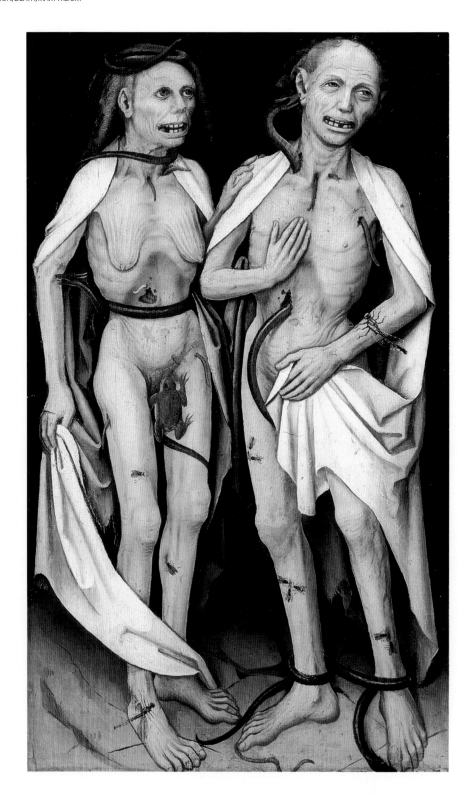

Other illustrated stories tell of three knights who in the woods meet three skeletons whose appearance is meant to be seen as a mirror held up to the near future that awaits all (the caption says 'We were as you are now, you will be as we are now!'). Sometimes they come across a decomposed body and a monk reminds them of the destiny that awaits them. Many frescoes are devoted to this theme, such as *The Encounter between the Three Living Men and the Three Dead Men* (fourteenth century), in the sacristy of St Luke's church in Cremona, or the now mutilated fresco on the façade of the Oratory of the Disciplines at Elusone (fifteenth century), in which we see the dual themes of the triumph of death and the Danse Macabre.

In modern times, perhaps also in concomitance with the experience of the first anatomy theatres, the still carnivalesque idea of the triumph gave way in penitential literature to the detailed and horrifying description of the death throes or the putrefying dead body (see for example the text by **Sebastiano Pauli**).

Modern literature offers countless variations on the triumph of death and by way of example here we need only mention **Baudelaire** and a recent work by **DeLillo**.

Another cultured but also popular form of the celebration of death was the Danse Macabre, held in holy places and in cemeteries. The etymology of the word macabre, a fairly recent term, is still a controversial issue (perhaps it comes from Arabic or Hebrew, or perhaps from the name of a person called Macabré) but the ritual probably arose following the widespread terror caused by the 'Black Death', the great outbreak of plague in the fourteenth century. The purpose of the death dance was not so much to increase the fear of waiting for the end as the need to exorcise that fear and get accustomed to the idea that it was coming. The danse Macabre shows popes, emperors, monks or young girls all dancing together led by skeletons, and it celebrates the transience of life and the levelling of all differences in wealth, age, and power. One of the oldest images (now lost) dates from 1424, in the cemetery of the Église des Innocents in Paris, and all that remains of it are engravings.

During the Renaissance a series of small-format books appeared complete with engravings of the Danse Macabre, the most famous of which (by Hans Holbein) are still reproduced to this day. In these books we see a sequence of scenes from everyday life (or biblical episodes) in which one or more skeletons accompany the human characters to remind us that death, ever in waiting, is the ineluctable companion to human existence.

Many of the first images projected using the 'camera obscura' technique in the seventeenth century take the skeleton as their theme, and perhaps the latest and most famous portrayal of the Danse Macabre is to be found in Ingmar Bergman's movie *The Seventh Seal*.

Master of the Upper Rhine,
The Deceased Lovers, Death and Lust,
sixteenth century,
Strasbourg,
Musée du Strasbourg

The Triumph of Death,
early fiftteenth
century,
Palermo, Palazzo
Abatellis, Museo
Regionale della Sicilia

following pages
Pieter Bruegel the Elder,
The Triumph of Death,
1562,
Madrid,
Prado Museum

The Dance of Death

Charles Baudelaire (1821–67)
The Flowers of Evil

Proud as a living person of her noble
stature,
With her big bouquet, her handkerchief
and gloves,
She has the nonchalance and easy manner
Of a slender coquette with bizarre ways.
Did one ever see a slimmer waist at a ball?
Her ostentatious dress in its queenly
fullness
Falls in ample folds over thin feet, tightly
pressed
Into slippers with pompons pretty as
flowers.
The swarm of bees that plays along her
collar-bones
Like a lecherous brook that rubs against
the rocks
Modestly protects from cat-calls and jeers
The funereal charms that she's anxious to
hide.
Her deep eye-sockets are empty and dark,
And her skull, skilfully adorned with
flowers,
Oscillates gently on her fragile vertebrae.
Charm of a non-existent thing, madly
arrayed!

Some, lovers drunken with flesh, will call
you
A caricature; they don't understand
The marvellous elegance of the human
frame.
You satisfy my fondest taste, tall skeleton!
Do you come to trouble with your potent
grimace
The festival of Life? Or does some old
desire
Still goading your living carcass
Urge you on, credulous one, towards
Pleasure's sabbath? [. . .]
The abyss of your eyes, full of horrible
thoughts,
Exhales vertigo, and discreet dancers
Cannot look without bitter nausea
At the eternal smile of your thirty-two
teeth.
Yet who has not clasped a skeleton in his
arms,
Who has not fed upon what belongs to
the grave?
What matters the perfume, the costume or
the dress?
He who shows disgust believes that he is
handsome.
Noseless dancer, irresistible whore.

When I am dead

William Shakespeare

Sonnets, 71 (1609)

No longer mourn for me when I am dead
Than you shall hear the surly sullen bell
Give warning to the world that I am fled
From this vile world with vilest worms to
dwell:
Nay, if you read this line, remember not
The hand that writ it, for I love you so,
That I in your sweet thoughts would be
forgot,
If thinking on me then should make you
woe.
O! if, I say, you look upon this verse,
When I perhaps compounded am with
clay,
Do not so much as my poor name
rehearse;
But let your love even with my life decay;
Lest the wise world should look into your
moan,
And mock you with me after I am gone.

Two Views of a Cadaver

Sylvia Plath (1932–63)

In Brueghel's panorama of smoke and
slaughter
Two people only are blind to the carrion
army:
He, afloat in the sea of her blue satin
Skirts, sings in the direction
Of her bare shoulder, while she bends,
Fingering a leaflet of music, over him,
Both of them deaf to the fiddle in the
hands
Of the death's-head shadowing their
song.
These Flemish lovers flourish; not for
long
Yet desolation, stalled in paint, spares the
little country
Foolish, delicate in the lower right-hand
corner.

Bruegel's *The Triumph of Death*

Don DeLillo

Underworld (1997)

The dead have come to take the living.
The dead in winding-sheets, the
regimented dead on horseback, the
skeleton that plays a hurdy-gurdy [. . .]
He studies the tumbrel filled with skulls.
He stands in the aisle and looks at the
naked man pursued by dogs. He looks at
the gaunt dog nibbling the baby in the
dead woman's arms. These are long
gaunt starveling hounds, they are war
dogs, hell dogs, boneyard hounds beset
by parasitic mites, by dog tumors and dog
cancers.
Dear germ-free Edgar, the man who has
an air-filtration system in his house to
vaporise specks of dust – he finds a
fascination in cankers, lesions and rotting
bodies so long as his connection to the
source is strictly pictorial.
He finds a second dead woman in the
middle ground, straddled by a skeleton.
The positioning is sexual, unquestionably.
But is Edgar sure it's a woman
bestraddled or could it be a man? He
stands in the aisle and they're all around
him cheering and he has the pages in his
face. The painting has an instancy that he
finds striking. Yes, the dead fall upon the
living. But he begins to see that the living
are sinners. The cardplayers, the lovers
who dally, he sees the kings in an ermine
cloak with his fortune stashed in
hogshead drums. The dead have come to
empty out the wine gourds, to serve a
skull on a platter to gentlefolk at their
meal. He sees gluttony, lust and greed
[. . .] The dead beating kettledrums. The
sackcloth dead slitting a pilgrim's throat.
The meatblood colors and massed bodies,
this is a census-taking of awful ways to
die. He looks at the flaring sky in the
deep distance out beyond the headlands
on the left-hand page – Death elsewhere,
Conflagration in many places, Terror
universal, the crows, the ravens in silent
glide, the raven perched on the white
nag's rump, black and white forever [. . .]

Chapter III

The Apocalypse, Hell and the Devil

1. A Universe of Horrors

The ugly, in the form of the terrifying and the diabolical, makes its entry into the Christian world with John the Evangelist's book of Revelation (the Apocalypse). Not that there was any lack of mention of the Devil and hell in the Old Testament and in the other books of the New Testament. But, more than anything else, in those texts the Devil is mentioned through his actions or through the effects they produce (for example, the description of the possessed in the Gospels), with the exception of Genesis, in which he assumes the form of a serpent. The Devil never appears with the 'somatic' features with which he was to be portrayed in the Middle Ages; and, regarding the hereafter, fairly generic terms are used to describe the pangs suffered by sinners (wailing and gnashing of teeth, eternal fire) but no lively or evident image was ever offered.

Revelation is a sacred representation (today we might even say a 'disaster movie') in which we are spared no detail. Of course, this holds as long as we don't attempt to make an allegorical interpretation of this text, as various exegetes have done, but merely read it as a literal account of 'true things' that will happen, because this is the way that popular culture has understood it or heard it referred to, and this is the way that it inspired artistic images over the centuries. Around the end of the first century of our era, on the island of Patmos, the apostle John (or in any case the author of the text) had a vision and talked about it according to the rules of the literary genre known as 'vision' (or *apokalypsis*, revelation) common to Jewish culture.

Saint Severus Battles against the Locusts of the Apocalypse, eleventh century, Paris, Bibliothèque Nationale

The author hears a voice that obliges him to write down what he will see and to send it to the seven Churches of the Asiatic province. He sees seven golden candelabra and in the middle of them there is someone like a son of man, with snow-white hair and burning feet like molten bronze and a voice like the sound of many waters. In his right hand he holds seven stars and a sword issues from his mouth. And he sees a throne with One sitting on it, enveloped in a rainbow resembling an emerald. Around the throne there are twenty-four Elders and four creatures: a lion, an ox, an animal with a human face and a flying eagle. In his right hand the One who sits on the throne holds a scroll with seven seals that no one can open. But then there appears a lamb with seven horns and seven eyes, worshipped by the Elders and the four creatures and, on the opening of the first seal, there appears a white horse mounted by a victorious knight; the second seal brings a sorrel mounted by a man wielding a huge sword; the third brings a greenish horse mounted by a man carrying a set of scales. When the fourth seal is opened there appears a greenish horse mounted by Death; the fifth seal brings the martyrs; the sixth a great earthquake: the sun grows black and the moon red as blood, the stars fall and the sky recedes like a scroll, rolling up. Before the opening of the seventh seal there appears the white-robed host of those chosen by God. Then the seal is opened, and the seven angels standing straight before God begin to sound their seven trumpets. At every blast of one of the trumpets hailstones and fire fall upon and devastate the earth, a third of the sea becomes blood, all creatures perish, the stars fall and all the planets are reduced to one-third. The pit of the Abyss opens, and smoke and locusts emerge like terrible warriors led by the Angel of the Abyss. Four angels, freed from the River Euphrates where they had been bound, move with armies of countless people with fiery breastplates, and horses with lions' heads, and a third part of the inhabitants of the earth perishes, wounded by the tails of the horses (which resemble serpents), and by their fierce mouths.

At the sound of the seventh trumpet, as the Ark of the Alliance appears, there comes a woman, clad in the sun and the moon, crowned with twelve stars. Then comes a red, ten-horned dragon whose seven heads are crowned with diadems. A child is born and ascends to heaven to sit at God's side. There is a terrible battle between Michael, the angels and the dragon. The dragon plunges to earth and tries to strike the woman, who escapes it thanks to the wonderful intervention of the forces of nature. Then the dragon stops on the seashore, and from the sea emerges a beast with ten horns and seven heads, resembling a panther with a bear's paws and a lion's mouth, and with the entire world, which now admires him, as he spouts horrible blasphemies against God, he makes war on the saints and vanquishes them, aided by another beast emerged from the earth. This last is a false prophet (which successive tradition was to identify with the Antichrist) who makes all men slaves to the first beast.

But the hour of the fight back has come: together with 140,000 of the elect who have remained chaste the lamb reappears and angels prophesy

The Whore of Babylon,
The Apocalypse of the
Beatus of Burgo de
Osma,
eleventh century,
Soria, The Cathedral
Archives

Albrecht Dürer,
*The Four Horsemen of the
Apocalypse,*
1511,
Paris, Louvre

the fall of Babylon. The supreme judge arrives on a white cloud. He resembles the son of man and bears a sharp scythe like the angels who assist him, and the result is a great, punitive massacre. Angels with seven scourges finish the job, and the beast is beaten. In the sky the Tabernacle of the Testimony opens and the angels with the seven scourges carry seven goblets full of the wrath of God and once more they spread death and terror and malignant sores all around. The waters of the sea and the rivers are changed into blood, the sun parches the survivors, darkness and drought torment the living, while from the mouths of the dragon, the beast and the false prophet emerge three impure spirits that resemble frogs. They marshal all the kings of the earth and there is the decisive battle between the forces of good and evil, in the place called Armageddon. The whore appears again on a scarlet beast with seven heads and ten horns, bearing a goblet full of her lewdness; but she will be brought to ruin by the rebellion of the crowd she had seduced. Babylon falls, and the wrath of God destroys the city. The angels, the Elders and the four creatures sing the victory of God and a warrior on a white horse appears in the sky. He is at the head of victorious white armies and all together they capture the beast and hurl him together with the false prophet into a lake of burning sulphur.

Apocalypse Tapestries,
*c.*1300,
Angers

facing page
The Beast that Came
from the Sea, The
Bamberg Apocalypse,
ms. 140,
eleventh century,
Bamberg, Staat
Bibliothek

At this point Chapter 20 says that an angel comes who chains the dragon in the Abyss, where it will remain for *one thousand years.* After that time, Satan, the dragon, will return for a short time to seduce the people, but he is doomed to ultimate defeat, after which he will be thrown again into the lake of sulphur, together with the false prophet and the beast, while Christ and the blessed will reign for a thousand years over the earth. Finally there will be the Last Judgement and from the heavens will descend the Holy City, the Celestial Jerusalem, glittering with gold and jewels (but this splendid vision, which would deserve a chapter to itself, belongs to a history of beauty).

It is clear that this vision introduced a huge repertory of monstrous creatures and terrifying events into the Christian imagination. But the thing that triggered centuries of argument is the substantial ambiguity of Chapter 20. According to one interpretation, the millennium during which the dragon will remain in chains has not yet begun and so we are still waiting for a golden age. Or, as Augustine says in *The City of God,* the millennium represents the period spanning the Incarnation to the end of history, therefore it is the period we are already living through. In this case, however, waiting for the millennium is replaced by waiting for its end, with the terrors that will ensue, the return of the Devil and his false prophet, the Antichrist, the second coming of Christ, and the end of the world.

This interpretation filled those living at the end of the first millennium with great distress. The story of the Apocalypse unfolds between these two possible interpretations, swinging between euphoria and despair together with a sense of perennial expectation and tension as we wait for something (marvellous or terrifying) that must occur. But the Apocalypse and its exegetes had only *talked* about this: so it had to be translated into images, accessible even to the illiterate. Of all the interpretations of John's text, the greatest success was enjoyed by a mammoth commentary, hundreds of pages long compared to the few dozen that make up the text interpreted. This text is the *Apocalipsin, Libri Duodecim* by the Beatus of Liébana (730–85), an abbot who lived in Visigothic Spain at the court of the king of Oviedo. There is no sense in pointing out the credulity and naivety of this farrago of a commentary: perhaps it caused a stir because of its prurience and lubricity. Numerous manuscript copies were made, each embellished with splendid decorations (masterpieces of Mozarabic art), and an impressive series of codices of fabulous beauty, all produced between the tenth and eleventh centuries. These illuminated manuscripts of the so-called 'Beatuses' inspired much of medieval representational art, first and foremost the sculptures of the Romanesque abbeys standing along the four pilgrimage routes to Santiago di Compostela, but also those of the Gothic cathedrals. The apocalyptic themes usually featured on the portals and gables of these churches were Christ enthroned surrounded by the four evangelists, the Last Judgement and the inferno. Diabolic images like those of the dragons of the Abyss, the beasts with seven heads and ten horns, and the whore of Babylon on her scarlet beast were spread by other means, through other illuminated manuscripts and various pictorial cycles. Thus, the visual translation of a splendid text in visionary terms (over and above the promise of final glory with which it ends) introduced the fear of the end into the medieval imagination.

The most visible historic effects of the Apocalypse were social and political and regard the so-called 'millennium fears' and the birth of the millenary movements.

For a long time it was thought that, on the fateful night of the last 31 December of the millennium, humanity had stayed awake in the churches waiting for the end of the world, only to erupt into songs of joy on the following morning, and Romantic historians dwelt at length on this legend. In reality, contemporary texts hold no trace of these terrors, and the only sources referred to by those who believed in them were the works of sixteenth-century authors. As the first millennium drew to a close, the humble of the earth didn't even know they were living in the year 1000, because the dating system starting with the birth of Christ, and not from the presumed beginning of the world, was not yet in current use. Recently, some have maintained that there were endemic fears, but secret ones, in popular circles stirred up by preachers suspected of heresy, and it was for this reason that official texts did not mention them.

Hell,
twelfth century,
Conques,
Abbey
of Sainte-Foy

Before the End

Vincent of Beauvais (twelfth–thirteenth century)

Speculum Historiale, XXXI, 111

On the first day the sea will rise forty cubits above the mountains and its surface will rise up like a wall. On the second day it will drop so far that it will be hard to see. On the third day sea monsters, appearing on the sea's surface, will send their roaring up to the sky. On the fourth day the sea and all waters will catch fire. On the fifth day the grass and trees will put forth drops of blood; on the sixth day the buildings will collapse. On the seventh day rocks will crash into each other. On the eighth day there will be a universal earthquake. On the ninth day the earth will be levelled. On the tenth day men will come out of the caverns and wander around as if maddened, unable to speak to one another. On the eleventh day the bones of the dead will arise. On the twelfth day the stars will fall. On the thirteenth day all the survivors will die, only to rise again with the dead. On the fourteenth day the sky and the land will burn. On the fifteenth day there will be a new sky and a new land and everything will arise anew.

Gog and Magog,
The Apocalypse of the
Beatus of Burgo de Osma,
eleventh century,
Soria,
The Cathedral Archives

Although many medieval writers did not deal with the terrors aroused by that fateful year's end, many, such as **Rodulfus Glaber,** wrote about millenarian fears and consequently anguish over the end of the world crops up constantly in medieval culture. This is understandable if you think that, for men tormented by the centuries of invasions and massacres that followed the collapse of the Roman Empire, John's vision was no mystical fantasy but a fairly faithful portrait of what was happening to them and a threat of what might continue to happen in the future.But, whereas the anxieties before the millennium were endured passively by peasant populations unable to conceive of any way out, the new millennium saw the advent of a whole range of social differences and new masses (which today we would call the 'lumpenproletariat') saw in Revelation the promise of a better future to be obtained through rebellion.

Millenarianism generated mystical movements like the propheticism of Joachim da Fiore (who talks of a community based on equality that would be established during the golden age to come) and the Franciscan rigour of the Friars Minor, but in variants of da Fiore's thinking the passage to this Third Age is often depicted as opposition to established power and the world of wealth. Mystical drives thus culminated in anarchy, while austerity and dissipation, the thirst for justice and banditry, came to characterise restive groups under the spell of charismatic leaders, in which the only aspect of apocalyptic inspiration to emerge was merely

a taste for purifying violence, not infrequently visited upon the Jews (identified as representatives of the Antichrist).

Millenarian movements have appeared in various centuries, and they are still being formed to this day, in marginal communities that have sometimes been the scene of mass suicides. As for the beginning of modern times, just consider episodes like the one where, during the Reformation, a peasants' revolt was transformed by Thomas Müntzer (who defined himself as the scythe that God had whetted to mow down His enemies, and saw Luther as the beast and the whore of Babylon) into the utopia of an egalitarian society; or the Anabaptists of Münster, who called their city New Jerusalem, proclaimed the end of the world before Easter, saw John of Leyden as the Messiah of the last days, and died in an appalling massacre, which seemed to have come straight out of Revelation itself.

These and other movements sprang up as a reaction to the monstrosities recounted by the visionary of Patmos, the intention being to outdo them and thus bring about a happy age in which Satan together with his works and his pomp would be definitively defeated.

The fact that, sometimes, the followers of the Apocalypse yielded once again to the allure of the beast and his violence, causing more rivers of blood to flow, is merely further evidence of the seductive power of that fearful text.

Around the Millennium

Rodulfus Glaber (tenth–eleventh century)
History of the Year One Thousand, IV, 9–10

Just before the year 1033 of our Lord, in other words one thousand years after the Saviour's passion, many famous people in the West died [. . .] Shortly thereafter, all over the world the effects of the famine began to make themselves felt, and almost the entire human race risked death. The weather had become so inclement that no one could find a propitious time to sow seeds or reap the harvest, especially because of the flooding. The elements seemed to be at war with one another: but they were undoubtedly the instrument God used to punish men's pride [. . .]

There was no one then who did not suffer for lack of food: great lords and the middle class were on the same level as the poor: hunger made everyone emaciated [. . .]

When there were no more animals or birds to eat, men, driven by terrible pangs of hunger, had to resort to feeding on every kind of carrion as well as other things that cause revulsion just to speak of. In order to escape death, some ate the roots of trees and weeds in the rivers, but it was no use, because there is no escaping the wrath of God save in God Himself.

It is horrifying to tell of the awful things men did during that era. Alas! As has been recorded only a few other times in history, this ravenous hunger drove men to eat human flesh. Wayfarers were attacked by those stronger than they, and their bodies were cut up into pieces, cooked over fires, and eaten. Even those who moved from one land to another in the hopes of escaping the famine, and were given hospitality along the way, had their throats cut during the night and were used to nourish the very same people who offered them shelter. Many, showing a piece of fruit or an egg to children, drew them aside in order to slaughter and eat them.

In many places the cadavers of the dead were dug up and used to allay people's hunger. This raving madness reached such excesses that untended beasts had more chance than men of escaping the clutches of thieves. When feeding on human flesh had become almost a customary practice, one man brought some meat that had already been cooked to the market in Tournus to sell it, as if it had been the flesh of some animal. When he was arrested, he did not deny his shameful crime: then he was bound and burned at the stake. Another man who had gone to the place where they had buried that flesh in order to disinter and eat it was burned as well.

2. Hell

facing page
Hans Memling,
*Triptych with the Last
Judgement*,
detail,
1467–71,
Danzig, Muzeum
Narodowe

Although Revelation ends with the vision of Satan hurled into the underworld, from where he will never emerge again, nevertheless this was not the text that introduced the concept of hell to the Christian world. Long before, many religions had conceived of a usually subterranean place where the shades of the dead wandered. In the pagan Hades, Demeter went to seek Persephone carried off by the lord of the underworld; Orpheus descended to save Eurydice; while Ulysses and Aeneas also ventured there. The Quran also talks of a place of punishment. In the Old Testament we find mention of an 'abode of the dead' but without any talk of punishments or torment, while the Gospels make more explicit mention of the Abyss, and especially Gehenna and its eternal fires, where there will be 'wailing and gnashing of teeth'.

The Middle Ages produced many descriptions of hell and many accounts of journeys to the underworld, from *The Navigation of St Brendan* to the *Vision of Tundall*, from Giacomino da Verona's *On the Infernal Babylonian State* to the *Book of the Three Scriptures* by Bonvesin de la Riva. From these men, from Virgil (*Aeneid*, VI), and probably from the Arab tradition too (there is a mention of a **Book of the Stair** from the eighth century that tells of a journey made by Mohammed to the realm of the underworld), **Dante** was to draw inspiration for his *Inferno*. Dante's work is a cardinal text for its account of all kinds of monstrosities and its catalogue of manifold deformities (Minos, the Furies, Geryon, Lucifer, with three faces and six huge bat wings) and its collection of unspeakable tortures–from the slothful who run naked stung by wasps and horseflies, to gluttons scourged by rain and disembowelled by Cerberus, from heretics who lie in fiery graves to men of violence plunged into a river of boiling blood, from blasphemers, sodomites and usurers struck by showers of fire to flatterers immersed in manure, from simoniacs stuck head down with their feet ablaze to swindlers submerged in boiling pitch and prodded with hooks by Devils, from hypocrites burdened with leaden cloaks to thieves transformed into reptiles, to forgers afflicted with scabies and leprosy to traitors immersed in ice ...

The influence both of apocalyptic literature and the various accounts of journeys to the underworld led to the proliferation in Romanesque abbeys and Gothic cathedrals, in illuminated manuscripts, in frescoes, of all those portrayals that reminded the faithful day by day of the punishments that awaited sinners.

Master of Catherine of Cleves,
The Mouth of Hell,
ms. 945, fol. 168v,
c.1440,
New York,
Pierpoint Morgan Library

Hell in the Old Testament

Psalms, 9:17
The wicked shall be turned into hell, and all the nations that forget God.

Job, 21:13
They spend their days in wealth, and in a moment go down to the grave.

Isaiah, 5:14
Therefore hell hath enlarged herself, and opened her mouth without measure: and their glory, and their multitude, and their pomp, and he that rejoiceth, shall descend into it.

Isaiah, 14:4, 9, 11
That thou shalt take up this proverb against the king of Babylon, and say [. . .] Hell from beneath is moved for thee to meet thee at thy coming: [. . .] Thy pomp is brought down to the grave, and the noise of thy viols [. . .]

Ezekiel, 26:20
When I shall bring thee down with them that descend into the pit, with the people of old time, and shall set thee in the low parts of the earth, in places desolate of old, with them that go down to the pit [. . .]

Hell in the Gospels

Matthew, 5:22
But I say unto you, That whosoever is angry with his brother without a cause shall be in danger of the judgement: and whosoever shall say to his brother, Raca, shall be in danger of the council: but whosoever shall say, Thou fool, shall be in danger of hell fire.

Matthew, 13:40
As therefore the tares are gathered and burned in the fire; so shall it be in the end of this world.

Matthew, 13:42
And shall cast them into a furnace of fire: there shall be wailing and gnashing of teeth.

Matthew, 18:8
Wherefore if thy hand or thy foot offend thee, cut them off, and cast them from thee: it is better for thee to enter into life halt or maimed, rather than having two hands or two feet to be cast into everlasting fire.

Matthew, 22:13
Then said the king to the servants, Bind him hand and foot, and take him away, and cast him into outer darkness, there shall be weeping and gnashing of teeth.

Matthew, 23:33
Ye serpents, ye generation of vipers, how can ye escape the damnation of hell?

Matthew, 25:41
Then shall he say also unto them on the left hand, Depart from me, ye cursed, into everlasting fire, prepared for the devil and his angels.

Matthew, 25:46
And these shall go away into everlasting punishment: but the righteous into life eternal.

Mark, 3:29
But he that shall blaspheme against the Holy Ghost hath never forgiveness, but is in danger of eternal damnation.

Mark, 9:43–8
And if thy hand offend thee, cut it off: it is better for thee to enter into life maimed, than having two hands to go into hell, into the fire that never shall be quenched: Where their worm dieth not, and the fire is not quenched. And if thy foot offend thee, cut it off: it is better for thee to enter halt into life, than having two feet to be cast into hell, into the fire that never shall be quenched: Where their worm dieth not, and the fire is not quenched. And if thine eye offend thee, pluck it out: it is better for thee to enter into the kingdom of God with one eye, than having two eyes to be cast into hell fire: Where their worm dieth not, and the fire is not quenched.

John, 5:29
And shall come forth; they that have done good, unto the resurrection of life; and they that have done evil, unto the resurrection of damnation.

Saint Brendan's Hell

Anonymous

The Voyage of St Brendan (tenth century, fifteenth century Tuscan version)

Having followed the north wind, they saw an island that was entirely covered with large rocks. This was a very dirty island that had neither trees nor leaves nor plants nor flowers nor fruits, but was full of forges and blacksmiths. Each forge had its own smith, and they had all the tools that blacksmiths use. Their forges burned brightly with red-hot fires, and each blacksmith hammered with such force and made so much noise that if this was not Hell, it seemed that it must be.

Then the priests felt a powerful wind and heard the sound of hammers, the clangour of hammers on anvils. And upon hearing this noise, Saint Brendan made the sign of the cross and said: 'O Lord God, save us from this island, if it be your will.' And having said this, immediately a man from the island came towards them; Old, with a long beard, he was black with ash and hairy like a pig, and stank terribly. Then, as soon as he saw these servants of God, the man immediately turned round, and the abbot made the sign of the cross, and imploring God said: 'O my sons, set

the sails and let us leave as quickly as we can so that we may escape this island of suffering as soon as possible.'

Having spoken thus, an ugly old bearded man suddenly came to the island's shore. In one hand he held a blacksmith's tongs and in the other a red-hot iron pole, and seeing that the ship had left, he threw that iron pole after them. By the grace of God it didn't strike them, but where it fell, the water began to boil powerfully. And having seen this happen they saw a great multitude of these men come to the shore, all horrible like the first; and each was holding in his hand an enormous club of burning iron that gave off a great stench. And of these clubs and the other things they threw, not one struck the ship, but they created a terrible stink, and made the water boil for three days; the priests also saw the island burn brightly, and as they were leaving, they heard a great yelling and noise come from those horrible men. And Saint Brendan, comforting his brothers, said: 'Don't be afraid, my sons, our Lord is, and will ever be, our saviour. I want you to know that we are near hell, and this island is a part of it, and you have seen its signs and therefore you must pray devoutly that we do not find ourselves here again.'

Nicola Pisano,
Hell,
1260,
Pisa, Baptistry

Gustave Doré
Geryon from Dante,
L'inferno,
1861,
Paris, Hachette

A Monstrous Metamorphosis

Dante (1265–1321)

Inferno, XXV, 34 sgg.

As I was holding raised on them my brows,
Behold! a serpent with six feet darts forth
In front of one, and fastens wholly on him.
With middle feet it bound him round the paunch,
And with the forward ones his arms it seized;
Then thrust its teeth through one cheek and the other;
The hindermost it stretched upon his thighs,
And put its tail through in between the two,
And up behind along the reins outspread it.
[. . .]
Then they stuck close, as if of heated wax
They had been made, and intermixed their colour;
Nor one nor other seemed now what he was;
[. . .]
Already the two heads had one become,
When there appeared to us two figures mingled
Into one face, wherein the two were lost.
Of the four lists were fashioned the two arms,
The thighs and legs, the belly and the chest
Members became that never yet were seen.
Every original aspect there was cancelled;
Two and yet none did the perverted image
Appear, and such departed with slow pace.
Even as a lizard, under the great scourge
Of days canicular, exchanging hedge,
Lightning appeareth if the road it cross;
Thus did appear, coming towards the bellies
Of the two others, a small fiery serpent,
Livid and black as is a peppercorn.
And in that part whereat is first received
Our aliment, it one of them transfixed;
Then downward fell in front of him extended.
The one transfixed looked at it, but said naught;
Nay, rather with feet motionless he yawned,
Just as if sleep or fever had assailed him. [. . .]
The legs together with the thighs themselves
Adhered so, that in little time the juncture
No sign whatever made that was apparent.
He with the cloven tail assumed the figure
The other one was losing, and his skin
Became elastic, and the other's hard.
I saw the arms draw inward at the armpits,
And both feet of the reptile, that were short,
Lengthen as much as those contracted were.
Thereafter the hind feet, together twisted,
Became the member that a man conceals,
And of his own the wretch had two created.
[. . .] Issued the ears from out the hollow cheeks;
What did not backward run and was retained
Of that excess made to the face a nose,
And the lips thickened far as was befitting.

Geryon

Dante (1265–1321)

Inferno, XVII, 7–27

And that uncleanly image of deceit
Came up and thrust ashore its head and bust,
But on the border did not drag its tail.
The face was as the face of a just man,
Its semblance outwardly was so benign,
And of a serpent all the trunk beside.
Two paws it had, hairy unto the armpits;
The back, and breast, and both the sides it had
Depicted o'er with nooses and with shields.
[. . .]
His tail was wholly quivering in the void,
Contorting upwards the envenomed fork,
That in the guise of scorpion armed its point.

Beato Angelico,
The Last Judgement,
1430–35,
Florence,
St Mark's Museum

Mohammed's Journey to the Inferno

The Book of Stairs, 79 (eighth century)
And when Gabriel had finished his report I, Mohammed, prophet and messenger of God, saw sinners tormented in hell in many different ways, and so I felt such enormous compassion for them that I began to sweat all over; and I saw several among them whose lips were being cut off with fiery scissors. Then I asked Gabriel who they were. And he told me that they were those who sow words of discord among the people. And others, whose tongues were being cut off, were those who had borne false witness. I saw others hanging by their members on fiery hooks, and they were the men who had committed adultery on earth. And afterwards I saw a great crowd of women, an almost incredible number, and all were suspended by their privates from great fiery beams. And these hung from fiery chains, so extraordinarily hot that no one could possibly express it. And I asked Gabriel who those women were. And he told me that they were the whores who had never abandoned fornication and lasciviousness.

And I saw many other men who were very handsome and very well dressed. And I understood that they were the rich among my people, and all of them were burning in the fire. And I asked Gabriel why they burnt thus, because I knew well that they gave a

great deal of charity to the poor. And Gabriel told me that even though they were charitable, they were swollen.

Cerberus

Dante (1265–1321)
Inferno, VI, 13–24
Cerberus, monster cruel and uncouth,
With his three gullets like a dog is barking
Over the people that are there submerged.
Red eyes he has, and unctuous beard and black,
And belly large, and armed with claws his hands;
He rends the spirits, flays, and quarters them.

The Furies

Dante (1265–1321)
Inferno, IX, 34–63
And more he said, but not in mind I have it;
Because mine eye had altogether drawn me
Tow'rds the high tower with the red-flaming summit,
Where in a moment saw I swift uprisen
The three infernal Furies stained with blood,
Who had the limbs of women and their mien,
And with the greenest hydras were begirt;
Small serpents and cerastes were their tresses,
Wherewith their horrid temples were entwined.

Baroque Infernos

Romolo Marchelli

Lenten Sermons (1682)

God, in order to further torment the damned, made Himself distiller, and inside those stills of hell He enclosed the pangs of the most ravenous hungers, the most burning thirsts, the most freezing cold, the firiest passions; the torments of those slaughtered by iron, choked by the hangman's noose, reduced to ashes by flames and torn apart by wild beasts; the flesh eaten alive by worms, devoured by serpents, flayed with knives, gashed and torn by the torturer's iron combs; the arrows of Saint Sebastian, the gridiron of Saint Lawrence, the oven in the form of a bronze bull of Saint Eustace, the lions of Saint Ignatius; and severed and shattered bones and dislocated joints and detached limbs; all the keenest pains, all the most vehement anxieties, all the most terrible pangs, all the longest death agonies and all the slowest, most laborious, most atrocious deaths. And distilling all these ingredients, He made such a brew, each drop of which contains the refined quintessence of all pains, in such a way that each flame, each ember, better yet each spark of that flame contains within itself the distillation of all torments within a single torment.

St Alphonsus Liguori

Preparation for Death, XXVI (1758)

What is this inferno? It is the place of torment [. . .] And the more someone has offended God in some way, the more torments he will suffer [. . .] The sense of smell will be tormented. What punishment would it be to find oneself closed in a room with a rotten corpse? [. . .] The damned must reside amidst many millions of other damned souls, alive for the punishment, but cadavers for the stench they give off. [. . .] They will suffer all the more (I say) for their stench, for the screaming, and for the crowds; because in hell they will be one on top of the other, like sheep crowded together in wintertime [. . .] From this then will come the punishment of immobility [. . .] Since the damned soul will then fall into hell on the last day, so he will have to remain, without ever changing his

place and without being able to move his foot, or his hand, as long as God is God.

His hearing will be tormented with the continuous screams and cries of those poor desperate souls. The demons will clamour continuously [. . .] What punishment is it when one wants to sleep and one hears an invalid who complains continuously, a dog barking, a little child crying? Wretched damned, who must hear the noise and cries of those tormented constantly and for all eternity! The throat will be tormented with hunger; the damned will be hungry as wolves [. . .] But he will never have so much as a crumb of bread. He will feel such thirst, that not even all the water in the sea would be enough to slake it; but he will not have so much as a drop: the glutton asked for a drop, but he hasn't had it yet, and he never, ever will [. . .]

The punishment that most torments the senses of the damned is the fire of hell, which torments the touch [. . .] In this land punishment by fire is the worst of all; but there is a great deal of difference between our fire and that of hell, which Saint Augustine has said makes ours seem as if painted [. . .] Therefore the wretched will be surrounded by fire, like wood inside a furnace. The damned soul will find himself with an abyss of fire below, an abyss above, and an abyss all around him. If he touches, sees, breathes; he does not touch, see or breathe anything but fire. He will exist in fire like a fish in water. But this fire will not only surround the damned, it will enter into his guts to torment him from within. His body will become entirely made of fire, so that his guts will burn inside his stomach, his heart inside his chest, his brain inside his skull, his blood inside his veins, even his bone marrow inside his bones: each damned soul will become a furnace of fire [. . .]

If hell were not eternal, it would not be hell. The punishment that does not last for long, is not much of a punishment. On an infirm man you may lance an abscess, on another gangrene breaks out; the pain is great, but because it ends quickly, it is no great torment. But what punishment would it be, if that cut or that

operation with fire continued for a week, for an entire month? When the punishment is very long, even when it is light, like discomfort in the eyes, or the pain of a great weight, it becomes unbearable. But why stop at pain? Even a play or music that lasts too long, or continues for an entire day, would be unbearably tedious. And what if it lasted a month? Or a year? What will hell be like? It is not the place where one watches the same play, or hears the same music: there is not only a discomfort in the eyes, or a great weight: one does not feel merely the torment of a cut, or a hot iron, but rather all the torments, all the pain; and for how long? For all of eternity [. . .]

[. . .] Death in this life is the thing most feared by sinners, but in hell it will become the most desired [. . .] And how long will their misery last? Forever and ever [. . .]

The damned will ask the demons: Where is the night? [. . .] When does it end? When do these shadows lift, when do these cries, this stench, these flames, these torments end? And they will answer: 'Never, never.' And how long will it last? 'For ever and ever.'

Modern Hell

Jean-Paul Sartre

In Camera (1945)

INEZ – *(Confronting him fearlessly, but with a look of vast surprise)* Well, well! *(A pause)* Ah, I understand now. I know why they've put us three together.

GARCIN – I advise you to . . . to think twice before you say any more.

INEZ – Wait! You'll see how simple it is. Childishly simple. Obviously there aren't any physical torments – you agree, don't you? And yet we're in hell. And no one else will come here. We'll stay in this room together, the three of us, for ever and ever . . . In short, there's someone absent here, the official torturer.

GARCIN – *(Sotto voce)* I'd noticed that.

INEZ – It's obvious what they're after – an economy of man-power . . . or devil-power, if you prefer. The same idea as in the cafeteria where customers serve themselves.

ESTELLA – What ever do you mean?

INEZ – I mean that each of us will act as torturer of the two others.

Lucas van Leyden,
*Triptych of the Last
Judgement*,
detail, 1527,
Leyden, Musée
Municipal de Lakenhall

But hell was also to obsess the centuries that followed, and in Baroque Lenten sermons (see the texts by **Marchelli** and **St Alfonso Maria de' Liguori**) the faithful were terrified by descriptions of the pangs of hell that exceed Dante in violence, in part because they are not redeemed by any artistic inspiration. The idea of hell even returns in an existentialist, atheist vein. **Jean-Paul Sartre**'s *In Camera* (*Huis clos*) is a representation of a modern inferno: although in life we are defined by Others, by their pitiless gaze that reveals our ugliness or our shame, nonetheless we can still fool ourselves into thinking that others do not see us as we really are. But in Sartre's inferno (a hotel room where the light is always on and the door closed, in which three people who had never seen one another before have to coexist for eternity) you cannot escape the eye of the Others and you live alone with their scorn. One of the characters shouts 'Open up, open up, for God's sake. I accept everything: the boot, the pincers, the molten lead, the tongs, the garrotte, everything that burns, that lacerates, I want to suffer properly ...' All is in vain: 'there's no need for red-hot gridirons; hell is other people.'

3. The Metamorphosis of the Devil

At the centre of hell sits Lucifer, or Satan. But satanic figures, Devils and fiends had been present since earliest times. Various kinds of demons, in the form of intermediary beings who are sometimes benevolent, other times malevolent, and, when wicked, of monstrous aspect (but even in Revelation the 'angels' are helpers both of God and the Devil), existed in various cultures: in Egypt the monster Ammut, a cross between a crocodile, a leopard and a hippopotamus, devoured the guilty in the afterworld; there are ferocious-looking beings in Mesopotamian culture; in various forms of dualistic religion there is a Principle of Evil in opposition to a Principle of Good. There are Devils like Al-Saitan inIslamic culture, described as having bestial characteristics, just as there are demonic tempters, the *gul*, who take on the appearance of beautiful women.

As for Jewish culture, which had a direct influence on Christian culture, the Devil of Genesis tempts Eve in the form of a serpent and within the tradition, on interpreting some biblical texts that seem to refer to other things, like **Isaiah** and **Ezekiel**, he was present at the beginning of the world as the Rebellious Angel, whom God cast down into hell.

In the Bible we also find mention of Lilith, a female monster of Babylonian origin, who in the Jewish tradition becomes a female demon with a woman's face, long hair and wings, and who in the Cabalistic tradition (seventh–eighth century) was held to be Adam's first wife, later transformed into a demon.

We might add the 'Meridian Devil' of Psalm 91, who appears at first as the angel of death but in the monastic tradition later became the tempter of the flesh, and the numerous mentions of Satan in various passages, where he appears as the Slanderer, the Adversary, as he who asks for Job to be put to the test, and finally as Asmodeus in the book of Tobias. In the book of Wisdom (2.24) we read: 'God created man for immortality, and he made him in His own image and likeness, but the envy of the Devil brought death into the world.'

In the Gospels the Devil is never described, only the effects that he causes. But, apart from tempting Jesus, on several occasions he is driven from the bodies of the possessed, he is mentioned by Jesus and variously defined as the Evil One, the Enemy, Beelzebub, the Liar and the Prince of this world.

Lucifer,
Codex Altonensis,
fol. 48r,
fourteenth century

The Fall of the King of Babylon
Isaiah, 14:12–15

How art thou fallen from heaven, O Lucifer, son of the morning! how art thou cut down to the ground, which didst weaken the nations! For thou hast said in thine heart, I will ascend into heaven, I will exalt my throne above the stars of God: I will sit also upon the mount of the congregation, in the sides of the north: I will ascend above the heights of the clouds; I will be like the most High. Yet thou shalt be brought down to hell, to the sides of the pit.

The Battle between Michael and the Dragon
Revelation, 12:1–5, 7–9

And there appeared a great wonder in heaven; a woman clothed with the sun, and the moon under her feet, and upon her head a crown of twelve stars: And she being with child cried, travailing in birth, and pained to be delivered. And there appeared another wonder in heaven; and behold a great red dragon, having seven heads and ten horns, and seven crowns upon his heads. And his tail drew the third part of the stars of heaven, and did cast them to the earth: and the dragon stood before the woman which was ready to be delivered, for to devour her child as soon as it was born.

[. . .] And there was war in heaven: Michael and his angels fought against the dragon; and the dragon fought him and his angels. And prevailed not; neither was their place found any more in heaven. And the great dragon was cast out, that old serpent, called the Devil, and Satan, which deceiveth the whole world.

It seems obvious, also for traditional reasons, that the Devil must be ugly. As such he is already evoked by St Peter ('Brothers, be sober and vigilant, because your adversary the Devil, like a roaring lion, is all around you seeking whom he might devour'). He is also described in animal forms in the lives of the hermits and, in a crescendo of ugliness, he gradually invades patristic and medieval literature, especially devotional works. The Devil appears before **Rodulfus Glaber**; swarms of Devils appear in travellers tales about exotic lands as in **Mandeville**, and for various centuries pious legends circulated about the 'pact with the Devil': the Devil tempts the good Christian and has him sign a pact that today we would call Faustian, but then the Christian usually manages to wriggle out of the trap.

A pact with the Devil is the basis of the medieval legend of Cyprian, a young pagan who, in order to have the girl he loves, Justine, sells his soul to the Devil. In the end, however, moved by the girl's faith, he converts and together they take the path to martyrdom. This same theme was later picked up by Calderon de la Barca in his *The Mighty Magician* (1637). But one of the most successful popular versions of the tale from the earliest Christian centuries was the *Legend of Theophilus*: a deacon in Cilicia, Theophilus was slandered by his bishop and deprived of his position.

To get it back, thanks to the help of a Jewish wizard, he meets the Devil who requires the deacon to sell him his soul and to abjure Christ and the Virgin. Once the pact is signed, Theophilus is restored to his former position. But after seven years of life in sin he repents and for forty days he prays to the Virgin. She intercedes through her son and manages to get back the fateful parchment, which she gives back to Theophilus. He burns it and publicly declares his fault and the miracle. This legend crops up in Paolo Diacono, in Vincent of Beauvais's *Speculum Historiale*, in Jacobus da Varagine's *Golden Legend*, in a poem by Roswitha, in Rutebeuf and in Spanish and English literature—not to mention Goethe's *Faust*.

One of the most efficacious portrayals of the miracle of Theophilus is to be found in the tympanum of the Romanesque church of Souillac, where a sequence of images (defined by some as a forerunner of the strip cartoon) tells the tale: on the bottom left the Devil proffers Theophilus the parchment, on the right the deacon signs it, while at the top we see the Virgin descending from heaven to get the document back from the Devil.

In this sculpture the Devil is already ugly but, judging by other images from this period, he is not yet represented in all his ugliness. A mosaic dated c. 520 in the church of St Apollinare Nuovo, in Ravenna, depicts him as a red angel. The monster with a tail, the ears of a beast, a goat-like beard, claws, hoof and horns began to appear from the eleventh century onwards, the bat wings being a slightly later addition.

Acta Sanctorum

Grim-looking, terrible in form, large-headed, long-necked, gaunt-faced, with a squalid beard, hairy-eared, with glowering brows, fierce-eyed, foetid-mouthed, horse-toothed, spitting fire from his mouth, grim-jawed, fat-lipped, fearful-voiced, with scorched hair, frothy-mouthed, large-chested, rake-ribbed, thin-legged, swollen-heeled.

Rodulfus Glaber and the Devil

Rodulfus Glaber (tenth–eleventh century) *Chronicles*, V, 2

Events of this kind have often happened to me, by the will of God, and even very recently. One night, just before morning, when I was staying in the Monastery of the Blessed martyr St Leger in Champeaux, there appeared before me at the foot of the bed a dark-looking little figure of a man. As well as I could make out, he was of modest height, with a narrow neck, a haggard face, dark black eyes, a forehead puckered with wrinkles, a squished nose, a protruding mouth, swollen lips, a thin, sharp chin, a goatee, hirsute ears that rose to a point, raised and unkempt hair, canine teeth, an elongated cranium, puffed-out chest, hunchbacked, a quivering arse, and filthy clothes; he was breathless and his whole body was agitated. He grabbed a hold of one corner of the straw mat where he was standing and shook the bed terribly violently; then he spoke: 'You'll stay no longer in this place.'

Waking up with a start, as sometimes happens, I saw the being I've described. Grinding his teeth, he repeated more than once: 'You'll stay here no longer.' I quickly jumped out of bed and ran into the monastery where, throwing myself at the foot of the altar of our Holy Blessed Father, I cowered for a long time, terrorised. I tried with the utmost concentration to recall to mind all the misdeeds and grave faults that I had committed since I was a youth, either voluntarily or through negligence. And since neither fear nor love of God had ever driven me to penitence nor to make amends for all of this, I lay there suffering and lost, and I could not come up with anything better to say than these simple words: 'Lord Jesus, you who have come to save the sinners, in virtue of your immense compassion, have pity on me!'

The Priest Theophilus makes a Pact with the Devil, twelfth century

Jacques Le Grant,
*Le livre des bonnes
moeurs*, ms. 297, f.
109v.,
fifteenth century,
Chantilly, Musée Condé

A devil taking away a nun, thirteenth century, Chartres Cathedral, south portal

The Vale of the Devils

Sir John Mandeville

The Travels of Sir John Mandeville (1366)

Beside that Isle of Mistorak upon the left side nigh to the river of Pison is a marvellous thing. There is a vale between the mountains, that dureth nigh a four mile. [. . .] This vale is all full of devils, and hath been always. And men say there, that it is one of the entries of hell. In that vale is great plenty of gold and silver. Wherefore many misbelieving men, and many Christian men also, go in oftentime for to have of the treasure that there is; but few come again, and namely of the misbelieving men, ne of the Christian men neither, for anon they be strangled of devils. And in mid place of that vale, under a rock, is an head and the visage of a devil bodily, full horrible and dreadful to see, and it sheweth not but the head, to the shoulders. [. . .] For he beholdeth every man so sharply with dreadful eyen, that be evermore moving and sparkling as fire, and changeth and stirreth so often in diverse manner, with so horrible countenance, that no man dare not neighen towards him. And from him cometh out smoke and stinking fire and so much abomination, that unnethe no man may there endure. But the good Christian men, that be stable in the faith, enter well without peril. For they will first shrive them and mark them with the token of the holy cross, so that the fiends ne have no power over them. But albeit that they be without peril, yet, natheles, ne be they not without dread, when that they see the devils visibly and bodily all about them, that make full many diverse assaults and menaces, in air and in earth, and aghast them with strokes of thunder-blasts and of tempests. And the most dread is, that God will take vengeance then of that that men have misdone against his will. And ye shall understand, that when my fellows and I were in that vale, we were in great thought, whether that we durst put our bodies in adventure, to go in or not, in the protection of God. And some of our fellows accorded to enter, and some not. [. . .] And then we entered fourteen persons; but at our going out we were but nine. And so we wist never, whether that our fellows were lost, or else turned again for dread. [. . .] And thus we passed that perilous vale, and found therein gold and silver, and precious stones and rich jewels, great plenty, both here and there, as us seemed. But whether that it was, as us seemed, I wot never. For I touched none, because that the devils be so subtle to make a thing to seem otherwise than it is, for to deceive mankind.

Bernardo Parentino,
The Temptations of Saint Anthony,
c.1490,
Rome,
Galleria Doria Pamphili

The Temptation of St Anthony

Athanasius of Alexandria (fourth century)
The Life of St Anthony
In the beginning [the devil] tried to draw
him away from his penitence by whispering
to him memories of his wealth, his affection
for his sister, love of money and glory, the
various pleasures of the table and other
comforts of life; and, finally, the difficulties
of virtue, reminding him that his body
would become weak, and of the duration of
his sacrifices [. . .] And one night he took
the form of a woman, imitating her ways of
seducing him.

Then that place was immediately filled
with the forms of lions, bears, leopards,
bulls, serpents, asps, scorpions and wolves,
and each of these moved around according
to its nature. The lion roared, impatient to
attack, the bull seemed ready to charge with
its horns, the serpent coiled itself up but
was unable to come any closer, and the
wolf seemed to leap, but then stopped [. . .]
All these noises and apparitions, along with
their angry cries, struck terror.

Because demons will do anything,
blather, confuse you, pretend to be innocent
in order to fool simpletons, cause an uproar,
laugh as if mad, and whistle, but if one pays
no attention to them they cry immediately
and lament as if vanquished [. . .]

And he was holding vigil in the night
when the devil sent against him ferocious
animals. Realising that this was an illusion
created by his enemy, he said to those
animals: 'If you have been given power
against me, I am ready to be devoured, but
if you have been sent against me by
demons, then leave at once because I am
Christ's servant.' And as soon as Anthony
said this, they ran away, struck by his words
as if whipped.

The Ecstasy of Torture

Gustave Flaubert
The Temptation of St Anthony (1847–49)
In the middle of the portico, in bright
sunlight, a naked woman was bound to a
pillar. Two soldiers were beating her with
their straps, and at every blow she writhed
[. . .] her body was beautiful [. . .]
marvellously so [. . .]

I could have been bound to the pillar
next to yours, face to face, before your
eyes, responding to your moans with my
sighs, and our suffering would have
blended into one, our souls entwined. (*He
scourges himself furiously*.) Take this, and
that, for you, again! – But hold, now I am
seized by a tremor. What a torment! What a
delight! Like kisses. My bones are melting!
I'm dying [. . .]

Félicien Rops,
*The Temptations
of Saint Anthony*,
1878

following pages
(p.98)
Salvator Rosa,
*The Temptations
of Saint Anthony*,
c.1646, Coldirodi
(Sanremo), Pinacoteca
Stefano Rambaldi
(p.99)
Salvador Dalí,
*The Temptations
of Saint Anthony*,
1946, Brussels, Musées
Royaux des Beaux-Arts
de Belgique

The Devil in all his monstrosity is not only the frightful dominant figure in illuminated manuscripts and frescoes, he had already been vividly evoked in accounts of the temptations of the hermits (see, for example, the *Life of Saint Anthony* by **Athanasius of Alexandria**). In such texts he also takes on the inviting aspect of ambiguous young men or voluptuous prostitutes, to the point that, in modern times, between the Romantic and Decadent movements, the theme is almost blasphemously turned on its head. Instead of emphasising the ugliness of the Devil and the strength of the hermit who resists him, the artist dwells on the image of the tempter and on the mushy posturing of the tempted (see, for example, **Flaubert**).

from left to right
J. Collin de Plancy,
Dictionnaire infernal:
Abracax, Belzebuth,
Baël, Deumus, Haborym,
Hambuscias,
1863,
Paris, Plon

A phantasmagorical collection of all forms of devilish ugliness is *Baldus* (1517) written by Teofilo Folengo under the pseudonym of Merlin Coccai. *Baldus* is a heroic-comic, grotesque, goliardic poem, and is both a parody of Dante's *Comedy* and a forerunner of Rabelais' *Gargantua*. Unfortunately we cannot give any anthological examples here because it really must be read in its original macaronic Latin, since it loses all its flavour in translation. Among the main character's and his friends' various picaresque adventures there is, in Book 19, a battle with a host of Devils, who appear in a collage of animal forms: foxes with no tails, bears and pigs with horns, mastiffs with three paws, bulls with four horns, giants with heads like wolves' snouts, monkeys, squirrels, cat-macaques, baboons, gryphons that are half lion, and eagles that are half dragon, big owls that are part bat, monsters with the beak of an owl and the limbs of a frog, creatures with billy goat horns and donkey's ears. Baldus and his friends defeat the devils by using Beelzebub as a cudgel until he is broken into 170,000 chunks leaving Baldus holding no more than a goose's foot. But the moral of that victorious battle is that Baldus realises that the Devil hasn't been defeated, because he returns in the vices of contemporary society, especially in the ambitions of ecclesiastics. This invective on the rebirth of the inferno within the bosom of the Church (whose presence we have already seen in the Joachimites and the millenarian heretics) was written just as the Protestant Reformation was getting under way.

The Dimensions of Devils

Jean-Joseph Surin
The Triumph of Divine Love Over the Powers of Hell (1829)

If he wants to, [a devil] can sit on the head of a pin; but they can manifest their being or substance in all the space they can, for example 15 leagues. One of the biggest, like Leviathan for example, can occupy a space of 30 leagues, another, 15, another again, 12, each according to his own natural capacity. One such as Leviathan cannot take up 30 square leagues, but may extend himself like a serpent to such a size; and one that can stretch for 30 leagues can stretch out, apart from in length, within a more modest space (for example a round measuring one quarter of a league), or fill a great city with its substance.

The Pope as Prince of Devils,
Protestant caricature, sixteenth century,

In his writings, Luther often identified both the Devil and the Antichrist with the Pope. Luther was obsessed by the Devil and legend has it that, during one of his apparitions, Luther drove him away by throwing an inkwell at him. But even without the legend, in his *Table Talk* we find invective of this type: 'I often drive away the Devil with a fart. When he tempts me with foolish sins, I say to him: Devil, I gave you a fart yesterday too: did you add it to the reckoning?' (122) Or: 'When I awake, the Devil comes right away and debates with me until I tell him: lick my arse ... Because he torments us most of all with doubt. On the other hand we have the treasure of the Word. Praise be to God' (141). Nonetheless, in Luther and in the Protestant tradition a certain concept was gaining ground (one that was certainly not shared by those fanatical Protestants who were later to launch the persecution of witches and warlocks suspected of having made pacts with the Devil (see Chapter XIX) according to which the Devil was identified by the vices of which he became the symbol. The biggest collection of demonological material published in Protestant circles is the *Theatrum diabolorum* (1569), a large volume of about seven hundred pages that deals with all aspects of demonology (the number of Devils is calculated as 2,665,866,746,664) but no traditional demons are mentioned, instead we have the Devils of blasphemy, dance, lust, hunting, drinking, tyranny, sloth, pride and gambling.

Hieronymus Bosch,
Detail from *Triptych of
The Temptations
of Saint Anthony*,
1505–06,
Lisbon, Museo Nacional
de Arte Antiga

Hieronymus Bosch died at the beginning of the Reformation. His infernal creatures are hybrids reminiscent of the diabolical collages in *Baldus*, but they are far removed from the previous iconography. They do not spring from a combination of known animal features but have their own nightmarish independence, and we don't know whether they come from the Abyss or whether they live, unobserved, in our world. The creatures that, in the *Triptych of the Temptations of Saint Anthony*, badger the hermit are not traditional demons, too evil to be taken seriously. Almost amusing, like carnival characters, they are far more persuasive. With regard to Bosch, people have talked of 'the demoniac in art' and in his works they have seen heretical ferments, references to the world of the unconscious, alchemical allusions and a prelude to surrealism. Antonin Artaud talks about him in his 'Theatre of Cruelty' as one of the artists capable of showing us the dark side of our psyche.

following pages
Hieronymus Bosch,
Detail from *Triptych of
The Temptations
of Saint Anthony*,
1505–06,
Lisbon, Museo Nacional
de Arte Antiga

Bosch was a member of a Confraternity of Our Lady, conservative in spirit but at the same time interested in a reform of the mores, and so we are inclined to think of his images as a series of moralising allegories on the decadence of his times. In the *Garden of Delights* or in *The Hay Wain* we have not only sulphurous visions of the afterlife, but also scenes that are apparently refined, sensual and idyllic. But those same scenes are also terribly disquieting as they show how the world of earthly pleasures leads to hell. Bosch almost seems to anticipate the *Theatrum diabolorum*: he gives us not so much visions of the Devils that live in the abysses of the earth, as images of the vices of the society in which he lived.

Chapter IV

Monsters and Portents

1. Prodigies and Monsters

The classical world was very sensible of portents or prodigies, which were seen as signs of imminent disaster. These included marvels such as blood raining down from the sky, disturbing incidents, flames in the sky, abnormal births, and babies with the genitalia of both sexes, as can be seen in the *Book of Prodigies* by **Julius Obsequens** (who in the fourth century AD recorded all the prodigious things that had happened in Rome over the preceding centuries).

It was probably on the basis of these anomalies that Plato imagined the original androgyne, and the same bases were partly the source of many of the monsters said to inhabit Africa and Asia, of which only scant and inaccurate information was available. On the other hand, those who ventured to those lands really did see hippopotami, elephants and giraffes – and in **Job** we find a creature that was probably a crocodile but went down in history as Leviathan. In the fourth century BC, Cstesias of Cnidos had already written about the wonders of India. Ctesias' work was lost, but there is a wealth of extraordinary creatures in Pliny's *Natural History* (first century AD), which inspired a series of successive compendia. In the second century AD, Lucian of Samostata, in his *True History*, albeit purely as a parody of traditional credulity, wrote of hippogryphs, birds whose wings were made of lettuce leaves, minotaurs, and flea-archers as big as twelve elephants.

Note too how in the **Romance of Alexander** (which appeared in Latin in the twelfth century but sprang from sources traceable back to Pseudo-Callisthenes, of the third century AD) the Macedonian conqueror had to face some frightening peoples.

Ulisse Aldrovandi,
in *Monstrorum historia*,
VI, 1642

Leviathan
Job 41:10–24, 26–32

None is so fierce that dare stir him up: who then is able to stand before me? Who hath prevented me, that I should repay him? Whatsoever is under the whole heaven is mine. I will not conceal his parts, nor his power, nor his comely proportion. Who can discover the face of his garment? or who can come to him with his double bridle? Who can open the doors of his face? his teeth are terrible round about. His scales are his pride, shut up together as with a close seal. One is so near to another, that no air can come between them. They are joined one to another, they stick together, that they cannot be sundered. By his neesings a light doth shine, and his eyes are like the eyelids of the morning. Out of his mouth go burning lamps, and sparks of fire leap out. Out of his nostrils goeth smoke, as out of a seething pot or caldron. His breath kindleth coals, and a flame goeth out of his mouth. In his neck remaineth strength, and sorrow is turned into joy before him. The flakes of his flesh are joined together: they are firm in themselves; they cannot be moved. His heart is as firm as a stone; yea, as hard as a piece of the nether millstone [. . .]

The sword of him that layeth at him cannot hold: the spear, the dart, nor the habergeon. He esteemeth iron as straw, and brass as rotten wood. The arrow cannot make him flee: slingstones are turned with him into stubble. Darts are counted as stubble: he laugheth at the shaking of a spear. Sharp stones are under him: he spreadeth sharp pointed things upon the mire. He maketh the deep to boil like a pot: he maketh the sea like a pot of ointment. He maketh a path to shine after him; one would think the deep to be hoary.

Earth Generates Many Scourges
Aeschylus (sixth century BC)
The Libation Bearers

Earth generates many scourges and terrible terrors: Dreadful monsters, enemies to mortals, fill the gulfs of the deep sea. Up high, between heaven and earth, flames streak through the air and every creature that flies or crawls can speak of the windy fury of storms.

The Androgyne
Plato (fifth–fourth century BC)
Symposium, 189d–191b

In the first place, let me treat of the nature of man and what has happened to it; for the original human nature was not like the present, but different. The sexes were not two as they are now, but originally three in number; there was man, woman, and the union of the two, having a name corresponding to this double nature, which had once a real existence, but is now lost, and the word 'Androgynous' is only preserved as a term of reproach. In the second place, the primeval man was round, his back and sides forming a circle; and he had four hands and four feet, one head with two faces, looking opposite ways, set on a round neck and precisely alike; also four ears, two privy members [. . .] and he could also roll over and over at a great pace, turning on his four hands and four feet, eight in all, like tumblers going over and over with their legs in the air; this was when he wanted to run fast. [. . .] Terrible was their might and strength, and the thoughts of their hearts were great, and they made an attack upon the gods [. . .] At last, after a good deal of reflection, Zeus discovered a way. He said: 'Methinks I have a plan which will humble their pride and improve their manners; men shall continue to exist, but I will cut them in two and then they will be diminished in strength and increased in numbers; this will have the advantage of making them more profitable to us [. . .]' He spoke and cut men in two, like a sorb-apple which is halved for pickling, or as you might divide an egg with a hair; and as he cut them one after another, he bade Apollo give the face and the half of the neck a turn in order that the man might contemplate the section of himself: he would thus learn a lesson of humility. Apollo was also bidden to heal their wounds and compose their forms. So he gave a turn to the face and pulled the skin from the sides all over that which in our language is called the belly, like the purses which draw in, and he made one mouth at the centre, which he fastened in a knot (the same which is called the navel); he also moulded the breast and took out most of the wrinkles, much as a shoemaker might smooth leather upon a last; he left a few, however, in the region of the belly and navel, as a memorial of the primeval state. After the division the two parts of man, each desiring his other half, came together, and throwing their arms about one another, entwined in mutual embraces, longing to grow into one, they were on the point of dying from hunger and self-neglect, because they did not like to do anything apart; and when one of the halves died and the other survived, the survivor sought another mate, man or woman as we call them – being the sections of entire men or women – and clung to that.

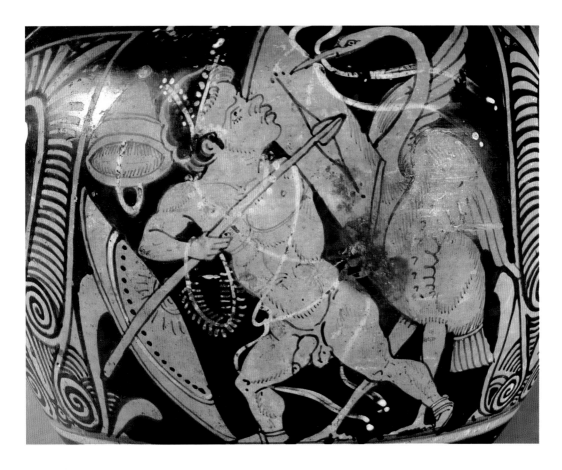

Pygmy and Crane, krater, detail, from church buildings in Volterra, fourth century, Florence, Museo Archaeologico

Portents

Julius Obsequens (fourth century)
The Book of Marvels

Nine days of prayer were observed, since in the area around Piceno it had rained rocks and in many places celestial fires, with the slightest of puffs, had burned the clothes of several persons. The temple of Jupiter on the Capitol Hill was struck by lightning. In Umbria, they found a hermaphrodite of around twelve years of age, and by order of the soothsayers, it was put to death. The Gauls, who had entered Italy through the Alps, were driven back without a fight [. . .]

Several statues on the Capitol Hill were knocked down by the continuous storms [. . .] At the banquet of Jupiter the heads of the Gods were shaken by an earthquake; a plate laden with things prepared to honour Jupiter fell over. Rats nibbled the olives on the table [. . .]

During the night lights were seen in the sky over Lanuvium. In Cassino, many buildings were destroyed by a bolt of lightning, and the sun shone for several hours during the night. In Teano Sidicino a child was born with four hands and four feet. After the purification, there was peace [. . .]

In Ceres a pig with human hands and feet was born, as well as children with four feet and four hands. In Foro Esino a flame, that issued from a bull's mouth, did not hurt the animal [. . .]

A phoenix and an owl were seen inside the city. In a stone cave one man was devoured by another [. . .] Many thousands of people were drowned in the floodwaters of the Po and the pond of Arezzo. It rained milk twice. In Norcia, twins were born of an unmarried woman: one female twin born with all her limbs intact, a male with its stomach open in the front, so that one could see its intestines, and with no opening behind; the child, after crying, died.

Alexander fights against wild men and beasts, from *Le livre et la vraye histoire du bon roi Alexandre*, Royal ms. 20 B. XX, fol. 51, fifteenth century, London, British Library

The Adventures of Alexander

Anonymous (twelfth century)

The Alexander Romance, II, 33

Then we reached a greyish land, in which there were savages, similar to giants, who were all around us; they had fiery eyes and seemed like lions. There were also other beings named Ochlites: their bodies were entirely hairless, they stood four cubits tall and were slender as spears. As soon as they saw us, they started running towards us: they were covered with lion furs, and were extremely strong and trained to fight without weapons. We struck them, but they struck back, and killed many of us with cudgels. I feared we would be overcome, and gave the order to set the forest alight: at the sight of fire, those extremely strong men fled; but before doing so they had killed no less then one hundred and eighty of our soldiers.

The following day I decided to go into their caverns: there we found wild beasts that seemed like lions, but with three eyes, chained to the doors [. . .] Then we left, and we reached the land of the Apple-eaters. There was a man whose body was entirely covered with hair, he was enormous and we were afraid. I gave orders to capture him: he was caught, but he continued to scrutinise us with his savage glare. Then I had a naked woman brought before him: he grabbed her and was about to eat her. The soldiers immediately ran in to take her away from him, and he began screeching in his own tongue. Upon hearing those cries, other beings of his species came out of the swamp and threw themselves at us. They came in their thousands and our army numbered forty thousand men: so I ordered the swamp to be set on fire, and those beings fled at the sight of fire. We captured three, but they refused to eat for eight days and finally died. These beings do not speak as men do, but rather howl, like dogs.

2. An Aesthetic of the Measureless

This and other information went to nourish what has been defined as the 'Hisperic Aesthetic'. Classical Latinists had already condemned the style known as 'Asian' (and then 'African'), in comparison with the balance of the 'Attic' style. This Hisperic style was considered 'ugly' by the Fathers of the Church, as is borne out by the following invective penned by St Jerome (*Adversus Jovinianum,* I): 'By now there are many barbarous writers and many discourses muddled by stylistic vices that one cannot understand any more either who is speaking or what he is speaking about. All swells and deflates like a diseased serpent that falls apart as it essays to make its coils [...] What is the use of this verbal witchcraft?'

But between the seventh and the eighth centuries there was a radical change in tastes, at least in an area stretching from Spain to the British Isles, and touching part of Gaul. The Hisperic aesthetic was the style of a Europe that was going through its 'Dark Ages', characterised by the decline of agriculture, the abandonment of the cities, the collapse of the great Roman aqueducts and roads. In a climate of general barbarity, in lands covered with forests, monks, poets and illuminators saw the world as a dense wood, inhabited by monsters, and criss-crossed by labyrinthine paths. Hisperic writing no longer obeyed the traditional laws of proportion: people enjoyed the new music of incomprehensible barbaric neologisms, writers opted for long alliterative chains that the classical world would have deemed pure cacophony, and what was appreciated was not measure but the gigantic and the measureless. Irish monks in particular, who in those difficult and disorderly centuries had conserved and brought back a certain literary tradition to Continental Europe, made their way through the worlds of language and visual imagination as if they were indeed forests, or the seas like those the Irishman St Brendan wandered through, anchored to a horrible whale he had taken for an island and thanks to which he met Judas imprisoned on a rock, lashed and tormented by the waves of the sea.

Between the seventh and the ninth centuries, perhaps in Ireland (but certainly in the British Isles), there appeared a *Liber monstrorum de diversis generibus* that, apart from describing all kinds of monsters, commented upon their variety.

Book of Kells,
VIII sec.,
Dublin,
Trinity College

In Book II we read: 'There is no doubt that there is an infinity of sea beasts, whose boundless bodies high as mountains violently shake even the most gigantic billows and the stretches of water all but ripped up from the sea bottom [...] Churning up with horrible eddies waters already agitated by the great mass of their bodies, they head for the beach offering those who look upon them a terrifying sight.' In this climate, in the eighth century there appeared in Ireland the *Book of Kells*, adorned with splendid enlarged initial letters that are a triumph of *entrelacs*, labyrinthine knotwork in which appear, together with divine figures, all kinds of monstrous creatures. There are stylised animal forms, small simian figures among impossible foliage that cover pages and pages, like the repetitive motifs of a carpet, whereas in reality every line, every corymb, represents a different invention. It is a complex swirling composition, deliberately at odds with all educated rules of symmetry, in a symphony of delicate colours, from pink to orange-yellow, from lemon to mauve. Quadrupeds, birds, greyhounds with swans' beaks, unbelievable humanoid figures contorted like circus athletes who stick their heads between their knees, throwing their heads back in this way to form the initial letter of a word. Malleable and flexible as coloured elastic bands, they weave their way through the intricate web of connections, peeping out from abstract decorations, entwining themselves around initial letters, and sidling in between one line and the next.

3. The Moralisation of Monsters

How did devoted monks see those 'extremely ugly' monsters? Certainly much the same way as, over the following centuries, people enjoyed other deformed beings in the margins of illuminated pages (the so-called marginalia) and on the capitals of Romanesque churches.

Medieval man found those monsters attractive just as we enjoy looking at exotic animals in a zoo; proof of this is the emphatic way in which a rigorist like St Bernard (in the *Apologia ad Guillelmum*) condemns the sculptures on capitals that the faithful evidently found too attractive by half (but he describes them so well that we are led to suspect that he himself had looked at them more closely than he should have done): 'What place is there in the cloisters [...] for that ridiculous monstrosity, that strange kind of deformed shape or shaped deformity? What are foul apes doing there? Or ferocious lions? Or monstrous centaurs? Or half-men? Or dappled tigers? [...] You can see many bodies beneath a single head and vice versa many heads atop a single body. On the one side you can see a quadruped with a serpent's tail, and on the other a fish with a quadruped's head. Here, a beast that looks like a horse with the hindquarters of a goat, there a horned animal with the hindquarters of a horse. In short there is everywhere such a great and strange variety of heterogeneous forms that there is more pleasure to be had in reading the marbles than the codices and in spending the whole day admiring one by one these images rather than meditating on the law of God.'

Monster devouring a man, central capital of the church of Saint-Pierre, eleventh–twelfth century, Chauvigny, Church of Saint-Pierre

Even Monsters are God's Children
St Augustine (fourth–fifth century)
The City of God, XVI, 8

Another problem arose: How can one believe that from the children of Noah, or better yet from that sole man from whom they too were created, a race of human monsters could originate? Even profane history speaks of them; we learn that some had only one eye; others had feet back to front; others were of both sexes, and had the right breast of a man and the left breast of a woman, and by coupling could either conceive or generate alternatively; others had no mouth and could only breathe through their nostrils; still others stood only one cubit high and therefore were called Pygmies by the Greeks; in some places women could conceive at five and didn't live past eight years.

They even tell that there existed a race of men who had only one leg and could not flex their knee, but were nevertheless very fast: they were called *Sciapods*, because during the summer, when they lay down on the ground, they protected themselves with the shade cast by their feet [. . .]

In any case, the same principle that explains the generation of monstrous men also explains the creation of monstrous peoples. God is the one who created all beings, He knows when and how He must or will have to create, because He knows the beauty of the universe and the similarity or diversity of its parts. But those who cannot contemplate the whole are disturbed by the deformity of one of its parts, because they are ignorant of the context that part refers to.

We know that men are born who have more than five fingers on their hands or feet; it is a rather unimportant anomaly, but nevertheless it should not lead us to be so foolish as to think that the Creator made a mistake in the number of those fingers, even though we cannot grasp the reason for the phenomenon! [. . .]

In Hippo-Diarrhytus there exists a man who has the soles of his feet and the palms of his hands in the form of a crescent, with only two fingers; if an entire race of these individuals existed, they would be added to the curious and the marvellous. But would this be a valid reason to deny that such a man is descended from the first man, created by God? [. . .]

We are presuming that the things we are told about the variety of those peoples and their differences from us are true. In fact, if we did not already know that apes, monkeys and chimpanzees are not men, but beasts, those historians who brag about their own erudition might fool us with their vainglorious nonsense, presenting them as a human race [. . .] For this reason, it seems to me that the safest way to resolve this issue would be the following: either that which has been written about these peoples is false; or, if it is true, they are not men; or, if they are men, then they descend from Adam.

The Christian world proceeded to an authentic 'redemption' of monsters. As we have already seen (in Chapter 2.1) with regard to the pancalistic vision, **Augustine** says that monsters are beautiful because they are creatures of God. In his *Christian Doctrine*, Augustine also tried to regulate the allegorical interpretation of Holy Writ by pointing out that you need to sense a spiritual meaning beyond the literal meaning when the holy book seems to lose itself in apparently superfluous descriptions of stones, herbs or animals. But to understand the spiritual meaning of a precious stone or an animal, you need an 'encyclopaedia' that explains the allegorical significance of those things. This led to the birth of the *moralised bestiaries*, in which every creature mentioned (no matter whether real or imaginary) was associated with a moral teaching. The first of these texts to enter the Christian world was the **Physiologus**, written in Greek between the second and third centuries of our era (and then translated into Latin as well as various oriental languages), which lists about forty animals, trees and stones. After having described these beings, the *Physiologus* shows how and why each of them is the vehicle of an ethical and theological message. For example, the lion, which according to legend wipes out its tracks with its tail to elude hunters, becomes a symbol for Christ who wipes out the sins of man.

From *The Physiologus*
Anonymous (second–third century)
The Physiologus

The unicorn is a small animal, similar to a goat, but extremely fierce. Hunters cannot come near it because of its extraordinary strength. It has a single horn located in the middle of its head.

How do you hunt one? They set out an immaculate virgin, the animal jumps into her lap and she breastfeeds it, and then leads it to the king's palace.

The unicorn is an image of the Saviour: in fact [. . .] it resides in the womb of the true, immaculate Virgin Mary.

In the mountains, an animal known as the elephant exists. He has no yearning for carnal relations: when elephants want to have young, they travel to the east, near paradise, where a tree known as the mandrake grows. The female picks the fruit first, and offers it to the male, tempting him with it until he takes the fruit. After having eaten, the male moves close to the female and mates with her . . . When the time has come to give birth, she wades into a pool until the water reaches her udders, and then gives birth to her offspring in the water, and the young beast climbs up on her knees and sucks her teat [. . .] This is the elephant's nature: if it falls down, it is unable to get back up again, because it has no joints in its knees. And how might it fall down? When it wants to sleep, it leans against a tree and hunters, who are familiar with the elephant's nature, go and saw the tree trunk halfway through. The animal comes to rest and then falls along with the tree, and begins to send forth loud

trumpeting. Another elephant hears this and comes to help, but it is not capable of lifting up its companion: therefore both begin trumpeting, and another twelve elephants arrive, but not even all of these together can lift up the fallen beast; therefore they all start trumpeting: finally a small elephant arrives, puts its trunk under the fallen elephant and lifts him up [. . .] Therefore, the elephant and its mate are images of Adam and Eve: when they were amid the blessings of paradise before the transgression, they knew neither carnal union nor mating. But once the woman had eaten the fruit of the tree, in other words of the spiritual mandrake, giving some to the man as well, then Adam knew the woman, and created Cain above the malignant waters [. . .] Then the great elephant arrived, in other words the Law, and it was unable to lift him; then the twelve elephants came (in other words the prophets), and they weren't able to lift the fallen man either; finally, the holy spiritual elephant arrived, and he lifted the man up.

The Physiologus says of the viper that the male has the face of a man, the female the face of a woman: they have human form down to their navels, while their tails are like that of a crocodile. The female has no vagina, simply a slit like the eye of a needle. When the male mates with the female, he ejaculates into her mouth, [. . .] Therefore, vipers are patricidal and matricidal, and Saint John did well to compare them with the Pharisees: in the same way as the viper murders its father and mother, they too killed their spiritual fathers, the prophets.

4. The *Mirabilia*

The Physiologus (duly enlarged and reorganised) was the model for the majority of the bestiaries, lapidaries, herbals and 'encyclopaedias' conceived along the lines laid down by Pliny; from *On the Nature of Things* by Rabanus Maurus (eighth–ninth century) to the great compilations of the twelfth and thirteenth centuries, such as *The Image of the World* by Honorius of Autun, *On the Nature of Things* by Alexander Neckham, *On the Property of Things* by Bartholomew Anglicus, the *Mirror of Nature* by Vincent of Beauvais, down to *The Book of the Treasure* and *The Little Treasure* by Brunetto Latini. Likewise, the animals in *The Physiologus* are sought for and sometimes described in accounts of imaginary journeys like Mandeville's *Travels* or *On the Composition of the World* by Ristoro d'Arezzo.

The list is incomplete but reveals the attraction felt by the ancient and medieval world for lands still unexplored and the stunned marvel with which readers of those books fantasised about all those wonders. Proof of this is the enormous success enjoyed by a twelfth-century fake, the **Letter of Prester John**, in which we read about a fabulous Christian realm in Asia, beyond the lands of the infidels, inhabited by virtuous peoples rich in gold and gems. The myth of Prester John fascinated many travellers (such as Marco Polo) who tried to find him and who politically encouraged Christian expansion eastwards (but the location of the fabulous realm was shifted from Asia to Africa at the beginning of the modern era, when it was identified with Christian Ethiopia). One of the reasons for the attraction exercised by this imaginary kingdom, almost a confirmation of the virtues and the riches it enjoyed, was precisely the description of the creatures who lived there, subject to John's power.

These monsters were certainly not considered examples of beauty, but not all were felt to be dangerous. The fearful ones included the Basilisk with its venomous breath; the Chimaera whose head was that of a lion and whose body was half-dragon, half-goat; the Leucrococa (the body of a donkey, the hindquarters of a deer, the thighs of a lion, horses' hoofs, a cloven horn, a mouth stretching from ear to ear from which a quasi human voice issued, and a single bone in the place of teeth); or the Manticore (with three rows of teeth, the body of a lion, the tail of a scorpion, blue eyes, blood-coloured complexion, and a hissing voice like that of a serpent).

*Monstrous races
of Ethiopia,*
Ms. 461, fol. 26v,
1460 ca., New York,
Pierpont Morgan Library

The Realm of Prester John
Anonymous (twelfth century)
The Letter of Prester John
I, Prester John, am lord of lords and in every richness found under the sun, and in virtue and power I am greater than every king on earth. [. . .]

The creatures that are born and live in Our dominion include elephants, dromedaries, camels, hippopotamuses, crocodiles, metacollinarum, cametennus, tensevetes, panthers, wild asses, white lions and red lions, white bears and white blackbirds, silent cicadas, gryphons, tigers, jackals, hyenas, wild oxen and horses, wild men, horned men, fauns, satyrs and females of the same species, pygmies, dog-headed men, giants standing forty cubits tall, one-eyed creatures, Cyclops, a bird known as the Phoenix, and almost every kind of animal that resides under the heavens [. . .]

In one of Our provinces there is a river they call the Indus. This river, whose source is in Paradise, branches out throughout the region, and in it can be found natural stones, emeralds, sapphires, carbuncles, topaz, chrysolites, onyx, beryl, amethysts, sardius, and many other precious stones [. . .]

In the extreme regions of the earth [. . .] We possess an island [. . .] upon which year-round, twice a week, God sends down abundant showers of manna that the population gathers and eats; the only food they need to survive. In fact they do not plough, they do not sow seeds, they do not harvest, nor do they dig the earth in any way to draw forth its richest fruits [. . .] All these peoples, who feed only on celestial food, live to be five hundred years old. Nevertheless, once they reach one hundred, they rejuvenate and gain strength by drinking thrice from the waters of a spring that flows from between the roots of a tree that can be found there [. . .] Among us, no one lies [. . .] Among us there are no adulterers. No sin has power over us.

117

A Wild Man

Luigi Pulci
Morgante, V, 38–45 (1481–82)

A head like a bear he had,
Furry and proud, and teeth like
tusks,
Strong enough to split a rock with one
bite;
His tongue was all covered with scales;
One eye he had in the middle of his
chest
A fiery orb two spans across;
His beard was shaggy, as was his hair,
Two ears like those of an ass
And long, strange, bristly arms.
His chest and body were all covered
with hair;
Long nails on his feet and hands.
No shoes he wore on dry land,
But, naked and unshod, he went about
barking like a dog:
No one ever saw a monster as ugly as
this;
And in his hand he carried a large club
of rowan wood
All weathered and black as a crow.

Pierre Boaistuau
*Mostre prins en une
forest aiant figure
humayne qui aymoit
les femmes,*
in *Storie prodigiose,*
ms. 136, fol. 140r,
sixteenth century,
London, Wellcome
Library

facing page
Raphael,
*Saint Michael
and the Dragon,*
c.1505,
Paris, Louvre

There were also evil-crested serpents who walked on legs and whose gullets were always open and dripping venom. Another terrifying creature was the dragon, represented in paintings when it met defeat at the hands of St George, while much knightly literature later showed it battling against knights, who might also have encountered the hirsute Wild Man of the woods, as we see in **Pulci**'s *Morgante*. But the same cannot be said of other gentle creatures whose form and habits were certainly extraordinary and equally far removed from every human ideal of beauty or fitness. These basically harmless creatures included headless men with eyes on their shoulders and two holes in their breasts by way of a nose and mouth; the Androgynes; the Astomori, entirely devoid of a mouth, who fed only on smells; two-headed men; men with straight legs and no knees, horses' hoofs and a phallus on their chests; men with extremely long necks and arms like saws; the Pygmies, forever at war with the cranes; or the likeable Sciapods (creatures with a single leg on which they run very fast indeed and which they hold upright when they sleep, in order to enjoy the shade cast by the single enormous foot). Finally, there was the Unicorn, a beautiful white stallion with a horn on its forehead, which could be captured only by leaving a virgin beneath a tree so that the animal, attracted by the odour of virginity, would go and lay its head in her lap.

Panotii, detail,
c.1120–30,
Vezelay, tympanum of
the Church of Sainte-
Madeleine

Sebastien Münster
Basilisk, in *Universal Cosmography*,
1558

following pages
The Master
of Boucicaut,
Unicorns, dragons,
cynocephalae,
blemmyae, sciapods
and one-eyed men,
in the *Book of Marvels*,
fifteenth century,
Paris, Bibliothèque
Nationale de France

The Basilisk

Pliny the Elder (23–79 AD)
Natural History, 33

There is the same power also in the serpent called the basilisk. It is produced in the province of Cyrenaica, being not more than twelve fingers in length. It has a white spot on the head, strongly resembling a sort of a diadem. When it hisses, all the other serpents fly from it: and it does not advance its body, like the others, by a succession of folds, but moves along upright and erect upon the middle. It destroys all shrubs, not only by its contact, but those even that it has breathed upon; it burns up all the grass too, and breaks the stones, so tremendous is its noxious influence. It was formerly a general belief that if a man on horseback killed one of these animals with a spear, the poison would run up the weapon and kill, not only the rider, but the horse as well. To this dreadful monster the effluvium of the weasel is fatal, a thing that has been tried with success, for kings have often desired to see its body when killed; so true is it that it has pleased Nature that there should be nothing without its antidote. The animal is thrown into the hole of the basilisk, which is easily known from the soil around it being infected.

Some Monsters

St Isidore of Seville (570–636)
Etymologies, XI, 3

The Greeks [. . .] consider the Giants to be *ghegheneis*, in other words *terrigeni*, which means *born of the earth*, because it was the earth herself, according to legend, who gave birth to them from her own immense girth [. . .] The *Cinocefali* are known as such insofar as they have the heads of dogs, and because their own howling proves them more beast than man: they are born in India. India also produces the *Cyclops*, called thus because it is believed they have a single eye in the middle of their foreheads [. . .] Some people believe that the *Blemmyae* are born in Libya.

These creatures have a body but no head, with eyes and a mouth on their chests. It has been written that in the extreme Orient, there exist people with monstrous faces: some have no noses, and deformed, completely flat faces; others possess such prominent lower lips that when they sleep, they use these lips to cover their entire face in order to protect themselves from the fierce sun; still others have gummed-up mouths, and can only nourish themselves through a small hole with the help of oatmeal straws. They say that among the Scythians there live the *Panotii*, who possess ears so enormous that they can use them to cover their entire bodies [. . .] It is said that the *Artabants* live in Ethiopia and walk on all fours like goats: none of them live beyond the age of forty. The *Satyrs* are little men with hooked noses, horns on their foreheads and goat's feet. Saint Anthony saw one in the solitude of the desert. When asked about his species by the servant of God, the satyr responded: 'I am a mortal, one of those who lives around the desert and whom the gentiles, fooled by numerous errors, venerate as Fauns and Satyrs.' [. . .] It is said that in Ethiopia live a people known as the *Sciapods*, gifted with special legs that give them extraordinary speed: the Greeks called them *skiópodes* because when they lie down supine on the ground in the sun's severe heat, they use their enormous feet to shade themselves. The *Antipodi*, inhabitants of Libya, have the soles of their feet pointing backwards, in other words turned behind their legs, and eight toes on each. The *Hippopods* live in Scythia: they have a human shape but with horse's feet. They say that in India there lives a people called the *Makròbioi*, who stand twelve feet tall. Also in India there lives a people whose stature is equal to one cubit, who the Greeks refer to as *Pygmaei* (Pygmies), a name derived in fact from the cubit, and about whom we spoke earlier: they live in the mountainous regions of India, near the ocean.

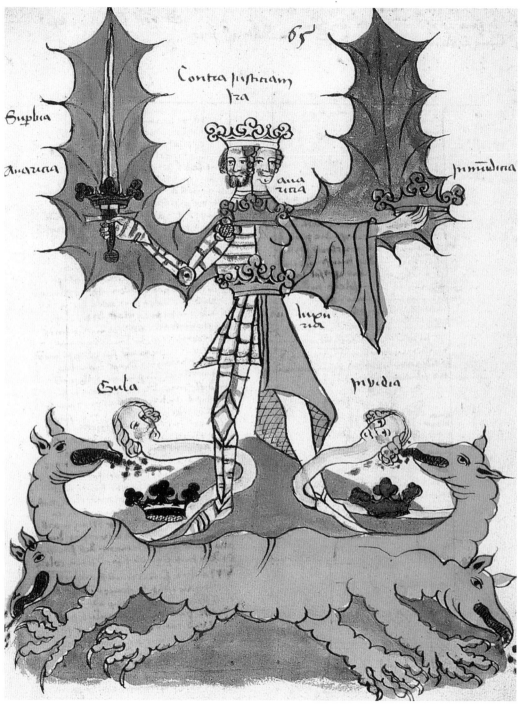

5. The Destiny of Monsters

Familiarity with monsters – right from the start – had also led the Christian world to use them to define the Divinity. As **Pseudo-Dionysus the Areopagite** says in *The Celestial Hierarchy*, the nature of God is ineffable, and since no metaphor no matter how poetically stunning could talk of Him, and since any discourse of ours would be powerless, capable only of talking about God by negation, saying not what He is but what *He is not*, then we might as well name Him through highly dissimilar images, such as those of animals and monstrous creatures. On the other hand there is a precedent for this in the vision of **Ezekiel**, where celestial creatures are described in animal form, thus providing the apostle John with the inspiration for the divine throne (and this explains why the tradition was later to associate the three evangelists with the figures of the ox, the lion and the eagle).

But even in the Renaissance period monsters had a friendly function, precisely because of their impressive ugliness. For example, in the *arts of memory*, since ancient times, those wishing to be able to recall words and concepts were advised to associate them with various rooms in a building or with various places in a city where there stood horrifying statues that were hard to forget. And so in the *Ars memorandi* of Petrus von Rosenheim (1502) we see mnemonic figures that are certainly akin to the monsters of the Apocalypse and the creatures of the bestiaries.

facing page
Hermaphrodite Lucifer,
from the Buch der
heiligen Dreifaltigkeit,
ms. 428,
1488,
Vaud, St Gallen

Finally, monsters were to find enormous fortune in the heterodox universe of the alchemists, where they came to symbolise the various processes required for obtaining the Philosopher's Stone or the Elixir of Long Life – and we can suppose that the adepts of the occult arts did not find them frightful but wonderfully seductive.

As we shall see in Chapter X, the taste for legendary marvels began to give way to a curiosity about what was scientifically *interesting*, and other kinds of monsters packed the cabinets of curiosities and other modern collections. By then, people were exploring places that were still legendary lands in the Middle Ages, and such undertakings left no further room for the monsters of the bestiaries. Monsters still have a place in the modern and contemporary imagination, but in other forms.

Petrus von Rosenheim,
Ars memorandi,
1502,
Pforzheim

God as Worm

Dionysius the Areopagite (fifth century)
The Celestial Hierarchy, II, 5

We will find that the interpreters of the
theology of the mysteries devoutly adapt
these symbols not only in the case of the
celestial orders, but sometimes even for
the very manifestations of the Deific
Principles. And sometimes they celebrate
the Divinity beginning with the most
precious things we see, like the sun of
justice [. . .] But other times, they
celebrate it with the names of middle
elements like fire that casts light without
doing damage, water the provider of vital
health and, to speak symbolically, like
water that enters the belly whence
unstoppable rivers gush forth. Finally,
they call it by the names of the basest
things, like fragrant ointment, corner
stones, even attributing to it the form of
wild beasts, adapting to it the

characteristics of the lion and the
panther, saying that it will be like a
leopard or an enraged bear.

I will also add the basest of all
comparisons, one that will also seem
the most shameful: in fact, all those
learned in matters divine have told us
that God also took on the form of a
worm. Thus the theosophists and the
interpreters of the mystical revelations
set apart in purity the 'Holy of Holies',
thereby keeping it from imperfect and
profane things, watching over the
various holy representations so that
divine things are not accessible to the
profane and so that those who
contemplate holy simulacra do not
mistake the form for the reality. And so
we may celebrate divinity through true
negations and through images of the
basest things that are in contrast with
the divine likeness.

Caliban

William Shakespeare

The Tempest, II, 2 (1611)

Trincolo: [. . .] [noticing Caliban] What have we here, a man or a fish? Dead or alive? A fish, he smells like a fish – a very ancient and fishlike smell, a kind of not-of-the-newest poor-John. A strange fish. Were I in England now, as once I was, and had but this fish painted, not a holiday fool there but would give a piece of silver. There would this monster make a man. Any strange beast there makes a man. When they will not give a doit to relieve a lame beggar, they will lay out ten to see a dead Indian. Legged like a man, and his fins like arms! Warm, o' my troth! I do now let loose my opinion, hold it no longer: this is no fish, but an islander that hath lately suffered by a thunderbolt [. . .]

Monstrous Breasts

Jonathan Swift

Gulliver's Travels (1726)

I must confess no object ever disgusted me so much as the sight of her monstrous breast, which I cannot tell what to compare with, so as to give the curious reader an idea of its bulk, shape, and colour. It stood prominent six feet, and could not be less than sixteen in circumference. The nipple was about half the bigness of my head, and the hue both of that and the dug, so varied with spots, pimples, and freckles, that nothing could appear more nauseous [. . .] This made me reflect upon the fair skins of our English ladies, who appear so beautiful to us, only because they are of our own size, and their defects not to be seen but through a magnifying glass; where we find by experiment that the smoothest and whitest skins look rough, and coarse, and ill-coloured.

Owing to the influence of navigators who came across (in reality) savage populations with savage customs, **Shakespeare** gave us the horrible (and unhappy) Caliban, and **Swift** gave us the creatures encountered in the course of his travels. Then, gradually, people's familiarity with monsters waned; they struck **Poe** as disquieting, they horrified **Arthur Conan Doyle** (who already knew something about prehistoric animals), while **Baudelaire** dreamed of erotic ecstasies on the body of a giantess.

In our own times, having passed through Dracula, Frankenstein's monster, Mr Hyde, King Kong, and finally surrounded by the living dead and aliens from outer space, there are new monsters around us, but we are merely afraid of them and do not see them as messengers of God. Nor do we think to tame them by placing a virgin beneath a tree. Perhaps the first hint of scepticism regarding the frequently benevolent creatures of the bestiaries is already to be found in Marco Polo's *Travels*, when he, who travelled in reality and not merely in the imagination, came across what were clearly rhinoceroses. These were animals he had never seen, and since his culture provided him with the idea of the unicorn as a quadruped with a horn on its snout, he tells us he saw unicorns. But, since he was an honest, punctilious chronicler, he hastens to explain that these unicorns were rather strange, unlike the traditional image of them: they were not slender and white but had 'hair like that of the buffalo and feet like those of the elephant'; the horn was black and ugly, the tongue spiny, and the head was like that of a wild boar. Polo concludes that this beast was not only 'a very ugly beast to behold' but also that 'it is not, as they say here, that it will allow itself to be taken by a maiden, but quite the contrary'.

Merian Cooper
and Ernest
B. Schoedsack
(directors),
King Kong,
1933

facing page
Arnold Böcklin,
Sirens,
1875,
Berlin, Staatliche
Museen

The Giantess
Charles Baudelaire
The Flowers of Evil (1857)
At the time when Nature with a lusty spirit
Was conceiving monstrous children each
day,
I should have liked to live near a young
giantess,
Like a voluptuous cat at the feet of a queen.
I should have liked to see her soul and
body thrive
And grow without restraint in her terrible
games;
To divine by the mist swimming within her
eyes
If her heart harboured a smouldering flame;
To explore leisurely her magnificent form;
To crawl upon the slopes of her enormous
knees,
And sometimes in summer, when the
unhealthy sun
Makes her stretch out, weary, across the
countryside,
To sleep nonchalantly in the shade of her
breasts,
Like a peaceful hamlet below a
mountainside.

Red in Tooth and Claw
Edgar Allan Poe
*The Narrative of Arthur Gordon Pym of
Nantucket*, 18 (1850)
We also picked up the carcass of a singular-
looking land-animal. It was three feet in
length, and but six inches in height, with
four very short legs, the feet armed with
long claws of a brilliant scarlet, and
resembling coral in substance. The body
was covered with a straight silky hair,
perfectly white. The tail was peaked like
that of a rat, and about a foot and a half
long. The head resembled a cat's with the
exception of the ears – these were flopped
like the ears of a dog. The *teeth* were of the
same brilliant scarlet as the claws.

The Lost World
Arthur Conan Doyle
The Lost World, 12 (1912)
Suddenly I saw it. There was movement
among the bushes at the far end of the
clearing which I had just traversed. A great
dark shadow disengaged itself and hopped
out into the clear moonlight. I say 'hopped'
advisedly, for the beast moved like a
kangaroo, springing along in an erect
position upon its powerful hind legs, while
its front ones were held bent in front of it. It
was of enormous size and power, like an
erect elephant, but its movements, in spite
of its bulk, were exceedingly alert. For a
moment, as I saw its shape, I hoped that it
was an iguanodon, which I knew to be
harmless, but, ignorant as I was, I soon saw
that this was a very different creature.
Instead of the gentle, deer-shaped head of
the great three-toed leaf-eater, this beast had
a broad, squat, toad-like face like that which
had alarmed us in our camp. His ferocious
cry and the horrible energy of his pursuit
both assured me that this was surely one of
the great flesh-eating dinosaurs, the most
terrible beasts which have ever walked this
earth.

129

Chapter V

The Ugly, the Comic, the Obscene

1. Priapus

Montaigne (*Essays* II, V) wondered: 'what has the sexual act ever done to mankind, what has this natural, necessary, and legitimate act done that men do not dare talk of it if not with shame and exclude it from all serious or pondered discourse? We are bold enough to say: *kill, steal, betray*, so why is that other thing pronounced only between gritted teeth?' In effect human beings (at least in Western society) have always felt ill at ease with all that is excremental and all that has to do with sex. We are disgusted by excrement (that of others, animals included, much more than our own) and hence consider it ugly. In his *Civilization and its Discontents* Freud observed that 'the genital organs in themselves, the sight of which is always exciting, are nonetheless never considered beautiful'. This embarrassment finds its expression in shame, i.e., the instinct or the duty to abstain from exhibiting and from referring to certain parts of the body and certain activities. The sense of shame has varied according to the various cultures and historical periods. There have been epochs, as was the case in ancient Greece or the Renaissance, in which the representation of sexual attributes did not appear repugnant but actually contributed to emphasising the beauty of a body, and there are cultures in which those same attributes are exhibited in public without any embarrassment. But in those cultures with a strong sense of shame a taste for its violation is manifested through its opposite, which is *obscenity*.

One can indulge in obscene behaviour out of anger or a spirit of provocation, but very often obscene behaviour or language simply *arouse laughter* – just think of the way children love to hear or make jokes about excrement.

Bartolomeo Passerotti,
Caricature,
sixteenth–seventeenth
century,
private collection

Since earliest antiquity, the cult of the phallus has united the characteristics of obscenity, a certain ugliness, and an inevitable comicality. A typical example of this is a minor deity like Priapus (who appears in the Greco-Latin world in the Hellenistic period), equipped with an enormous genital organ. The son of Aphrodite, he was a protector of fertility and his images, usually made of fig wood, were placed in the fields and in the orchards both to protect the crops and to serve as a scarecrow; it was thought that he could drive off thieves by sodomising them. He was certainly obscene, he was considered ridiculous because of that huge member (and it's no accident that today priapism is an illness), and he was not thought to be handsome. In fact he was defined as *amorphos*, ugly (*aischron*) because his was not the correct form. In a bas-relief in Aquileia dating from Trajan's day (a piece known also to Freud, who mentions it in a letter in 1898) he is portrayed as Aphrodite, disgusted by the features of this ill-favoured child, rejects him. Finally, he was not a happy god: he was also defined as 'monolithic' because he was carved out of a single piece of wood and stuck in the field unable to move and devoid of the capacity to change his shape proper to many other mythological characters. He was oppressed by loneliness and his incapacity to seduce a nymph, despite his hypertrophic possibilities. And we can hardly fail to note the tome of commiseration reserved for him by **Horace** in the *Satires*.

Invocation to Priapus, first century AD, Pompeii, Casa dei Vettii

Yet he was basically an amusing and likeable deity, a friend to wayfarers, and as such he is portrayed by various poets, from **Theocritus** to the **Priapea** (an anonymous collection probably from the first century AD, written in a burlesque, lewd tone) down to the **Palatine Anthology.**

Thus Priapus symbolises the close relationship established since early times between ugliness, lewdness and comicality (as we can also see in passages from **Aristophanes** and the **Life of Aesop**).

Priapus's Lament
Horace (first century BC)
Satires, I, 8
Once upon a time I was a trunk of fig
tree wood
Timber both useless and no good,
When a carpenter uncertain whether to
make
A bench or a Priapus,
Chose the God.
And a God I've been ever since,
A peerless bogeyman for birds and
thieves:
I keep sticky fingers away with my right
And the red pole
That rises obscenely from my groin,
While a sheaf of reeds atop my head
Frightens harmful birds
And keeps them from alighting in new
gardens.
Once upon a time, slaves had their
friends'

Corpses brought here in wretched boxes,
Tossing them out of their cramped cells;
Here you could find the derelicts' local
bone yard [. . .]
Now, above the reclaimed Esquiline hill
People can live
And walk in the sun along the ramparts,
Where once you'd have been horrified to
see
Bleached bone and desolate earth;
And I'm no longer bothered so much,
By the thieves and animals
That usually live in these places,
But by the witches, who with potions and
magic
Play havoc with the human mind:
And to tell the truth I can't stamp them
out
And stop them from gathering bones
Or poisonous weeds, when the moon,
Wandering through the night
Boasts a face full of light.

Priapus

Priapea, 6, 10, 24

Though I am, as you can see, but a
wooden Priapus,
with a wooden scythe and a wooden
penis;
I'll grab you and hold you still,
And once you're caught I'll enjoy you,
my girl.
And this big thing, large and stiff as a
lyre
I'll bury up to your seventh rib, or higher.
Why laugh, you foolish girl? Neither
Praxiteles
Nor Scopas nor Phidias has shaped me.
A villain from a shapeless log carved me
thus
And then cried out: 'Yes! You're Priapus!'
Now you stare at me, and laugh
repeatedly?
It seems you find it pleasurable and fun,
This column springing straight up from
my groin!
The custodian of this fertile garden has
ordered me
To guarantee this place is let alone, let be
So accept your punishment, thief, though
you'll indignantly say,
'For so little verdure, such exorbitant
pay?'
'Yes, of course! Now pay!'

Priapeum

Theocritus (third–fourth century AD)
Epigrams, 4

Along that path, where the oak trees are,
O goatherd, on turning a corner, you will
find a crude simulacrum made of fig
wood. With three legs, it's still covered
with bark, and has no ears. But its vital
member is capable of performing the
work of Venus. A holy fence surrounds it,
and a stream flows out from the rocks,
surrounded by laurel, myrtle, and fragrant
cypress trees. And there a vine winds its
way, bearing grapes – and the blackbirds
of spring sing various songs in their sharp
voices. And nightingales respond with
their honeyed music. Stop there, and ask
gracious Priapus to take away my desire
for Daphne, and I'll sacrifice a fine little
goat right away. But if he refuses, I'm
prepared to make a triple sacrifice: I will
sacrifice a heifer, a hairy goat, and a lamb
I keep indoors. May the god hear my
prayer!

Dijon Painter,
The Prodigious Birth of Venus,
fourth century BC,
Bari, Museo
Archaeologico della
Provincia

Poor Socrates

Aristophanes
The Clouds, 169 (423 BC)
Chaerephon said that the gut of the gnat was narrow, and that, in passing through this tiny passage, the air is driven with force towards the breech; then after this slender channel, it encountered the rump, which was distended like a trumpet, and there it resounded sonorously.
Strepsiades: So the arse of a gnat is a trumpet.
Disciple: One night, when he was studying the course of the moon and its revolutions and was gazing open-mouthed at the heavens, a lizard crapped upon him from the top of the roof.
Strepsiades: A lizard crapping on Socrates! That's rich!

Crapping Common Sense

Anonymous (first–second century)
The Aesop Romance
'Can you explain to me why, when we defecate, we often examine our excrement?' Aesop explained: 'In olden days there was a king's son who, because of his life of ease and luxury,

spent most of his time sitting and shitting. Once he remained seated thus so long that, having forgotten what he was doing, he shat his own common sense. From that day forward, men shit hunched over, being careful not to crap away their own common sense. But don't you worry: you can't shit something you don't possess!'

Against Laughter

St Basil
Lesser Rules (fourth century)
The Lord took upon himself all the corporeal functions inseparable from human nature, [. . .] But nevertheless, as the Gospels tell us (*vae vobis qui ridetis nunc, quia lugebitis et flebitis*, Luke 6:25), he never gave in to laughter. On the contrary, he defined those who allow themselves to be dominated by laughter as unhappy [. . .]

Rules of the Four Fathers (fifth century)
If anyone is discovered laughing or telling jokes [...] we will order that man, in the name of the Lord, to be repressed with the whip of humility in every way possible for two whole weeks.

2. Satires on the Peasantry and Carnival Festivities

There are forms of art that express *lost harmony* (hence the sublime or the tragic, which cause anxiety and tension), *possessed harmony* (hence the beautiful and the fair, which induce serenity) or *lost and failed harmony*, which brings us to the comic as the loss and *diminution*, or also as the *mechanisation* of normal behaviour patterns. Thus we can laugh at the arrogant stuffed shirt who slips on a banana skin, at the stiff movements of marionettes, and we can laugh at various forms of expectations frustrated, at the animalisation of human features, at the bungling of an incompetent, or at amusing word play. These and other forms of comicality play on deformation, but not necessarily on obscenity.

But comicality and obscenity come together either when we make fun of someone we hold in contempt (for example when we mock or make coarse jokes about cuckolds) or when we indulge in some cathartic act with respect to something or someone who is oppressing us. In this case, by arousing laughter at the expense of the oppressor, the comic-obscene also represents a sort of compensatory rebellion.

This form of rebellion (even when authorised, and hence understood as a safety valve for tensions that otherwise would be uncontrollable) is to be found in the Roman Saturnalia, during which slaves were permitted to take the place of their masters, and during triumphs, where veterans were allowed to bombard the hero of the day with the most scurrilous quips and loaded allusions.

The early Christian world was not indulgent when it came to laughter, considered to be a quasi diabolical licence. A tradition derived from an apocryphal gospel, the *Epistle of Lentulus*, taught that Christ had never laughed and the debate on Jesus and laughter went on for centuries. But such documents **against laughter** must not let us forget that other fathers and doctors of the Church defended the right to a healthy merriment and that right from the early medieval centuries there were humorous texts in circulation. These included *The Supper of Cyprianus* (a phantasmagorical parody that was extremely popular in the monasteries and that portrayed biblical characters in a decidedly irreverent light) or the *Joca monachorum* (Monks' Jokes). There were also moments explicitly devoted to comic licence, like the *riso pasquale* (literally, the Easter laugh), when during the celebrations of the Resurrection it was permitted to make jokes in church even during the sermons.

Tricouillard,
fifteenth century,
Angers, wooden house

An Embarrassing Husband

Anonymous

'The Black Scrotum' (twelfth–fourteenth century)

My Lord, in your presence
I want to say before everyone here
the reason why I have come to court.
I've been married for seven years now
with a peasant, whom I never fully knew,
until last night, when for the first time
I discovered

the reason why I can no longer stay with him,
nor remain in his company.
You'll find what I say is true:
my husband has a prick blacker
than iron, and a scrotum blacker
than any monk's or priest's cassock;
and it's hairy like the skin of a bear,
and furthermore no old moneylender's purse
was ever so swollen as his scrotum.
I've told you the truth;
I don't know how to tell it any better.

The Peasant's Fart

Rutebeuf (thirteenth century)

Jesus Christ has no wish
For peasants to find hospitality
In his sainted Mother's home [. . .]
Peasants cannot win Paradise
With money or other stuff,
While they cannot even go to Hell,
Because even the devils find them
revolting [. . .]
One day a peasant
Fell ill
And in Hell all were ready
To receive his soul.
I tell you with absolute certainty.
A devil came to him
To take him downstairs, as was his right,
And he attached a leather bag to the man's
bum,
Because it was his firm belief
That the soul fled from that part there.
But that evening the peasant had taken
A potion for his malady,
And had eaten beef with garlic
With hot fat broth
So that his belly wasn't soft
But tighter than a drumskin.

He was going to die, no doubt,
But if he could drop a fart, all would be
well.
So he set to straining with a will,
And he gave the job his all,
So doggedly did he go to it,
Tossing and turning,
That he let rip the loudest fart,
Filling up the bag, which the devil tied,
For by way of penitence the devil
Had trodden upon the man's belly;
And the proverb rightly says
'Push too hard and you'll get shit'.
Then the Devil headed for the door
With the fart closed inside the bag.
He tossed it into hell,
But the fart escaped the bag.
All the devils were dancing with rage
And cursed the peasant's soul.
The next day they held an assembly
And came to an agreement:
That never more would they
Take a peasant's soul,
For it'll stink for sure.
And this is why peasants
Will go neither to heaven nor to hell:
And you will have understood this well.

The Middle Ages was a period full of contradictions, in which public shows of piety and austerity were accompanied by generous concessions to sin, as is revealed to us by many short stories from the period, and there were places where prostitution was tolerated (even villages-gynaecea, known as *columbaria*, patronised by feudal lords). Nor must we forget the eroticism of courtly poetry and the songs of the goliards, who were clerics at that. Moreover the sense of shame was certainly different from the modern one, especially among the poor, where families lived in promiscuity, sleeping all in the same room or even in the same bed, while bodily functions were performed in the fields without anyone worrying overmuch about privacy. Obscenity (and praise of the deformed and the grotesque) appears in the **satires on the peasantry** and in the carnival festivities in relation to the lives of the humble. These are two fairly different phenomena. There are many texts, from the French *fabliaux* to the Italian short stories and Chaucer's *Canterbury Tales*, in which the villein is shown as a fool, ever ready to swindle his master, dirty and stinking (in one story, on passing in front of a perfumer's workshop, a donkey driver was so overcome by the scents that he fainted, coming to only when they had him smell some manure). Sometimes, peasants were also portrayed as Priapus, disfigured by disgusting genital attributes.

But this was not an example of popular comicality; it was more of an expression of the contempt and diffidence in which peasants were held by the feudal and ecclesiastical worlds, who took sadistic pleasure in the peasant's deformities and laughed *at* him rather than *with* him.

Crapping on the doughnut, on church stall, 1531, Walcourt, the Church of Sainte-Materne

facing page
The Flag of the Mad Mother, fifteenth or sixteenth century, Dijon

The Cowherd
Chrétien de Troyes
Yvain, the Knight of the Lion (1180 ca.)
A peasant that looked like a Moor, incredibly deformed and horrible, a creature so ugly that you can't describe him in words, was sitting on a stump holding a large club. I approached and saw that his head was bigger than that of an old nag or any other animal. His tousled hair was balding on his forehead and he had hairy ears over two spans broad and big as those of an elephant. This yokel had bushy eyebrows, a flat face, eyes like an owl's, a nose like a cat's, jowls like those of a wolf, sharp, yellowish fangs like those of a wild boar, a red beard, twisted moustache, and his chin seemed stuck to his chest. His back was long, but twisted and humped. He was leaning against his club and wearing a very strange outfit. It was made neither of linen nor wool, but, attached at the neck, there hung down two freshly flayed bull or ox hides.

Flatulence
Karl Rosenkrantz
The Aesthetics of Ugliness, III (1853)
Flatulence is an ugly business in all circumstances. But since it is a sign that the liberty of man is not always entirely under his control, and since it often takes him by frightful surprise in the wrong place, rapidly slipping away from him unguarded, it resembles a goblin that, without warning and *sans gêne* puts him in an embarrassing situation. And so comedians have always made use of it in grotesques and burlesques, at least by allusion [. . .] Since we men, immaterial of the age, education, social class and rank that distinguish us, are all part of this involuntary baseness of nature, allusions in this regard seldom fail to make the public laugh: this is why low comedy is extraordinarily fond of all the boorishness, filth, and nonsense associated with this matter.

For their part, the common townsfolk were the stars of grotesque parodies during carnival and other similar events, such as the Feast of the Ass and the *charivari*, processions held when a widower remarried, characterised by shouting, obscene gestures, and dressing up in disguise, during which people made an enormous racket using cauldrons, casserole dishes and other kitchen utensils. But at carnival time the main element was the grotesque representation of the human body (hence the masks), parodies of sacred things and complete licence in language, blasphemy included. The triumph of all that during the rest of the year was considered ugly or forbidden, these festivities nonetheless were an interlude granted and tolerated only on specific occasions. For the rest of the year there were the official religious holidays. On these occasions the traditional order and respect for the hierarchy were reconfirmed, while during carnival the social order and hierarchy was allowed to be overturned (they even elected the king or the bishop of the festivities) and the clownish and 'shameful' traits of popular life emerged. The people took gleeful revenge on the feudal and ecclesiastical powers and, through parodies of devils and the underworld, they tried to react against the fear of death and the afterlife, and against the terror of the plagues and catastrophes that would dominate the rest of the year.

The Charivari,
Ms. Fr. 146, fol. 34,
fourteenth century,
Paris, Bibliothèque
Nationale de France

And so one might say, paradoxically, that seriousness and gloominess were the prerogative of those who practised a healthy optimism (we have to suffer but then eternal glory will be ours), while laughter was the medicine of those who pessimistically lived a wretched and difficult life.

These events also included the Feast of Fools, and it's obvious how the figure of the fool (who can also be the bearer of unexpected wisdom) was characterised by a grimace of madness that was immediately transformed into a clownish mask.

On such occasions a farcical role was also assigned to the excrement that in church, during the burlesque election of a false bishop, was used instead of incense, while during the charivari excrement was tossed at the crowds. In this way ugliness was in a certain sense redeemed, perhaps partly owing to the fact that the star of carnival, hungry and oppressed by disease, was no more beautiful than the character he represented – and hence, though an act of defiance, the ugly person was accepted and imposed as a model.

The Prince of Fools
Pierre Gringoire
(fifteenth–sixteenth century)
Moody fools, befuddled fools, wise fools; city fools, fools from castles and villages; stultified fools, simple fools, subtle fools; loving fools, solitary fools, wild fools, fools old, new and foolish of every age; barbarous fools, foreign fools, considerate fools, reasonable fools, perverse fools, stubborn fools [. . .], foolish dames and foolish ladies-in-waiting; foolish old women and fresh foolish girls; all female fools who love men; courageous, cowardly, ugly and beautiful fools; sprightly fools, sweet fools, rebellious fools; female fools who want their pay; fools trotting down the path; thin fools, red fools, fat fools and pale fools; on Mardi Gras the Prince will host you all at Les Halles.

3. The Renaissance and Liberation

All these phenomena were, in a sense, turned on their head during the Renaissance. The clearest example of this process is in Rabelais's *Gargantua and Pantagruel*, which began to appear in 1532. In this book, not only did **Rabelais** revisit and pillage the most risqué forms of the old popular culture with extraordinary originality, but his obscenity no longer appeared (or not solely) as a plebeian characteristic, becoming rather the language and behaviour of a royal court. What's more, the ostentation of scurrility (with unsurpassed comic results) was no longer practised in the ghetto of the barely tolerated carnival festivities. It was transferred into cultivated literature, it was exhibited officially, it became a satire on the world of the learned and ecclesiastical customs. In short, it had taken on a philosophical function. It was no longer a matter of an occasional anarchic popular rebellion, but a genuine cultural revolution. In a society that had come to advocate the prevalence of the human and of the earthly over the divine, obscenity became the proud assertion of the rights of the body – and as such Rabelais was splendidly analysed by **Bachtin**. According to classical medieval criteria, the giants Gargantua and his son Pantagruel were deformed because they were out of proportion, but their deformity becomes glorious. They are no longer the fearsome giants who rebelled against Jupiter, inexorably condemned by classical mythology, nor are they the monstrous inhabitants of India of medieval legend: in their incontinent and 'enormous' greatness, they become the heroes of a new day.

Pantagruel's Fart
François Rabelais
Gargantua and Pantagruel, II, 27 (1532)
Then, getting up, he gave a fart, a leap, and a whistle, and joyously cried aloud: 'Long live Pantagruel!'

At this sight, Pantagruel tried to do the same. But with the fart he blew the earth trembled for twenty-seven miles round, and with the fetid air of it he engendered more than fifty-three thousand little men, misshapen dwarves; and with a poop, which he made, he engendered as many little bowed women, such as you see in various places, and who never grow, except downwards like cows' tails, or in circumference, like Limousin turnips. 'What now?' exclaimed Panurge. 'Are your farts so fruitful? By God, here are fine clumpish men, fine stinking women. Only let them be married together, and they'll breed horseflies.'

Gustave Doré,
Illustration
for *Gargantua
and Pantagruel*,
1873,
Paris, Garnier

following pages
François Rabelais
Illustration for *Les songes
drôlatiques de
Pantagruel*,
1565,
Paris, Richard Breton

How Panurge Crapped Himself

François Rabelais

Gargantua and Pantagruel, IV, 67 (1532)
As Panurge came near, Friar John smelt
an odour of some sort which was not
gunpowder. So he turned Panurge round
and saw that his shirt was all mucky and
newly shitten. The retentive power of the
nerve which controls the sphincter muscle
– Panurge's arse-hole that is – had been
relaxed by the extreme fear which had
accompanied his fantastic visions. On top
of this had come the thunder of the
cannonading, which is more terrifying in
the bowels of the ship than on the deck.
Now one of the symptoms and
concomitants of fear is that it usually
opens the gate of the seraglio in which
the fecal matter is temporarily stored.

Some of Panurge's Good Customs

François Rabelais

Gargantua and Pantagruel, II, 16 (1532)
As for the poor masters of art and the
theologians, he persecuted them most of
all. When he saw any of them in the
street, he never failed to play them some
trick. Sometimes he would put dung in
their graduate hoods, sometimes he
would tie little fox-tails or hare's-ears
behind them, and at other times he
would do them some other mischief.
One day, when all the theologians were
summoned to meet in the Rue du Feurre,
he made a mud pie composed of garlic,
galbanum, asafoetida, and castoreum in
quantity and of turds that were still warm.
This he steeped in the runnings from
sores. Then, very early in the morning, he
smeared and anointed the pavement, so
that the devil himself could not have
endured it.

The Invention of the Arse-wipe

François Rabelais

Gargantua and Pantagruel, I, 13 (1532)

'By long and curious experiments,' replied Gargantua, 'I have invented a method of wiping my arse which is the most lordly, the most excellent, and the most convenient that ever was seen.'

'What's that?' asked Grandgousier.

'I shall tell you in a moment,' said Gargantua. 'Once I wiped myself on a lady's velvet mask, and I found it good. For the softness of the silk was most voluptuous to my fundament. Another time on one of their hoods, and I found it just as good. Another time on a lady's neckerchief; another time on some ear-flaps of crimson satin. That trouble passed when I wiped myself on a page's bonnet, all feathered in the Swiss fashion.

'Then, as I was shitting behind a bush, I found a March-born cat; I wiped myself on him, but his claws exulcerated my whole perineum. I healed myself of that next day by wiping myself on my mother's gloves, which were well scented with *maljamin*. Then I wiped myself with sage, fennel, anise, marjoram, roses, gourd leaves, cabbage, beets, vineshoots, marsh-mallow, mullein – which is red as your bum – lettuces, and spinach leaves. All this did very great good to my legs. Then with dog's mercury, persicaria, nettles and comfrey. But that gave me the bloody-flux of Lombardy, from which I was cured by wiping myself with my codpiece.

'Then I wiped myself on the sheets, the coverlet, the curtains, with a cushion, with the hangings, with a green cloth, with a table-cloth, with a napkin, with a handkerchief, with an overall. And I found more pleasure in all those than mangy dogs do when they are combed.'

'Yes,' said Grandgousier. 'But which wiper did you find the best?'

'[. . .] But to conclude, I say and maintain that there is no arse-wiper like a well-downed goose, if you hold her neck between your legs. You must take my word for it, you really must. You get a miraculous sensation in your arse-hole, both from the softness of the down and from the temperate heat of the goose herself; and this is easily communicated to the bum-gut and the rest of the intestines, from which it reaches the heart and the brain. Do not imagine that the felicity of the heroes and demigods in the Elysian Fields arises from their asphodel, their ambrosia, or their nectar, as those ancients say. It comes, in my opinion, from their wiping their arses with the neck of a goose, and that is the opinion of Master Duns Scotus too.'

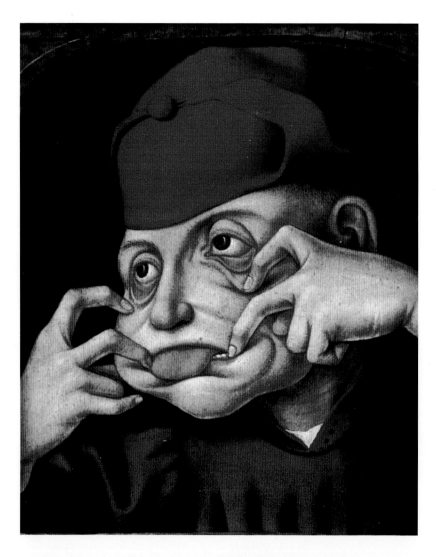

A Satirical Table from a Flemish Triptych, c.1520, Liège, Bibliothèque Centrale

At the beginning of the seventeenth century satires on the peasantry were also turned on their heads with *Bertoldo* (1606) by **Giulio Cesare Croce.** With this character, again very ugly and coarse, the villein was no longer depicted as foolish but astute as the author dipped into the legend of Aesop, whose ill-favoured aspect concealed wisdom and cunning. Nor did we really have to wait for Bertoldo, because in 1553 we find the *History of the Peasant Campriano* where the ingenious peasant, who had hidden his money in the backside of his own donkey, fools some stupid merchants by letting them see his donkey defecate money before selling it to them for a high price. In the meantime, even the fool had been transformed from a carnival character to a philosophical symbol: each of the various madmen sailing towards the land of Cockaigne had already become a caricature of a different vice in the *Ship of Fools* by Sebastian Brant (1494) and Erasmus of Rotterdam has Folly in person rail against the customs of his own day in his *In Praise of Folly* (1509).

Hieronymus Bosch,
The Ship of Fools,
c.1500,
Paris, Louvre

The Mouth and the Nose

Mikhail Bachtin

The Work of Rabelais and Popular Culture,
V (1965)

Of all the features of the human *face*, only
the *mouth* and the *nose*, and this last as a
substitute for the phallus, play a major role
in grotesque images of the body. The eyes
are of no importance in the grotesque
image of the face. They merely express the
purely *individual* life, or, so to speak, the
inner life of man, and hence they have no
importance for the purposes of the
grotesque. The grotesque deals only with
goggling eyes [. . .] just as it takes an interest
in all that *sprouts, protrudes, or emerges
from the body*, everything that tries to flee
the confines of the body. In the grotesque a
particular significance is attached to all
excrescences and ramifications, everything
that prolongs the body and unites it with
other bodies or to the non-corporeal world.
One might also add that goggling eyes are
of interest to the grotesque because they
bear witness to a *purely bodily tension*. But
for the grotesque the most important part of
the entire face is the mouth. It dominates
all. A grotesque face can basically be
reduced to a *gaping mouth* and all the rest
serves merely as a *frame for this mouth*, for
this *bodily abyss that gapes wide and
swallows*.

Bertoldo

Giulio Cesare Croce

The Extremely Subtle Slyness of Bertoldo,
1 (1606)

In the time when Alboino, King of the
Lombards, had become lord over almost all
of Italy, setting up his royal capital in the
beautiful city of Verona, a peasant called
Bertoldo happened to come to his court. He
was a deformed and extremely ugly man,
but where his shape was lacking, the
vivacity of his mind bridged the gap: he
was very witty and quick to answer, and in
addition to the sharpness of his intellect, he
was also astute, malicious and nasty by
nature. And his stature was such as is
described here. First, he was a small man,
with a head as fat and round as a ball; his
forehead was furrowed and wrinkled; his
eyes red as fire; his lashes long and rough
as a pig's bristles; his ears were asinine; his
mouth large and rather misshapen, with his
lower lip hanging down like a horse's; his
beard grew thick on his chin and droopy as
a billygoat's; his nose was hooked and
upturned, with enormous nostrils; and his
teeth stuck out like a boar's. Under his chin
he had three or even four goitres that, while
he talked, danced around like lids atop
boiling pots; he had goat's legs like a satyr,
long, broad feet, and his entire body was
covered with hair; his hose was a very dull
grey, and all patched on the knees, he wore
shoes with large high heels. To sum up: he
was truly the exact opposite of Narcissus.

A contemporary of Rabelais was Pieter Bruegel the Elder, thanks to whom the world of the peasantry, with its festivities, its coarseness and its deformities, became the subject of great art. As in the satires on the villeins, Bruegel's painting represented the people but was not intended for them. As Hauser observed in his *Social History of Art*, those who want to portray their own lives are social groups satisfied with their condition, not those who are still oppressed and would like a different life. Bruegel's art was intended for the town and not for the country. But, despite this, no one can deny that Bruegel was scrupulously attentive regarding rustic customs while his portrayal of the peasantry was certainly not ferocious and derisive like that of the medieval satires.

Portrait of Falstaff
William Shakespeare
Henry IV, II, 4 (1598–1600)
HENRY: [...] There is a devil haunts thee in the likeness of an old fat man; a tun of man is thy companion. Why dost thou converse with that trunk of humours, that bolting-hutch of beastliness, that swollen parcel of dropsies, that huge bombard of sack, that stuffed cloak-bag of guts, that roasted Manningtree ox with the pudding in his belly, that reverend vice, that grey iniquity, that father ruffian, that vanity in years? Wherein is he good, but to taste sack and drink it? wherein neat and cleanly, but to carve a capon and eat it? wherein cunning, but in craft? wherein crafty, but in villany? wherein villanous, but in all things? wherein worthy, but in nothing?

The Good Ugliness of Nature
Antonio Rocco
On Ugliness (1635)
In Nature the ugliest things are putrefaction, the dead, famine, poverty and so forth. In addition to these, there are also others; which, if you look closely, are rather the most wonderful things in the world. Putrefaction, which is a deprivation, also gives life to every new generation, to everything under the sun, all of which can be found in peripatetic philosophy; now, if the beginnings are bad, what follows will be even worse; but if they are good, then what follows will be excellent. In one of the principles Aristotle called base, *appetit enim, ut turpe, etc. de generatione animalium*, he too notes that there is undoubtedly nothing uglier nor more unpleasant than the procreation of animals, and especially of man himself. In fact, anyone who witnesses those repulsive mixtures of dark blood, filthy seed, dirty menses and putrid sperm would be profoundly nauseated. If you consider births, purgation, excretion, and so forth, you will clearly see that what I say is true, and despite this, these things are absolutely important and necessary, and are the beginnings of every good; now isn't Nature's ugliness good?

The consideration of ugliness then began to take on realistic aspects, as was to happen with seventeenth-century painting. In *On Ugliness* (1635) **Antonio Rocco** states polemically that he wants to deal with ugly things because things that are always sweet and pretty are inevitably nauseating in the end. Rocco has fun expressing moralistic and anti-feminist paradoxes, showing how in women ugliness is 'the custodian of honesty, a remedy for lust, and a chance for equity and justice' and hence only ugly women do not arouse desire and anguish in lovers, while they are not wanton like beautiful women. Rocco also praises natural disasters, which lead to regeneration, and defines as a principle of all good many things that some people find disgusting, such as childbirth, menstruation, sperm and purgatives. With the Renaissance obscenity entered a new phase. The presence of the genitalia in representations of human bodies no longer scandalised anyone, and they were seen as an element of beauty, while writers like Aretino extolled acts hitherto considered unmentionable (and to this day decency still forbids us to include them in the anthology). Such material eventually found its way into court – the papal court included – and was no longer deemed distasteful, but a bold and unashamed invitation to enjoyment. The art of the cultivated classes publicly claimed the same right that was previously granted almost on the quiet to the plebeian rabble, with the exception that this right was exercised with grace and not violence – and it brought about the disappearance of the *mentionable* and the *unmentionable*. In claiming to make a 'beautiful' portrayal not only of innocent ugliness but also of that considered to be taboo, this new art separated the obscene from the ugly.

President de Curval
The Marquis de Sade
The 120 Days of Sodom, Introduction
(1785)

The President de Curval was a pillar of society; almost sixty years of age, and worn by debauchery to a singular degree, he offered the eye not much more than a skeleton. He was tall, he was dry, thin, had two blue lustreless eyes, a livid and unwholesome mouth, a prominent chin, a long nose. Hairy as a satyr, flat-backed, with slack, drooping buttocks that rather resembled a pair of dirty rags flapping upon his upper thighs; the skin of those buttocks was, thanks to whipstrokes, so deadened and toughened that you could seize up a handful and knead it without his feeling a thing. [. . .] Similarly untidy about all the rest of his person, the President, who furthermore had tastes at the very least as nasty as his appearance, had become a figure whose rather malodorous vicinity might not have succeeded in pleasing everyone [. . .]. Few mortals had been as free in their behaviour or as debauched as the President; but, entirely jaded, absolutely besotted, all that remained to him was the depravation and lewd profligacy of libertinage. Above three hours of excess, and of the most outrageous excess, were needed before one could hope to inspire a voluptuous reaction in him [. . .] Curval was to such a point mired down in the morass of vice and libertinage that it had become virtually impossible for him to think or speak of anything else. He unendingly had the most appalling expressions in his mouth, just as he had the vilest designs in his heart, and these with surpassing energy he mingled with blasphemies and imprecations supplied him by his true horror, a sentiment he shared with his companions, for everything that smacked of religion. This disorder of mind, yet further augmented by the almost continual intoxication in which he was fond of keeping himself, had during the past few years given him an air of imbecility and prostration which, he would declare, made for his most cherished delight.

Félicien Rops
Pornokrates,
1878,
Namur, Musée
Provincial Félicien Rops

Obscenity provided an opportunity for urbane entertainment in the licentious literature of the seventeenth and eighteenth centuries, even though in a 'maudit' like **De Sade** it regained all its most repugnant features. Again, decency prevents us from including in the anthology the *entire* description of M. De Curval as it appears in *120 Days of Sodom*. Curval is a libertine made horrible, fetid, and disgusting by disgustingly lewd acts, described without sparing the reader a single detail. In stepping over the boundary between the mentionable and the unmentionable, Sade goes beyond the normal exercise of bodily functions: in an attempt to be cathartic, he uses obscenity to overstep the mark, to aim at enormity and the intolerable. In any event, obscenity came to play a dominant role in much of the literature of the late nineteenth century and in that produced by the avant-garde movements of the twentieth century, with a view to demolishing the taboos of the self-righteous and at the same time to gain acceptance for all aspects of corporality. But in the nineteenth century things that had been previously considered obscenely ugly were unhesitatingly dealt with in realistic art and literature, which wanted to portray all aspects of everyday life. In any case, proof of the relativity of the concept of decency is that many works now read even in schools such as Flaubert's *Madame Bovary* and Joyce's *Ulysses*, or the novels of Lawrence and Miller, caused a scandal when they first came out and were occasionally banned.

4. Caricature

One of the forms of the comic is the caricature. The idea of caricature is basically a modern one, and some say that it begins with certain grotesques by Leonardo. But Leonardo 'invented' types rather than select recognisable targets, just as in previous times portrayals were made of beings already deformed by definition, such as satyrs, devils, or peasants. But modern caricature came into being as a polemical device against a real person or a recognisable social category, and it exaggerates an aspect of the body (usually the face) to deride or denounce a moral blemish through a physical one.

In this sense caricature never refines its object, but makes it uglier, emphasising a trait to the point of deformity. Thus, moralists like **Hans Sedlmayr** (in *The Lost Centre*) have talked of a process that deprives man of his equilibrium and dignity.

Some caricatures are certainly made with the intention of humiliating the target and making it hateful (see Chapter 7 for the various techniques used to demonise political, religious, or racial enemies).

Nonetheless, by emphasising some characteristics of the subject, caricature is often intended to arrive at a deeper understanding of the character.

Nor does it always aim at exposing an 'inner' ugliness but at highlighting physical or intellectual features or behaviour patterns that make the character likeable. Hence while the ferocious caricatures of Daumier or Grosz expose the moral baseness of personalities and types of their day, the caricatures of thinkers or artists created by the Italian artist Tullio Pericoli are genuine portraits of great psychological insight, which often reach a celebratory level.

This is why **Rosenkranz** held that caricature is an aesthetic redemption of ugliness, insofar as it is not limited to emphasising a disproportion, nor to focusing on all the anomalous elements present (in which case, as with Swift's giants and pygmies, we wouldn't be dealing with a caricature but a different form). Good caricature employs exaggeration 'as a dynamic factor that involves its totality', and ensures that the element of formal disorganisation becomes 'organic'. In other words it is a 'beautiful' portrayal that makes harmonious use of deformation.

Quentin Metsys,
The Bill of Sale,
sixteenth century,
Berlin, Gemäldegalerie,
Staatliche Museen

Leonardo da Vinci,
*Caricature of an Old
Man's Head*,
1500–05,
Hamburg, Kunsthalle

John Hamilton
Mortimer,
Caricature of a Group,
c.1776,
Yale Center for British
Art, Paul Mellon
Collection

facing page
Honoré Daumier,
Two Lawyers and Death,
nineteenth century,
Winterthur, Oskar
Reinhart Collection

Harmony in Caricature

Karl Rosenkranz

The Aesthetics of Ugliness, III (1853)

[The Ugly] transforms the sublime into the vulgar, the agreeable into the repugnant, and absolute beauty into caricature in which dignity becomes emphasis, and charm coquettishness. Caricature is hence the acme of formal ugliness but precisely because, thanks to its reflection determined by the positive image of which it is a distortion, it slips over into comedy. Until now we have always seen the point at which the ugly can become ridiculous. In destroying themselves, the informal and the incorrect, the vulgar and the repugnant can produce an apparently impossible reality, which has a comic effect. All these factors are a part of caricature. It too becomes informal and incorrect, vulgar and repugnant, according to all the graduations of these concepts. It has an inexhaustible capacity to transform and connect them with the ability of a chameleon. This enables the creation of paltry grandeur, rational nonsense, empty fullness, and thousands of other contradictions [. . .].

Caricature consists in *exaggerating* a form until it becomes deformed. Yet this definition should be limited a little more [. . .] To explain caricature you need to add another concept to exaggeration, that of a disproportion between the form and its totality, and hence a negation of the unity that should exist according to the concept of form. That

is to say, if the entire form were enlarged or diminished to an equal extent in all its parts, then the proportions would remain the same in themselves and consequently – as is the case with Swift's characters – nothing really ugly would result. But if a part escapes from the unity so as to negate the normal correlation, and since this last still exists in the other parts, all is displaced and disordered, which is ugly. Disproportion constantly implies the proportionate form. A prominent nose, for example, can be a great beauty. But it if becomes too big, the rest of the face disappears too much by comparison with it. A disproportion is created. Involuntarily we compare its size with that of the other part of the face and we conclude that it should not be so big. The excessive size not only makes a caricature of the nose, but of the entire face of which it is a part [. . .] But here too, yet again, we must establish a boundary. A simple disproportion might produce as a consequence a simple ugliness, but one that we would be quite unable as yet to define as caricature [. . .]

The exaggeration that disfigures form must operate as a dynamic factor involving the totality of the form. Its disorganisation must become organic. This concept is the secret of the production of caricature. In its disharmony, through the ill-intentioned exaggeration of a part of the whole, a certain harmony arises anew.

facing page
Tullio Pericoli,
Albert Einstein,
1959

George Grosz,
A Grey Day,
1921,
Berlin, Staatliche
Nationalgalerie

Against Caricature
Hans Sedlmayr
The Loss of the Centre, V (1948)

Caricatures have existed since the most remote times. We know of them since the end of late Alexandrine culture. In caricature physical ugliness is emphasised. During the Baroque period there were personal and private caricatures, as for example in Caracci, Mitelli, Ghezzi, and Bernini too. As Baudelaire rightly pointed out, the so-called caricatures of Leonardo da Vinci are not authentic caricatures. In the middle ages they had the slanderous political picture, which is a form of capital punishment in effigy.

It was only from the end of the eighteenth century – in England at first – that caricature appeared as a genre in itself, and only in the nineteenth century, with Daumier, did a great artist adopt it as the central feature of his work. The important symptom is not the simple birth of caricature, but its elevation to the rank of a high and meaningful artistic force. From 1830 onwards, the magazine 'La caricature' was published. It had a political slant: 'A Walpurgis Night, pandemonium, a guzzling satanic drama, sometimes mad, sometimes revolting'. The allusion here is to the slums whence caricature springs. By its nature it is a disfigurement of the human character and, in extreme cases, an introduction of the infernal element (which is none other than the totality of images opposite to human ones) to the human element. This disfigurement can take various paths: the man is disfigured, for example, by a mask [. . .] But in general the thoughtless process of disfigurement makes use of two methods, one of which may be called positive and the other negative. This last deprives man of his balance, his form and his dignity; it shows him as ugly, poorly formed, wretched, and ridiculous. Man, the crown of creation, is debased and lowered, but he keeps his human character. [. . .]. At the beginning of the twentieth century [. . .] together with a new, ruthless caricature that denigrates men internally, the image of the disfigured man who subjugates the artist in an irresistible manner was to show himself with no mask in the human images of modern art, in those images that the ingenuous man saw as frightful caricatures but are in truth engendered in the deepest darkness of the abyss [...]

Chapter VI

The Ugliness of Woman Between Antiquity and the Baroque Period

1. The Anti-female Tradition

Between the Middle Ages and the Baroque period, *vituperatio* with regard to women – whose ugliness reveals their inner malice and pernicious powers of seduction – was a theme that enjoyed great success. Previous to this, in classical literature **Horace, Catullus** and **Martial** had already provided us with repulsive portraits of women, while Juvenal's *Sixth Satire* was fiercely misogynous. In the *Medicamina faciei femineae* (Medicaments for the Female Countenance), a fragment devoted to cosmetics, Ovid warns that woman is made more beautiful by virtue than by make-up. The problem of cosmesis cropped up again in the Christian world with **Tertullian**, who remarks with ruthless severity that 'according to the Scriptures, the allurements of beauty are always as one with the prostitution of the body'. Apart from moral condemnation (and clear disagreement with the licence of the pagan world), Tertullian is insinuating that women plaster themselves with make-up and other artifices to conceal their physical defects, in the vain illusion that by so doing they may be more pleasing to their husbands or, worse, to strangers.

Patrizia Bettella (in *The Ugly Woman*, which ranges from the Middle Ages to the Baroque period) pinpoints three phases in the development of the theme of the ugly woman. In the Middle Ages there were many portrayals of the *old woman*, a symbol of physical and moral decay, in opposition to the canonical praise of youth as a symbol of beauty and purity. But during the Renaissance female ugliness became the subject of lampoons containing ironic praise of models that did not conform to the dominant aesthetic canons. In the Baroque period, however, we finally come to a positive reassessment of female imperfections as elements of attraction.

Bernardo Strozzi,
Vanitas,
1630,
Moscow, Pushkin
Museum

Big-nosed Girl

Gaius Valerius Catullus (84–54 ca. BC)
Carmina, 43
Hi, girl, neither with the smallest nose,
Nor with beautiful feet or black eyes
Or long fingers or dry lips
Or refined of speech.
Girlfriend of that bankrupt from Formiae,
So the provincials say you are beautiful?
They compare you to my Lesbia?
What a stupid, vulgar world!

Nasty Stench

Horace (65–8 BC)
Epodes, XII
What are you after, woman, some black
elephant? Why do you send gifts and love
letters to me? I am no exuberant youth, with
a stuffy nose. You know, I've got a really
sharp sense of smell and I'm better than any
hound, who can sniff out where the boar is
hiding, so I know if there's a polyp in that
nose, or some stink lurking in those hairy
armpits! What a sweaty, foul stench rises
from her shagged-out limbs when, my penis
drooping, she hastens to satiate her
unbridled lust; with her make-up dripping
off her cheeks, and her hair dye, made from
crocodile shit, is running; rutting openly,
she breaks the mattress, and with it the
whole four-poster bed . . .

Vetustilla

Martial (first century)
Epigrams, 94
You have outlived three hundred consuls,
Vetustilla,
You old hag; you have three hairs and four
teeth left,
A cicada's chest, the legs (and colouring) of
an ant.
You walk around with a forehead more
wrinkled than your stole
And breasts like cobwebs; the Nile crocodile
Has a tiny mouth compared with your maw,
the frogs
Of Ravenna and the mosquitoes of Adria,
for all their noise, are less
Irritating and more melodious than you.
Your
Vision is that of an owl in the morning
sunlight and
You stink like a billy goat; your backside is
drier than
A duck's arse, and not even an old cynic
Is scrawnier than your vagina. The attendant
at the baths lets you in
Along with the graveyard prostitutes, but
only after
Blowing out the lamp [. . .] And you're still

considering
Marriage after two hundred husbands have
died on you? [. . .]
The only thing capable of penetrating that
vagina of yours
Is a funeral candle.

Women, Wear a Veil

Tertullian (third century)
On the Apparel of Women, 4–7
You must please your husbands, and your
husbands alone. And the more you please
them, the less you'll worry about pleasing
others. Don't worry, O blessed ladies, no
woman is ugly to her own husband; she
was pleasing enough when she was chosen
for her manners and beauty. Nor are there
any among us who think that, if a woman
dresses up with greater moderation, her
husband might find her hateful and reject
her. Every husband demands the tribute of
chastity, but not beauty (if he is Christian),
because we are not slaves to those things
that pagans value as important [. . .]

I am not telling you this to suggest that
you adopt an entirely coarse and savage
look, nor do I wish to persuade you that it
is good to be slovenly and dirty, but I
advise you to use good sense and correct
restraint in taking care of your bodies. You
do not have to go beyond what is required
by simple and sufficient propriety: no more
than is pleasing to God.

In fact, those women who torment their
skin with make-up, or stain their cheeks red
and extend the line of their eyes with soot
sin against Him. There can be no doubt that
these women dislike what God has created,
and in themselves they reproach and
criticise the creator of all things. They
criticise Him when they remove blemishes,
when they add things, and they
undoubtedly get these things from the
enemy creator, in other words the devil
[. . .] I even see some who dye their hair
the colour of saffron. They are ashamed of
their nation: ashamed they were not born in
Germany or Gaul. Therefore they change
their nationality thanks to their hair
colour [. . .]

It has been said that no one can
increase his height. You certainly increase
your weight, building up atop your heads
certain buns and woven constructions [. . .]
Renounce all this slavery to ornaments of
your own free will. In vain you struggle to
appear ornate, in vain you go to the most
talented hairdressers: God commands you
to wear veils, I believe, so that the heads of
some of you cannot be seen.

Statue of an old market
lady,
first century AD,
New York, Metropolitan
Museum of Art

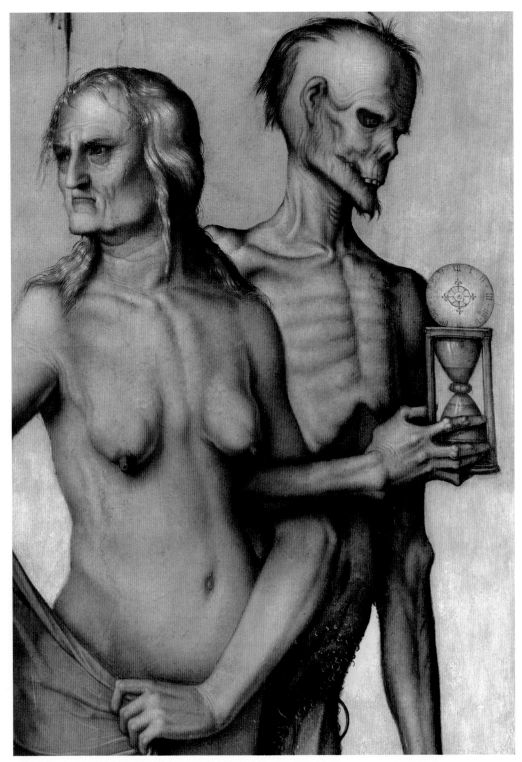

I Am the Siren Sweet
Dante (1265–1321)
Purgatory, XIX, 7–33
There came to me in dreams a stammering
woman,
Squint in her eyes, and in her feet distorted,
With hands disseevered and of sallow hue.
[. . .] 'I am,' she sang, 'I am the Siren sweet
Who mariners amid the main unman,
So full am I of pleasantness to hear.
I drew Ulysses from his wandering way
Unto my song, and he who dwells with me
Seldom departs so wholly I content him.'
Her mouth was not yet closed again, before
Appeared a Lady saintly and alert
Close at my side to put her to confusion. [. . .]
She seized the other and in front laid open,
Rending her garments, and her belly showed
me; This waked me with the stench that issued
from it.

Anti-Beatrice
Cecco Angiolieri (thirteenth-fourteenth century)
Rhymes 398
Hey, take a look, Ciampol! See how
Wizened that old lady is,
And how she looks when she straightens up,
How much her body stinks all over,
And how she resembles a Barbary ape
In face, shoulders and posture,
And how, when we look at her, she gets mad,
Grinding and gnashing her teeth.
Looking at her, you shouldn't feel so much
Ire, anguish, breathlessness, or love,

Hans Baldung Grien,
*Death and the
Age of Man*, detail,
1540,
Madrid, Prado Museum

Nor even great happiness,
But rather marvel that she doesn't make
You lose every amorous feeling in your heart.

Smelly Old Lady
Rustico di Filippo (thirteenth century)
'Everywhere you go, you take your bog along,'
You smelly, deceitful old lady,
So that anyone who comes near you
Has to hold his nose and run for it.
Your teeth and gums are full of tartar,
Because your stinking breath clogs them up;
Chamber pot seats seem like cypress wood
Compared to the terrific fragrance you give off.
When you open your horrendous snout,
It seems as if a thousand graves have opened
up:
Why don't you kick the bucket or get yourself
buried,
So that no one has to see or hear you again?
Because the whole world fears you, I think
you're like a fox
You give off such a tremendous stench, you
filthy beast.

Malignant Old Woman
Burchiello (fifteenth century)
'Malignant Old Woman'
Rotten, perfidious and malignant old woman
Enemy of all good, envious,
A spell-weaving, crafty old witch,
Nasty and contorted, you are nothing but
trouble.

In the Middle Ages, **Dante** (*Purgatory*, XIX, 7–9) saw the siren as a horrible, stammering woman, and this 'vituperation of the old woman' appears in many texts such as *The Art of the Versemaker* by Matthew of Vendome, in which we find a disgusting portrait of the old and depraved Beroes (bald, wrinkled face, rheumy eyes, with repellent breath and mucus dripping from her nose), and in *On the Secrets of Women* by Pseudo-Albertus Magnus, in which the author accepts the widespread belief that the gaze of an old woman (made lethal by the retention of menstrual blood) poisoned children in the cradle. On occasion, the *topos* of anti-female invective appears as a reaction to the *dolce stil novo* vision of the *donna angelicata*, or 'woman-angel', and so the ugly woman as described by **Rustico di Filippo** or by **Cecco Angioleri** becomes an anti-Beatrice.

At the dawn of the humanist movement, the acme of misogyny was reached in **Boccaccio**'s *Corbaccio*. The narrator loves, unrequited, a beautiful widow and his evident resentment is expressed by the soul of her husband, which ascends from purgatory to tell him about the licentiousness and the perfidy of this woman, revealing to this already ageing Lothario (of forty-two!) that she conceals her fifty years with creams and other revolting muck and dwelling at length upon the disgusting details of her physical ugliness.

The Nature of Women
Giovanni Boccaccio
Corbaccio (1363–66)

The female is an imperfect animal, stirred by thousands of passions both unpleasant and abominable even to think of, let alone to consider: if men looked upon women as they should, they would go to them solely for the pleasure that nature merits; otherwise, freed of all superfluous burdens, they would take care to steer clear of them [. . .] No other animal is less clean than she: not even pigs, wallowing in the mud, are as ugly as women; and, if someone might wish to refute this, let him examine her parts, let him search out the secret places where she, ashamed, hides the horrid instruments with which women remove their superfluous humours.

When she got out of the bed in the morning her face was, and I believe still is, the revolting greenish colour of the fumes given off by a stagnant pond, while her skin was as coarse as that of moulting birds, wrinkled, scabby, and flaccid all over. So entirely was she the opposite of how she looked as soon as she had time to beautify herself that no one – unless he had seen her as I have, a thousand times before – would believe his eyes. Who doesn't know that whitewash applied to smoky walls, just like women's faces, can take on the colour the painter desires? And who doesn't know that the more you mix dough (an unfeeling thing), the more it rises, just as a woman's living flesh, which once appeared lifeless, now seems full? She painted her skin so heavily, creating such a thick outer skin, that when the night arrived to reveal her true self to me, I, who had seen her before all this, could only wonder and marvel. And if you had seen her, as I did pretty much every morning, her hairnet pulled down over her ears, a scarf wound round her neck, her face as muddied as I described here above, squatting on her heels over the chamber pot, a quilted robe wrapped tight about her body, bluish bags under her eyes, coughing up gobs of catarrh, I have no doubts that not even the many virtues your friend has attributed to her would be enough to make you love her [. . .] You saw her tall and slim, and I believe I can safely say, just as I am sure of the blessings that await me, that, gazing upon her bosom, you were sure that what you saw was true; just as you believed that her face was real, not having seen those drooping jowls concealed by rouge and powder [. . .] In that bulge you saw above her belt, you must realise there was no pleasant padding, but rather the flesh of two deformed fruits, that were perhaps once firm plums pleasant both to touch and behold, as I believe she inherited directly from her mother's body [. . .] Those breasts, for whatever reason, whether from having been tugged upon too much by lovers, or having been crushed too often beneath another's weight, have become so elongated, that perhaps (better yet, without the perhaps), if she let them fall as they would, they would reach her navel, empty and wrinkled as a burst blister; and undoubtedly if that kind of breast were as fashionable in Florence as certain hats are in Paris, she, with elegance and grace, could have flung them over her shoulders in the French manner. What more can I tell you? Her belly is also flabby and sagging, unlike her cheeks, pulled taut by her make-up, and is deeply wrinkled like the skin of young goats. It looks like an empty sack, no different than the dewlap of a bull's throat; it is in her best interests to keep that loose skin held up high, just as she does with the rest of her body, when nature calls upon her to relieve herself or, if she so pleases, to pop a man's hot loaf in her oven.

Andres Serrano,
Budapest (The Model),
1994,
Courtesy of the Paula
Cooper Gallery

Fine Silver Hair

Joachim du Bellay (sixteenth century)
The Regrets
Fine silver hair gracefully twisted.
A serene, wrinkled brow, and gilded face,
Fair eyes of crystal, a large mouth
honoured
By the vast wrinkles that form its twisted
border
Beautiful ebony teeth, oh precious treasure
That with just one smile my soul torments
me
And you, ample tits, worthy of such a size,
You wrinkles in that sumptuous damask
throat!
O chubby hands with yellowing nails!
O fine, lean thigh, you fleshy calf,
And that for modesty, alas, I may not
mention!
Fair transparent body, you numbed limbs,
May you please forgive me, prodigious
miracle,
If, being mortal, I do not dare to love you.

Silvery Locks

Francesco Berni (sixteenth century)
'Sonnet for his Lady'
Fine silvery locks, fuzzy and twined with
no art
Round a beautiful golden face;
A wrinkled forehead, that I pale on
beholding,
Upon which the arrows of Love and Death
appear;
Eyes of grey pearl, snowy eyelashes,
And those large, stubby fingers,
That even I am sweetly attracted to;
Milk white lips, a large, divine mouth;
Wobbling teeth of rare ebony;
Of unheard of, ineffable harmony;
Proud and grave in her ways: to you,
Divine servants of love, I manifest
The beauties of my love.

When I was Beautiful

Pierre de Ronsard (sixteenth century)
Sonnets for Hélène
When you will be an old woman, of an
evening,
By candlelight, sitting by the fire,
unravelling and spinning,
You will say my poems anew, marvelling:
Ronsard sang my praises when I was
beautiful.
Then you will have no maid to listen to
you,
Overcome with tiredness and already half
asleep,
Who will not open her eyes at the sound
of my name

And praise yours for being so lucky.
I will be under the ground, a spirit among
naked spirits,
Resting beneath the shade of the myrtle
bushes.
You by the hearth a bent old woman
You will weep for my love and your
proud disdain,
Live, listen, wait not for tomorrow:
Pluck now the rose of life [. . .]

Disgusting Tit

Clément Marot
'Blazon of the Ugly Tit' (1535)
Tit that is nothing but skin,
Scrawny flag limply flapping
Big tit, long tit,
Squashed tit, tit like a bun
Tit with a pointy nipple
Like the sharp end of a funnel,
You jounce about at every move
Without any need for a shake ...
Tit, we might say that he who fondles you
Knows he has a finger in the pie.
Toasted tit, hanging tit
Wrinkled tit, tit that gives
Mud instead of milk,
The devil wants you in his
Infernal family, to nurse his daughter.
Tit to be thrown over one shoulder
Like those broad shawls of olden times
If you are spotted, lots of men feel like
Grasping you with gloves on
So as not to soil themselves, and to use
you,
Tit, to slap the big ugly nose of her
Who has you dangle below the armpit.

Señora Aldonza

Diego Hurtado de Mendoza
(sixteenth century)
'To an Old Woman who Thinks She's
Beautiful'
Señora Aldonza, you're three times thirty
years old,
You've no more than three hairs and a
single tooth,
And a cicada for a breast
Made of spider webs, at best.
In those clothes you're wearing you hide
All the wrinkles I can see on your
forehead;
Your mouth is as rickety as a bridge
And wide as two doors.
You sing like a frog or a woodcock,
Your paw is snot from a corpse,
And you look just like a barn owl
You stink like a fish set to soak,
With that twisted goat's back of yours,
You look like a plucked chicken to me.

Better Ugly than Beautiful
Ortensio Lando
Paradoxes II (1544)
Some people think that sometimes it's better to be ugly than to be beautiful [. . .] It seems to me that there can be no doubt that if Helen the Greek and Paris the Trojan had been ugly rather than beautiful, the Greeks would have had fewer troubles and the Trojans would not have suffered siege and successive destruction [. . .] We often see that ugly people are wiser and cleverer than beautiful people. Let's start with Socrates, who, we are told, and his sculpted portrait certainly shows, was terribly ugly, yet he was such a worthy person that even the oracle pronounced him the wisest of men. Aesop of Phrygia, a famed storyteller, was almost monstrous to look at; [. . .] but despite this (as everyone knows), he had virtues in abundance, and was of superior intelligence. Zeno the philosopher and Aristotle were both monstrously ugly, Empedocles likewise. Galba was terribly ugly too, but all of these most illustrious men struck people as intelligent and eloquent [. . .] And how many beautiful women in Italy today behave honestly? I am more than certain that in my country the nicest and most beautiful women are likewise reputed the most lascivious and dishonest. [. . .] I am extremely surprised by those women who complain that they are not beautiful, and fight bitterly against nature for this reason, trying so diligently and laboriously to make themselves more beautiful, no matter what the cost or effort. [. . .] Oh ugliness, therefore, you saintly friend of chastity, shield against scandal, and protector from dangers, you certainly know the easiest conversations; you remove all bitterness from pleasant talk, you crush evil suspicions, you are the only remedy for jealousy [. . .]

The Ugliness of Men
Lucretia Marinelli
The Nobility and Excellence of Women (1591)
Therefore, we can say that the beauty of women is a marvellous spectacle, as well as a notable miracle that men never appropriately honour or revere. But I want to go even further, and demonstrate that while men are obliged and forced to love women, women are not required to love them back, if not out of simple courtesy [. . .] Men are supposedly obliged to love beautiful things: but what is more beautiful in this world than women? Nothing, truly nothing, as all men rightly say when they describe the grace and the splendour of Paradise in the enchanting faces of women, due to which, they say, they are obliged to love them: but not for this are women obliged to love men: because the less handsome, or the ugly, are not by nature worthy of love. I say that all men are ugly compared with women; therefore they are unworthy of being loved in return by women, if not thanks to the natural courtesy of the female character. [. . .] So let men stop their arguing, complaining, sighing, and protesting because – in spite of the ways of the world – they want women to return their love and call them cruel, disagreeable, and heartless when they don't: all laughable accusations that fill the poetry books.

In Renaissance times the ugly woman looks more like an anti-Laura; in divertissements like those by **Berni**, Doni or Aretino – as in similar French texts (**Ronsard**, **du Bellay** or **Marot**) – there is a manifest anti-Petrarchism.

In these poems there is no longer any rancour: the view of deformity is either playfully ironic or affectionate. The fading looks of an old woman become a melancholy reflection on the waning of beauty. And during the Renaissance we witness the appearance of some reflections that once more call into question the condemnation of ugliness. Whereas **Ortensio Lando**, even before Rocco's eulogy of ugliness (mentioned in the previous chapter), reflects satirically on the advantages of female ugliness, **Lucrezia Marinelli**, in what we might now define as a pre-feminist spirit, turns the previous tradition on its head and extols the beauty of women in opposition to the ugliness of men.

2. Mannerism and the Baroque

While the Renaissance marked the success of a classical concept of art, based on the imitation of the harmonies of nature, the advent of Mannerism ushered in a change. Today we tend to fix the beginning of Mannerism with a conventional date, 1520, the year of Raphael's death. Whereas previously *manner* had been used to designate the style of a given author, and later a repetitive way of referring to the great models of the past, now Mannerism was defined as the phase in which the artist, afflicted by angst and 'melancholy', was no longer interested in beauty as imitation but in *expressiveness*. Theorists of Mannerism expounded the doctrine of the Genius and the *Idea*, conceived in the artist's mind, was the expression – endowed with creative power – of the divine aspects that inform it. Deformity was therefore justified as a rejection of uninspired imitation and of the *rules*, which do not determine genius but spring from it. Mannerists tended to render their vision subjectively and while Renaissance artists aimed at reconstructing a scene as if it were seen by a mathematically objective eye, Mannerists dissolved the structure of classical space in the crowded scenes devoid of a centre favoured by Bruegel, in the distorted and 'astigmatic' figures of El Greco, and in the restless and unrealistically stylised faces of Parmigianino. We have a choice of the *expressive* as opposed to the *beautiful*, a tendency to the bizarre, the extravagant and the deformed, as in Arcimboldo's fantastic figures.

The Baroque period witnessed a growing taste for the extraordinary, for those things that arouse wonder and, in this cultural climate, artists explored the worlds of violence, death and horror, as happened with the works of Shakespeare and of the Elizabethans in general, or in Quevedo's *Dreams*, all the way down to morbid reflections of the corpse of one's beloved, as in **Gryphius**. In this way, Mannerism and the Baroque had no fear of using elements that classical aesthetics found irregular. Hence even the theme of the ugly woman was seen from a different point of view: a woman's imperfections were described as elements of interest, sometimes as sensual stimuli – and we shall see how this attitude was revisited both in Romanticism and in Decadentism by authors – just to give one example – such as Baudelaire.

Giuseppe Arcimboldo,
Winter,
1563, Vienna,
Kunsthistorisches
Museum

IThe Attraction of the Lame
Michel de Montaigne
Essays, III, 11 (1595)
A common Italian proverb says that no
man knows Venus in all her most perfect
sweetness if he hasn't gone to bed with a
lame woman [. . .] I would have thought
it was the disjointed movement of a lame
woman that gave some new pleasure to
the event, and some touch of sweetness
to those who try it out, but I recently
learned that even ancient philosophy
established as much: it says that since the
legs and thighs of a lame woman do not
receive the nourishment they are
supposed to, the genitalia, which lie just
above, are fuller, more nourished and
more vigorous. Or perhaps it is that,
given that this defect hinders the act,
those afflicted with lameness squander
less strength and reach the games of
Venus more integral and whole [. . .]
Given the sole authority established by
the ancient and public use of this
proverb, once I even came to believe that
I had enjoyed more pleasure with a
woman because she was lame, and I
counted this among her graces.

Pallor of a Beautiful Woman
Giovan Battista Marino
The Lyre, 14 (1604)
O wan little sun of mine,
The bright red dawn loses
Its colours before your sweet pallor.
O dear pallid death of mine,
Vanquished, the rose loses
Its red, amorous colour before your
Sweet and pallid violets.
Oh, let it please destiny
That I might become as pallid as you,
My sweet wan love!

The Handsome Old Lady
Giuseppe Salomoni
Rhymes, 4 (1615)
Already a liar and a fool,
I criticised, sweet and gentle old lady,
Your breasts, your hair, and your fair face.
Now, having changed my mind, I'll
change my tune as well
And for each of my lies, have you listen
to
A poem of retraction [. . .]
Your hair is silver, but even so
It is more attractive to me than gold
Be it braided, or hanging free [. . .]
Your serene brow,
Once beautiful, smooth as a welcoming
beach

Strewn with white flowers, is furrowed,
yes,
By the chill plough of old age, but those
same furrows,
Give other hearts
A blend of pleasure and pain
Like the sweet smell of harvest and the
spiked ear of grain.
Your curved eyelashes,
And your arched eyebrows
Have kindled great love,
But now seem (Oh wonder!)
Useless weapons, frail instruments;
Yet more powerful than ever
They march forth with their reapers and
archers,
To harvest souls and pierce hearts.
Your enrapturing gaze
Is fading, but though fading
It still sends forth looks that steal the
heart,
And so I continue to burn with love for
you [. . .]
Your rosy lips,
A treasure trove of kisses
And source of sweet talk,
Have no fear of age's rapacious claw
[. . .]
Your white breast,
The happy, pleasurable and well-kept
garden
Of wanton apples,
Sweet and beautiful and lively to behold,
You dare uncover, even though these
fruits of yours are no longer young [. . .]
Your hand, beautiful and white,
Is touched by age,
And seems weary from long use;
But in its languishing, it languishes not,
and has not lost
The fame of beauty it once held, indeed
its beauty grows [. . .]
Wrinkled is your throat, wrinkled are your
cheeks,
And wrinkled your breasts,
But they are, thanks to love, wrinkled
trophies of beauty,
And no blemish [. . .]
Yes, yes, my pretty old lady,
You are old but lovely,
And in your beauty, youth is mirrored
once again [. . .]
By your side, this cupid grows old,
Yet continues to love and desire you,
Even the sun grows old and fades
alongside you.
Song, time is flying
But fear not its shafts,
For even as you grow old,
You become ever more beautiful.

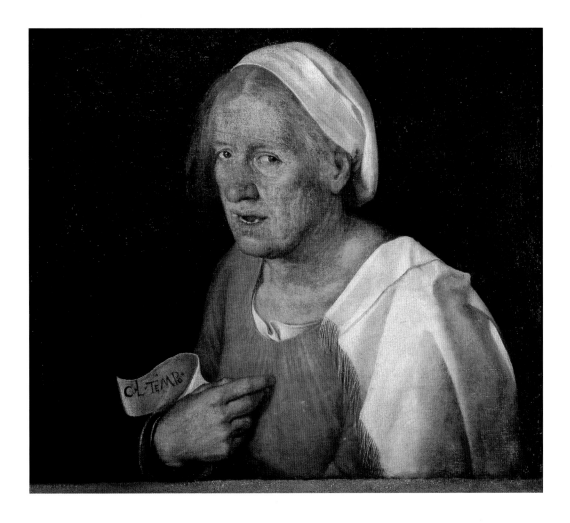

Giorgione,
The Old Woman,
1506–07,
Venice,
Galleria dell'Accademia

following pages
Quentin Metsys (attrib.),
Grotesque Woman,
1525–30,
London,
National Gallery

Between the sixteenth and seventeenth centuries we find two significant texts: **Montaigne** wrote an affectionate eulogy to lame women and **Shakespeare** apparently belittled his Dark Lady through a series of negations of the traditional characteristics of beauty, but ends with a 'yet': despite everything, he loves his muse. But the Baroque poets went further: poems appeared in praise of women who stammered, or were dwarfs, hunchbacks, cross-eyed, pockmarked, and, in contrast to the medieval tradition of highly coloured or rosy cheeks, **Marino** extolled the pallor of his beloved. Whereas previous canons of female beauty required blonde hair, now women with black hair were eulogised. In his *Rhymes*, Tasso wrote: 'You are dark, but beautiful', and Marino praised the beauty of a black slave girl. There is a touching tribute to the *beautiful old woman* in **Salomoni** and, while **Quevedo**'s text still seems traditionally rancorous, this is not the case with **Burton**, where the exuberant description of a horrendous woman reiterates the notion that love can go beyond the opposition between beautiful and ugly.

171

A Hallucination

Francisco de Quevedo

Fin del mundo por de dentro (1612)

Do you see this hallucination? Laida went to bed and this morning she put on her make-up by herself. Now she is acting a bit odd. You should know that women, as soon as they wake up, first put on their faces, their decolleté and their two hands, and then their clothes. Everything you see in her is shop bought and is not the work of nature. You see her hair? Well she bought that too, it didn't grow by itself. Her eyelashes are more sooty than black, and if noses were made like eyelashes she wouldn't have one at all. Those teeth you can see, and her mouth, are black as an inkwell thanks to the concoctions she uses. Her ear wax has been shifted from her ears to her lips, which are now two little candles. And what about her hands? What looks white is really grease. What a sight it is to see a woman, who the next day must go out to be admired, sousing herself in brine the night before, and going to sleep with her face covered in cream, only to paint her living flesh the next day at her pleasure! What a sight is an ugly woman or a dirty old lady who like the famous necromancer [Enrique de Villena] want to be resuscitated in a phial! Do you see them? Well, it's not their stuff. If they washed their faces you wouldn't recognise them. Believe me, in the world there is nothing as well tanned as the hide of a beautiful woman, when their make-up dries, more plaster breaks off than the number of skirts they wear. They mistrust their bodies and when they wish to stimulate someone's nose they immediately fall back on essences, fumigations, and perfumes and even the sweat of their feet is concealed by amber slippers. I assure you that our senses are left devoid of what a woman is, and sated with what she appears to be. If you kiss her your lips are bedaubed; if you embrace her you hug slats and crush cardboard; if you sleep with her you leave half of her under the bed in the form of high heels; if you court her you end up exhausted; if you win her you get bored, and if you keep her you face bankruptcy; if you leave her she persecutes you; if you love her she leaves you. Show me what you find good in her, and consider this superb creature of our weakness, made powerful by our needs, who would be of more use to us whipped and mortified rather than

satisfied, and you will clearly see your folly. Think of when she has her menses and she will disgust you; and when she doesn't have them remember that she has had them before and will have them again, and she who enchants you will horrify you. And be ashamed for being bewitched by things that in any old wooden statue would have a less disgusting essence.

Loving an Ugly Woman

Robert Burton

The Anatomy of Melancholy (1621)

Love is blind, as they say, Cupid's blind, and so are all his followers. *Quisquis amat ranam, ranam putat esse Dianam* [whoso loves a frog, thinks that frog a Dian]. Every lover admires his mistress, though she be very deformed of herself, ill-favoured, wrinkled, pimpled, pale, red, yellow, tanned, tallow-faced, have a swollen juggler's platter face, or a thin, lean, chitty face, have clouds in her face, be crooked, dry, bald, goggle-eyed, blear-eyed, or with staring eyes, she looks like a squis'd cat, hold her head still awry, heavy, dull, hollow-eyed, black or yellow about the eyes, or squint-eyed, sparrow-mouthed, Persian hook-nosed, have a sharp fox-nose, a red nose, China flat, great nose, *nare simo patuloque* [snub and flat nose], a nose like a promontory, gubber-tushed, rotten teeth, black, uneven brown teeth, beetle-browed, a witch's beard, her breath stink all over the room, her nose drop winter and summer, with a Bavarian poke under her chin, a sharp chin, lave-eared, with a long crane's neck, which stands awry too, *pendulis mammis,* 'her dugs like two double jugs', or else no dugs, in that other extreme ... a vast virago, or an ugly tit, a slug, a fat fustilugs, a truss, a long lean rawbone, a skeleton, a sneaker [. . .], and to thy judgment looks like a mard in a lanthorn, whom thou couldst not fancy for a world, but hatest, loathest and wouldest have spit in her face, or blow thy nose in her bosom, *remedium amoris* [a cure for love] to another man, a dowdy, a slut, a scold, a nasty, rank, rammy, filthy, beastly quean, dishonest peradventure, obscene, base, beggarly, rude, foolish, untaught, peevish [. . .], if he love her once, he admires her for all this, he takes no notice of any such errors or imperfections of body or mind, he had rather have her than any woman in the world.

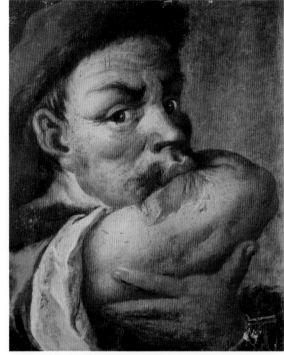

Caliban
William Shakespeare
The Tempest, I, 2 (1623)

PROSPERO: Thou poisonous slave, got by the devil himself
Upon thy wicked dam, come forth!
(*Enter CALIBAN*)
CALIBAN: As wicked dew as e'er my mother brush'd
With raven's feather from unwholesome fen
Drop on you both! A south-west blow on ye
And blister you all o'er!
PROSPERO: For this, be sure, to-night thou shalt have cramps,
Side-stitches that shall pen thy breath up; urchins
Shall forth at vast of night that they may work,
All exercise on thee; thou shalt be pinch'd
As thick as honeycomb, each pinch more stinging
Than bees that made 'em.
CALIBAN: I must eat my dinner.
This island's mine, by Sycorax my mother,
Which thou tak'st from me. When thou cam'st first,
Thou strok'st me and made much of me, wouldst give me
Water with berries in't, and teach me how
To name the bigger light, and how the less,
That burn by day and night; and then I lov'd thee,
And show'd thee all the qualities o' th' isle,
The fresh springs, brine-pits, barren place and fertile.
Curs'd be I that did so! All the charms
Of Sycorax, toads, beetles, bats, light on you!
For I am all the subjects that you have,
Which first was mine own king; and here you sty me
In this hard rock, whiles you do keep from me
The rest o' th' island.
PROSPERO: Thou most lying slave,
Whom stripes may move, not kindness! I have us'd thee,
Filth as thou art, with human care, and lodg'd thee
In mine own cell, till thou didst seek to violate
The honour of my child.
CALIBAN: O ho, O ho! Would't had been done.
Thou didst prevent me; I had peopl'd else
This isle with Calibans.
MIRANDA: Abhorred slave,
Which any print of goodness wilt not take,
Being capable of all ill! I pitied thee,
Took pains to make thee speak, taught thee each hour ·
One thing or other. When thou didst not, savage,
Know thine own meaning, but wouldst gabble like
A thing most brutish, I endow'd thy purposes
With words that made them known.
But thy vile race,
Though thou didst learn, had that in't which good natures
Could not abide to be with; therefore wast thou
Deservedly confin'd into this rock, who hadst
Deserv'd more than a prison.
CALIBAN: You taught me language, and my profit on't
Is, I know how to curse. The red plague rid you
For learning me your language!

on the previous pages
Lucas Cranach,
The Fountain of Youth,
1546,
Berlin,
Gemäldegalerie

facing page
Georges de La Tour,
The Hurdy-Gurdy Player,
1628–30,
Nantes, Musée des
Beaux Arts

Bartolomeo Passerotti,
Man Eating His Arm,
sixteenth century,
Milan, private collection

Old Michelangelo

Michelangelo
Rhymes (1623)
I keep a hornet in a little jar,
Bones and some rope in a leather bag,
Three pills of pitch in a little bottle.
Lilac-coloured eyes now milky and
shadowed,
My teeth like the keys of an instrument
Whose movement gives me voice or
silence.
My face has a fearful look.
My clothes are so threadbare and ragged,
That I could scare the crows from a field.
I'm hard of hearing in one ear,
And in the other a cricket chirrups all
night long;
When I sleep the catarrh makes breathing
difficult [. . .]
What's the point in my making all those
puppets,
If in the end, I've wound up like
That fellow who managed to cross the sea
Only to drown in his own snot?
My great art, for which I became so
famous,
Has led me to be, in the end, a poor old
man
At the mercy of others,
So much so that if I don't die soon,
I'll just fall to pieces.

To Himself

Andreas Gryphius (seventeenth century)
'Night, Luminous Night' I, 48
I have a horror of myself: my limbs
tremble
When I observe through lashes spent by
now
My lips and nose and the caverns of my
eyes
Blinded by wakefulness and my laboured
breathing

My tongue, black with thirst, stumbles
over words
And mutters something; my weary soul
calls
The great consoler, my flesh smacks of
the grave,
The doctors leave, the pains return,
My body is nothing but veins, skin and
bone.
Sitting is a sufferance, lying down a
torment.
My very thighs need crutches.
What price fame, honours, youth, and art?
When this hour comes all is smoke and
fog.
It is an agony bent on killing us.

Richard III

William Shakespeare
Richard III, I, 1 (1597)
But I, that am not shaped for sportive
tricks,
Nor made to court an amorous looking-
glass;
I, that am rudely stamp'd, and want love's
majesty
To strut before a wanton ambling nymph;
I, that am curtail'd of this fair proportion,
Cheated of feature by dissembling nature,
Deformed, unfinish'd, sent before my time
Into this breathing world, scarce half
made up,
And that so lamely and unfashionable
That dogs bark at me as I halt by them;
Why, I, in this weak piping time of peace,
Have no delight to pass away the time,
Unless to spy my shadow in the sun
And descant on mine own deformity:
And therefore, since I cannot prove a
lover,
To entertain these fair well-spoken days,
I am determined to prove a villain
And hate the idle pleasures of these days.

But right from the start of the Mannerist period there was a steady increase in melancholy reflections on ageing in men, and a sorrowful compassion runs though the verses in which **Michelangelo** or **Gryphius** portray the ugliness of their old age. The same period also marked a compassionate consideration of the ugliness that produces suffering and at the same time wickedness – another theme later picked up by the Romantic movement. Note the bitter sympathy with which **Shakespeare** shows us the sufferings of Caliban or Richard III, suggesting that what made them wicked was the rancorous way in which others looked upon their ugliness. The same understanding for human blemishes also appears in the works of many painters, where ill-favoured faces were depicted not to mock the unfortunate or to represent evil, but to show disease or the mortal work of time.

Chapter VII

The Devil
in the Modern World

1. From Rebellious Satan to Poor Mephistopheles

The Christian tradition had tried to forget that, if Satan had been an angel, then presumably he must have been most beautiful. Around the seventeenth century, however, Satan began to undergo a transformation. In *Hamlet*, **Shakespeare** showed that the Devil can also present himself in beautiful forms, and **Marino,** in *The Slaughter of the Innocents* (1632), presents Satan as a being weighed down by a gloomy despondency – thus to a certain extent arousing our compassion. Compare the Lucifer depicted by **Dante** (fourteenth century) with the Pluto of *Jerusalem Delivered* by **Tasso** (sixteenth century). Both are horrible; yet Tasso did not deny his Pluto a 'horrid majesty'.

The text that marks the definitive redemption of Satan is Milton's *Paradise Lost* (1667). Some have talked of political reasons (Milton had taken part in the Puritan revolution later defeated by the Restoration) and so the poet saw Satan as a model of rebellion against established power. But – even without granting, as Blake does (*The Marriage of Heaven and Hell*, 1790–93), that Milton was 'on the devil's side without knowing it', the Miltonian Satan prevalently possessed the traits of degenerated beauty and indomitable pride. He is no revolutionary, because he lacks an ideal goal beyond the desire for revenge and the affirmation of his own ego, but he is certainly a model of pure, rebellious energy, so much so that Schiller (in his critique of his own play *The Robbers*) wrote that the reader would side with the vanquished, and Shelley, in his *Defence of Poetry*, said that Milton's Devil was superior to the God he fought against. Satan will not repent out of a sense of honour, he will not subject himself to his conqueror, and refuses to ask for mercy: 'Better to reign in Hell than serve in Heaven.'

Heinrich Füssli,
*Satan Emerging
from Chaos*, from
Milton's *Paradise Lost*, III,
1010 ff., 1794–96,
Zurich,
private collection

William Blake,
Satan Smiting Job with Sore Boils, illustration from the *Book of Job*,
RA 2001.68,
1826,
New York, Pierpoint Morgan Library

facing page
Joseph Anton Koch,
The Inferno,
1825–29,
Rome, the Dante Room, Casino Massimo

Lucifer in Dante

Dante (1265–1321)
Inferno, XXXIV, 28–57
The Emperor of the kingdom dolorous
From his mid-breast forth issued from the ice,
And better with a giant I compare
Than do the giants with those arms of his;
[. . .]
O, what a marvel it appeared to me,
When I beheld three faces on his head!
The one in front, and that vermilion was;
Two were the others, that were joined with this
Above the middle part of either shoulder,
And they were joined together at the crest;
And the right-hand one seemed 'twixt white and yellow
The left was such to look upon as those
Who come from where the Nile falls valley-ward.
Underneath each came forth two mighty wings,
Such as befitting were so great a bird;
Sails of the sea I never saw so large.

Tasso's Pluto

Torquato Tasso

Jerusalem Delivered, IV, 7 (1581)
The tyrant proud frowned from his lofty cell,
And with his looks made all his monsters tremble,
His eyes, that full of rage and venom swell,
Two beacons seem, that men to arms assemble,
His feltered locks, that on his bosom fell,
On rugged mountains briars and thorns resemble,
His yawning mouth, that foamed clotted blood,
Gaped like a whirlpool wide in Stygian flood.

Satan in Marino

Giovan Battista Marino
The Slaughter of the Innocents (1632)
In his eyes, where evil dwells and death,
A murky crimson light blazes.
His sidelong gaze and twisted pupils
Seem comets, and lanterns his brows.
And from his nostrils and bloodless lips
He vomits soot and stench;
Irate, Proud, and Desperate,
Thunderclaps are his sighs,
And lightning bolts his breath.

The Appeal of the Rebel

John Milton

Paradise Lost, I, 62–151 (1674)

Nine times the space that measures
day and night
To mortal men, he, with his horrid
crew,
Lay vanquished, rolling in the fiery
gulf,
Confounded, though immortal. But his
doom
Reserved him to more wrath; for now
the thought
Both of lost happiness and lasting pain
Torments him: round he throws his
baleful eyes,
That witnessed huge affliction and
dismay,
Mixed with obdurate pride and
steadfast hate.
At once, as far as Angels ken, he views
The dismal situation waste and wild.
A dungeon horrible, on all sides
round,
As one great furnace flamed; yet from
those flames
No light; but rather darkness visible
Served only to discover sights of woe,
Regions of sorrow, doleful shades,
where peace
And rest can never dwell, hope never
comes
That comes to all, but torture without
end
Still urges, and a fiery deluge, fed
With ever-burning sulphur
unconsumed.
Such place Eternal Justice has prepared
For those rebellious; [. . .] into what
pit thou seest
From what height fallen: so much the
stronger proved
He with his thunder; and till then who
knew
The force of those dire arms? Yet not
for those,
Nor what the potent Victor in his rage
Can else inflict, do I repent, or change,
Though changed in outward lustre,
that fixed mind,
And high disdain from sense of injured
merit,
That with the Mightiest raised me to
contend,
And to the fierce contentions brought
along
Innumerable force of Spirits armed,
That durst dislike his reign, and, me
preferring,
His utmost power with adverse power
opposed
In dubious battle on the plains of
Heaven,
And shook his throne. What though
the field be lost?
All is not lost – the unconquerable
will,
And study of revenge, immortal hate,
And courage never to submit or
yield:
And what is else not to be overcome.
That glory never shall his wrath or
might
Extort from me. To bow and sue for
grace
With suppliant knee, and deify his
power,
Who, from the terror of this arm, so
late
Doubted his Empire – that were low
indeed;
That were an ignominy and shame
beneath
This downfall.

Lewis Morrison,
Faust, theatre poster,
1896

Gérard Philipe in *La beauté du diable* (*Beauty and the Beast*),
René Clair (director),
1950

A Poor Devil
Johann Wolfgang von Goethe
Faust, I (1773–74)
Mephistopheles – I am a portion of that Energy,
That still devising ill, still causes good to be.
[. . .] I am the spirit that still denies;
And rightly so: for whatsoe'er is wrought
Is only fit to come to naught:
And it were best, if there were no creation;
Thus all that you call sin, annihilation,
Evil, in short, is solely my vocation.
[. . .]
'Tis but the modest truth I speak to you:
Although to foolish man's conceit
His world is perfect and complete.
I am a part o' the part, that once was everything;
Part of the darkness, whence the light did spring,
That haughty power, that now from Mother Night
Would wrest the realm of space, her ancient right:
Yet howsoe'er it strives, 'tis all in vain,
In matter prisoned it must still remain [. . .].
Faust – Your noble rôle is plain to me at length:
Since all that's great defies your strength,
You try your hand on what is small.
Mephistopheles – And I confess I've had no luck at all!
This universe, this gross Creation,
Which fights against annihilation,
Has always managed to evade
The utmost efforts I have made;
I've worked with earthquake, inundation, storm,
Yet land and ocean still retain their form;
While as for man and beast – accursed breeds –
They've proved the toughest job of any;
Already I have buried – ah! How many!
Yet still a new and lusty race succeeds:
So on things go; it drives one to despair!
From earth, from water and from air
A myriad germs are ever working free,
In moisture and in drought, in warmth and cold;
And if on fire I had not kept my hold,
There would be nothing left for me!

While in Marlowe's *Dr Faustus* (1604) Mephistopheles is still ugly, and while, in the eighteenth century, he is portrayed in the form of a camel in *The Devil in Love* by **Cazotte**, in **Goethe**'s *Faust* he makes his appearance as a well-dressed gentleman. True, he does present himself to Faust in the guise of a black dog before transforming himself into a hippopotamus with blazing eyes and horrid tusks, but finally he appears dressed as a wandering scholar and a respectable intellectual.

He is diabolical only in the sense that he is dialectically persuasive and convincing and plays 'cat and mouse' with Faust. On the other hand he doesn't have to try too hard to seduce Faust, who was already prepared to traffic with spirits, almost as if it were he who wanted to meet the Devil and not vice versa.

Hence Mephistopheles heralds a third metamorphosis of the Devil. In the twentieth century the evil one becomes absolutely 'secular' (see the texts by **Dostoevsky**, **Papini** and **Mann**); neither terrifying nor glamorous, infernal in his drabness and in his apparent petit bourgeois nastiness, he becomes more dangerous and worrying because he is no longer innocently ugly as he was once portrayed.

Cazotte's Devil

Jacques Cazotte
The Devil in Love (1772)
I spoke the invocation in a clear, strong voice, then, reinforcing the sound, I repeated three times quickly: Beelzebub.

A chill ran through my veins, and the hair stood up on my head. I had just finished when on the vaulted ceiling right in front of me a double window opened up: from that opening a torrent of light brighter than day poured forth: a camel's head, horrible in size, came to the window: its ears were the largest thing about it.

The odious ghost opened its jaws, and in a tone in keeping with the rest of the apparition, said to me:
'What do you want?' [. . .]

The first idea that came to mind was a dog – Come – I said – in the form of a spaniel. – As soon as I'd given that order, the frightful camel extended its neck sixteen feet, lowered its head to the centre of the room, and vomited a spaniel that had glossy fur and ears that reached down to the floor.

The Devil in Dostoevsky

Fyodor Dostoevsky
The Brothers Karamazov (1879–80)
He was a gentleman, or to put it better, a sort of Russian gentleman, no longer young, *qui frisait la cinquantaine*, as the French say, with a touch of grey in his dark hair, still fairly long and thick, and in his goatee.

Papini's Devil

Giovanni Papini
'The Devil Told Me' (1906)
He is very tall and very pale: he is still young, but his is the kind of youth that has lived through too much and is sadder than old age. His extremely white, elongated face has no particular features apart from a thin mouth, closed and clenched tight, and a single, very deep wrinkle running perpendicular up from in between his eyebrows, and ending almost at the roots of his hair. [. . .] He always wears black and his hands are always impeccably gloved.

Mann's Devil

Thomas Mann
Doctor Faustus (1947)
He is a rather scrawny man, not very tall and even shorter than I am, wearing a casual beret pulled down over one ear, while on the other side reddish hair sprouts at his temple. He has reddish eyelashes, flushed eyes, and an ashen face, and the tip of his nose curves downwards a little. Over a stitched shirt with diagonal stripes he wears a check jacket, with sleeves that are too short, from which stubby-fingered hands emerge. His trousers are too tight and his shoes so beaten up that they can no longer be cleaned. A pimp, a parasite, with the voice of a theatre actor.

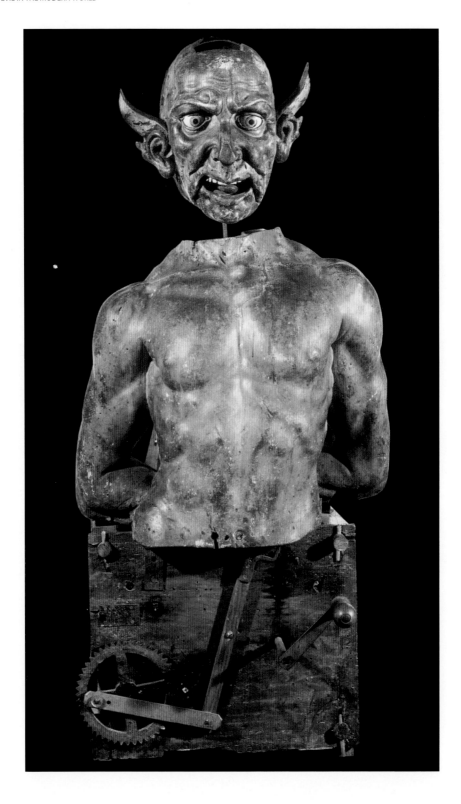

2. The Demonisation of the Enemy

As Satan's features were gradually neutralised, there was a growing tendency to demonise the enemy, who was assigned satanic characteristics. And although it was the modern world that came to pay particular attention to this enemy (who took the place of Satan), the enemy had always existed.

Since ancient times, the enemy was always the Other, the foreigner. His features did not appear to correspond to our criteria of beauty and if he had different dietary habits then people were struck by his smell. Without going too far back in time, we should remember that Westerners find it unacceptable that the Chinese eat dogs and the English feel the same about the French eating frogs. Not to mention the incomprehensible sounds of a foreign tongue. The Greeks defined as *barbarians* (literally, stutterers) all those who did not speak Greek, and in Roman sculpture the barbarians defeated by the legions have shaggy beards and pug noses.

The first enemy Christianity found itself up against was the vicar of Satan, the Antichrist, and all known texts on the **face of the Antichrist** (inspired, moreover, by biblical sources such as **Daniel**), from the early centuries to the *Letter on the Origin and Time of the Antichrist* by **Adso of Montier-en-Der** and to **Hildegard of Bingen**, insist on his obscene ugliness (occasionally justified by his coming from Jewish stock).

The second enemy, right from the start, was the heretic, and one of the weapons used by Western and Eastern Christianity against heretics was the description of their diabolical customs. Consider a Byzantine text like *On the Activity of Demons* by **Michael Psellos** (eleventh century), copied ad infinitum over the years by every kind of heretical sect, and regarding ritual infanticide, often used as an accusation against the Jews.

The Schismatics were also enemies. In a report by **Liutprand of Cremona** (tenth century) on the Byzantine court (which we remember for its sumptuousness) we find a horrified description of local dress, foods and that resinated wine that many people today consider a delicacy.

Obviously, the **Saracens** were always seen as horrendous.

Finally, another constant was the horror of lepers and **plague victims** because, as they were incurable and tainted, such unfortunates were seen as adversaries of society.

Manfredo Settala,
The Slave in Chains
(automa of the devil),
seventeenth century,
Milan, Civiche Raccolta
di Arte Applicata,
Sforza Castle

following page
Luca Signorelli,
*The Preaching of the
Antichrist,*
detail of fresco,
1499–1504,
Orvieto, Madonna
di San Brizio Chapel,
Orvieto Cathedral

185

The Prophecy of Daniel
Daniel 7:2–8, 15–18, 23
Daniel spake and said, I saw in my vision by night, and, behold, the four winds of the heaven strove upon the great sea. And four great beasts came up from the sea, diverse one from another. The first was like a lion, and had eagle's wings: I beheld till the wings thereof were plucked, and it was lifted up from the earth, and made stand upon the feet as a man, and a man's heart was given to it. And behold another beast, a second, like to a bear, and it raised up itself on one side, and it had three ribs in the mouth of it between the teeth of it: and they said thus unto it, Arise, devour much flesh. After this I beheld, and lo another, like a leopard, which had upon the back of it four wings of a fowl; the beast had also four heads; and dominion was given to it. After this I saw in the night visions, and behold a fourth beast, dreadful and terrible, and strong exceedingly; and it had great iron teeth: it devoured and brake in pieces, and stamped the residue with the feet of it: and it was diverse from all the beasts that were before it; and it had ten horns. I considered the horns, and, behold, there came up among them another little horn, before whom there were three of the first horns plucked up by the roots: and, behold, in this horn were eyes like the eyes of man, and a mouth speaking great things [. . .] I Daniel was grieved in my spirit in the midst of my body, and the visions of my head troubled me. I came near unto one of them that stood by, and asked him the truth of all this. So he told me, and made me know the interpretation of the things. These great beasts, which are four, are four kings, which shall arise out of the earth. But the saints of the most High shall take the kingdom, and possess the kingdom for ever, even for ever and ever [. . .] The fourth beast shall be the fourth kingdom upon earth, which shall be diverse from all kingdoms, and shall devour the whole earth, and shall tread it down, and break it in pieces.

The Birth of the Antichrist
Adso de Montier-en-Der (tenth century)
On the Birth and Times of the Antichrist
The Antichrist will be born of the Jewish people [. . .], from the union between a father and a mother like all men and not, as some maintain, from a virgin alone. In this manner, he will be entirely conceived in sin, generated in sin, and born in sin. At the beginning of his conception the devil will enter the maternal uterus, he will be nourished in the mother's womb through diabolic means, and the power of the devil will always be with him. And just as the Holy Ghost came down and filled the body of the mother of our Lord Jesus Christ with his virtue, in such a way that he was born of the Holy Spirit and born holy and divine; in the same manner the devil will enter into the mother of the Antichrist, filling her up completely, surrounding her, making her his, possessing her outside and inside in such a manner that she, thanks to diabolic cooperation, will conceive as humans do, and he who is born will be entirely iniquitous, wicked, and lost. For this reason he will be called the son of perdition [. . .] He will have sorcerers, witches, soothsayers and enchanters who, through diabolic inspiration, will teach him every iniquity, falsehood, and evil art.

On the Antichrist's Face
Syriac Testament of Our Lord Jesus Christ, I, 4 (fifth century)
This is what he looks like: his head is like a burning flame, his right eye is bloodshot, his left is green as a cat's and has two pupils, his eyelids are white, his lower lip is large, his right femur is weak, he has big feet, and his thumb is flattened and elongated.

The Apocalypse of Elias, 3:15–17 (third century)
He is delicate, with thin legs, tall, a tuft of grey hair on his bald forehead, his eyebrows stretch all the way to his ears, he has signs of leprosy on the backs of his hands. He transforms himself before those who see him: sometimes he appears young, other times old.

The Apocalypse of St John the Divine (fifth century)
He has a glowering look, his hair is like arrowheads, he frowns, his right eye is like the morning star, and his left like that of a lion. His mouth is one cubit wide, his teeth are a span in length, and his fingers are like sickles. His footprints are two cubits long and he has 'Antichrist' written across his forehead.

Manuscript from the Monastery of Mont Saint-Michel (tenth century)
The disciples said to Jesus: 'Lord, tell us what he will be like.' And Jesus said to them: 'He will stand nine cubits tall. He will have black hair tied back with an iron chain. He will have an eye as bright as dawn on his forehead. His lower lip will be large and he will have no upper lip. The little finger of his hand will be the longest, and his left foot broader than his right.

Hildegard of Bingen
Liber Scivias III, 1, 14 (twelfth century)
The son of perdition, in his folly, will come with all the craftiness of the first seduction, and monstrous turpitudes, and black iniquities: he will have two fiery eyes, an ass's ears, the nose and mouth of a lion, and send out among men acts of folly of the most criminal kind from amid the fires and the most shamefully contradictory voices, making them renounce God, spreading the most horrible stenches among them, attacking the institutions of the Church with the cruellest rapacity; grinding his horrible iron teeth together in an enormous rictus.

Anonymous
Cursor Mundi, 22.391–22.398 (fourteenth century)
The splendour will be such at the advent of Christ that when faced with the Lord's powerful light the Antichrist will get such a terrible fright that all the filth of his guts will come pouring out his arse from fear of Christ, ashamed and full of terror and pain, thus he shall die shit-stained.

The Ugliness of the Byzantines
Liutprand of Cremona (tenth century)
Embassy Report from Constantinople
On 4 June [968], we reached
Constantinople and, after having been
received dishonourably to cause You insult,
we were further abused most shamefully
[. . .] Greek wine, mixed with pitch, resin
and chalk, is undrinkable [. . .] On 7 June,
on the Pentecostal holy day, I found
myself before Nikephoros, a monstrous
being, a pygmy with an enormous head,
who seemed like a mole because of his
tiny eyes. He was made even uglier thanks
to a long, thick and grizzled beard, had a
neck as long as a finger, and thick, bristly
hair, an Ethiopian in colour, 'whom you
wouldn't want to run into in the middle of
the night,' with an obese stomach, tiny
buttocks, with thighs too long for his small
stature, short legs, flat feet, a threadbare
outfit that had been worn so often it had
become ill-smelling and discoloured, shod
in Sicyonian shoes, possessing an
impertinent tongue, with the crafty
character of a fox, a true Ulysses for
perjury and lies [. . .]

A copious multitude of merchants and
low-born people gathered together in that
solemn space to welcome and praise
Nikephoros, amassing along the road from
the palace all the way to the Church of
Saint Sophia, practically creating a wall;
poorly equipped with small shields that
were too light and worthless lances. And
added to this ugly spectacle was the fact
that most of the populace, clamouring for
him, came forward barefooted [. . .] But
even his dignitaries, who paraded with him
in the middle of that shoeless mob, were
wearing clothes that were too big and full
of holes from overuse [. . .] During that
vile and disgusting dinner, fit only for
drunkards, oily and seasoned with a
certain horrible fish liquor, he asked me
various questions concerning Your
Highness, specifically about reigns and
soldiers. And while I answered each
sincerely, he said: 'You're lying: your king's
soldiers don't know how to ride horses
and they don't know a thing about fighting
on foot; the large size of their shields, the
weight of their armour, the length of their
swords and the weight of their helmets
makes it impossible for them to fight [. . .]
Your lord doesn't even have much of a sea
fleet. I alone possess the scourge of
maritime forces, and I'll attack him with my
ships, destroy his coastal cities and reduce
to ashes those along his rivers.'

Mathias Grünewald,
*The Temptations of
Saint Anthony*, detail
from the altar at
Isenheim,
1515,
Colmar, Musée
Unterlinden

facing page
Sarcophagus of the
Emperor Hostilian
decorated with scenes
of battles between the
Romans and the
barbarians,
AD 251,
Rome, Museo Nazionale
Romano

The Plague Victim
Tommaso Fasano
'On the Epidemic Fever That Afflicted
Naples in the Year 1764' (1765)
Anyone who wishes to better understand
the strength of the putrid smell of the
infirm, and that of ulcers, filthy sores,
rotten and cancerous flesh in particular,
need only consider that a single man
afflicted with a malignant ulcer, thanks to
the pus generated and gathered in his
body, gives off a disgustingly putrid
odour, so nauseating that it will offend
anyone who comes in and breathes it.
Nature, will fall down in a faint. This
atmosphere pollutes the air around it,
and successively all the air that fills the
small rooms, and then the entire ward;
then it contaminates the clothes and in a
certain sense the very pavement and
walls [. . .]

The Sweet Stench of the Saracens
Felix Fabri (fifteenth century)
*Evagatorium in Terrae Sanctae, Arabiae
et Egypti Peregrinationem*
The Saracens give off a certain horrible
stench, due to which they continuously
practice ablutions of various kinds; and
given that we do not stink, they do not
care whether we bathe with them or not.
But they are not so indulgent with the
Jews, who stink even worse. They
welcome us into their baths because –
just as even a leper will cheer up when a
healthy man joins his company, because
this man is not despised and because the
leper believes that contact with a healthy
man might somehow improve his own
health – in the same manner the
malodorous Saracens are happy to enjoy
the company of people like us who do
not stink.

Thomas Murner,
'The pastor of the
Lutheran church makes
a pact with a buffoon or
a madman and the
devil', in *Von der Grossen
Lutherischen Narren*,
1522

The modern world, which has always represented religious or national enemies with grotesque or wicked-looking features, is the birthplace of political caricature. At the time of the Reformation the caricatures produced by Protestants and Catholics to portray the Pope or Luther were truly ferocious. French legitimists at the time of the Revolution lampooned the sans-culottes showing them as bloodthirsty cannibals. Between the nineteenth and twentieth centuries we have anticlerical caricatures and nineteenth-century Italian patriots made savage caricatures of their Austrian oppressors (although a delightful text like **Giusti**'s first describes the ugliness of the occupying forces, then waxes sentimental over those soldiers far from home, busily praying to a common God). But in every war the enemy was depicted as monstrous. During the First World War a certain Berillon wrote *La polychesie de la race*, in which he attempted to demonstrate that not only did the average German produce more faecal matter than his French counterpart, but the smell was worse.

There was also a rich crop of anti-Nazi and anti-fascist caricatures but, especially during the Cold War, anti-communist caricatures were equally vitriolic.

'The Allied Armies
against the Kaiser', from
Le petit journal,
29 September 1914

James Gillray,
*A family of sans-culottes
taking refreshment after
the fatigues of the day,*
1792,
Published by Hannah
Humphrey

Un petit Souper, a la Parisienne: ___ or ___ *A Family of Sans-Culotts refreshing, after the fatigues of the day.*

The Austrians

Giuseppe Giusti
'Saint Ambrose' (1846)

Your Excellency, you who glare at me
For those common jokes,
Labelling me as anti-German
Because I denounce scoundrels' misdeeds,
I beg you listen to what has just happened
To me. Taking a stroll one morning,
I happened to find myself in Saint Ambrose,
In that old church on the outskirts of Milan [. . .]
I went in, and found it full of soldiers,
Soldiers from the north,
In other words Bohemians and Croatians,
Sent here to our rich land to stand around like poles:
And in fact they all stood at rigid attention,
As they do when on review.
With their enormous moustaches and those snouts,
All ramrod straight before God.
I stayed at the back of the church;
because there by chance
Amidst that rabble, I won't deny
I felt a sense of revulsion
That You can't feel thanks to your position.
I felt a heavy atmosphere, and a certain stink:
Pardon me, Excellency, but
In that beautiful house of the Lord,
Even the candles on the main altar
Seemed to be made of tallow.
But in that moment in which the priests
Prepare to consecrate the host
Suddenly my heart was struck
By the sweet sounds of a band near the altar.
From their war trumpets issued forth notes
Like the voice of a people
Praying and weeping for the
Difficulties of life, recalling better days.
It was a chorus by Verdi; the chorus we Lombards,
Wretched and thirsty for justice,
Raised up to God: O Lord, You have moved
And intoxicated so many hearts at the thought of this nation.
Then I began to feel my opinions change.
Now, it was as if those soldiers
Had become people like my own
And unwittingly I joined the crowd.
What can I say, Excellency, it is beautiful music,
Furthermore, it is ours, and it was played

well;
With art and thought,
And where there is art, even prejudice can be put aside.
But once the song was done, I felt as before;
When suddenly, almost as if on purpose,
From those mouths that seemed dumb as logs,
There issued forth a slow German canticle
Rising up within the sacred atmosphere of that church:
It was a prayer, and seemed to me to be a
Grave, mournful, solemn lament
So much so that I felt it in my soul;
And I was stunned that those pigskins,
Those exotic wooden puppets,
Could raise harmony to such heights.
In that anthem, I heard the bittersweet feelings
Of the songs I'd listened to as a child; those we
Learn in the tranquillity of home,
And which return to mind during the dark days;
Sad thoughts for a dear, distant mother,
A desire for peace and love,
A deep sadness for distance and separation [. . .]
All of this struck deeply into my heart.
And when they finished, I was left to mull
Over the strongest and sweetest thoughts.
These people, I said to myself, have been forced
From Croatia and Bohemia
By a fearful king, to invade and enslave us,
But they too have become slaves,
Just like the herds who winter in the Maremma.
Forced by a hard life and hard discipline,
To be mute, derided, and solitary,
The blind instruments of shrewd robbery
That probably affords them nothing and
of which they're not aware;
And this hate, that keeps the Lombards
From growing any closer to the Germans,
Serves those who reign by division,
Who fear that diverse peoples might live in brotherhood.
Poor people! Far from their own,
Deep in a country that hates them,
Who knows, perhaps in their hearts
They hate their sovereigns too!
I think that in the end they feel as we do.
In this church, if I don't leave quickly,
I'll end up embracing a corporal,
That brave pole of hazel wood,
All tough and planted there stiff as a ramrod.

An anticlerical cartoon
from *L'Asino*,
15 January 1899

Anti-communist
electoral poster,
1948

John Heartfield,
'Have no fear, he's a
vegetarian', a
photomontage from
the magazine
Regards,
7 May 1936,
Germany, Snark
Archives

*Italian capitalism puts
on Mussolini's face*,
February 1923,
Giovanni Galantara
Collection

Gino Boccasile,
Anti-American
propaganda cartoon
from the Repubblica
Sociale Italiana,
1943–44

Doctor Fu Manchu

Sax Rohmer

The Bride of Fu Manchu (1933)

He wore a plain yellow robe and walked in silent, thick-soled slippers. Upon his head was set a little black cap surmounted by a coral bead. His hands concealed in the loose sleeves of his robe, he stood there, watching me. And I knew that this man had the most wonderful face that I had ever looked upon. It was aged, yet ageless. I thought that if Benvenuto Cellini had conceived the idea of executing a death-mask of Satan in gold, it must have resembled very closely this living-dead face upon which my gaze was riveted. [. . .] *This was Dr Fu Manchu!*

The Negro

'Negro', *Encyclopaedia Britannica* (first American edition, 1798)

Negro, *Homo pelli nigra,* a name given to a variety of the human species, who are entirely black, and are found in the torrid zone, especially in that part of Africa that lies within the Tropics. In the complexion of negroes we meet with various shades; but they likewise differ far from other men in all the features of their face. Round cheeks, high cheek bones, a forehead somewhat elevated, a short, broad, flat nose, thick lips, small ears, ugliness and irregularity of shape, characterise their external appearance. The negro women have the loins greatly depressed, and very large buttocks, which give the back the

shape of a saddle. Vices the most notorious seem to be the portion of this unhappy race: idleness, treachery, revenge, cruelty, impudence, stealing, lying, profanity, debauchery, nastiness and intemperance, are said to have extinguished the principles of natural law, and to have silenced the reproofs of conscience. They are strangers to every sentiment of compassion, and are an awful example of the corruption of man when left to himself.

Anatomy of Race

Cesare Lombroso

The White Man and the Black Man: Essays on the Origins and Variety of the Human Races, I and II (1871)

The European cranium is distinguished by the stupendous harmony of its forms: it is not too long, nor too round, nor too pointy or pyramid-shaped. On its forehead (Fig. 2) – smooth, broad, erect upon the face – you can clearly distinguish the strength and supremacy of thought: the zygomas, or cheekbones of the face, are not too far apart, and the jawbone does not stick out very far: this is why he calls himself *Orthognathous*.

The cranium of a Mongolian on the other hand is round, or pyramid-shaped, with cheekbones quite far apart from each another, and thus he is called *Eurygnathous*; these characteristics are associated with their scanty beards and hair, the obliqueness of their eyes, and their more or less yellow or olive-coloured skin [. . .]

But the Hottentots form an even more singular variety of the human race. The Hottentot is, one might say, the duck-billed platypus of humanity, because he brings together the most disparate forms of the black and yellow races with some entirely his own, which he shares with just a few animals (those that swarm near him). He blends the flat face of the Chinese with the protuberant one of the Negro. His incisors are shaped like anvils. His ulna, which is the bone of the forearm, still displays (as in some animals), that opening, known as the olecranic fossa, present in our foetuses. His hair grows all around the head, sprouting in little strips, in tufts like the bristles of a clothes brush, in such a manner that a barber who gives a Bushman a close shave would find himself looking down upon a head marbled here and there like a mahogany table sprinkled with pepper grains.

Alex Raymond,
Ming, from *Flash
Gordon*,
© King Features
Syndicate Inc.

One constant of the white man's civilising mission has always been a
merciless portrayal of the African, not only in narrative and in painting, but
also in scientific texts like those of **Lombroso**. The ideology of the 'white
man's burden' prompted many writers to create greasy characters who
belong to some non-European ethnic group, from the treacherous Arab to
the devotees of Indian cults such as *thuggee*. Not to mention the countless
Chinese with sinister faces who are masters of all forms of cruelty. This
happened in comics too; see Alex Raymond's Ming, in the *Flash Gordon*
saga, whose perfidy is made clear by his Asiatic features. Then there are the
enemies of James Bond in the novels of **Ian Fleming** who, more so than
in the films, are almost always of mixed blood or communist agents, and are
out-and-out monsters who seem to have been assembled in the laboratory
of a mad scientist.

Goldfinger
Ian Fleming
Goldfinger, 3 (1959)
When he stood up, the first thing that had struck Bond was that everything was out of proportion. Goldfinger was short, not more than five feet tall, and on top of the thick body and blunt, peasant legs was set almost directly into the shoulders a huge and it seemed exactly round head. It was as if Goldfinger had been put together with bits of other people's bodies.

The Soviet Lesbian
Ian Fleming
From Russia with Love, 9 (1957)
Outside the anonymous, cream-painted door, Tatiana could already smell the inside of the room. When the voice told her curtly to come in, and she opened the door, it was the smell that filled her mind while she stood and stared into the eyes of the woman who sat behind the round table under the centre light.

It was the smell of the Metro on a hot evening – cheap scent concealing animal odours. People in Russia soak themselves in scent, whether they have had a bath or not, but mostly when they have not [. . .]

[. . .] the bedroom door opened and the 'Klebb woman' appeared in the opening. 'What do you think of this, my dear?' Colonel Klebb opened her dumpy arms and twirled on her toes like a mannequin. She struck a pose with one arm outstretched and the other arm crooked at her waist.

[. . .] Colonel Klebb was wearing a semi-transparent nightgown in orange *crêpe de chine*. It had scallops of the same material round the low square neckline and scallops at the wrists of the broadly flounced sleeves. Underneath could be seen a brassière of two large pink satin roses. Below, she wore old-fashioned knickers of pink satin with elastic above the knees. One dimpled knee, like a yellowish coconut, appeared thrust forward between the half-open folds of the nightgown in the classic stance of the modeller [. . .] Rosa Klebb had taken off her spectacles and her naked face was now thick with mascara and rouge and lipstick.

She looked like the oldest and ugliest whore in the world. [. . .] She reached up an arm and turned on a pink-shaded table-lamp whose stem was a naked woman in sham Lalique glass. She patted the couch beside her. 'Turn out the top light, my dear. The switch is by the door. Then come and sit beside me. We must get to know each other better.'

Doctor No
Ian Fleming
Doctor No, 13, 14 (1958)
Doctor No was at least six inches taller than Bond, but the straight, immovable poise of his body made him seem still taller. The head was also elongated and tapered from a round, completely bald skull down to a sharp chin so that the impression was of a reversed raindrop – or rather oildrop, for the skin was of a deep almost translucent yellow. It was impossible to tell Doctor No's age: as far as Bond could see, there were no lines on the face. It was odd to see a forehead as smooth as the top of the polished skull. Even the cavernous indrawn cheeks below the prominent cheekbones looked as smooth as fine ivory. There was something Dali-esque about the eyebrows, which were fine and black and sharply upswept as if they had been painted on as make-up for a conjuror. Below them, slanting jet black eyes stared out of the skull. They were without eyelashes. They looked like the mouths of two small revolvers, direct and unblinking and totally devoid of expression. The thin fine nose ended very close above a wide compressed wound of a mouth which, despite its almost permanent sketch of a smile, showed only cruelty and authority. The chin was indrawn towards the neck. Later Bond was to notice that it rarely moved more than slightly away from centre, giving the impression that the head and the vertebra were in one piece.

The bizarre, gliding figure looked like a giant venomous worm wrapped in grey tin-foil, and Bond would not have been surprised to see the rest of it trailing slimily along the carpet behind.

Doctor No came within three steps of them and stopped. The wound in the tall face opened. 'Forgive me for not shaking hands with you,' the deep voice was flat and even. 'I am unable to.' Slowly the sleeves parted and opened. 'I have no hands.'

Mr Big
Ian Fleming
Live and Let Die, 7 (1954)
It was a great football of a head, twice the normal size and very nearly round. The skin was grey-black, taut and shining like the face of a week-old corpse in the river. It was hairless, except for some grey-brown fluff above the ears. There were no eyebrows and no eyelashes and the eyes were extraordinarily far apart so that one could not focus on them both, but only on one at a time. Their gaze was very steady and penetrating. When they rested on something, they seemed to devour it, to encompass the whole of it. They bulged slightly and the irises were golden round black pupils which were now wide. They were animal eyes, not human, and they seemed to blaze.

The nose was wide without being particularly negroid. The nostrils did not gape at you. The lips were only slightly everted, but thick and dark. They opened only when the man spoke and then they opened wide and drew back from the teeth and the pale pink gums.

PRUNEFACE
1943

MRS. PRUNEFACE
1943

FLATTOP SR.
1944

SHAKEY
1945

Chester Gould,
Characters
from *Dick Tracy*,
1941–46

LITTLEFACE
1941

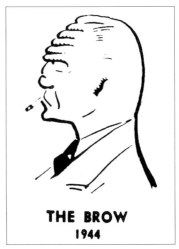

THE BROW
1944

The 'Thing'

H.P. Lovecraft

The Dunwich Horror (1927)

The building was full of a frightful stench which Dr Armitage knew too well, and the three men rushed across the hall to the small genealogical reading-room whence the low whining came. For a second nobody dared to turn on the light, then Dr Armitage summoned up his courage and snapped the switch. [. . .]

The thing that lay half-bent on its side in a foetid pool of greenish-yellow ichor and tarry stickiness was almost nine feet tall, and the dog had torn off all the clothing and some of the skin. It was not quite dead, but twitched silently and spasmodically while its chest heaved in monstrous unison with the mad piping of the expectant whippoorwills outside. [. . .] It would be trite and not wholly accurate to say that no human pen could describe it, but one might properly say that it could not be vividly visualised by anyone whose ideas of aspect and contour are too

200

closely bound up with the common life-forms of this planet and of the three known dimensions. It was partly human, beyond a doubt, with very man-like hands and head, and the goatish, chinless face had the stamp of the Whateleys upon it. But the torso and lower parts of the body were teratologically fabulous, so that only generous clothing could ever have enabled it to walk on earth unchallenged or uneradicated. Above the waist it was semi-anthropomorphic; though its chest, where the dog's rending paws still rested watchfully, had the leathery, reticulated hide of a crocodile or alligator.

The back was piebald with yellow and black, and dimly suggested the squamous covering of certain snakes. Below the waist, though, it was the worst; for here all human resemblance left off and sheer phantasy began. The skin was thickly covered with coarse black fur, and from the abdomen a score of long greenish-grey tentacles with red sucking mouths protruded limply. Their arrangement was odd,

and seemed to follow the symmetries of some cosmic geometry unknown to earth or the solar system. On each of the hips, deep set in a kind of pinkish, ciliated orbit, was what seemed to be a rudimentary eye; whilst in lieu of a tail there depended a kind of trunk or feeler with purple annular markings, and with many evidences of being an undeveloped mouth or throat. The limbs, save for their black fur, roughly resembled the hind legs of prehistoric earth's giant saurians; and terminated in ridgy-veined pads that were neither hooves nor claws. [. . .] Of genuine blood there was none; only the foetid greenish-yellow ichor which trickled along the painted floor beyond the radius of the stickiness, and left a curious discoloration behind it. [. . .]

When the medical examiner came, there was only a sticky whitish mass on the painted boards, and the monstrous odour had nearly disappeared. Apparently Whateley had had no skull or stable skeleton [. . .]

Frank Frazetta,
Beauty and the Beast,
1995,
private collection

facing page
Karel Thole,
Cover for *It Crept
Along the Sand*
by Hal Clement,
1962,
Edizioni Urania

Our journey through the ugliness of the enemy can only end with the first real apparition of what was to become the galactic enemy, The Thing, The Inconceivable. In **Lovecraft**, this amorphous or slimily polymorphous being is still of this world and represents our unconscious fears, but in science fiction (novels and films) it is presented as the 'alien' invader, the bug-eyed monster, the creature with insect eyes that comes from space, a barbarian in the most ancestral sense of the term, menacing and impossible to assimilate because totally non-human.

As such, the bug-eyed monster is the personification of all enemies and confirms the human tendency to portray what we *must* hate as being devoid of all form, thus always making it the ultimate incarnation of the Devil.

Chapter VIII

Witchcraft, Satanism, Sadism

1. The Witch

Diabolical beings capable of casting spells, making magic philtres and other enchantments have existed since the earliest days of antiquity; they are mentioned in the *Codex Hammurabi*, which dates from the beginning of the second millennium BC; in Egyptian culture; in the temples of Ashurbanipal (the seventh century BC); in the Bible, where we read of the lapidation of necromancers and fortune tellers. Greek culture had sorceresses like Medea and Circe, the Roman laws of the Twelve Tables condemned black magic, and we find more still on this subject in **Horace** and **Apuleius**. Right from the start, although it was recognised that black magic was practised both by men (warlocks) and women (witches), a deep-rooted misogyny tended to identify the malefic creature with women. In the Christian world, a union with the Devil could only be perpetrated by a woman. In the Middle Ages there was already talk of the Sabbat as a diabolical assembly in which witches not only cast spells but also indulge in full-blown orgies, having sexual relations with the Devil in the form of a goat, a symbol of lust. Finally the image of the witch astride a broomstick (even though this was later transformed into the Befana, a kindly witch who brings Italian children treats on the evening of twelfth night) is clearly a phallic reference.

Legends are not created from nothing. The so-called witches were old 'wise women' who claimed to know about medicinal herbs and philtres. Others were poor charlatans who fed on the gullibility of the people, others again were genuinely convinced that they had had relations with the Devil. Clinical cases, obviously. Overall, however, witches represented a form of popular subculture.

Francisco Goya,
The Witches' Sabbat,
1797–98,
Madrid,
Museo Lazaro Galdiano

U. Molitor,
'Three witches with the
heads of a donkey,
a cockerel and a goat
leave for the Sabbat',
a woodcut in *Von den
Unholden oder Hexen*,
1489,
Konstanz

Witchcraft in the Bible
Leviticus 20:27
A man also or woman that hath a familiar
spirit, or that is a wizard, shall surely be put
to death: they shall stone them with stones:
their blood shall be upon them.

The Fates
Dante
Inferno, XX, 121–3
Behold the wretched ones, who left the
needle,
The spool and rock, and made them
fortune-tellers;
   They wrought their magic spells with
herb and image.

Horace's Witches
Horace (65–68 BC)
Sermons, 8

I myself saw Canidia, howling with Sagana.
Their deathly pallor gave each witch a
terrible look. They started digging in the
earth with their fingernails and tearing at a
young lamb with their bare teeth: the blood
flowed into the hole, where they could call
up the souls of the ancestors who would
give them the answers they sought. And
there was an effigy made of wool, and
another of wax: the woollen effigy was the
larger of the two, who used torments to
keep the other at bay; the smaller effigy
stood in a supplicant's position, with the
resigned expression of one who is about to
die. One called upon Hecate, the other
upon ferocious Tisiphone: and you would
have seen packs of wandering serpents and
infernal dogs, and the reddening moon,
hiding behind large sepulchres so as not to
witness these events.

Turned into an Ass
Apuleius (125–80)
The Golden Ass, I, 13; III, 24
She drove the sword up to the hilt into the
left side of his neck. Then she took a small
leather bag and collected all the blood that
gushed forth, taking great care not to spill
even a single drop. The good Meroe stuck
her hand through the wound all the way
down to the innards, rummaging around,
and pulled out my poor companion's heart,
while from the throat slashed by that
tremendous blow issued forth a voice,
better yet an indistinct gurgling, from the
bubbling of his breath. Meanwhile, Panthia
used a sponge to plug the wound where it
was broadest, and said: 'O sea-born
sponge, beware of passing by running
water.'
   Once that was done they were about to
leave, but first, having pushed aside my
bunk, they both planted themselves open-
legged above my face, and emptied their
bladders, inundating me with foul-smelling
piss.
   My hairs became as thick as bristles, my
skin became as hard as leather, and at the
ends of my hands the fingers were no
longer separated, but had come together in
a single hoof, and at the bottom of my
spine a big tail now stuck out. My face was
enormous, my mouth wide as could be, my
nostrils dilated, my lips drooped down: and
enormous, horribly hairy ears grew upon
my head. And I could take no comfort from
my disastrous transformation if not this:
now that I could no longer even embrace
my dear Fotis, my rod had become
enormous!

The French School,
*Preparing for
the Witches' Sabbat*,
first half of the
nineteenth century,
Meudon,
Musée Rodin

Documents condemning witches already existed in the Middle Ages, such as the bull issued by Pope Alexander V in 1258. Theologians also talked of witches and necromancers. St Bonaventure, for example, warns us that 'in proportion to their subtlety or spirituality, demons can introduce themselves into a man's body and torment him, unless prevented from doing so by a superior power' (*Commentary on the Sentences*, III, 8).

Nonetheless, witches were not an obsession for the ecclesiastical world. Contrary to current opinion, witch trials were not widespread in the Middle Ages. Such things really began in the modern world, and proof of this lies in the fact that most of the iconographic material on witches dates from the fifteenth century. The Inquisition was established in the thirteenth century, but it was more interested in heretics. In 1484, however, a bull was issued by Innocent VIII against witchcraft, *Summis desiderantibus affectibus*, and the Pope ordered two inquisitors, Heinrich Kramer and Jakob Sprenger, to take drastic action against witches.

It was these two who some years later published the *Malleus maleficarum* (Hammer of the Witches), the supreme treatise on witchcraft, in which they taught how to recognise these poor wretches, how to question them, and how to use torture to make them confess to their pact with the Devil.

Histoire de Merlin,
manuscript,
folio 62v.,
fifthteenth century

The Witch Believes She's a Witch

Episcopal Canons (ninth century)
Certain depraved women, who have
turned to Satan and have been led astray
by his illusions and seductions, believe
and claim to ride certain beasts through
the night, in the company of a multitude
of women, following Diana [. . .]

Priests must constantly preach to
God's people that these things are
completely false, and that these fantasies
are not produced in the minds of the
faithful by the divine spirit, but rather by
evil. Satan, in fact, transforms himself into
an angel of light and takes possession of
the minds of these sorry women,
subjugating them by means of their weak
faith and credulity. He takes on the
appearance and looks of different people
[. . .] and despite the fact that a faithless
woman experiences this in spirit alone,
she believes that it takes place in the
body and not merely in the mind.

The Witch Truly is a Witch

Papal Bull issued by Innocent VIII
Summis desiderantes affectibus (1484)
We have only recently heard – to our great
displeasure – that in several regions in
Germany [. . .] people of both sexes,
forgetful of their own salvation and straying
from the Catholic faith, do not fear to give
themselves over carnally to devils, incubi
and succubi, thereby causing the progeny
of women, animals, and the fruits of the
earth to die or waste away [. . .] by means
of enchantments, charms, spells, and other
execrable magical practices [. . .] With the
intent of acting upon this, as our position
requires, with remedies suited to
preventing the scourge of heretical
depravity from spreading its poison and
hurting innocent people, the
aforementioned inquisitors Sprenger and
Kramer are hereby charged with
conducting inquisitions in that land, in such
a manner that they may proceed with the
correction, incarceration, and punishment
of these people [. . .]

Histoire de Merlin,
manuscript,
folio 63v.,
fifthteenth century

So the witch trials and the subsequent sentences to the stake or to the gallows exploded between the sixteenth and eighteenth centuries, not only in the Catholic world but also and especially in the Protestant world (given that Luther defined them as 'the Devil's whores' and accused them of stealing milk, raising storms, riding goats and tormenting babies in the cradle) and not only in Europe, but also – and with particular virulence – in New England, where the notorious Salem witch trials of 1692 led to the hanging of nineteen women. Witches are a common presence in literature; prime examples being the witches in **Shakespeare** and those of Walpurgisnacht in **Goethe**'s *Faust*. But the bulk of the literature regards the polemic about witchcraft. In 1557, **Cardano** maintained that witches were merely superstitious old women (thus anticipating the interpretation of modern psychiatry), but diehard believers in witchcraft (to mention only a few) included Ian Weir (*De praestigiis daemonum*, 1564), Jean Bodin (*La démonomanie des sorciers*, 1580), Martino del Rio (*Disquisitionum magicarum libri sex*, 1599), Francesco Maria Guazzo (*Compendium maleficarum*, 1608), Joseph Glanvil (*Saducismus triumphatus*, 1681), and Cotton Mather, who had played a (controversial) role in the Salem trials and who gave various sermons on witchcraft in that same century – while attempts to explode the myth were not made until the eighteenth century by authors such as Tartarotti (*On the Nocturnal Meetings of Witches*).

Louis Maurice Boutet de Monvel, *The Lesson before the Sabbat*, c.1880, Nemours, Château de Nanteau-sur-Lunain

The Hammer of the Witches

Jakob Sprenger and Heinrich Kramer

Malleus Maleficarum (1486)

To begin with, we will speak of how they interact with men, then with animals and ultimately with the fruits of the earth. As far as men are concerned, we are interested first and foremost in the ways witches use their craft to keep them from reproducing or engaging in the sexual act, in such a way that the woman cannot conceive and the man cannot perform the act. In the second place how, sometimes, this act may not be performed with one woman while it can with another. Third, how virile members are removed, as if completely torn away from the body. Fourth, how it is possible to recognise when a thing comes solely from the power of the devil, acting on his own without the help of witches. Fifth, how witches use their miraculous arts to transform people of either sex into beasts. Sixth, the various ways in which midwife witches kill the foetus in a mother's womb, or, when they do not do so, offer the child to devils. [. . .]

In conclusion, all these things arise from carnal lust, which is insatiable in them [. . .] It should come as no surprise that among those who are infected with the heresy of witches there are more women than men [. . .] And may the Almighty be blessed for having thus far saved the male sex from such a great scourge! [. . .]

Poor Women

Gerolamo Cardano

On the Variety of Things, XV (1557)

They are poor women in wretched circumstances, who eke out a living in the valleys feeding on chestnuts and herbs. If they didn't drink a little milk, they couldn't survive at all. Therefore they are emaciated, deformed, ashen, with protruding eyes, and through their looks reveal their melancholic, ill natures. They are taciturn, dreamy, and little different from those who are possessed by the devil. They are so sure of their own opinions that anyone listening to the yarns they spin with such conviction would take as true things that have never happened and never will happen.

Theodore Chassériau,
*Macbeth and
the Three Witches*,
detail,
1855,
Paris, Musée d'Orsay

The Witches in *Macbeth*

William Shakespeare

Macbeth, Act IV, scene 1 (1623)

FIRST WITCH: Thrice the brinded cat hath mew'd.

SECOND WITCH: Thrice and once the hedge-pig whined.

THIRD WITCH: Harpier cries 'Tis time, 'tis time.

FIRST WITCH: Round about the cauldron go;
In the poison'd entrails throw.
Toad, that under cold stone
Days and nights has thirty-one
Swelter'd venom sleeping got,
Boil thou first i' the charmed pot.

ALL: Double, double toil and trouble;
Fire burn, and cauldron bubble.

SECOND WITCH: Fillet of a fenny snake,
In the cauldron boil and bake;
Eye of newt and toe of frog,
Wool of bat and tongue of dog,
Adder's fork and blind-worm's sting,
Lizard's leg and owlet's wing,
For a charm of powerful trouble,

Like a hell-broth boil and bubble.

ALL: Double, double toil and trouble;
Fire burn and cauldron bubble.

THIRD WITCH: Scale of dragon, tooth of wolf,
Witches' mummy, maw and gulf
Of the ravin'd salt-sea shark,
Root of hemlock digg'd i' the dark,
Liver of blaspheming Jew,
Gall of goat, and slips of yew
Silver'd in the moon's eclipse,
Nose of Turk and Tartar's lips,
Finger of birth-strangled babe
Ditch-deliver'd by a drab,
Make the gruel thick and slab:
Add thereto a tiger's chaudron,
For the ingredients of our cauldron.

ALL: Double, double toil and trouble;
Fire burn and cauldron bubble.

Sepulcru samuelis

When the persecution was over, the image of the witch did not wane; it continued to survive in fairy tales and crops up in the works of horror writers like **Lovecraft**.

What interests us here is that in most cases the many victims of the stake were accused of witchcraft *because they were ugly*. And, with regard to this ugliness, some people even imagined that during their hellish Sabbats they were able to transform themselves into attractive creatures, but always characterised by ambiguous features that revealed their inner ugliness.

Salvator Rosa,
The Witch,
1640–49,
Milan,
private collection

Walpurgis Night

Johann Wolfgang von Goethe
Faust, Part I, 'Walpurgis Night' (1887)
*Faust, Mephistopheles, Ignis Fatuus
(singing in alternation)* – To-whit! To-whoo! It sounds more near;
Plover, owl and jay appear,
All awake, around, above?
Paunchy salamanders too
Peer, long-limbed, the bushes through!
And, like snakes, the roots of trees
Coil themselves from rock and sand,
Stretching many a wondrous band,
Us to frighten, us to seize;
From rude knots with life embued,
Polyp-fangs abroad they spread,
To snare the wanderer! 'Neath our tread,
Mice, in myriads, thousand-hued,
Through the heath and through the moss!
And the fire-flies' glittering throng,
Wildering escort, whirls along,
Here and there, our path across. [. . .]
All things round us whirl and fly;
Rocks and trees make strange grimaces,
Dazzling meteors change their places,
How they puff and multiply! [. . .]
Mephistopheles – *A murky vapour thickens night.*
Hark! Through the woods the tempests roar!
The owlets flit in wild affright.
Hark! Splinter'd are the columns that upbore
The leafy palace, green for aye:
The shivered branches whirr and sigh,
Yawn the huge trunks with mighty groan.
The roots upriven, creak and moan!

In fearful and entangled fall,
One crashing ruin whelms them all,
While through the desolate abyss,
Sweeping the wreck-strewn precipice,
The raging storm-blasts howl and hiss!
[. . .]
Hark! the mountain ridge along,
Streameth a raving magic-song!
Witches (in chorus) – Now to the Brocken the witches hie,
The stubble is yellow, the corn is green;
Thither the gathering legions fly,
And sitting aloft is Sir Urian seen:
O'er stick and o'er stone they go whirling along,
Witches and he-goats, a motley throng,
[. . .]
The way is broad, the way is long;
What mad pursuit! What tumult wild!
Scratches the besom and sticks the prong;
Crush'd is the mother, and stifled the child.
Wizards (half chorus) – Like house-encumber'd snail we creep;
While far ahead the women keep,
For when to the devil's house we speed,
By a thousand steps they take the lead.
The Other Half – Not so, precisely do we view it;
They with a thousand steps may do it;
But let them hasten as they can,
With one long bound 'tis clear'd by man. [. . .]
Chorus of Witches – Salve gives the witches strength to rise;
A rag for a sail does well enough;
A goodly ship is every trough;
To-night who flies not, never flies.

The Village of Witches

H.P. Lovecraft

The Dunwich Horror (1927)

Two centuries ago, when talk of witch-blood, Satan-worship, and strange forest presences was not laughed at, it was the custom to give reasons for avoiding the locality. In our sensible age – since the Dunwich horror of 1928 was hushed up by those who had the town's and the world's welfare at heart – people shun it without knowing exactly why. It is that the natives are now repellently decadent, having gone so far along that path of retrogression so common in many New-England backwaters. They have come to form a race by themselves, with the well-defined mental and physical stigmata of degeneracy and inbreeding. The average of their intelligence is woefully low, whilst their annals reek of overt viciousness and half-hidden murders, incest, and deeds of almost unnameable violence and perversity.

The old gentry, representing the two or three armigerous families which came from Salem in 1692, have kept somewhat above the general level of decay; though many branches are sunk into the sordid populace so deeply that only their names remain as a key to the origin they disgrace. [...] No one, even those who have the facts concerning the recent horror, can say just what is the matter with Dunwich; though old legends speak of unhallowed rites and conclaves of the Indians, amidst which they called forbidden shapes of shadow out of the great rounded hills, and made wild orgiastic prayers that were answered by loud crackings and rumblings from the ground below. In 1747 the Reverend Abijah Hoadley, newly come to the Congregational Church at Dunwich Village, preached a memorable sermon on the close presence of Satan and his imps, in which he said: 'It must be allow'd, that these Blasphemies of an infernall Train of Daemons are Matters of too common Knowledge to be deny'd; the cursed Voices of *Azazel* and *Buzrael*, of *Beelzebub* and *Belial*, being heard now from under Ground by above a Score of credible Witnesses now living. I my self did not more than a Fortnight ago catch a very plain Discourse of evil Powers in the hill behind my House; wherein there were a Rattling and Rolling, Groaning, Screeching and Hissing, such as no things of this Earth cou'd raise up, and which must needs have come from those Caves that only black Magick can discover, and only the Divell unlock.'

Imagining Witches

Patrick McGrath

Spider (1990)

When I was growing up we lived on Kitchener Street, [...] All the rooms in the house were small and cramped, with low ceilings; the bedrooms had been wallpapered so many years before that the paper was moist and peeling, and badly discoloured in patches; the large spreading stains, with their smell of mildewed plaster (I can smell it now!) formed weird figures on the fading floral pattern and stimulated in my childish imagination many fantastic terrors. [...]

Later I would go up to my bedroom, and I think I should tell you about that room, for so much of all this is based on what I saw and heard, and even *smelled*, from up there. I was at the back of the house, at the top of the stairs, and I had a view of the yard and the alley beyond. It was a small room, and probably the dampest in the house. There was a large patch on the wall opposite my bed where the paper had come away and the plaster had started literally to erupt – there were crumbly, greenish lumps of moist plaster swelling from the wall, like buboes or cankers, that turned to powder if you touched them. My mother was constantly at my father to do something about it, and though he'd replastered the wall once, within a month they were back, the problem being leaky drainpipes and decaying mortar in the brickwork, all of which my mother thought he should be able to fix but which he never had. I would lie awake at night and by whatever moonlight penetrated the room I would gaze at these shadowy lumps and nodules, and in my boyish imagination they became the wens and warts of some awful humpbacked night-hag with an appalling skin disease, a spirit damned for her sins against men to be trapped, tormented, in the bad plaster of an old wall in a slum. At times she left the wall and entered my nightmares (I was plagued by nightmares, as a boy), and then when I woke in the night in terror I would see her sneering in the corner of the room, turned away from me, her head cloaked in shadow and her eyes glittering from that horrible knobbly skin, the smell of her breath befouling the air; then I would sit up in bed, screaming at her, and it was only when my mother came in and turned the light on that she returned to her plaster, and I would then have to have the light on for the rest of the night.

Francesco Salviati,
The Three Fates,
*c.*1550,
Florence, Galleria
Palatina

Walt Disney,
*Snow White and the
Seven Dwarfs*,
David Hand (director),
1937,
© Disney

2. Satanism, Sadism and the Taste for Cruelty

Witches were accused of holding blasphemous ceremonies in which they worshipped the Devil, but the liturgy of Satan is not just a part of the legend, even though Devil worship has always been attributed to heretical sects or called up in order to condemn the Knights Templar. Numerous satanist cults exist to this day and they occasionally hit the headlines thanks to the criminal (and real) activities of those held to be members.

Experts divide modern satanist sects into four schools: rationalist and atheist groups, who consider Satan to be a symbol of reason and the search for pleasure, over and beyond any moral or religious constraints; occultists, who turn religious rites and beliefs on their heads; 'acid' Satanists, whose rituals are always orgies accompanied by the use of drugs (a trend turned into theatre by many rock bands); and finally the Luciferians, with their ancient Manichaean and Gnostic influences, for whom the Devil is a positive principle.

The reasons for the adoration of the Devil, when they do not spring from psychiatric syndromes, or merely serve to justify orgiastic and sexually excessive behaviour, may be ascribed to the same reasons that lead many people to believe in magical practices. In real life the gap between what we desire and what we obtain is usually fairly wide, even when science steps in, whereas magic ensures success through a sort of instant short circuit (you can harm your enemy by sticking a pin into a wax dummy, you can ward off evil through an amulet, you can win the love of one who does not love you through a philtre). In such cases satanism is a form of pact with the Devil.

The fundamental rite of Satan worshippers is usually the black mass, which according to various reports is celebrated not on an altar stone but on the naked body of a woman, while a priest, apostate but regularly ordained, consecrates the holy wafers so that they may be profaned.

Since such ceremonies are the subject of many fantastic tales and since witnesses have always been reluctant to talk about them, the text that best describes these rites is to be found in *Là-bas* by **Huysmans**, who probably had contacts in satanic circles.

Heinrich Füssli,
*Titania Caressing
Bottom with the Head
of a Donkey*,
1793–94,
Zurich, Kunsthaus

Odilon Redon,
The Deformed Octopus,
c.1883,
Saint-Germain-en-Laye,
Musée Départementale
Maurice Denis 'La Prieuré'

Giacomo Grosso,
A study for
The Supreme Meeting,
1894,
Camino Monferrato (AL),
Enrico Colombotto Rosso
Collection

The Black Mass
J.-K. Huysmans
Là-Bas (1891)

Then the altar became visible. It was an ordinary church altar on a tabernacle above which stood an infamous, derisive Christ. The head had been raised and the neck lengthened, and wrinkles, painted in the cheeks, transformed the grieving face to a bestial one twisted into a mean laugh. He was naked, and where the loincloth should have been, there was a virile member projecting from a bush of horsehair. [. . .] Preceded by the two choir boys the canon entered, wearing a scarlet bonnet from which two buffalo horns of red cloth protruded. Durtal examined him as he marched toward the altar. He was tall, but not well built, his bulging chest being out of proportion to the rest of his body. His peeled forehead made one continuous line with his straight nose. The lips and cheeks bristled with that kind of hard, clumpy beard which old priests have who have always shaved themselves. The features were round and insinuating, the eyes, like apple pips, close together, phosphorescent. [. . .]

The canon solemnly knelt before the altar, then mounted the steps and began to say mass. Durtal saw then that he had nothing on beneath his sacrificial habit. His black socks and his flesh bulging over the garters, attached high up on his legs, were plainly visible. The chasuble had the shape of an ordinary chasuble but was of the dark red colour of dried blood, and in the middle, in a triangle around which was an embroidered border of colchicum, savin, sorrel, and spurge, was the figure of a black billy-goat presenting his horns [. . .] Indeed, at that moment the choir boys passed behind the altar and one of them brought back copper chafing-dishes, the other, censers, which they distributed to the congregation. All the women enveloped themselves in the smoke. Some held their heads right over the chafing-dishes and inhaled deeply, then, fainting, unlaced themselves, heaving raucous sighs. The sacrifice ceased. The priest descended the steps backward, knelt on the last one, and in a sharp, tripidant voice cried: 'Master of Slanders, Dispenser of the benefits of crime, Administrator of sumptuous sins and great vices, Satan, thee we adore, reasonable God, just God! [. .] Thou determinest the mother to sell her daughter, to give her son; thou aidest sterile and reprobate loves; Guardian of strident Neuroses, Leaden Tower of Hysteria, bloody Vase of Rape! [. . .]

'And thou, thou whom, in my quality of priest, I force, whether thou wilt or no, to descend into this host, to incarnate thyself in this bread, Jesus, Artisan of Hoaxes, Bandit of Homage, Robber of Affection, hear! Since the day when thou didst issue from the complaisant bowels of a Virgin, thou hast failed all thine engagements, belied all thy promises. Centuries have wept, awaiting thee, fugitive God, mute God! Thou wast to redeem man and thou hast not, thou wast to appear in thy glory, and thou sleepest. [. . .] We would drive deeper the nails into thy hands, press down the crown of thorns upon thy brow, bring blood and water from the dry wounds of thy sides [. . .]' 'Amen!' trilled the soprano voices of the choir boys. Durtal listened in amazement to this torrent of blasphemies and insults. The foulness of the priest stupefied him.

A silence succeeded the litany. The chapel was foggy with the smoke of the censers. The women, hitherto taciturn, flustered now, as, remounting the altar, the canon turned toward them and blessed them with his left hand in a sweeping gesture. And suddenly the choir boys tinkled the prayer bells. It was a signal. The women fell to the carpet and writhed. One of them seemed to be worked by a spring. She threw herself prone and waved her legs in the air. Another, suddenly struck by a hideous strabism, clucked, then becoming tongue-tied stood with her mouth open, the tongue turned back, the tip cleaving to the palate. Another, inflated, livid, her pupils dilated, lolled her head back over her shoulders, then jerked it brusquely erect and belaboured herself, tearing her breast with her nails. Another, sprawling on her back, undid her skirts, drew forth a rag, enormous, meteorized; then her face twisted into a horrible grimace, and her tongue, which she could not control, stuck out, bitten at the edges, harrowed by red teeth, from a bloody mouth. Suddenly Durtal rose, and now he heard and saw Docre distinctly. Docre contemplated the Christ surmounting the tabernacle, and with arms spread wide apart he spewed forth frightful insults, and, at the end of his forces, muttered the Billingsgate of a drunken cabman. One of the choir boys knelt before him with his back toward the altar. A shudder ran around the priest's spine. In a solemn but jerky voice he said, 'Hoc est enim corpus meum,' then, instead of kneeling, after the consecration, before the precious Body, he faced the congregation, and appeared tumefied, haggard, dripping with sweat. He staggered between the two choir boys, who, raising the chasuble, displayed his naked belly. Docre made a few passes and the host sailed, tainted and soiled, over the steps.

Durtal felt himself shudder. A whirlwind of hysteria shook the room. While the choir boys sprinkled holy water on the pontiff's nakedness, women rushed upon the Eucharist and, grovelling in front of the altar, clawed from the bread humid particles and drank and ate divine ordure. Another woman, curled up over a crucifix, emitted a rending laugh, then cried to Docre, 'Father, father!' A crone tore her hair, leapt, whirled around and around as on a pivot and fell over beside a young girl who, huddled to the wall, was writhing in convulsions, frothing at the mouth, weeping, and spitting out frightful blasphemies. And Durtal, terrified, saw through the fog the red horns of Docre, who, seated now, frothing with rage, was chewing up sacramental wafers, taking them out of his mouth, wiping himself with them, and distributing them to the women, who ground them underfoot, howling, or fell over each other struggling to get hold of them and violate them.

The Attraction of the Horrendous
Friedrich Schiller
'On Tragic Art' (1792)

It is a general phenomenon of our nature, that that which is sad, terrible, and even horrendous holds an irresistible attraction for us; we feel ourselves repulsed and at the same time attracted by scenes of pain and terror [...] How numerous the crowd that accompanies a criminal to the scene of his execution!

Neither the pleasure of a love for justice gratified, nor the ignoble taste of a bloodthirsty yearning for vengeance can explain this phenomenon. The wretch may even arouse forgiveness in spectators' hearts, the sincerest compassion may take an interest in favour of his salvation; but nevertheless the spectator is moved, to a greater or lesser extent, by a curious desire to view and listen to the expression of his suffering. If the educated man, the man of refined sentiments, is an exception, it is not because this instinct does not exist in him, but rather because it has been overcome by the sorrowful power of pity, or is curbed by the rules of decorum. The coarse son of nature, unbridled by any genteel sentiments, abandons himself unashamedly to this powerful impulse. Which must, therefore, have its foundation in the natural disposition of the human soul.

One case of pseudo-satanism that leads us to other reflections is the story of Gilles de Rais. A marshal of France while still a young man, de Rais fought alongside Joan of Arc and wound up hanged at thirty-six after a **trial** in which (thanks to numerous witnesses) he was shown to be guilty of sodomy and other abuses of young people whom he first lured into his castle before slaughtering them and burying their dismembered corpses. As usually happens in such cases, it was said that Gilles had established a relationship with the Devil, but it is hard to attribute his crimes to Satan worship. He was simply a sick man, whose war experiences had inured him to a taste for blood. And it is precisely this propensity of his for torture that makes us wonder whether it is the Devil who drives people to be cruel or whether it is not a natural tendency to cruelty that leads people to imagine, by way of a justification and a reason for arousal, a relationship with the Devil. Human beings have always loved cruel spectacles, from the days of the Roman amphitheatres, and one of the first descriptions of a horrifying torment is to be found in **Ovid**, where he tells the story of how Apollo had the faun Marsyas flayed alive after the latter had beaten him in a musical contest.

Schiller defined this 'natural disposition' to the horrific very well, and let us not forget that in every period people have always rushed excitedly to witness executions. If today we think of ourselves as 'civilised', perhaps it is only because the cinema has provided us with 'splatter' movies, which do not disturb the spectator's conscience given that they are presented as fictitious.

Titian,
*The Punishment
of Marsyas,*
1570–76,
Kromeriz,
Archbishop's Palace

following pages
'The 'notorious'
Gilles de Rais practising
black magic
and sacrificing children',
engraving,
nineteenth century

The Fate of Marsyas
Ovid (42 BC–18 AD)
Metamorphoses, 383
Scarce had the man this famous story told,
Of vengeance on the Lycians shown of old,
When straight another pictures to their view
The Satyr's fate, whom angry Phoebus slew;
Who, rais'd with high conceit, and puff'd
with pride,
At his own pipe the skilful God defy'd.
Why do you tear me from my self, he cries?
Ah cruel! must my skin be made the prize?
This for a silly pipe? he roaring said,
Mean-while the skin from off his limbs

was flay'd.
All bare, and raw, one large continu'd
wound,
With streams of blood his body bath'd the
ground.
The blueish veins their trembling pulse
disclos'd,
The stringy nerves lay naked, and expos'd;
His guts appear'd, distinctly each express'd,
With ev'ry shining fibre of his breast.

221

The Pleasures of Gilles de Rais

Georges Bataille

'The Deposition of Etienne Corillart', *The Trial of Gilles de Rais* (1998)

Moreover the witness said and deposed that the said Sillé, Henriet, and himself, found and took to the room occupied by the said Gilles de Rais, the accused, numerous girls and boys with whom the said Gilles held his lecherous orgies, as is said hereinunder in greater detail. This they did on the orders of the said Gilles, the accused. [. . .]

Questioned about the number of children handed over to the said Gilles, the accused, in each of the said places, by him, and by the said Sillé and Griart, witness replied that in Nantes he saw fourteen or fifteen, at Machecoul most of the said forty, but that he couldn't otherwise be more precise about the exact number.

Also, witness said and deposed that the said Gilles de Rais, in order to indulge in his unnatural perversions and satisfy his libidinous desires with these children, would first take his rod or virile member in his hands, handling it or making it erect or holding it out, after which he would place it between the thighs and the legs of the said girls and boys, ignoring the natural orifices of the said girls, rubbing the said rod or virile member on the bellies of the said girls and boys with great pleasure, eagerness and lecherous lust until his sperm flowed across their bellies.

Also, witness said and deposed that before perpetrating his debauchery on the said girls and boys, with a view to preventing them from crying out, and so that they would not be heard, the said Gilles de Rais would sometimes hang them up with his own hands; on other occasions he would have others hang them up by the neck, with ropes or cords, in his room, from a pole or a hook; then he would lower them or have them lowered, pretend to cosset them, and reassure them that he didn't want to hurt them or injure them and that, on the contrary he wanted to have fun and, in this fashion, he

prevented them from crying out.

Also, when the said Gilles de Rais committed his horrid debauchery and his sins of lust on the said girls and boys he would afterwards kill them or have them killed.

Questioned in order to find out who did the killing, witness replied that sometimes the said Gilles, the accused, would murder them with his own hands, and on other occasions he would have them killed by the said Sillé or Henriet or by him, the witness, or by one of them, together or separately.

Questioned as to how this was done, witness replied: sometimes by decapitation, other times by slitting the throat, other times again by quartering them and breaking their necks with a club; and that there was a sword specially used for killing them, vulgarly known as the 'slasher'. [. . .]

Also, witness moreover said and deposed that the said Gilles de Rais would sometimes vent his lusts on the said girls and boys before hurting them, but this only seldom; other times, and often, after having hung them up or hurt them in other ways; other times again after having slit or after having had someone else slit the veins of their necks or throats, as the blood gushed out; on other occasions while they were in the languor of death or even after death or when their heads had been cut off, as long as the bodies were still warm.

Also, witness said and deposed that the said Gilles de Rais practised his lustful perversions with girls in the same way as he abused the boys, scorning and ignoring their nature, and that he had heard it said that he enjoyed it far more when he indulged in such depravity with the said girls, as is said hereinbelow, rather than use their natural orifice in the normal way. [. . .]

One André Buchet, who is mentioned hereinabove, handed over to Gilles de Rais a boy of about ten, on whom the said Gilles committed and perpetrated his abominable sins of lust in the fashion described hereinabove. The

boy was delivered by a certain Boetden, whose house stood hard by the market of Vannes, fairly near the house of the said Lemoine, and that the ostlers of the said Gilles, the accused, were lodged in the home of the said Boetden. The boy was taken there because the house of the said Lemoine had no place safe enough in which to murder the boy. The boy was killed in a room of the said Boetden's house, and his head was cut off and burned in the said room. The body, bound with the child's own belt, was thrown into the cesspit of the said Boetden's house, where he, the witness, with difficulty climbed down to ensure that the said body sank. The witness added that the said Buchet knew all about these things.

Also, witness said and deposed that the said Gilles, the accused, after the veins of the necks or throats of the said children had been slit, or after other parts of their bodies had been cut, and when the blood began to gush forth, or even after decapitation, carried out as mentioned hereinabove, would sometimes sit on their bellies and take pleasure in watching them die, sometimes sitting astride them the better to observe their death throes and then death itself.

Also, witness said and deposed that sometimes and indeed fairly often, after the decapitation and death of the said children, brought about in this way or in other ways, as is said hereinabove, the said Gilles would take pleasure in looking at them and in having the witness look at them, as well as the others who were privy to his secrets, and he would show them the heads and the limbs of the said murdered children, and ask which of the children had had the handsomest limbs, the fairest face, the finest head. Often he would enjoy kissing one or the other of these murdered children, whose limbs he was examining, or one of those who had already been examined and had struck him as having the most beautiful face.

Jacques Callot,
table from
The Wretchedness of War,
1633

The 'Ballad of the Gibbet' by **Villon** was certainly inspired by compassion towards those executed, but it reminds us that the sight of bodies humiliated by torture or capital punishment was a customary thing in times gone by.

Similarly, Callot's etching shows us clusters of hanged men, a daily spectacle during the wars of the seventeenth century. Another notorious character was Vlad Dracula, the voivode of Wallachia in the fifteenth century. Although Dracula had fought valiantly against the Turks, he was fond of impaling people on sharpened stakes, but the story that he used to make a cheerful dinner in the midst of a host of impaled victims is probably a legend.

Familiarity with death led to syndromes of cruelty even with regard to the saints. Today, in the cathedral of St Vitus in Prague, we can see display cabinets with the craniums of St Adalbert and St Wenceslas, one of St Margaret's teeth, a fragment of St Vitalius' tibia, one of St Sophia's ribs, and St Eoban's shin bone. In the treasury of the Hofburg Palace in Vienna there is one of John the Baptist's teeth and a bone from the arm of St Anne, while the treasury of Milan Cathedral conserves the larynx of St Charles Borromeo.

These exhibits look like the work of a contemporary artist, and the history of relics offers a wealth of fakes, the work of skilled craftsmen. But when they were authentic, these yellowing strips of mystically repugnant, pathetic and mysterious bits of cartilage, these scraps of crumbling matter whose nature and origin is hard to say, are the result of a complete dismemberment of venerated bodies, of the boiling away of flesh to obtain skeletons to break up, and of out-and-out profanation of bodies due to an excess of popular devotion.

Sometimes popular devotion was merely the victim of a trade that grew up for reasons of tourism, to attract crowds of the faithful to a city or a sanctuary. And so we can see that cruelty may spring not only from hatred or from a perverse taste for disfigurement but often also from excessive feelings of love and veneration.

Vlad III Dracula
has his victims impaled,
1476–77

The Ballad of the Gibbet

François Villon

The Ballad of the Gibbet (1489)

Brothers and men that shall after us be,
Let not your hearts be hard to us:
For pitying this our misery
Ye shall find God the more piteous.
Look on us six that are hanging thus,
And for the flesh that so much we cherished
How it is eaten of birds and perished,
And ashes and dust fill our bones' place,
Mock not at us that so feeble be,
But pray God pardon us out of His grace.
Listen, we pray you, and look not in scorn,
Though justly, in sooth, we are cast to die;
Ye wot no man so wise is born
That keeps his wisdom constantly.

Be ye then merciful, and cry
To Mary's Son that is piteous,
That His mercy take no stain from us,
Saving us out of the fiery place.
We are but dead, let no soul deny
To pray God succour us of His grace.
The rain out of heaven has washed us clean,
The sun has scorched us black and bare,
Ravens and rooks have pecked at our eyne,
And feathered their nests with our beards and hair.
Round are we tossed, and here and there,
This way and that, at the wild wind's will,
Never a moment my body is still;
Birds they are busy about my face.
Live not as we, nor fare as we fare;
Pray God pardon us out of His grace.

The Death of Andronicus

Nicetas the Choniate (1150 ca–1217)
Chronological Narration, XI, 8, 5–10
Appearing in this manner before the Emperor Isaac, they abused him, slapping him on his cheeks, kicking him in the rear, pulling out his beard, knocking out his teeth, ripping out his hair, making a public laughing-stock of him [. . .] Then, after his right hand was struck off with an axe, he was thrown back in the same cell without food, drink or any help from anyone.

After several days an eye was gouged out of his head and, seated on a mangy camel, he was paraded in triumph (for dishonour) around the *agora*: like an old oak tree stripped of its leaves, his skull was completely bare and more clean-shaven than an egg, and he wore nothing more than a cloth rag [. . .] Some struck him in the head with clubs, others smeared bull excrement in his nostrils, others squeezed sponges impregnated with the intestinal filth of humans and cows on his face. Others lashed out at him, spitting foul insults about his mother and father. A few punctured his sides with skewers. The most brazen among them threw rocks at him and called him a rabid dog. A dissolute whore grabbed a vase full of hot water from a kitchen and emptied it over his cheeks. There wasn't a single person who did not mistreat Andronicus.

Led in this ignominious manner into the theatre in a ridiculous triumphal parade, he was lifted up miserably and with great mockery from atop the camel, he who had once been on high was now in the dust. He was immediately hung by his feet, bound together with a cork cord, to the two little columns which, surmounted by a stone, rise up alongside bronze statues of a wolf and a wry-necked hyena. Despite suffering these many torments and enduring an infinite number of others which I won't tell you here, Andronicus, being a strong soul, courageously resisted these disgraceful attacks.

Turning to face those who were coming to strike him, he said nothing but: '*Kyrie, eleison,*' and 'why break a reed that has already been torn asunder?' Not even after having hung him by his feet did that crowd of stupid fools draw away from the mangled Andronicus or take pity on his body but, tearing away his rags, they proceeded to massacre his genitals. A villain drove a long sword into his guts through his jaws; a few Latin types planted a scimitar into his anus and, spreading out around him, drew out their swords, testing them to see which was sharpest and glorying in their own dexterity after a well-placed blow.

After so many travails and such suffering, in the end he breathed his last, painfully raising his right arm and lifting it to his mouth, so that to those assembled it seemed as if he wished to suck the blood that still oozed hot from a recent wound.

The Execution of Damiens

The Amsterdam Gazette,
1 April 1757
In the end, he was quartered. This last operation took a very long time, because the horses they used were not accustomed to pulling; in fact instead of four, they had to use six [. . .] You can be certain that, although he had always been a great blasphemer, not a single curse escaped his lips; only the excessive pain made him burst out with horrible cries, and often he repeated: 'My God, have pity on me; Jesus save me' [. . .] Sulphur was lit, but the flame was so weak that with the exception of the backs of his hands, his skin was relatively undamaged. Then, an executioner's assistant, his sleeves rolled up above his elbows, took some specially made pincers around a foot and a half in length, and clamped down first on the fat of the right leg, then the thigh, then the two fatty parts of the right arm; finally the breasts. Despite his strength and robustness, this assistant had a hard time ripping off pieces of flesh, and had to grab with his pincers two or three times in the same place, twisting until a wound the size of a six-lira coin was created where he had torn the flesh away.

After this pincer torture Damiens, who cried out very loudly though without swearing, raised his head and looked at himself; then the same pincer-bearer went to a large cauldron and with an iron spoon scooped out some boiling hot drug and poured great gobs of it into each wound. Then the slender ropes were tied to the ropes to be attached to the horses, and then a horse was attached to each of his limbs, at the thighs, legs and arms [. . .]

The horses lunged, each pulling a limb out straight, each horse's reins held by an assistant. After fifteen minutes, the same ordeal, but finally after many attempts they were forced to move the horses: in other words, leading the one attached to the right arm up towards the head, those attached to the thighs moving up towards the arms, which finally broke the arms at the joints. This procedure was repeated several times without success [. . .]

Finally the executioner Samson went to tell monsieur Le Breton that there was no way nor any hope of succeeding, and he asked him to ask the Lords if they wanted Damiens cut into pieces [. . .] Monsieur Le Breton, upon his return from the city, gave the order to try harder, which was done; but the horses shied and one of those attached to the thighs fell down on the pavement [. . .]

After three or four attempts, the executioner Samson and the assistant who had used the pincers each took a knife from their pockets and cut the thighs from the trunk of the body; the four horses pulling dragged away the two thighs, the one on the right side first, then the other; after which the same operation was conducted on the arms and shoulders and underarms and for the four parts; they had to cut the flesh almost down to the bone; the horses, pulling with all their might, tore the first arm off and then the other.

Once these four parts were detached, the confessors went down to talk to him. The executioner's assistant told them that he was dead, but the truth is that I saw the man shudder and his lower jaw moved back and forth as if he were speaking.

Hieronymus Bosch,
The Garden of Delights,
detail from
the right-hand
panel showing Hell,
c.1500,
Madrid, Prado Museum

When it comes to the dismemberment of living bodies we have two sources regarding royal executions, that of the Byzantine emperor Andronicus (as told by **Nicetas the Choniate**) and the quartering of **Damiens** (who had attempted to assassinate Louis XV in 1757); the first was put to death at the hands of a street mob, while the execution of the second was followed with excited interest by the crowd. The taste for cruelty did not spare even animals: **Poe** gives us a fantastic tale of the torture and killing of a cat, but **Eco** gives an account of a real idea, inspired by an experiment actually proposed in the seventeenth century in order to find a sure way of establishing longitude on board a ship. Such episodes today would prompt us to talk of sadism, but it was to show how the taste for cruelty was rooted in human nature that **Sade** celebrated his contempt for the bodies of others. And if Sade advocated violence partly by way of a philosophical provocation, Romantic and Decadent literature (see **Maturin**) often referred to it as a supreme form of sensuality.

No less horrible things may be found in other narratives, some due to a mere taste for the sensational, as in **Fleming**, others written as a condemnation of the cruelty of the world, as in **Conrad** (whose work inspired the horrors of the film *Apocalypse Now*). **Orwell** reminds us that torture is still at home under dictatorial regimes, and **Kafka** tells us of an ever-present metaphysical violence, a phenomenon still manifested today in the course of conflicts in which the belligerents lose all sense of humanity. The Devil no longer has any function regarding these practices, nor do we try any longer to evoke his name by way of justification. By now, the taste for cruelty is entirely a human feature.

227

Francesco Del Cairo,
*The Martyrdom
of Saint Agnes*,
c.1634–35,
Venice, Pier Luigi Pizzi
Collection

facing page
The Master
of the Holy Blood,
Lucrezia,
c.1520

depravation by abusing me all the more [...] Alas, while sometimes my imagination had dwelled on these pleasures, I believed them as chaste as the God who had inspired them, gifted by nature to serve as consolation for men, born of love and tenderness; I was far from believing that man, like a ferocious beast, could not experience joy if not by terrifying his female companions. I experienced all of this, and to a degree of violence that the pangs of the natural laceration of my virginity proved the least I would have to bear over the course of this assault. But it was the moment of orgasm, when Antoine had finished crying out furiously, finished the brutal assaults on every part of my body, with bites so similar to the bloody caresses of a tiger, that for a moment I believed myself the prey of some ferocious beast that would not be satisfied until it had devoured me. Once these horrors ended, I fell back onto the altar where I had been offered up as a sacrifice, almost devoid of consciousness and all but lifeless.

The Pleasure of Execution
Marquis de Sade
Justine (1791)
Aren't our public places packed full every time someone is assassinated in accordance with the law? And the strangest thing is that more often than not, they are women: women are more inclined to cruelty than we are because they possess a more sensitive constitution. That's what fools don't understand.

Sadism
Marquis de Sade
Justine (1791)
But what details [...] Great God [...] It's impossible for me to describe them; one might have said that this wicked person, the greatest libertine of the four for all he seemed the closest to the ways of nature, agreed to approach her, to show more restraint in his worship of her, only to compensate for this semblance of lesser

Amateurs in Suffering
Charles Robert Maturin
Melmoth the Wanderer (1820)
'It is actually possible to become *amateurs in suffering*. I have heard of men who have travelled into countries where horrible executions were to be daily witnessed, for the sake of that excitement which the sight of suffering never fails to give, from the spectacle of a tragedy, or an *auto-da-fé*, down to the writhings of the meanest reptile on whom you can inflict torture, and feel that torture is the result of your own power. It is a species of feeling of which we never can divest ourselves – a triumph over those whose sufferings have placed them below us [...]

'You will call this cruelty, I call it curiosity – that curiosity that brings thousands to witness a tragedy, and makes the most delicate female feast on groans and agonies. [...]'

And Melmoth, as he spoke, flung himself on a bed of hyacinths and tulips that displayed their glowing flowers, and sent up odorous breath right under Isidora's casement. 'Oh, you will destroy my flowers!' cried she, while a reminiscence of her former picturesque existence when flowers were the companions alike of her imagination and her pure heart, awoke her exclamation. 'It is my vocation – I pray you pardon me!' said Melmoth, as he basked on the crushed flowers, and darting his withering sneer and scowling glance at Isidora.

The Torture Garden
Octave Mirbeau
The Torture Garden, III, 3 (1899)

She cuddled up close to me, all of her, supple and tender.

'You don't want to listen to me, you nasty thing!' she continued. 'And you won't even caress me! Caress me darling. Feel my breasts, how cold and firm they are!'

And in a flatter tone, gazing at me with eyes flashing with green fire, voluptuous and cruel, she said:

'Only eight days ago I saw something extraordinary. Oh, my love, I saw them whipping a man because he had stolen some fish [. . .] It happened in the torture garden. Try to imagine the scene. The man was kneeling, his head resting on a kind of block, all black with dried blood. His back and flanks were bare: a back and flanks the colour of old gold. I arrived just as a soldier was tying the man's long pigtail to a ring fixed to a paving stone. Beside the patient, another soldier was heating an iron rod in the flames of a forge. And now mark my words! Are you listening to me? . . . When the rod was red hot, the soldier brandished it in the air and then brought it down on the back of the condemned man. The rod made a whistling sound before penetrating the muscles, which sizzled, and from which a reddish aura arose . . . do you see? The soldier let the iron cool in the flesh, which swelled and closed up again; then, when it was cold, he wrenched it violently away taking some bleedings scraps of flesh with it . . . And the man let out frightful cries of pain. Then the soldier started again. He did it fifteen times. And, my love, at every blow it seemed to me as if the rod were penetrating my back too . . . Atrocious and delightful!'

And since I said nothing, she repeated: 'Atrocious and delightful! If you only knew how handsome and strong that man was! Sculpted muscles . . . Embrace me, my dear love, embrace me!'

The Prisoner of Dream
Giovanni Papini
'The Sick Gentleman's Final Visit' (1906)

He was, truly, *a spreader of fear.* His presence lent fantastic colour to the simplest things – when his hand touched some object, it seemed that this thing became part of the world of dreams. His eyes did not reflect things present, but rather unknown and distant things that those who were with him did not see. No one ever asked him what his evil was and why he seemed not to cure himself of it [. . .]

– I am not a real man. [. . .] I am – and I want to tell you this despite the fact that you may not believe me – nothing less than *a figment of dream.* One of William Shakespeare's images has become literally and tragically exact for me: I *am made of the stuff your dreams are made of!* I exist because there is *someone* who is dreaming me; there is *someone* sleeping and dreaming who sees me act and live and move and in this very moment is dreaming that I am telling you all of this. When *this someone* began dreaming me, I began to exist; when he wakes up I will cease to exist. [. . .]

– But finally I grew tired and humiliated at the thought of having to serve as entertainment for this unknown and unrecognisable master; I realised that fictitious life wasn't worth so much baseness and low flattery. Then I began to ardently wish for that which used to horrify me, in other words that he would wake up. I forced myself to fill my life with spectacles horrifying enough to wake a body up from fear. I tried everything in the attempt to achieve the repose of nothingness; I did everything I could to interrupt this sad comedy of my apparent life, to destroy this ridiculous larva of life that makes me resemble men!

– No crime was unknown to me: no iniquity was new; I drew back from no terrors. I murdered innocent old people with refined torture; I poisoned the waters of an entire city; I burned in the same instant the hair of a multitude of women; rendered savage by my yearning for nothingness, I tore apart with my own teeth all the youngsters I encountered along my way. At night I sought out the companionship of the gigantic, black, whispering monsters that men no longer recognise; I took part in the incredible deeds of gnomes, nightmares, kobolds, phantasms; I dived from the heights of a mountain down into a valley naked and distraught, surrounded by caverns full of bleached bones; and the witches taught me the screams of desolate beasts such as would make the strongest men shudder at night. But it seems that the man who dreams me is not afraid of that which would make the rest of you tremble. Oh appreciate the sight of that which is most horrible to you, otherwise care not and have no fear.

Arturo Martini,
A Portrait of the Marchesa Luisa Casati,
1912,
Milan,
private collection

Arf Arf

Umberto Eco

The Island of the Day Before, 19 (1996)

Well shielded from curious eyes, in an enclosure made to his measure, on a bed of rags, lay a dog.

He was perhaps of good breed, but his suffering and hunger had reduced him to mere skin and bones. And yet his tormentors showed their intentions to keep him alive: they had provided him with abundant food and water, including food surely not canine, subtracted from the passengers' rations.

He was lying on one side, head limp, tongue lolling. On that exposed side gaped a broad and horrible wound. At once fresh and gangrenous, it revealed a pair of great pinkish lips, and in the centre, as along the entire gash, was a purulent secretion resembling whey. Roberto realised that the wound looked as it did because the hand of a chirurgeon, rather than sew the lips together, had deliberately kept them parted and open, attaching them to the outer side.

Bastard offspring of the medical art, that wound had not only been inflicted but wickedly treated so it would not form a scar and the dog would continue suffering – who knows for how long. Further, Roberto saw in and around the wound a crystalline residue, as if a doctor (yes, a doctor, so cruelly expert!) every day sprinkled an irritant salt there. [...] From what Roberto had seen, from what a man with his knowledge could infer, the dog had been wounded in England, and Byrd was making sure he would remain wounded. Someone in London, every day at the same, agreed hour, did something to the guilty weapon, or to a cloth steeped in the animal's blood, provoking a reaction, perhaps of relief, but perhaps of still greater pain, for Dr Byrd himself had said that the Weapon Salve could also harm.

Thus on the *Amaryllis* they could know at a given moment what time it was in Europe. And knowing the hour of their transitory position, they were able to calculate the meridian! [. . .]

The waiting lasted hours, made longer by the moans of the hapless creature, but finally he heard other sounds and discerned lights.

A little later, he found himself witnessing an experiment taking place only a few steps from him, in the presence of the doctor and his three assistants.

'Are you taking notes, Cavendish?'

'Aye, aye, doctor.'

'We will wait then. He is whining too much this evening.'

'It is the sea.'

'Good dog, good old Hakluyt,' the doctor said, calming the animal with some hypocrite petting. 'It was a mistake not to establish a set sequence of actions. We should always begin with the lenitive.'

'Not necessarily, doctor. Some evenings he is asleep at the proper hour and has to be wakened with an irritant.'

'Careful . . . he seems to be stirring . . . Good dog, Hakluyt . . .Yes, he's upset!' The dog was emitting unnatural yelps. 'Then have exposed the weapon to the fire. Are you recording the time, Withrington?'

'It's almost half eleven.'

'Look at the clocks. About ten minutes should go by.'

The dog continued howling for an interminable time. Then he made a different sound, which after an arf arf grew gradually weaker until it was replaced by silence.

'Good,' Dr Byrd was saying. 'Now what time is it, Withrington?'

'It should correspond. A quarter before midnight.' [. . .]

'That seems enough to me. Now, gentlemen,' Dr. Byrd said, 'I hope they stop the irritation at once. Poor Hakluyt cannot bear it. Water and salt, Hawlse, and the cloth. Good dog, Hakluyt, now you're better . . .

'Tomorrow morning, Hawlse, salt on the wound, as usual. Let us sum up, gentlemen. At the crucial moment, here we were close to midnight, and from London they signalled us that it was noon. We are on the antimeridian of London, and therefore on the one-hundred-ninetieth of the Canaries. If the Islands of Solomon, as tradition has it, are on the antimeridian of the Isla de Hierro, and if we are at the correct latitude, sailing towards the west with a following wind, we should land at San Cristoval, or however we choose to rebaptise that ghastly island.' [. . .]

Was the destiny of the world thus affected by the way these madmen interpreted the language of a dog? Could a grumbling in the poor animal's belly make the villains decide that they were approaching or moving away from a place desired by Spanish, French, Dutch Portuguese, all equally villainous?

Sam,
winner of the Ugliest
Dog in the World
Contest,
www.essentialnews.net

Caravaggio,
*Judith Cutting
off the Head of
Holofernes,*
detail,
1599,
Rome, Galleria Nazionale
d'Arte Antica,
Palazzo Barberini

The Black Cat
Edgar Allan Poe
'The Black Cat' (1839)
One night, returning home, much intoxicated, from one of my haunts about town, I fancied that the cat avoided my presence. I seized him; when, in his fright at my violence, he inflicted a slight wound upon my hand with his teeth. The fury of a demon instantly possessed me. I knew myself no longer. My original soul seemed, at once, to take its flight from my body; and a more than fiendish malevolence, gin-nurtured, thrilled every fibre of my frame. I took from my waistcoat-pocket a pen-knife, opened it, grasped the poor beast by the throat, and deliberately cut one of its eyes from the socket! [...]

In the meantime the cat slowly recovered. The socket of the lost eye presented, it is true, a frightful appearance, but he no longer appeared to suffer any pain. He went about the house as usual, but, as might be expected, fled in extreme terror at my approach. I had so much of my old heart left, as to be at first grieved by this evident dislike on the part of a creature which had once so loved me. But this feeling soon gave place to irritation. And then came, as if to my final and irrevocable overthrow, the spirit of PERVERSENESS. Of this spirit philosophy takes no account. Yet I am not more sure that my soul lives, than I am that perverseness is one of the primitive impulses of the human heart – one of the indivisible primary faculties, or sentiments, which give direction to the character of Man. It was this unfathomable longing of the soul to vex itself – to offer violence to its own nature – to do wrong for the wrong's sake only – that urged me to continue and finally to consummate the injury I had inflicted upon the unoffending brute. One morning, in cool blood, I slipped a noose about its neck and hung it to the limb of a tree; – hung it with the tears streaming from my eyes, and with the bitterest remorse at my heart; – hung it because I knew that it had loved me, and because I felt it had given me no reason of offence; – hung it because I knew that in so doing I was committing a sin [...]

Noel Quidu,
The head of a member
of the LURD armed
movement,
2003,
Monrovia

following page
Gaudenzio Ferrari,
*The Martyrdom of Saint
Catherine,*
1539–40,
Milan,
Pinacoteca di Brera

Skulls

Joseph Conrad
Heart of Darkness (1899)

You remember I told you I had been struck at the distance by certain attempts at ornamentation, rather remarkable in the ruinous aspect of the place. Now I had suddenly a nearer view, and its first result was to make me throw my head back as if before a blow. Then I went carefully from post to post with my glass, and I saw my mistake. These round knobs were not ornamental but symbolic; they were expressive and puzzling, striking and disturbing – food for thought and also for vultures if there had been any looking down from the sky; but at all events for such ants as were industrious enough to ascend the pole. They would have been even more impressive, those heads on the stakes, if their faces had not been turned to the house. Only one, the first I had made out, was facing my way. I was not so shocked as you may think. The start back I had given was really nothing but a movement of surprise. I had expected to see a knob of wood there, you know. I returned deliberately to the first I had seen – and there it was, black, dried, sunken, with closed eyelids – a head that seemed to sleep at the top of that pole, and, with the shrunken dry lips showing a narrow white line of the teeth, was smiling, too, smiling continuously at some endless and jocose dream of that eternal slumber.

[...]

Curious, this feeling that came over me that such details would be more intolerable than those heads drying on the stakes under Mr Kurtz's windows. After all, that was only a savage sight, while I seemed at one bound to have been transported into some lightless region of subtle horrors, where pure, uncomplicated savagery was a positive relief, being something that had a right to exist – obviously – in the sunshine.

In the Penal Colony
Franz Kafka

'In the Penal Colony' (1919)
'However,' the Officer said, interrupting himself, 'I'm chattering, and his apparatus stands in front of us. As you see, it consists of three parts. With the passage of time certain popular names have been developed for each of these parts. The one underneath is called the Bed, the upper one is called the Inscriber, and here in the middle, this moving part is called the Harrow.' (. . .)

'So now, only the most important things. When the man is lying on the Bed and it starts quivering, the Harrow sinks onto the body. It positions itself automatically in such a way that it touches the body only lightly with the needle tips. Once the machine is set in this position, this steel cable tightens up into a rod. And now the performance begins.

'Someone who is not an initiate sees no external difference among the punishments. The Harrow seems to do its work uniformly. As it quivers, it sticks the tips of its needles into the body, which is also vibrating from the movement of the bed. Now, to enable someone to check on how the sentence is being carried out, the Harrow is made of glass. That gave rise to certain technical difficulties with fastening the needles securely, but after several attempts we were successful. We didn't spare any efforts. And now, as the inscription is made on the body, everyone can see through the glass. Don't you want to come closer and see the needles for yourself.' The Traveller stood slowly, moved up, and bent over the Harrow. 'You see,' the Officer said, 'two sorts of needles in a multiple arrangement. Each long needle has a short one next to it. The long one inscribes, and the short one squirts water out to wash away the blood and keep the inscription always clear. The bloody water is then channelled here in small grooves and finally flows into these main gutters, and the outlet pipe takes it to the pit.' The Officer pointed with his finger to the exact path which the bloody water had to take. (. . .)

'Now I know all about it,' said the Traveller, as the Officer turned back to him again. 'Except the most important thing,' said the latter, grabbing the Traveller by the arm and pointing up high. 'There in the Inscriber is the mechanism which determines the movement of the Harrow, and this mechanism is arranged according to the diagram on which the sentence is set down. I still use the diagrams of the previous Commandant. Here they are.' He pulled some pages out of the leather folder. 'Unfortunately I can't hand them to you. They are the most cherished thing I possess. Sit down, and I'll show you them from this distance. Then you'll be able to see it all well.' He showed the first sheet. The Traveller would have been happy to say something appreciative, but all he saw was a labyrinthine series of lines, criss-crossing each other in all sort of ways. These covered the paper so thickly that only with difficulty could one make out the white spaces in between. 'Read it,' said the Officer. 'I can't,' said the Traveller. 'But it's clear,' said the Officer. It's very elaborate,' said the Traveller evasively, 'but I can't decipher it.'

'Yes,' said the Officer, smiling and putting the folder back again, 'it's not calligraphy for school children. One has to read it a long time. You too will finally understand it clearly. Of course, it has to be a script that isn't simple. You see, it's not supposed to kill right away, but on average over a period of twelve hours. The turning point is set for the sixth hour. There must also be many, many embellishments surrounding the basic script. The essential script moves around the body only in a narrow belt. The rest of the body is reserved for decoration. [. . .]

'Do you understand the process? The Harrow is starting to write. When it's finished with the first part of the script on the man's back, the layer of cotton wool rolls slowly onto the body slowly onto its side to give the Harrow a new area. [. . .] In this way it keeps making the inscription deeper for twelve hours. For the first six hours the condemned man goes on living almost as before. He suffers nothing but pain. After two hours, the felt is removed, for at that point the man has no more energy for screaming. Here at the head of the Bed warm rice pudding is put in this electrically heated bowl. From this the man, if he feels like it, can help himself to what he can lap up with his tongue. No one passes up this opportunity. I don't know of a single one, and I have had a lot of experience. He first loses his pleasure in eating around the sixth hour. I usually kneel down at this point and observe the phenomenon. The man rarely swallows the last bit. He turns it around in his mouth and spits it into the pit. When he does that, I have to lean aside or else he'll get me in the face. But how quiet the man becomes around the sixth hour! The most stupid of them begin to understand. It starts around the eyes and spreads out from there. A look that could tempt one to lie down under the Harrow. Nothing else happens. The man simply begins to decipher the inscription. He purses his lips, as if he is listening. You've seen that it's not easy to figure out the inscription with your eyes, but our man deciphers it with his wounds. True, it takes a lot of work. It requires six hours to complete. But then the Harrow spits him right out and throws him into the pit, where he splashes down into the bloody water and cotton wool. Then the judgement is over, and we, the Soldier and I, quickly bury him.'

Pier Paolo Pasolini
(director),
*Salò and the 120
Days of Sodom*,
1975

Room 101

George Orwell

1984, Part Three, 3, 5 (1949)

'Do anything to me!' he yelled. 'You've been starving me for weeks. Finish it off and let me die. Shoot me. Hang me. Sentence me to twenty-five years. Is there somebody else you want me to give away? Just say who it is and I'll tell you anything you want. I don't care who it is or what you do to them. I've got a wife and three children. The biggest of them isn't six years old. You can take the whole lot of them and cut their throats in front of my eyes, and I'll stand by and watch it. But not Room 101!'

'Room 101,' said the officer.

The man looked frantically round at the other prisoners, as though with some idea that he could put another victim in his own place. His eyes settled on the smashed face of the chinless man. He flung out a lean arm. 'That's the one you ought to be taking, not me!' he shouted. 'You didn't hear what he was saying after they bashed his face. Give me a chance and I'll tell you every word of it. He's the one that's against the Party, not me.' […] The two sturdy guards had stooped to take him by the arms. But just at this moment he flung himself across the floor of the cell and grabbed one of the iron legs that supported the bench. […]

Then there was a different kind of cry. A kick from a guard's boot had broken the fingers of one of his hands. They dragged him to his feet. […]

'You asked me once,' said O'Brien, 'what was in Room 101. I told you that you knew the answer already. Everyone knows it. The thing that is in Room 101 is the worst thing in the world.'

The door opened again. A guard came in, carrying something made of wire, a box or basket of some kind. He set it down on the further table. Because of the position in which O'Brien was standing, Winston could not see what the thing was.

'The worst thing in the world,' said O'Brien, 'varies from individual to individual. It may be burial alive, or death by fire, or by drowning, or impalement, or fifty other deaths. There are cases where it is some quite trivial thing, not even fatal.'

He had moved a little to one side, so that Winston had a better view of the thing on the table. It was an oblong wire cage with a handle on top for carrying it by. Fixed to the front of it was something that looked like a fencing mask, with the concave side outwards. Although it was three or four metres away from him, he could see that the cage was divided lengthways into two compartments, and that there was some kind of creature in each. They were rats. 'In your case,' said O'Brien, 'the worst thing in the world happens to be rats.'

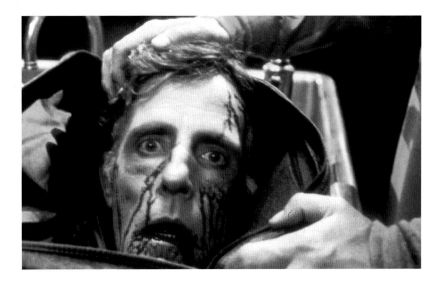

Stuart Gordon (director), *Re-Animator*, 1985

Devoured by Sharks

Ian Fleming

Live and Let Die (1954)

Once he saw a great snout come out of the water and smash down on something. The fins threw up spray as they flashed among the tidbits. Two black arms suddenly stuck up in the air and then disappeared. There were screams. Two or three pairs of arms started to flail the water towards the reef. One man stopped to bang the water in front of him with the flat of his hand. Then his hands disappeared under the surface. Then he too began to scream and his body jerked to and fro in the water. Barracuda hitting into him, said Bond's dazed mind. [...]

It was a large head and a veil of blood streamed down over the face from a wound in the great bald skull.

Bond watched it come on.

The Big Man was executing a blundering breast-stroke, making enough flurry in the water to attract any fish that wasn't already occupied. [...]

The surging head came nearer. Bond could see the teeth showing in a rictus of agony and frenzied endeavour. Blood half veiled the eyes that Bond knew would be bulging in their sockets. He could almost hear the great diseased heart thumping under the grey-black skin. [...]

The Big Man came on. His shoulders were naked, his clothes stripped off him by the explosion, Bond supposed, but the black silk tie had remained and it

showed around the thick neck and streamed behind the head like a Chinaman's pigtail.

A splash of water cleared some blood away from the eyes. They were wide open, staring madly towards Bond. They held no appeal for help, only a fixed glare of physical exertion.

Even as Bond looked into them, now only ten yards away, they suddenly shut and the great face contorted in a grimace of pain.

'Aarh,' said the distorted mouth.

Both arms stopped flailing the water and the head went under and came up again. A cloud of blood welled up and darkened the sea. Two six-foot thin brown shadows backed out of the cloud and then dashed back into it. The body in the water jerked sideways. Half of the Big Man's left arm came out of the water. It had no hand, no wrist, no wristwatch.

But the great turnip head, the drawn-back mouth full of white teeth almost splitting it in half was still alive. And now it was screaming, a long gurgling scream that only broke each time a barracuda hit into the dangling body. [...]

The head floated back to the surface. The mouth was closed. The yellow eyes seemed still to look at Bond.

Then the shark's snout came right out of the water and it drove in towards the head, the lower curved jaw open so that light glinted on the teeth. There was a horrible grunting scrunch and a great swirl of water. Then silence.

Chapter IX

Physica curiosa

1. Lunar Births and Disembowelled Corpses

above
D.C. Courcelles,
*Icones musculorum
capitis*,
1743

left
Lavinia Fontana,
*Portrait of Antonietta
Gonzales*, oil on canvas,
1594–95,
Blois,
Musée du Chateau
de Blois

Monsters did not disappear with the medieval *mirabilia*, but returned in the modern world, albeit in another form and with another function. Since the Middle Ages, there have been debates about the difference between the two kinds of monstrosity that, if abstracted from many terminological variables, we might define as *portents* and *monsters*. Portents were amazing and prodigious but natural events (like the birth of hermaphroditic or two-headed babies). Many authors have tried to explain the cause of such things (for example, Renaissance doctors like Ambroise Paré, whom we will come across later), although it was apparently hard not to see them (as the ancients had done) as premonitory signs of some extraordinary event – and in this sense the *Prodigiorum ac ostentorum chronicon* of Conrad Lycosthenes (1557) is still a celebrated example.

In any event, right from the first centuries of the Middle Ages, it was maintained that portents were not to be considered as against nature (as if they had eluded divine control) but, and this was the view of Isidore of Seville, *against nature as we know it*. In antiquity and the Middle Ages the real monsters were non-human individuals born in the normal way to parents who were the same as them (as we saw in Chapter IV) and permitted or wanted by God to serve as signs of some allegorical message on his part. From the Renaissance onwards, as voyages of exploration began to open up other continents, inhabited by savages and very strange animals (but all of which could be imported into the courts of Europe), but not by legendary monsters never encountered in reality, the word monster came to stand for portentous individuals, whether products of anomalous births, or unusual animals that explorers and travellers came across.

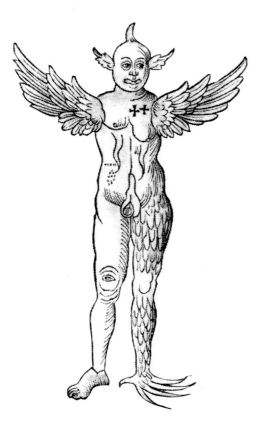

The Monster of Ravenna
Luca Landucci
Florentine Diary (1512)
In Ravenna a woman gave birth to a
monster, of which we give a drawing here;
it had a horn on its head, standing straight
up like a sword, and instead of arms it
had two wings like a bat's, and on a level
with the breasts it had a Y-shaped mark
on one side and a cross on the other, and
lower down at the waist, two serpents,
and where the natural organs are it was
both male and female; its upper body was
female and the lower body male. On the
right knee it had an eye, and its left foot
was like an eagle's talons. I saw it painted,
and anyone who wanted to could see this
painting in Florence.

Monster in the Form of a Monk
Ambroise Paré
On Monsters and Marvels (1573)
In his book *On Fish*, Rondelet says that in
the sea off Norway they saw a sea
monster that, when it was caught,
everyone called the 'monk', because that's
what it looked like.

The attitude towards these creatures was no longer fright or an attempt
to decipher their mystical significance, but of *scientific curiosity*, or at least
pre-scientific curiosity, and I chose to call this chapter 'Physica Curiosa'
because that was the title of a monumental work (1,600 pages with dozens
and dozens of engravings) published by the Jesuit Caspar Schott in 1662,
which contains a description of all the natural monstrosities known at the
time. These were exotic animals like elephants and giraffes, freaks of nature,
and certain creatures that the sailors or travellers who saw them from a
distance (and who superimposed upon them memories of tales about
legendary monsters) found reminiscent of monsters of the bestiaries. As a
result dugongs were taken for mermaids or sirens.

On the other hand, in similar texts, on many occasions the illuminator or
engraver made literal interpretations of the names, already bizarre in
themselves, given by Pliny and others, and so the seal (*Vitulus marinus*) became
a sort of fish-shaped veal calf, the crustacean (*Mus marinus*) a mouse with fins,
the octopus a fish with legs, while the ostrich (*Struthio camelus*) became a
winged camel. Among the many books on monsters we might mention *Des
monstres et prodiges* by Ambroise Paré (1573), the *Monstrorum historia* by Ulisse
Aldrovandi (1642) and *De monstris* by Fortunato Liceti (the first edition of
which came out in 1616). But Aldrovandi's eleven volumes dealt with zoology
in general and other authors had worked along the same lines.

Ulisse Aldrovandi,
Monstrum foemina,
in *Monstrorum Historia,*
1658,
Bolgona, Ferroni

Ambroise Paré,
'Bishop fish', in *Opera chirurgica,*
1594,
Frankfurt, Feyerabend

Fundamental contributions to the development of the biological sciences (even though they contained representations of monstrous creatures) were made by Conrad Gessner's *Historium animalium* (1551–58) and Johann Johnston's *Historia naturalis* (1653), just to name two. In the same period this interest in extraordinary things led to the advent of the *Wunderkammern,* or wonder cabinets, the forerunners of our natural science museums, where rather than try to collect systematically all the things that ought to be known, people tended to collect things that struck them as extraordinary or unheard of, including bizarre objects such as the horns of unicorns (usually narwhal horns) or stuffed crocodiles. In many of these collections, such as the one put together by Peter the Great in St Petersburg, monstrous foetuses were carefully preserved in spirits.

Sometimes, the discovery of an anomalous birth caused a chain reaction, as happened with the Monster of Ravenna. This creature was probably born in Florence in 1506, and, after the first news of it was given by Landucci in 1512, it triggered a series of portrayals that became more and more similar to the monsters of the old legends. Similar marvels were dealt with by authors such as **Paré**, whom we have already mentioned, **Montaigne**, **Lemnius** and others, and in all these cases it would appear that the spectacle of deformity was not seen as disgusting, but as intellectually exciting.

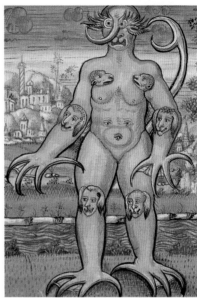

Ulisse Aldrovandi,
Monstro tribum capitis,
in *Monstrorum Historia,*
1698,
Bologna, Ferroni

Pierre Boaistuau
'A monstrous creature
engendered by
respectable parents',
in *Prodigious Stories,*
French ms. 136, f.29v,
sixteenth century,
London,
Wellcome Library

facing page,
Edvard Munch,
Heredity I,
1897–99,
Oslo, Munch Museet

The Origin of Monsters

Ambroise Paré

On Monsters and Marvels (1573)

Various causes give rise to monsters. The first is the glory of God. The second is His wrath. The third, a superabundance of semen. The fourth, an insufficient quantity of it. The fifth, the imagination. The sixth, hypertrophy, or the reduced dimensions of the uterus. The seventh, an incorrect way of sitting on the mother's part, for example when she is pregnant and spends too much time sitting with legs crossed or pulled up towards her belly. The eighth, on account of a fall or as a result of blows to the belly of the pregnant woman. The ninth, hereditary or accidental illnesses. The tenth, the putrefaction or corruption of the semen. The eleventh, the mixing or blending of semen. The twelfth, deceit on the part of wicked scoundrels. The thirteenth, demons or devils.

On a Monstrous Child

Michel de Montaigne

Essays, II, 30 (1595)

Two days ago I saw a child that two men and a nurse, who said they were the father, the uncle, and the aunt of it, carried about to get money by showing it, by reason it was so strange a creature. It was, as to all the rest, of a common form, and could stand upon its feet; could go and gabble much like other children of the same age; it had never as yet taken any other nourishment but from the nurse's breasts, and what, in my presence, they tried to put

into the mouth of it, it only chewed a little and spat it out again without swallowing; the cry of it seemed indeed a little odd and particular, and it was just fourteen months old. Under the breast it was joined to another child, but without a head, and which had the spine of the back without motion, the rest entire; for though it had one arm shorter than the other, it had been broken by accident at their birth; they were joined breast to breast, and as if a lesser child sought to throw its arms about the neck of one something bigger. The juncture and thickness of the place where they were conjoined was not above four fingers, or thereabouts, so that if you thrust up the imperfect child you might see the navel of the other below it, and the joining was betwixt the paps and the navel. The navel of the imperfect child could not be seen, but all the rest of the belly, so that all that was not joined of the imperfect one, as arms, buttocks, thighs, and legs, hung dangling upon the other, and might reach to the mid-leg. The nurse, moreover, told us that it urined at both bodies, and that the members of the other were nourished, sensible, and in the same plight with that she gave suck to, excepting that they were shorter and less [. . .]

Those that we call monsters are not so to God, who sees in the immensity of His work the infinite forms that He has comprehended therein; and it is to be believed that this figure which astonishes us has relation to some other figure of the same kind unknown to man.

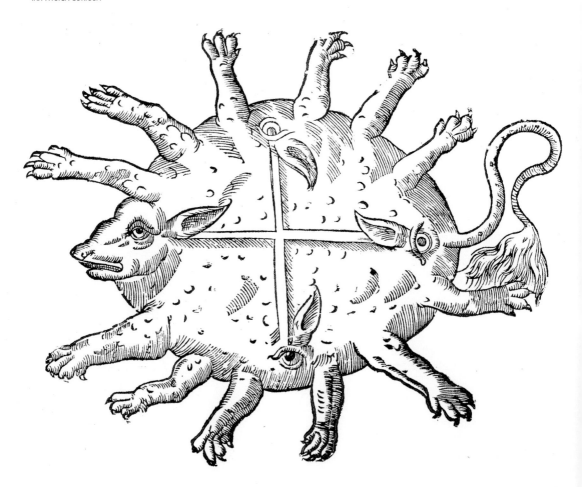

Ambroise Paré,
*On Monsters
and Prodigies,*
1573, Paris

With Twelve Paws

Ambroise Paré

On Monsters and Marvels (1573)

I have found in the *Description of Africa* by Leo Africanus a monstrously formed animal, like a tortoise. On its back there are two lines that meet at right angles in the form of a cross and at the extremity of each line there is an eye and an ear. Consequently these animals see and hear in four directions and on all sides with their four eyes and four ears. In addition they have only one mouth and one stomach, into which their food and drink descends. These beasts have many feet around their bodies thanks to which they can walk in any direction they wish without having to turn round. Their tails are very long and the tips are covered in thick hair. The inhabitants of that country say that the blood of these creatures has an extraordinary power to heal wounds and that no balsam has the power to do this better. But who would not be amazed on contemplating this animal with so many eyes, ears, and feet and [on seeing] that each of these carries out its appointed task? As far as I am concerned, to tell the truth, I have lost my reason and cannot say anything else, if not that Nature made it for sport in order to admire the greatness of its works.

Hydrocephalous Baby,
etching,
late eighteenth century

Lunar Birth

Levinus Lemnius (sixteenth century)
The Secret Miracles of Nature
Similar to this [abortion] is another flux that comes to women with much painful and convulsive writhing of the body, in which emerge many formless fleshy things, which is called lunar birth since a woman gets pregnant during the new moon when the flow of blood inside her is very great. This monstrous and ugly conception sometimes occurs without the help of a man, and usually occurs in very libidinous women whose powerfully active imaginations ensure that they need only stare at or touch a man and semen mixes with her menstrual blood and the result is a lump of flesh that looks like [. . .] a living creature [. . .] Some years ago I treated a woman who had been made pregnant by a sailor [. . .]; the space of nine months having gone by and the midwife having been called in, the woman first expelled with great effort a mass of completely formless flesh, which I believed to have been engendered after the legitimate coupling. But it had two long pieces of flesh resembling arms and, by palpitating, it revealed that it possessed some form of life, not unlike the jellyfish and foam that can be seen floating in the Ocean in the summer [. . .] After this piece of flesh she gave birth to a monster with a round, long neck, a twisted, hooked snout, frightening shining eyes, a sharp pointed tail and very fast on its feet. As soon as this monster emerged and saw the light, it instantly set to shrieking, and emitting the most terrible sounds, it ran here and there about the room seeking a place to hide. But the women in attendance seized up some pillows and threw them over it, and smothered it.

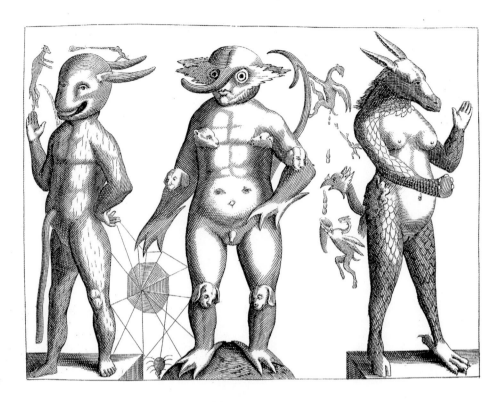

Fortunato Liceti,
From *De monstris*,
1668,
Pavia, Frambotti

Caspar Schott,
From *Physica curiosa*,
1662,
Würzburg, Endter

Ulisse Aldrovandi,
*Monstrum marinum
rudimenta habitus
episcopi referens*,
in *Monstrorum Historia*,
1698,
Bologna, Ferroni

Ulisse Aldrovandi,
*Monstrum marinum
humana facie*,
in *Monstrorum Historia*,
1698,
Bologna, Ferroni

In those same centuries culture had become familiar with the inside of the human body. Whereas the first anatomical experiments had already begun in the fourteenth century with Mondino de' Liuzzi, it was only from the Renaissance onwards, and notably with Vesalius's *On the Structure of the Human Body*, complete with splendid and blood-chilling images of creatures that had been skinned, reduced to a skeleton or a mere network of nerves and veins, that art turned its attention to the bodies dissected in the anatomy theatres, while shocking exhibitions of internal organs enjoyed a hyperrealistic triumph in the anatomical waxwork museums. Artists began to portray with undoubted satisfaction the 'Hippocratic face', which heralds the advent of death on the face of the dying, but now the grimacing of the moribund excited painters and sculptors in the same way as they reacted to the devastated features of the incurably ill. There is a passage in Schlegel (*On the Study of Greek Poetry*, 1797) in which he suggests that this new attention to the less pleasing aspects of the human body is in some way similar to the Shakespearean style: 'As it is in nature, Shakespeare creates the beautiful and the ugly without separating them and with the same exuberant abundance; none of his plays are *entirely* beautiful, and beauty is never the criterion that determines the structure of the whole. As it is in nature, only rarely are single beauties free of *impurities* [...] Shakespeare strips away the flesh from his subjects and uses the surgeon's scalpel to probe into the disgusting putrescence of the moral cadaver.' 249

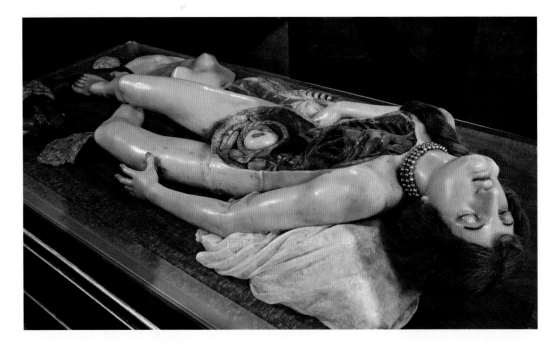

Clemente Susini,
Modular statue
of a young woman
showing the
cardiorespiratory,
digestive, and urogenital
apparatus (Venerina),
late eighteenth century,
Bologna, Institute
of Human Anatomy

facing page,
Gérard David,
The Flaying of Sisamnes,
1498,
Bruges, Groeninge
Museum

The Hippocratic Face

Hippocrates (fourth century BC)
The Book of Prognostics, 2
He should observe thus in acute diseases:
first, the countenance of the patient, if it
be like those of persons in health, and
more so, if like itself, for this is the best
of all; whereas the most opposite to it is
the worst, such as the following; a sharp
nose, hollow eyes, collapsed temples; the
ears cold, contracted, and their lobes
turned out: the skin about the forehead
being rough, distended, and parched; the
colour of the whole face being green,
black, livid, or lead-coloured. If the
countenance be such at the
commencement of the disease, and if this
cannot be accounted for from the other
symptoms, enquiry must be made
whether the patient has long wanted
sleep; whether his bowels have been
very loose; and whether he has suffered
from want of food; and if any of these
causes be confessed to, the danger is to
be reckoned so far less; and it becomes
obvious, in the course of a day and a
night, whether or not the appearance of
the countenance proceeded from these
causes. But if none of these be said to
exist, if the symptoms do not subside in
the aforesaid time, it is to be known for
certain that death is at hand. And, also, if
the disease be in a more advanced stage

either on the third or fourth day, and the
countenance be such, the same enquiries
as formerly directed are to be made, and
the other symptoms are to be noted,
those in the whole countenance, those
on the body, and those in the eyes; for if
they shun the light, or weep
involuntarily, or squint, or if the one be
less than the other, or if the white of
them be red, livid, or has black veins in
it; if there be a gum upon the eyes, if
they are restless, protruding, or are
become very hollow; and if the
countenance be squalid and dark, or the
colour of the whole face be changed –
all these are to be reckoned bad and fatal
symptoms. The physician should also
observe the appearance of the eyes from
below the eyelids in sleep; for when a
portion of the white appears, owing to
the eyelids not being closed together,
and when this is not connected with
diarrhoea or purgation from medicine, or
when the patient does not sleep thus
from habit, it is to be reckoned an
unfavourable and very deadly symptom;
but if the eyelid be contracted, livid, or
pale, or also the lip, or nose, along with
some of the other symptoms, one may
know for certain that death is close at
hand. It is a mortal symptom, also, when
the lips are relaxed, pendent, cold, and
blanched.

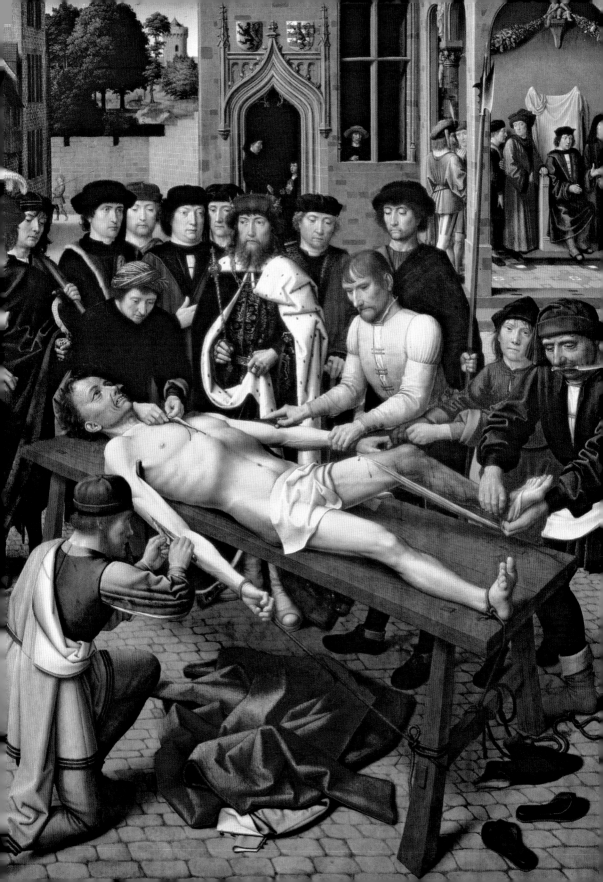

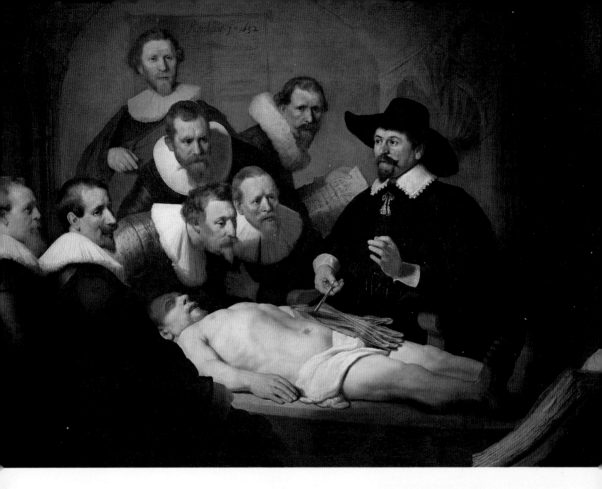

Rembrandt,
*The Anatomy Lesson
of Nicolaes Tulp*,
1632,
The Hague, Mauritshuis

Andrea Vesalius,
*De humani corporis
fabrica*,
1568,
Venice, Criegher

facing page
William Hogarth,
The Reward of Cruelty
from *The Four Stages
of Cruelty*, table IV,
1799,
Paris, Musée d'Histoire
de la Médécine

following pages
Gaetano Zumbo,
The Plague,
1691–94,
Florence,
Museo della Specula

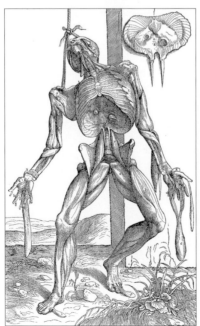

The Autopsy

Charles Baudelaire (on Hogarth)
'Some Foreign Caricaturists' (1861)
One of the oddest, certainly, is the one
that shows us a corpse flattened, rigid and
stretched out on a dissecting table. On a
pulley or some such mechanism, fastened
to the ceiling, the intestines of the rake's
corpse are being unwound. This dead
man is horrible to see, and nothing could
produce a more singular contrast with the
corpse, cadaverous above all corpses, than
the high foreheads, the long scraggy or
rotund faces, grotesquely serious, of all
these British doctors, in their enormous
curled wigs. In a corner, a dog greedily
sticks his snout into a bucket and filches a
few human bits from it. Hogarth, the
death of the comic! I would rather say he
is the comic in death. This cannibalistic
dog has always made me dwell in my
mind on that historic pig that got
shamelessly drunk on the blood of the
hapless Fualdès, whilst the barrel-organ
ground out the funeral service, so to
speak, of the dying man.

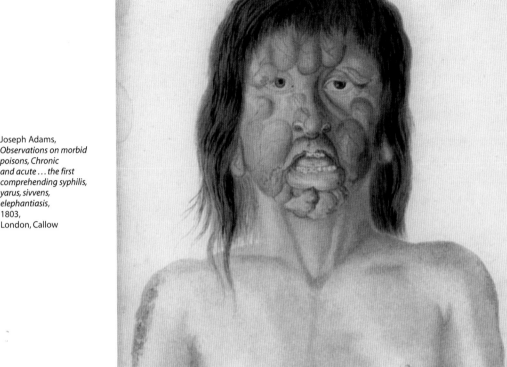

Joseph Adams,
*Observations on morbid
poisons, Chronic
and acute … the first
comprehending syphilis,
yarus, sivvens,
elephantiasis,*
1803,
London, Callow

Syphilis

Karl Rosenkrantz

The Aesthetics of Ugliness, 'Introduction'
(1853)

Illness is always a cause of ugliness when it involves the deformation of bones, skeleton, or muscle, as when the bones swell up in syphilis, and in the devastation of gangrene. It also leads to ugliness when it colours the skin, as in jaundice; when it covers the skin with a rash, as in scarlet fever, plague, certain forms of syphilis, leprosy, herpes, and trachoma. But there is no doubt that the most horrendous deformities are caused by syphilis because this disease does not merely cause nauseating eruptions on the skin, but also putrescent sores and devastating bone damage. Exanthemas and abscesses are assimilable to the sand worm, which digs its tunnels under the skin; they are, to a certain extent, parasitical individuals, whose existence contradicts the nature of the organism as a unity and in which it disintegrates. The sight of a similar contradiction is therefore extremely ugly. In general, illness is a cause of ugliness when it modifies form in an abnormal manner: this is also the case with dropsy, tympanitis, and so on. But this is not the case when – in cachexia, tuberculosis, and fever – it gives the organism a transcendent air that makes it seem ethereal. Weight loss, the burning gaze, pale cheeks or those reddened by fever afford a more immediate glimpse of the essence of the spirit. It is as if the spirit were already separated from the organism. It still dwells within it, but only to transform it into pure sign. The body with its transparent 'softness' is already emptied of significance, it is wholly and entirely an expression of the spirit that is about to leave it, independently of nature. What a truly luminous sight it is to see a young girl or a young man on their death bed, victims of tuberculosis: nothing of this kind is possible among animals. For the same reasons, death does not necessarily always make the features of the face ugly; it can also leave behind it a beautiful, blissful expression.

2. Physiognomy

An important chapter in any history of ugliness is the question of physiognomy, a pseudoscience that associated facial features (and the form of other organs) with character and moral disposition. Aristotle (in the *Prior Analytics*, II, 70b) observed that large extremities are the external sign of leonine courage and he concluded that a man with big feet could only be courageous. During the Renaissance, Barthélemy Coclès (*Physiognomonia*, 1533) drew the foreheads of irascible, cruel and avaricious men, and even portrayed the beard typical of a brutal, domineering man; Jean d'Indagine (*Chiromancer*, 1549) showed how cruel men have protruding teeth and how the eyes could make it possible to recognise licentious, traitorous and mendacious types. In *On Human Physiognomy* (1586) Giovan Battista della Porta compares the faces of various animals with human faces, bequeathing us fascinating pictures of sheep-men, lion-men, and donkey-men, starting from the philosophical persuasion that the divine power manifested its regulating wisdom even in physical features, thus establishing analogies between the human and animal worlds.

Further, convinced that subtle harmonies existed between body and mind, and that virtue embellishes where vice deforms, Johann Kaspar Lavater (*Physiognomische Fragmente*, 1775–78) also examined the lineaments of historical personages.

Petit Bernard
'The mouths
of audacious, bold,
shameless and
mendacious men',
etching, in Jean
d'Indagine,
Chiromancer,
1549,
Lyon

Temperaments and the Soul

Giovan Battista della Porta
On the Physiognomy of Man, I, 6
(1610)

The signs of a cold temperament: flesh that feels glabrous, fat, and cold to those who touch it; ruddy flesh and hair; and, when the temperament is very cold, a bluish colour, some say pallid. Other signs are narrow veins, and whitish eyes. Others add that those with a cold temperament develop late; have occult, sluggish breathing; a firm, shrill voice. Poor at running, they eat little [. . .] The hair is long, fine, and delicate [. . .] The signs of a moist temperament are: a full, fleshy body, soft and smooth, with occult joints: Such people sleep little. Parts that are usually hairy have little hair, the eyes weep easily, and the hair is blond. Other signs are: whitish eyes; weak natures; hidden joints and cavities. Not very strong, such people cannot bear effort, and so they immediately become soft, corpulent, weak, hairless, and sleep a lot.

Pointed Head

Giovan Battista della Porta
On the Physiognomy of Man, II, 1
(1610)

According to Polemon and Adamantius, the insensate fool has a narrow, pointed head. And those with a pointed head have no sense of shame. Alberto says: a head too dishonestly long is a sign of effrontery, and of insolence if the head is long in front. And if it is legitimate to compare this [shape] with some animal, it resembles birds with curved talons. But I reckon that these birds with curved talons are crows and quails, which have pointed heads and are most impudent.

High, Rounded Brow

Giovan Battista della Porta
On the Physiognomy of Man, II, 2
(1610)

Those with high rounded brows are stupid and their intelligence can be compared to that of the Ass, as Aristotle says in his *Physiognomy*. So if you observe the brow of the ass you will see that it is high, rounded and gibbous [. . .] In

addition, Aristotle does not only attribute the ignoramus with a rounded brow, but a large, fleshy one too. Polemon and Adamantius, most excellent Physiognomists, so that none may be deceived, use very clear language: the high, gibbous, rounded brow reveals the stupid, ignorant man. And they add that the ignorant man has a rounded brow. Alberto says that the high, rounded brow is a sign of stolidity.

Thick Lips

Giovan Battista della Porta
On the Physiognomy of Man, II, 12
(1610)

Thick slips reveal stupidity, as Aristotle wrote to Alexander. At the end of the book Polemon says: thick lips demonstrate ignorance. Conciliatore says: thick lips are a mark of the stupid and the ignorant. Aesop had thick, protruding lips, as Planudes said. Those who have thick lips [. . .] are considered ignorant, because thus are the lips of the Ass and the Ape. In fact the lower lips of Asses and Apes protrude more than their upper lips [. . .]

Agostino Carraci,
*Arrigo Peloso, Pietro
Matto e Amor Nano*,
1598–1600,
Naples,
Museo di Capodimonte

facing page
Giovan Battista
Della Porta,
*De humana
physiognomonia*,
1586,
Vico Equense, Cacchio

In the course of that same century there appeared Franz Joseph Gall's *Phrenology*: all the mental faculties, the instincts and the feelings are represented on the surface of the brain, and, for example, those gifted with outstanding memories have a round cranium with eyes set flush to the face and far apart. In his own way Gall anticipated research on the pinpointing of the various brain areas, but by going in search for *cranial bumps* that purported to express the predominance of one or the other faculty. Accused of materialism, his ideas led to scientific and philosophical disputes, and, in the *Phenomenology of Mind* (1807) Hegel remarked sarcastically: 'natural phrenology does not only think that a shrewd man should have a protuberance as big as a fist behind his ears, but also that an unfaithful wife must have, not on her face, but on that of her legitimate spouse, protuberances on the forehead.' Hegel admitted that, at most, the conformation of the cranium established an initial predisposition, but denied that this could prevail over spiritual activity, the only active force capable of defining the brain in which it resides. Both Gall and Hegel went too far in maintaining their positions unilaterally, but we must give Hegel credit for having perceived that, if we take physiognomic features too seriously, we risk branding an individual or a race in an irremediable fashion.

An image taken
from Gaspar Lavater,
*The Art of Knowing Men
from Physiognomy,*
vol. IX,
1735,
Paris, Depelafol

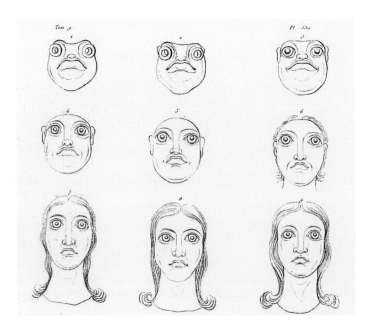

The Born Criminal

Cesare Lombroso

The Criminal Man, III, 1 (1876)

Many characteristics of primitive men, the coloured races, are very frequently found in born criminals. These include, for example, scant body hair, minimal cranial capacity, a receding forehead, highly developed frontal sinuses, greater frequency of wormian bones, especially the epactal ossicles, precocious synostoses, especially frontal synostoses, a prominently arched temporal bone, simplicity of the sutural bones, thicker cranial bones, massively overdeveloped jaws and cheekbones, prognathism, oblique eyes, darker skin, thicker, curlier hair, large ears; we may add the Lemurian appendix, anomalies of the ear, increased volume of the facial bones, dental diastema, great agility, poorly developed tactile sense and a high pain threshold, sharp eyesight, a certain incapacity for affection, a precocious tendency to wine and the pleasures of the flesh and an excessive passion for both [. . .], less chance of correction in women (Spencer), insensitivity to pain, complete moral insensitivity, idleness, the absence of any remorse, impulsiveness, psycho-physical excitability, and above all recklessness, which looks like courage at times, and courage that alternates with baseness, enormous vanity, a passion for gambling, alcohol, or surrogates for these, passions as fleeting as they are violent, superstitious by nature, excessively touchy about his own *ego* and even the relative concept of divinity and morality.

'Different criminal types',
in Cesare Lombroso,
The Criminal Man,
1876,
Turin, F.lli Bocca

Nonetheless, in the positivist nineteenth century, the field of criminal anthropology witnessed the success of the ideas of Cesare Lombroso, who in his *Criminal Man* tried to show how the traits of the criminal personality were always associated with somatic anomalies. Lombroso didn't simplify things to the point of saying that ugly people are always criminals, but he did associate physical stigmata with moral stigmata, employing arguments that purported to be scientific. At least as far as concerns the popularisation of these theories, it was easy not to pay sufficient attention to the fact that many hereditary taints were found more frequently in social classes afflicted by malnutrition and other disorders, and that asocial behaviour was obviously more frequent among these social outcasts. From here to the encouragement of the prejudice whereby 'ugly people are bad by nature' is but a short step. Not to mention the next step, in which – even in popular literature – labels like ugly and bad are applied to all those pariahs whom society cannot integrate or control or does not intend to redeem – as **Nietzsche** once said about Socrates. This was the lot of the poor. Just consider the ruthless portrait of the little proletarian Franti made by **De Amicis**. Equally merciless treatment was reserved for homosexuals (see **Foucault**), the demented and prostitutes, inexorably marked by their vice (see **Rosenkranz**), and thieves (see **Mastriani**).

Hugh Welch Diamond,
Portraits of Madwomen,
c.1852–5 3,
Paris, Musée d'Orsay

Thomas Couture,
The Madman,
nineteenth century,
Dijon, Musée Magnin

The Birth of the Homosexual
Michel Foucault
The History of Sexuality, II, 2 (1976)
The nineteenth-century homosexual became a personage, a past, a case history, and a childhood, in addition to being a type of life, a life form and a morphology, with an indiscreet anatomy and possibly a mysterious physiology. Nothing that went into his total composition was unaffected by his sexuality. It was everywhere present in him: at the root of all his actions because it was their insidious and indefinitely active principle; written immodestly on his face because it was a secret that always gave itself away.

It was consubstantial with him, less as a habitual sin than as a singular nature [. . .] Homosexuality appeared as one of the forms of sexuality when it was transposed from the practice of sodomy onto a kind of interior androgyny, a hermaphrodism of the soul. The sodomite had been a relapsed criminal; the homosexual was now a species.

Nietzschean Physiognomy
Friedrich Nietzsche
'The Problem of Socrates' (1911)
To judge from his origin, Socrates belonged to the lowest of the low: Socrates was the mob. You know, and you can still see it for yourself, how ugly he was. [. . .] Ugliness is not infrequently the expression of thwarted development, or of development arrested by crossing. In other cases it appears as a decadent development. The anthropologists among the criminal specialists declare that the typical criminal is ugly: *monstrum in fronte, monstrum in animo*. But the criminal is a decadent. Was Socrates a typical criminal? – At all events this would not clash with that famous physiognomist's judgement which was so repugnant to Socrates' friends. While on his way through Athens a certain foreigner who was no fool at judging by looks, told Socrates to his face that he was a monster, that his body harboured all the worst vices and passions. And Socrates replied simply: 'You know me, sir!'

Not only are the acknowledged wildness and anarchy of Socrates' instincts indicative of decadence, but also that preponderance of the logical faculties and that malignity of the mis-shapen which was his special characteristic. Neither should we forget those aural delusions which were religiously interpreted as 'the demon of Socrates'. Everything in him is exaggerated, *buffo*, caricature, his nature is also full of concealment, of ulterior motives and of underground currents.

Thieves

Karl Rosenkrantz
The Aesthetics of Ugliness, 'Introduction'
(1853)
Women thieves have a diffident gaze
that slips away to one side, with a
movement the French call 'fureter' (from
the Latin *fur*). When you visit large
prisons and enter the big shed where
sixty to a hundred of them are often
assembled to spin you can perceive this
particular look in their malicious eyes,
characteristic of this type of person.
Ugliness naturally becomes even more
pronounced when people want evil in
and for itself [. . .] Occasional lapses into
vice can often have an even more
displeasing, crude expression than evil
par excellence, which in its negativity is,
anew, a wholeness. Gross vice is evident
in its unilateral nature; the profundity –
or rather the non-profundity – of
absolute evil penetrates with its intensity
the appearance and the face equally,
and can exist even without developing
into criminal conduct.

The Prostitute

Francesco Mastriani
The Worms (1896)
This girl possessed all the physical and
moral characteristics that constitute the
prostitute type, characteristics found in
90 out of every 100 individuals of this
wretched species. Physical
characteristics: we have said that she
had the right temperament. And here we
should note that plumpness in these
wretched creatures does not begin to
develop (at least in the class who enjoy
a decent standard of living) until the age
of twenty-five to thirty years of age [. . .]
The voice . . . Oh! This is what
betrays the woman who has fallen

abjectly into prostitution . . . You see a
young girl of pleasing appearance, who
seems to possess the angelic candour of
virginity [. . .] Well, listen to her speak.
In one moment, the veil of illusion will
fall aside; the simulacrum of virginity has
vanished! In place of the genteel,
modest girl you will find the whore. The
voice, the voice alone will let you know
what kind of woman this girl really is.

The hoarseness of the voice: this is the
peculiar characteristic of these unhappy
women. 'This is no longer,' says the
abovementioned Duchatelet, 'the timbre
that adds so much appeal to a woman's
charms: from their mouth there issues
only raucous, discordant sounds that
pierce the ear, and that not even a carter
could hope to imitate.'

True, this characteristic is found
more frequently in women of the
lowest classes; but while in them it is
more developed and evident, it is no
less noticeable in those young ladies
whom the aristocracy of vice has placed
in the more splendid and luxurious
bordellos [. . .]
Grey eyes. This is the colour of eyes
most commonly found in these poor
creatures.

Dante Alighieri,
'Sodomites',
in *The Divine Comedy*,
ms. 597, fol. 114,3,
canto XV,
Chantilly,
Musée Condé

Emile Bayard,
Mattia, from Hector
Malot, *Sans famille,*
1880,
Paris, Hertzel

facing page
Medardo Rosso,
Sick Child,
Dresden,
Skulpturensammlung,
Staatliche
Kunstsammlungen

Poor and Bad

Edmondo de Amicis

Heart: A Schoolboy's Diary (1886)

(25 October, Tuesday) The classmate who sits on my left is also an odd bird. Stardi, small and stocky, without a neck, a grouch who never talks to anyone. It seems as if he doesn't understand much, but he listens carefully to the teacher without batting an eyelid, frowning and clenching his teeth. If you ask him something when the teacher is talking, the first and second times he doesn't answer, the third time he gives you a kick. Beside him sits a boy with a hard, nasty face, a certain Franti, who has already been expelled from another section [. . .]

(21 January, Saturday) Only one of us could have laughed while Derossi was talking about the King's funeral, and Franti laughed. I detest him. He is a bad lot. When a father comes to school to scold his son, Franti enjoys it; when someone cries, he laughs. He's scared of Garrone, and he hits the one they call 'the little bricklayer' because he is small; he picks on Crossi because he has a bad arm; he mocks Precossi, whom everyone else respects. He even makes fun of Robetti, in the second year, who is on crutches because he hurt himself saving a little boy's life. He provokes anyone weaker than he, and when he gets into a fight, he gets furious and punches to hurt. There is something revolting about his low forehead and his muddy eyes, which he keeps almost concealed beneath the visor of his waxed cloth cap. He fears nothing, laughs in the teacher's face, steals when he can, denies it shamelessly, and is always at loggerheads with someone; he brings large pins to school to prick his classmates with; he rips the buttons off his jacket, and rips them off other people's jackets, and then plays with them. His schoolbag, notebooks, and books are all crumpled, torn, and dirty; his ruler is full of notches, and his pen is all chewed and bitten, as are his nails, while his clothes are all stained and torn from fighting. They say that he has made his mother ill with all the worries he gives her, and that his father has kicked him out of the house three times. Every so often his mother comes to ask how he is getting along and she always goes away weeping. Franti hates school, hates his classmates, and hates the teacher. The teacher sometimes pretends not to see his monkey business, and he gets even worse. He tried to win him over with kindness, but all he got in return was derision. The teacher said some terrible things to him, and Franti covered his face with his hands as if he were crying, and laughed. 'You are suspended from school for three days', and he came back nastier and more insolent than before. One day Derossi told him: 'Cut it out, can't you see the teacher is suffering too much?' Franti threatened to stick a nail in his guts. But this morning, finally, he got himself kicked out like a dog. As the teacher was giving Garrone the rough copy of the 'Sardinian Drum', the short story for January, to transcribe, Franti tossed a firework on the floor that went off with a bang that echoed round the school like a shotgun blast.

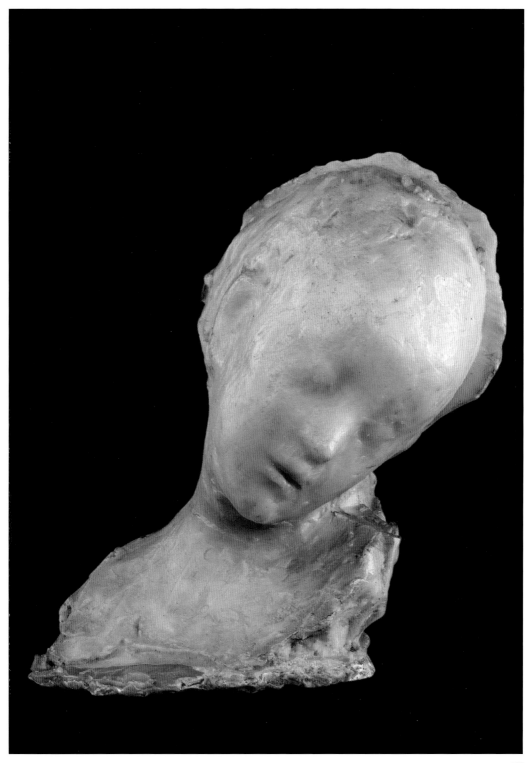

The Child Killers
Geoffrey Chaucer
'The Prioress' Tale' (1532)

As I have said, throughout the Jewery,
This little child, as he came to and fro,
Full merrily then would he sing and cry,
O Alma redemptoris, evermo';
The sweetness hath his hearte pierced so
Of Christe's mother, that to her to pray
He cannot stint of singing by the way.
Our firste foe, the serpent Satanas,
That hath in Jewes' heart his waspe's nest,
Upswell'd and said, 'O Hebrew people, alas!
Is this to you a thing that is honest,
That such a boy shall walken as him lest
In your despite, and sing of such sentence,
Which is against your lawe's reverence?'
From thenceforth the Jewes have conspired
This innocent out of the world to chase;
A homicide thereto have they hired,
That in an alley had a privy place,
And, as the child gan forth by for to pace,
This cursed Jew him hent, and held him fast
And cut his throat, and in a pit him cast.
I say that in a wardrobe he him threw,
Where as the Jewes purged their entrail.
O cursed folk! O Herodes all new!
What may your evil intente you avail?

Murder will out, certain it will not fail,
And namely where th' honour of God shall spread;
The blood out crieth on your cursed deed.
[. . .]
This gem of chastity, this emeraud,
And eke of martyrdom the ruby bright,
Where he with throat y-carven lay upright,
He Alma Redemptoris gan to sing
So loud, that all the place began to ring.
The Christian folk, that through the streete went,
In came, for to wonder on this thing:
And hastily they for the provost sent.
He came anon withoute tarrying,
And heried Christ, that is of heaven king,
And eke his mother, honour of mankind;
And after that the Jewes let he bind.
With torment, and with shameful death each one
The provost did these Jewes for to sterve
That of this murder wist, and that anon;
He woulde no such cursedness observe
Evil shall have that evil will deserve;
Therefore with horses wild he did them draw,
And after that he hung them by the law.
The child, with piteous lamentation,
Was taken up, singing his song alway:
And with honour and great procession,
They carry him unto the next abbay.

Over the centuries, the identification between ugliness and wickedness reached its peak in the analysis of the features of the Jew. This is not the place to write a history of anti-Semitism – from the first Christian condemnations of the 'perfidious Jews' to forms of popular anti-Semitism responsible for the medieval pogroms unleashed during the Crusades all the way down to the modern massacres in Slavic countries. Nonetheless, anti-Semitism began as a result of religious 'anti-Judaism', and not only on the part of the Church of Rome, because Martin Luther (in his *On the Jews and their Lies* of 1543) was ruthless in his treatment of the Jews, even though in the preceding years he had hoped to convert them en masse to Protestantism. But this religious anti-Judaism gradually melded with an ethnic anti-Semitism that became established in Europe after the Diaspora and, even more so, after the Jews were expelled from Spain when the Moors were finally driven out in 1492.

Although it is commonly held that this anti-Semitism sprang from contact with an ethnic group that had retained its own identity and expressed itself in an unknown tongue, in reality it was based largely on traditional stereotypes. See anti-Semitic texts such as 'The Prioress' Tale' in **Chaucer**'s *Canterbury Tales*, Marlowe's *Jew of Malta*, or Shakespeare's *The Merchant of Venice*.

Gino Boccasile,
anti-Semitic postcard
produced by the fascist
propaganda apparatus,
1943–44

It has been pointed out that the Jews were expelled from England in 1290 (and readmitted only in the seventeenth century by Cromwell) and so it's most unlikely that any of the three English authors mentioned above ever met a Jew. The image of the Jew spread as a pure stereotype and as such we find him again even in texts by an 'enlightened' author like the Abbé **Grégoire** and, as Fagin, in the nineteenth-century novel *Oliver Twist* by Charles Dickens. But a far more ferocious phenomenon (in the nineteenth and twentieth centuries) was the anti-Semitism based on the supposedly 'scientific' concept of *race*. To see the truth of this one should read, in order, the texts written by **Wagner** (it has been suggested that the Jewish stereotype was the basis for the evil dwarf Mime in the **Tetralogy**, who was portrayed with Jewish features by illustrators such as Rackham), by **Hitler**, Céline and the Italian fascist magazine *La difesa della razza* (The Defence of the Race) to understand that those who described Jews and their characteristics with such visceral rancour were the victims of undoubted psychological problems and unresolved complexes.

The facial features, the voice, and the actions of the 'ugly' Jew became (seriously this time) unequivocal signs of the moral deformity of the anti-Semite. To play on one of Brecht's sayings, hatred for justice 'distorts the face'.

The Jew According to the Enlightenment Scholar
Baptiste-Henri Grégoire
Essay on the Physical, Moral and Political Regeneration of the Jews (1788)
In general they have a leaden complexion, a hooked nose, deep-set eyes, a prominent chin and pronounced constrictor muscles around the mouth [. . .] In addition Jews are prone to diseases that point to the corruption of the blood, like the leprosy of the old days and scurvy today (which is akin to leprosy), scrofula, and so on [. . .]

Some say that the Jews constantly give off a bad smell [. . .] Others attribute these effects to the frequent use of vegetables with a pungent odour like onion and garlic, and some also talk of mutton; others again say that it is goose flesh, of which they are very fond, that makes them jaundiced and melancholy, given that this food contains an abundance of coarse, viscous sugars.

The Jew According to Wagner
Richard Wagner
'Hebraism in Music' (1850)
There is something foreign about the outward appearance of the Jew that is supremely repugnant to this nationality; one wishes to have nothing in common with a man who looks like that [. . .] It is impossible for us to imagine a character from Antiquity or from modern times, be he hero or lover, played by a Jew without feeling involuntarily struck by the degree of unseemliness, nay, of the ridiculous in such a performance [. . .] The man whose appearance, not when masquerading as some character or another, but solely on account of his race, seems incongruous to us in an artistic portrayal, must also be recognised as incapable of producing any work of art whose origin lies in the very nature of man [. . .] But the thing that disgusts us most is the particular accent that marks Jewish speech [. . .] Our ears are particularly irritated by the acute, sibilant, strident tones of this idiom. The Jews use words and syntax in a manner contrary to our national tongue [. . .]

On listening to them, without meaning to, we pay more attention to the way they speak than to what they say. This point is of great importance in explaining the impression produced by the musical works of Jews. On listening to a Jew talking, despite ourselves we are vexed when we find his discourse devoid of any truly human expression [. . .] It's natural that the congenital aridity of the Jewish personality, which we find so displeasing, finds its natural expression in song, which is the most vivacious and the most authentic manifestation of individual feelings. One might grant the Jews an aptitude for any other art rather than that of song, which seems denied them by their very nature.

The Jew According to Hitler
Adolf Hitler
Mein Kampf, II, 2 (1925)
Especially in regard to young people clothes should take their place in the service of education. The boy who walks about in summer-time wearing long baggy trousers and clad up to the neck is hampered even by his clothes in feeling any inclination towards strenuous physical exercise [. . .]

The young girl must become acquainted with her sweetheart. If the beauty of the body were not completely forced into the background today through our stupid manner of dressing, it would not be possible for thousands of our girls to be led astray by Jewish mongrels, with their repulsive crooked waddle [. . .]

The Jewish Eye
Doctor Celticus
Les 19 tares corporelles visibles pour reconnaître le juif (1903)
The Jewish eye is very particular. If it is true that the eye is the mirror of the soul, then we must say that the soul of the Jew is most cunning and perfidious; no eyes are duller or brighter than those of the Jews, depending on the occasion [. . .] The lids are always very puffy. The Jewish eye, around twenty years of age, folds at the commissures to form a thousand tiny wrinkles that are accentuated with age, so that the Jew always gives the impression that he is laughing and, young as he may be, he seems as wizened as an old man. Anyone, no matter how inexperienced, can easily note this peculiarity on looking at photographs of Jews. I call this eye the 'toad's eye', partly because the Jew has something of the toad about him. But I have no wish to slander that small pustular creature that renders such sterling service to agriculture and horticulture. The Jewish eye flashes. When a Jew starts to smile or laughs, his puffy eyelids come so close together as to leave only a barely perceptible and very brilliant line, a sign of shrewdness and cunning say expert physiognomists, and, I might add, of lechery [. . .]

Josef Fenneker,
Pogrom, poster,
1919,
Berlin, Deutsches
Historisches Museum

The Jew According to Fascist Racism
Giorgio Montandon
'How to Recognise a Jew', *The Defence
of the Race*, III, 21–2 (1940)
What are the characteristics of the
Jewish type?

– A strongly hooked nose, differing
according to the individual, often with
a prominent nasal septum, and
markedly flaring nostrils. Certain
individuals from Southern and Eastern
Europe have vulturine profiles so
pronounced as to make one think of a
selected type [. . .]

– Fleshy lips, the lower one often
protuberant, sometimes very noticeably,
eyes not deep set in the sockets with,
usually, a gaze that is rather moister
and clammier than that of other types,
and more hooded eyelids. [. . .]

– Less common and less decisive

characteristics of the Jewish type are:
woolly hair [. . .] and, regarding the
body: slightly curved shoulders and flat
feet, not to mention rapacious gestures
and a slouching gait.

Chapter X

Romanticism and the Redemption of Ugliness

1. The Philosophies of Ugliness

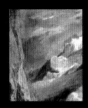

The first example of a thorough aesthetic consideration of ugliness is Lessing's *Laocoon* (1766). The statue of Laocoon (first century AD) represents the moment in which the Trojan priest, who had tried to warn his compatriots about the peril concealed inside the horse, is devoured together with his sons by two terrible serpents sent by Minerva. The inevitable reference was to the account of this event given by Virgil in the second book of the *Aeneid*, where the monsters tear the flesh of the two young men to pieces and envelop the hapless priest in their coils as he, struggling to get out of their deadly embrace, emits atrocious bellows like a flayed bull. Winckelmann (*Thoughts on Imitation*, 1755), in support of his neoclassical poetics, had noted how the statue expressed the suffering of Laocoon in a classically composed manner, in 'a repressed and anguished murmur'. But Lessing's idea was to attribute the difference between the poetic rendition and the sculptural one to the fact that poetry, the art of time, describes an action, in the course of which one can evoke repugnant events without making them unbearably evident, while sculpture (like painting, the art of space) can only portray an instant, and in fixing it could not show a disgustingly distorted face because the disfiguring violence of physical pain would not be reconcilable with the beauty of the portrayal.

But here we are interested not so much in the kernel of the debate as in the fact that, in order to back up his position, Lessing worked out a complex phenomenology of ugliness, analysing its various expressions in the various arts and reflecting upon the difficulties of making an artistic representation of the disgusting.

Laocoon,
50 BC,
Rome, Vatican Museum

Poetic Ugliness and Pictorial Ugliness
Gotthold Ephraim Lessing
Laocoonte (1766)

The poet makes use of the ugliness of forms: what use of this is granted to the painter? Painting, as an imitative faculty, can express ugliness: painting as a fine art cannot express it. In the first case all visible objects belong to it; in the second it includes only those visible objects that arouse pleasurable feelings
[. . .]

The same holds for the ugliness of forms. This ugliness offends our eyes, clashes with our taste for order and harmony, arousing repugnance without our taking into account the real existence of the object we perceive as ugly. We should not like to see Thersytes, either in nature or in an image; and although his image displeases us less, this happens not because the ugliness of his form ceases to be ugly in an imitation, but because we possess the faculty of abstracting from ugliness, and we delight only in the painter's art. But even this delight is constantly interrupted by the reflection on how art has been badly employed, and seldom will this thought fail to bring with it the devaluation of the artist [. . .]

Hence, given that the ugliness of forms cannot be in and of itself a subject for painting as a fine art, because the feelings it arouses are unpleasant and nonetheless not the kind of unpleasant feelings that become pleasing thanks to imitation, it is again a matter of seeing whether ugliness may not be useful to painting, or poetry too for that matter, to strengthen other feelings.

Can painting make use of ugly forms to attain the ridiculous and the terrible? I don't want to risk answering this with an immediate no. It is undeniable that innocuous ugliness can become ridiculous in painting too; especially when it is associated with an affected air of grace and respect. But it is equally undeniable that harmful ugliness, as it is in nature, will arouse terror even in a painting; and that that ridiculousness and that terror, which are already mixed feelings, obtain thanks to imitation a new degree of penetration and pleasure.

I must however observe that, despite this, painting is not at all in the same situation as poetry. In poetry, as I have already observed, the ugliness of form, owing to the transformation of its consistent parts into progressive ones, loses almost all of its repugnant effect.

David Caspar Friedrich,
Monk by the Sea,
1810,
Berlin, Nationalgalerie,
Staatliche Museen

following pages
William Turner,
*The Devil's Bridge
in the St Gothard Pass*,
nineteenth century,
Birmingham,
Birmingham Museums
and Art Gallery

John W. Waterhouse,
Miranda,
1916,
private collection

During the same century various writers dealt with the Sublime, which imposed a radical change in the way people saw the ugly, the disagreeable and even the horrendous. The theme of the Sublime had been proposed in the Hellenistic period by Pseudo-Longinus and rediscovered through some modern translations, including one made by Boileau (*A Treatise on the Sublime*, 1674), as a rhetorical reflection on ways of making poetic expressions about great, overwhelming passions. In the eighteenth century the debate on beauty shifted from the search for rules with which to define it to a consideration of the effects it produces, and the first works on the Sublime are not concerned so much with artistic effects as with our reaction to those natural phenomena dominated by the formless, the painful and the terrifying. Significantly, the aesthetic of the Sublime came just before the advent of the so-called Gothic novel (see the following chapter) and was accompanied by a new sensibility towards ruins.

See in particular Edmund Burke's *Philosophical Enquiry into the Origin of our Ideas of the Sublime and Beautiful* (1756–59). We sense the Sublime on seeing a storm, a rough sea, rugged cliffs, glaciers, abysses, boundless stretches of land, caves and waterfalls, when we can appreciate emptiness, darkness, solitude, silence and the storm – all impressions that can prove delightful when we feel horror for something that cannot possess us and cannot harm us.

The Sublime

Arthur Schopenhauer
The World as Will and Idea, III, 39 (1818)

Nature convulsed by a storm; the sky darkened by black threatening thunder-clouds; stupendous, naked, overhanging cliffs, completely shutting out the view; rushing, foaming torrents; absolute desert; the wail of the wind sweeping through the clefts of the rocks. Our dependence, our strife with hostile nature, our will broken in the conflict, now appears visibly before our eyes. Yet, so long as the personal pressure does not gain the upper hand, but we continue in aesthetic contemplation, the pure subject of knowing gazes unshaken and unconcerned through that strife of nature [...] and quietly comprehends the Ideas even of those objects which are threatening and terrible to the will. In this contrast lies the sense of the sublime.

But the impression becomes still stronger, if, when we have before our eyes, on a large scale, the battle of the raging elements [...] or, if we are abroad in the storm of tempestuous seas, where the mountainous waves rise and fall, dash themselves furiously against steep cliffs, and toss their spray high into the air; the storm howls, the sea boils, the lightning flashes from black clouds, and the peals of thunder drown the voice of storm and sea. Then, in the undismayed beholder, the two-fold nature of his consciousness reaches the highest degree of distinctness. He perceives himself, on the one hand, as an individual, as the frail phenomenon of will [...] and on the other hand, as the eternal, peaceful, knowing subject [. . .]

The Interesting

Friedrich Schlegel
On the Study of Greek Poetry (1797)

The dominion of the interesting can only destroy itself and is therefore a *transitory crisis of taste*. But the two possible catastrophes facing it are very different: whereas art is prevalently oriented towards aesthetic energy, taste, steadily more inured to old stimuli, will constantly ask for more stimuli, ever stronger and more violent: it will waste no time in passing from the piquant to the amazing. The *piquant* is that which convulsively excites numbed sensibilities, while the *amazing* is a stimulus and a goad for the imagination. Both are harbingers of imminent death. The *vapid* is the miserly nourishment of impotent taste, while *that which produces a shock* within the bosom of the public (in its eccentric, repugnant, and horrible modes) is the final convulsion of taste in its death throes [. . .]

Beauty is so far from being the dominant principle of modern poetry that many of the most splendid modern works are clearly portrayals of *ugliness*, so much so that one is obliged to admit (unwillingly) that there exists an immense richness of reality at the peak of its disorder and there is a desperation caused by the excess of energies and the conflict between them, whose portrayal requires an equal, if not a greater creative power and artistic wisdom than that which is required for the portrayal of that richness and those energies when they are in perfect harmony. [. . .] The public, even the most cultivated, wholly indifferent to form and exclusively athirst for *content*, asks only that the artists provide *interesting individuality*. As long as it produces an effect and that this effect is strong and new, the public is indifferent to the ways and materials that bring this about, precisely because that same public is indifferent to the harmony of the single effects in a completed whole.

The Tyger
William Blake
'The Tyger'(1794)
Tyger! Tyger! burning bright
In the forests of the night
What immortal hand or eye
Could frame thy fearful symmetry?
In what distant deeps or skies
Burnt the fire of thine eyes?
On what wings dare he aspire?
What the hand dare sieze the fire?
And what shoulder, & what art,
Could twist the sinews of thy heart?
And when thy heart began to beat,
What dread hand? & what dread feet?
What the hammer? what the chain?
In what furnace was thy brain?
What the anvil? what dread grasp
Dare its deadly terrors clasp?
When the stars threw down their spears,
And water'd heaven with their tears,
Did he smile his work to see?
Did he who made the Lamb make thee?
Tyger! Tyger! burning bright
In the forests of the night,
What immortal hand or eye,
Dare frame thy fearful symmetry?

The Medusa
Percy Bysshe Shelley
'On the Medusa of Leonardo da Vinci in
the Florentine Gallery' (1819)
[...] Its horror and its beauty are divine.
Upon its lips and eyelids seems to lie
Loveliness like a shadow, from which
shine,
Fiery and lurid, struggling underneath,
The agonies of anguish and of death.
[...]
And from its head as from one body
grow,
As . . . grass out of a watery rock,
Hairs which are vipers, and they curl
and flow
And their long tangles in each other
lock,
And with unending involutions show
Their mailed radiance, as it were to
mock
The torture and the death within, and
saw
The solid air with many a ragged jaw.

Arnold Böcklin,
Plague,
1898,
Basel, Kunstmuseum

In contrasting Beauty with the Sublime, Kant (*Critique of Judgement*, 1790) talks of a Mathematical Sublime, one example of which would be the sight of a starry sky, where we have the impression that what we see goes beyond our sensibilities and our reason leads us to postulate an infinity that the sense cannot grasp but the imagination manages to embrace in a sole intuition. Then there is the Dynamic Sublime, for example the sight of a storm, when the soul is stirred by an impression of boundless power and our sensible nature is humbled – hence a sense of disquiet, compensated for by our sense of moral greatness, against which the forces of nature are powerless. In *On the Sublime* (1800) Schiller saw the Sublime as something that makes us aware of our limitations but at the same time makes us feel that we are independent of all limits. For his part, Hegel saw the Sublime as an attempt to express the infinite without finding in the realm of phenomena any object commensurate with this representation (*Aesthetics*, II, 2, 1836–38). By that time beauty was no longer the dominant idea of an aesthetic. Moreover, Romantic thinkers shifted their attention to the nature of art, which is the only thing that allows us to realise an aesthetic value, even by talking about those things in nature that repel us. As Nietzsche was to say later (*The Birth of Tragedy*, 7, 1872) the Sublime 'subjugates terror by means of art'.

Théodore Géricault,
A Study of Severed Limbs,
1818–19,
Montpellier, Musée
Fabre

The fundamental text in this sense is *On the Study of Greek Poetry* (1795) by Friedrich Schlegel, in which modern art is contrasted with ancient art. Note that pre-Romantic and Romantic thinkers associate the beginnings of modern art with Christianity (as Hegel did), in opposition to the classic ideal of the Greek world. But it's hard to avoid the impression that these thinkers, in reliving the past in accordance with the sensibilities of modern times, are really talking about the new poetics of Romanticism.

Schlegel complained that until then no one had attempted a theory of ugliness, indispensable for an understanding of the gap between the classical and modern worlds. He came out in favour of classical art and bemoaned the modern advent of the ugly as a 'disagreeable sensible form of that which is bad'. Nonetheless, his writings reveal a kind of fascination for the characteristics of the new art – allied to the hope that it contained within itself the principles of its own obsolescence. In it he saw a prevalence of the *interesting* over the beautiful and of the *characteristic* and the *individual* over the ideal typicality celebrated in ancient art, and delineated the poetics of the Romantic character we shall be discussing shortly. Even though the ugly became a sort of 'aesthetic malefactor' against which Schlegel suggested we apply a 'criminal code', this diffidence – as Remo Bodei pointed out – also reveals his support for the spirit of a century marked by the French Revolution and the attractiveness of the idea of the 'regenerating chaos' of possible

Ilija Repin,
*Ivan the Terrible
with the Corpse
of his Son Ivan*,
1851,
Moscow,
Tret'jakov State Gallery

new orders. Over and above his intentions, Schlegel reminds us that the interesting and the characteristic require (to keep us in a continuous state of excitement and to represent 'the immense richness of the real at the height of its disorder') the irregular and the deformed. Otherwise one could not understand why expressions such as the 'absolute acme of modern poetry' were applied to Shakespeare, an artist who blended beauty and ugliness as happens in nature, where individual beauties are never free of impurities, and both his works and his characters possess a wealth of these impurities. In his *System of Aesthetics* (1839), Weiss saw ugliness as an integral part of beauty, a presence that the artistic imagination must take into account. In the *Aesthetics*, which we have already quoted with regard to the advent of ugliness in Christian iconography, Hegel talks of ugliness as if it were a *necessary moment* that comes into collision with beauty. In post-Hegelian circles, ugliness was dealt with by other authors such as Solger, Wischer, Ruge, Fischer and, especially, Karl Rosenkranz who, in his *Aesthetics of Ugliness* (1853) works out a phenomenology that ranges from the description of the *unseemly* to that of the *repugnant*, via the horrendous, the vacuous, the nauseating, the criminal, the eldritch, the demoniac, the witchlike, down to the celebration of caricature, which can transform the repugnant into the ridiculous and whose deformation becomes beautiful thanks to the *wit* that amplifies it, to the fantastic.

William Hogarth,
*David Garrick as
Richard III*,
1745,
Liverpool,
National Museum

The most ardent Romantic eulogy of ugliness came with Victor Hugo's preface to his play *Cromwell* (1827). Hugo too talks of modernity as something that begins with Christianity, but all his references to the past can be summed up in what has been defined the *manifesto of Romanticism*. His view of the Middle Ages, as a host of those monstrous infernal images that appear in cathedral sculptures, refer back to the neo-Gothic Middle Ages he was later to recreate in *The Hunchback of Notre Dame*.

The ugliness that Hugo saw as typical of the new aesthetic was the *grotesque* ('a deformed, horrible, repellent thing transported with truth and poetry to the realm of art'), the most fecund of the sources that nature makes available to artistic creation. In his *Discourses on Poetry* (1800) Schlegel had talked of the free eccentricity of images typical of the grotesque or arabesque as the destruction of the customary order of the world. In his *Preschool of Aesthetics* (1804) Jean Paul talks of this as *destructive humour*, and he starts from the Feast of Fools to arrive at the 'mockery of the entire world' in Shakespeare, and hence humour is transformed into something terrible and unjustifiable (so that *we feel as if the ground has been swept out from under our feet*).

But in Hugo the grotesque becomes the category (even though he is talking about artistic phenomena spread over about ten centuries) that explains, ushers in and in part promotes a gallery of characters that between the late eighteenth century and our own times appear marked by a satanic or pathetic absence of beauty. As Bodei observed, Hugo 'makes beauty turn full circle, thus leading it to coincide with ugliness'.

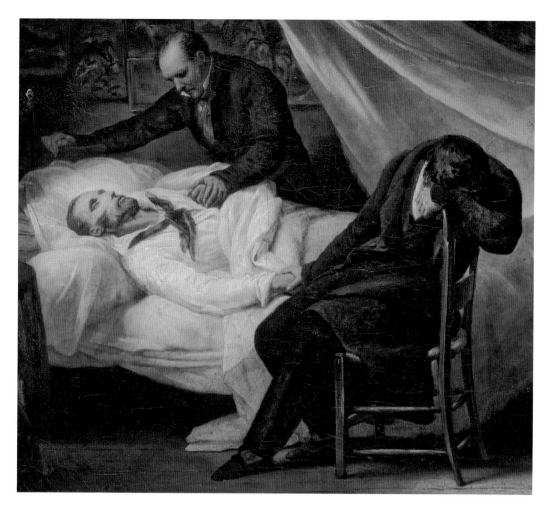

Ary Scheffer,
The Death of Géricault,
1824,
Paris, Louvre

The Twilight of Beauty

Victor Hugo
'Preface' to *Cromwell* (1827)

We have pointed out the characteristic trait, the fundamental difference that separates, in our view, modern art from ancient art, today's form from dead form, or – to use vaguer but better accredited words – *Romantic* literature from *classical* literature [. . .] Not that it would be correct to say that comedy and the grotesque were absolutely unknown to the ancients: which would be impossible [. . .] [But] in modern thinking the grotesque plays an immense part. It is everywhere: on the one hand it creates the deformed and the horrible; on the other the comic and the clownish. [. . .] The modern spirit has not lost the myth of supernatural creators, but it has brusquely conferred upon them a completely opposite character that produces a completely different effect: it has transformed giants into dwarfs and makes gnomes out of cyclops [. . .] Contact with the deformed has conferred something greater, more sublime, upon the modern sublime as compared to the beauty of ancient days [. . .] Beauty has only one type, ugliness has thousands [. . .]. From the human point of view, beauty is none other than form seen in its most elementary relationships, in its most absolute symmetry, and in its deepest harmony with our organism. [. . .] What we call ugly, on the other hand, is a detail from a great whole that eludes us, and that harmonises not so much with man alone but with all of creation. This is why ugliness constantly reveals new, but incomplete aspects of it.

2. Ugly and Damned

In *On Tragic Art* (1792) Schiller observed that 'it is a general phenomenon of our nature that sad, terrible, even horrific things are irresistibly attractive to us; and that scenes of suffering and terror repel and attract us with equal power' and that we greedily devour ghost stories that make our hair stand on end.

It was this spirit that led, a few decades previously, to the Gothic novel with its ruined castles and monasteries, terrifying vaults, bloody crimes, diabolic apparitions, ghosts and decomposed bodies. Works such as *The Castle of Otranto* by Horace Walpole (1764), **Beckford**'s *Vathek* (1786), **Lewis**' *The Monk* (1796), **Ann Radcliffe**'s *The Italian* (1797) and Maturin's *Melmoth the Wanderer* offer a gallery of characters who are either darkly handsome or whose faces bear the stigmata of their wickedness.

But the damned hero (often the heir to the Miltonian Devil) that Praz defined as the 'metamorphosis of Satan' continued to feature in painting and literature beyond the Gothic genre, and was present in Romanticism, Realism and Decadentism. Such characters include **Byron**'s Giaour and the various 'villains' found in **Sue**, **Balzac**, **Emily Brontë**, **Hugo** and **Stevenson**, down to our own day.

Whereas Kant (*Critique of Judgement*, 48) still maintained that the ugliness that arouses disgust cannot be represented without destroying all aesthetic enjoyment, with Romanticism this limitation was overcome. Lady Josiane, in *The Man Who Laughs* by **Hugo**, desires Gwynplaine precisely because he is disgusting and repugnant.

Eugène Delacroix,
*The Battle of Giaour
and Hassan*,
1835,
Paris,
Musée du Petit-Palais

Vathek's Journey
William Beckford
The History of the Caliph Vathek (1786)
In the midst of this immense hall, a vast multitude was incessantly passing. Their eyes, deep sunk in their sockets, resembled those phosphoric meteors, that glimmer by night, in places of interment. Some stalked slowly on; absorbed in profound reverie: some shrieking with agony, ran furiously about like tigers, wounded with poisoned arrows; whilst others, grinding their teeth in rage, foamed along more frantic than the wildest maniac. They all avoided each other; and, though surrounded by a multitude that no one could number, each wandered at random, unheedful of the rest, as if alone on a desert where no foot had trodden. [. . .] Upon a globe of fire, sat the formidable Eblis. His person was that of a young man, whose noble and regular features seemed to have been tarnished by malignant vapours. In his large eyes appeared both pride and despair: his flowing hair retained some resemblance to that of an angel of light.

The Evocation of the Devil

Matthew G. Lewis

The Monk (1796)

She led him through various narrow passages; and on every side, as they passed along, the beams of the lamps displayed none but the most revolting objects; skulls, bones, graves, and images whose eyes seemed to glare on them with horror and surprise. [...]

'He comes!' exclaimed Matilda in a joyful accent.

Ambrosio started, and expected the daemon with terror. What was his surprise when, the thunder ceasing to roll, a full strain of melodious music sounded in the air! At the same time a cloud disappeared, and he beheld a figure more beautiful than fancy's pencil ever drew. It was a youth seemingly scarce eighteen, the perfection of whose form and face was unrivalled. He was perfectly naked: a bright star sparkled on his forehead, two crimson wings extended from his shoulders, and his silken locks were confined by a band of many-coloured fires, which played round his head, formed themselves into a variety of figures, and shone with a brilliance far surpassing that of precious stones. Circlets of diamonds were fastened round his arms and ankles, and in his right hand he bore a silver branch imitating myrtle. His form shone with dazzling glory: he was surrounded by clouds of rose-coloured light, and, at the moment that he appeared, a refreshing air breathed perfumes through the cavern. Enchanted at a vision so contrary to his expectations, Ambrosio gazed upon the spirit with delight and wonder: yet, however beautiful the figure, he could not but remark a wildness in the daemon's eyes, and a mysterious melancholy impressed upon his features, betraying the fallen angel, and inspiring the spectators with secret awe.

The Doomed Hero

Lord Byron

The Giaour (1813)

Dark and unearthly is the scowl
That glares beneath his dusky cowl.
The flash of that dilating eye
Reveals too much of times gone by;
Though varying, indistinct its hue,
Oft will his glance the gazer rue,
For in it lurks that nameless spell,
Which speaks, itself unspeakable,
A spirit yet unquell'd and high,
That claims and keeps ascendency;
[...]
From him the half-affrighted Friar
When met alone would fain retire,
As if that eye and bitter smile
Transferr'd to others fear and guile:
Not oft to smile descendeth he,
And when he doth 'tis sad to see
That he but mocks at Misery.
[...]
But sadder still it were to trace
What once were feelings in that face:
Time hath not yet the features fix'd,
But brighter traits with evil mix'd;
And there are hues not always faded,
Which speak a mind not all degraded
Even by the crimes through which it waded:
The common crowd but see the gloom
Of wayward deeds, and fitting doom;
The close observer can espy
A noble soul, and lineage high:
Alas! though both bestow'd in vain,
Which Grief could change, and Guilt could stain,
It was no vulgar tenement
To which such lofty gifts were lent,
And still with little less than dread
On such a sight is riveted.

The Schoolmaster
Eugène Sue
The Mysteries of Paris (1842–43)
You couldn't imagine anything more terrifying than the face of this brigand.

His face was covered with deep, bluish scars; his lips swollen from the corrosive action of vitriol; the cartilagenous parts of his nose slit and his nostrils replaced by two shapeless holes. His tiny light grey eyes, round as could be, brimmed over with ferocity. His brow, flat like that of a tiger, was almost hidden by a leather cap with a long, reddish fur [. . .] it put you in mind of a monster's mane. No more than five foot two or three, the teacher had an enormously large head sunk between broad, powerful, meaty shoulders that were visible even beneath the flapping folds of his grey cloth smock. He had long, muscular arms and large stubby hands covered in hair as far as his fingers. His legs were a bit bandy but his huge calves suggested athletic power.

In short, this man embodied the exaggeration of all that is short, massive, and stocky, in the mould of the Farnese Hercules type. We must forgo describing the ferocious expression that would erupt on this frightful face, in those restless, mobile eyes that burned like those of a wild beast.

Vautrin
Honoré de Balzac
Father Goriot (1835)
The chief walked straight up to him, and commenced operations by giving him a sharp blow on the head, so that the wig fell off, and Collin's face was revealed in all its ugliness. There was a terrible suggestion of strength mingled with cunning in the short, brick-red crop of hair, the whole head was in harmony with his powerful frame, and at that moment the fires of hell seemed to gleam from his eyes. In that flash the real Vautrin shone forth, revealed at once before them all; they understood his past, his present, and future, his pitiless doctrines, his actions, the religion of his own good pleasure, the majesty with which his cynicism and contempt for mankind invested him, the physical strength of an organisation proof against all trials. The blood flew to his face, and his eyes glared like the eyes of a wild cat. He started back with savage energy and a fierce growl that drew exclamations of alarm from the lodgers. At that leonine start the police caught at their pistols under cover of the general clamour. Collin saw the gleaming muzzles of the weapons, saw his danger, and instantly gave proof of a power of the highest order. There was something horrible and majestic in the spectacle of the sudden transformation in his face; he could only be compared to a cauldron full of the steam that can send mountains flying, a terrific force dispelled in a moment by a drop of cold water. The drop of water that cooled his wrathful fury was a reflection that flashed across his brain like lightning. He began to smile, and looked down at his wig.

Heathcliff
Emily Brontë
Wuthering Heights (1847)
'Heathcliff did not glance my way, and I gazed up, and contemplated his features almost as confidently as if they had been turned to stone. His forehead, that I once thought so manly, and that I now think so diabolical, was shaded with a heavy cloud; his basilisk eyes were nearly quenched by sleeplessness, and weeping, perhaps, for the lashes were wet then: his lips devoid of their ferocious sneer, and sealed in an expression of unspeakable sadness. Had it been another, I would have covered my face in the presence of such grief. In his case, I was gratified.'

Loving Ugliness
Victor Hugo
The Man Who Laughs (1869)
'I feel degraded in your presence, and oh, what happiness that is! How insipid it is to be a grandee! I am noble; what can be more tiresome? Disgrace is a comfort. I am so satiated with respect that I long for contempt. [. . .]' She paused; then with a frightful smile went on, 'I love you, not only because you are deformed, but because you are low. I love monsters, and I love mountebanks. A lover despised, mocked, grotesque, hideous, exposed to laughter on that pillory called a theatre, has for me an extraordinary attraction. It is tasting the fruit of hell. An infamous lover, how exquisite! To taste the apple, not of Paradise, but of hell – such is my temptation. It is for that I hunger and thirst. I am that Eve, the Eve of the depths. Probably you are, unknown to yourself, a devil. I am in love with a nightmare. You are a moving puppet, of which the strings are pulled by a spectre. You are the incarnation of infernal mirth. You are the master I require. [. . .] Gwynplaine, I am the throne; you are the footstool. Let us join on the same level. Oh, how happy I am in my fall! I wish all the world could know how abject I am become. It would bow down all the lower. The more man abhors, the more does he cringe. It is human nature. Hostile, but reptile; dragon, but worm. Oh, I am as depraved as are the gods! [. . .] Now, you are not only ugly; you are deformed. Ugliness is mean, deformity is grand. Ugliness is the devil's grin behind beauty; deformity is the reverse of sublimity [. . .] I love you!' she cried. And she bit him with a kiss.

The Golem

Gustav Meyrink
The Golem: 'Fear' (1915)

It was a horrible creature, with broad shoulders and a burly physique, leaning upon a knobbly spiral stick made of white wood. Where its head should have been all I could make out was a fuzzy globe of diaphanous mist. The apparition gave off a strong smell of sandalwood and wet slate. The sensation that I was completely defenceless and in his power almost made me faint. The torment that had unnerved me for all that period of time now condensed into mortal dread, congealed in the being standing in front of me.

The instinct of self-preservation told me that I would go mad with horror and fear, were I to see the face of that phantasm [. . .] yet I was attracted to it as if by a powerful magnet, and I couldn't tear my eyes away from the diaphanous globe of mist, and I tried to make out its eyes, nose, and mouth. But despite my strenuous attempts to understand it, the mist stayed where it was, motionless and impenetrable. I certainly managed to put all sorts of heads on that trunk, but each time I was aware that they were figments of my imagination. All the heads vanished, almost in the very moment I created them. Only the form of an Egyptian ibis head lingered for a fairly long time. The outlines of the phantasm, emerging spectrally from the darkness, contracted in a barely perceptible way before expanding again, as if it were the work of the slow breathing that pervaded the entire figure, the only movement I was able to see. In place of feet, bony stumps rested on the floor, on which the grey, bloodless flesh had retreated to form concentric swellings.

The Monsters of the Terror

Victor Hugo
Ninety-three, II, 1 (1873)

On the 28th of June 1793 three men were sitting around a table in that backshop. Their chairs were set apart, with each man sitting at one side of the table with the fourth side empty. It was about eight in the evening. Outside in the street it was still day, but night had fallen in the backshop, where an oil lamp hanging from the ceiling, a luxury in those days, illuminated the table. The first of these three men was pale, young, and serious with thin lips and a cold gaze. In his cheek he had a nervous tic that must have bothered him when he smiled. He was powdered, gloved, groomed, and buttoned up. He was wearing a light blue suit with no creases, trousers in nankeen, white stockings, a high cravat, a pleated jabot, and shoes with silver buckles. Of the other two men, one was a kind of giant, and the other a kind of dwarf. The tall one was badly dressed in a large suit in scarlet cloth, his neck was bare and his loosened cravat hung down farther than his jabot. His jacket was open and missing some buttons and his fuzzy hair betrayed no trace of the hairdresser's art. His wig had something of the mane about it. His face bore the traces of smallpox, and he had an anger line between his eyebrows, a goodness line at the corners of his mouth, big lips and teeth, a fist like a porter's, and a glittering eye. The small one was a yellowish man who, seated, looked deformed; his head was thrown back, his eyes bloodshot, bluish growths on his face, and he was wearing a knotted handkerchief in his greasy straight hair. He had no forehead and his enormous mouth was a frightening sight. His shoes were large and his waistcoat seemed to be in what was once white satin, above which he wore a shirt among whose folds a hard straight line suggested the presence of a knife. The first of these men was called Robespierre, the second Danton, and the third Marat.

Mr Hyde

Robert Louis Stevenson
Dr Jekyll and Mr Hyde (1886)

Mr Hyde was pale and dwarfish, he gave an impression of deformity without any nameable malformation, he had a displeasing smile, he had borne himself to the lawyer with a sort of murderous mixture of timidity and boldness, and he spoke with a husky, whispering and somewhat broken voice; all these were points against him, but not all of these together could explain the hitherto unknown disgust, loathing and fear with which Mr Utterson regarded him. 'There must be something else,' said the perplexed gentleman. 'There is something more, if I could find a name for it. God bless me, the man seems hardly human! Something troglodytic, shall we say? or can it be the old story of Dr Fell? or is it the mere radiance of a foul soul that thus transpires through, and transfigures, its clay continent? The last, I think; for, O my poor old Harry Jekyll, if ever I read Satan's signature upon a face, it is on that of your new friend.'

Pierre Souvestre and
Marcel Allain,
Cover of *Fantômas*,
1912,
Florence, Salani

Lon Chaney in *The
Phantom of the Opera*,
Rupert Julian (director),
1925

Heinrich Füssli,
The Nightmare,
c.1781,
Frankfurt,
Goethe Museum

facing page
Gustav Klimt,
Silver Fishes,
1899,
private collection

Ugly and Exciting

J.-K. Huysmans
Against the Grain (*A Rebours*), IX
(1884)

She was a brunette, a little lean
woman, with black eyes and black
hair worn in tight bandeaux, that
looked as if they had been plastered
on her head with a brush, and
parted on one side near the temple
like a boy's. He had made her
acquaintance at a café-concert,
where she was giving performances
as a ventriloquist. Des Esseintes had
been fascinated; a crowd of new
thoughts coursed through his brain
[. . .] The lecherous caprices that
appeal to old men dominated him.
Feeling himself growing more and
more inefficient as a lover, he had
recourse to the most powerful
stimulus of aged voluptuaries
uncertain of their powers – fear.
While he held the woman clasped
in his arms, a hoarse, furious voice
would burst out from behind the
door: 'Let me in, I say! I know you
have a lover with you. Just wait a

minute, and I'll let you know, you
trollop.' – Instantly, like the
libertines whose passions are
stimulated by terror of being caught
in *flagrante delicto* in the open air,
on the river banks, in the Tuileries
Gardens, in a summer-house or on a
bench, he would temporarily
recover his powers, throw himself at
the ventriloquist, whose voice went
storming on outside the room, and
he found an abnormal satisfaction in
this rush and scurry, this alarm of a
man running a risk, interrupted,
hurried in his fornication. Unhappily
these sittings soon came to an end.
In spite of the extravagant prices he
paid, the ventriloquist sent him
about his business, and the same
night gave herself to a good fellow
whose requirements were less
complicated and his back stronger.

The Son of Evil

H.P. Lovecraft
The Dunwich Horror (1927)

Less worthy of notice was the fact
that the mother was one of the

decadent Whateleys, a somewhat
deformed, unattractive albino
woman of thirty-five, living with an
aged and half-insane father about
whom the most frightful tales of
wizardry had been whispered in his
youth. Lavinia Whateley had no
known husband, but according to
the custom of the region made no
attempt to disavow the child;
concerning the other side of whose
ancestry the country folk might –
and did – speculate as widely as
they chose. On the contrary, she
seemed strangely proud of the dark,
goatish-looking infant who formed
such a contrast to her own sickly
and pink-eyed albinism, and was
heard to mutter many curious
prophecies about its unusual powers
and tremendous future.[…]
He was, however, exceedingly ugly
despite his appearance of brilliancy;
there being something almost
goatish or animalistic about his thick
lips, large-pored, yellowish skin,
coarse crinkly hair, and oddly
elongated ears.

The Death of *She*

H. Rider Haggard

She (1887)

The smile vanished, and in its place
there came a dry, hard look; the
rounded face seemed to grow pinched,
as though some great anxiety were
leaving its impress upon it. The glorious
eyes, too, lost their light, and, as I
thought, the form its perfect shape and
erectness. I rubbed my eyes, thinking
that I was the victim of some
hallucination, or that the refraction from
the intense light produced an optical
delusion; and, as I did so, the flaming
pillar slowly twisted and thundered off
whithersoever it passes to in the bowels
of the great earth, leaving Ayesha
standing where it had been. As soon as
it was gone, she stepped forward to
Leo's side – it seemed to me that there
was no spring in her step – and
stretched out her hand to lay it on his
shoulder. I gazed at her arm. Where was
its wonderful roundness and beauty? It
was getting thin and angular. And her
face – by Heaven! – *her face was
growing old before my eyes!* I suppose
that Leo saw it also; certainly he recoiled
a step or two. [...] 'Oh, *look! – look! –
look!* shrieked Job, in a shrill falsetto of
terror, his eyes nearly dropping out of
his head, and foam upon his lips. '*Look!
– look! – look!* she's shrivelling up! she's
turning into a monkey!' and down he
fell upon the ground, foaming and
gnashing in a fit. True enough – I faint
even as I write it in the living presence
of that terrible recollection – she *was*
shrivelling up; the golden snake that had
encircled her gracious form slipped over
her hips and to the ground; smaller and
smaller she grew; her skin changed
colour, and in place of the perfect
whiteness of its lustre it turned dirty
brown and yellow, like a piece of
withered parchment. She felt at her
head: the delicate hand was nothing but
a claw now, a human talon like that of a
badly preserved Egyptian mummy, and
then she seemed to realise what kind of
change was passing over her, and she
shrieked – ah, she shrieked! – she rolled
upon the floor and shrieked! Smaller she
grew, and smaller yet, till she was no
larger than a monkey. Now the skin was
puckered into a million wrinkles, and on
the shapeless face was the stamp of
unutterable age. I never saw anything
like it.

292

3. Ugly and Unhappy

We can remain handsome and dissolute without ever growing old, but we can also be unhappy because our real decline and our inner ugliness are ruthlessly exposed by a portrait that is corrupted in our stead, as happens in **Wilde**'s *Portrait of Dorian Gray*. Nonetheless, the search for the *interesting* and the *individual*, or the grotesque, also leads us to imagine the deformity that drags towards a tragic destiny those who may be meek by nature but are condemned by their own bodies. Perhaps the first 'unhappy ugly man' of Romanticism is the monster in **Mary Shelley**'s *Frankenstein* (1818), followed by the pathetic freaks of nature created by **Hugo**, such as Quasimodo in *The Hunchback of Notre Dame* and Gwynplaine in *The Man Who Laughs*. Other unhappy ugly persons include heroes of Verdi's melodramas like Rigoletto – although Verdi also found stage room for the ugly and the damned, from Lady Macbeth to Iago, and in a letter wrote that he would have liked to see this last played by 'a rather tall, thin man with thin lips and small eyes close to the nose like a monkey's, and with a high, receding brow and a head that bulges at the back'.

The unhappiest of all are ugly women, like **Tarchetti**'s Fosca (and the same would also hold for **Gozzano**'s Felicita, had she not accepted her lot with melancholy good grace). In a short story by Zola ('Le repoussoir'), a certain Durandeau realises that, on seeing two women walking together and when one of them is visibly ugly, then by contrast everyone finds the other one pretty. So he decides to *make ugliness a business* and sets up an agency where ladies can hire an ugly female partner to stroll along at their side and thus highlight their own good looks – even though sometimes the client is even uglier than whatever companion is offered to her, and hence she discovers her own scarce attractiveness only in that moment. It is awful to read about the recruitment process and the way in which ugly women are told about the reason and the purpose for their being hired. But what is even worse is the suffering of the chosen candidates who, after enjoying a day spent dressed elegantly, at the theatre or an expensive restaurant in the company of a high-society lady, must return to their lonely lodgings of an evening, faced with a mirror that reminds them of the atrocious truth. The same mirror that reminded the young Sartre of his own condition as an irremediably unattractive man and an ugly duckling beyond redemption.

facing page
Franz von Stuck,
Sin,
1893,
Munich,
Neue Pinakothek

Quasimodo

Victor Hugo

The Hunchback of Notre Dame,
I, 5, 1832

We shall not try to give the reader an idea of that tetrahedral nose, that horseshoe mouth; that little left eye obstructed with a red, bushy, bristling eyebrow, while the right eye disappeared entirely beneath an enormous wart; of those teeth in disarray, broken here and there, like the embattled parapet of a fortress; of that callous lip, upon which one of these teeth encroached, like the tusk of an elephant; of that forked chin; and above all, of the expression spread over the whole; of that mixture of malice, amazement, and sadness [. . .]

A huge head, bristling with red hair; between his shoulders an enormous hump, a counterpart perceptible in front; a system of thighs and legs so strangely astray that they could touch each other only at the knees, and, viewed from the front, resembled the crescents of two scythes joined by the handles; large feet, monstrous hands; and, with all this deformity, an indescribable and redoubtable air of vigour, agility, and courage, strange exception to the eternal rule which wills that force as well as beauty shall be the result of harmony. Such was the pope whom the fools had just chosen for themselves.

The Man Who Laughs

Victor Hugo

The Man Who Laughs, II, 1 (1869)

Nature had been prodigal of her kindness to Gwynplaine. She had bestowed on him a mouth opening to his ears, ears folding over to his eyes, a shapeless nose to support the spectacles of the grimace maker, and a face that no one could look upon without laughing [. . .]

But was it nature? Had she not been assisted? Two slits for eyes, a hiatus for a mouth, a snub protuber-ance with two holes for nostrils, a flattened face, all having for the result an appearance of laughter; it is certain that nature never produces such perfection single-handed [. . .] But is laughter a synonym of joy?

Such a face could never have been created by chance; it must have resulted from intention [. . .] Had Gwynplaine when a child been so worthy of attention that his face had been subjected to transmutation? Why not? Needed there a greater motive than the speculation of his future exhibition? According to all appearance, industrious manipulators of children had worked upon his face. It seemed evident that a mysterious and probably occult science, which was to surgery what alchemy was to chemistry, had chiselled his flesh, evidently at a very tender age, and manufactured his countenance with premeditation. That science, clever with the knife, skilled in obtusions and ligatures, had enlarged the mouth, cut away the lips, laid bare the gums, distended the ears, cut the cartilages, displaced the eyelids and the cheeks, enlarged the zygomatic muscle, pressed the scars and cicatrices to a level, turned back the skin over the lesions whilst the face was thus stretched, from all which resulted that powerful and profound piece of sculpture, the mask, Gwynplaine.

Frankenstein's Monster

Mary Shelley

Frankenstein, 10 (1818)

As I said this I suddenly beheld the figure of a man, at some distance, advancing towards me with superhuman speed. He bounded over the crevices in the ice, among which I had walked with caution; his stature, also, as he approached, seemed to exceed that of man. I was troubled; a mist came over my eyes, and I felt a faintness seize me, but I was quickly restored by the cold gale of the mountains. I perceived, as the shape came nearer (sight tremendous and abhorred!) that it was the wretch whom I had created. I trembled with rage and horror, resolving to wait his approach and then close with him in mortal combat. He approached; his countenance bespoke bitter anguish, combined with disdain and malignity, while its unearthly ugliness rendered it almost too horrible for human eyes. But I scarcely observed this; rage and hatred had at first deprived me of utterance, and I recovered only to overwhelm him with words expressive of furious detestation and contempt. 'Devil,' I exclaimed, 'do you dare approach me? And do not you fear the fierce vengeance of my arm wreaked on your miserable head? Begone, vile insect! Or rather, stay, that I may trample you to dust! And, oh! That I could, with the extinction of your miserable existence, restore those victims whom you have so diabolically murdered!' 'I expected this reception,' said the daemon. 'All men hate the wretched; how, then, must I be hated, who am miserable beyond all living things! Yet you, my creator, detest and spurn me, thy creature, to whom thou art bound by ties only dissoluble by the annihilation of one of us. You purpose to kill me. How dare you sport thus with life? Do your duty towards me, and I will do mine towards you and the rest of mankind. If you will comply with my conditions, I will leave them and you at peace; but if you refuse, I will glut the maw of death, until it be satiated with the blood of your remaining friends. [...] How can I move thee? Will no entreaties cause thee to turn a favourable eye upon thy creature, who implores thy goodness and compassion? Believe me, Frankenstein, I was benevolent; my soul glowed with love and humanity; but am I not alone, miserably alone? You, my creator, abhor me; what hope can I gather from your fellow creatures, who owe me nothing? They spurn and hate me. The desert mountains and dreary glaciers are my refuge. I have wandered here many days; the caves of ice, which I only do not fear, are a dwelling to me, and the only one which man does not grudge. These bleak skies I hail, for they are kinder to me than your fellow beings. If the multitude of mankind knew of my existence, they would do as you do, and arm themselves for my destruction. Shall I not then hate them who abhor me? I will keep no terms with my enemies. I am miserable, and they shall share my wretchedness.'

Paul Leni (director),
The Man Who Laughs,
1928

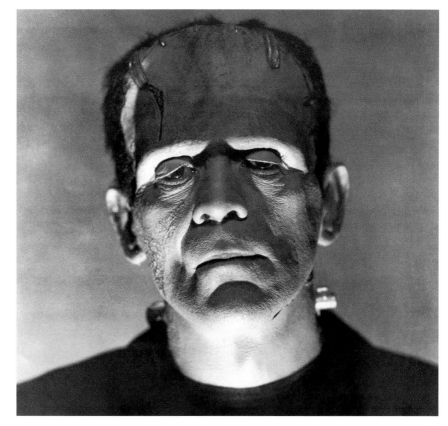

Boris Karloff in
Frankenstein,
James Whale
(director),
1931

facing page
Otto Dix,
Sylvia von Harden,
1926,
Paris, Centre Pompidou

Egon Schiele
Young Woman Sitting,
1914,
Vienna, Albertina

Miss Felicity
Guido Gozzano
La Signorina Felicita (1911)
You're almost ugly, nothing flattering
About your country-style clothing,
But your good, homely face
And your fine hair the colour of the sun,
Twisted into the tiniest braids,
Make you a kind of Flemish beauty [. . .]
And I see again your scarlet lips
Gaping wide in laughter and drink,
And your square face, with no eyebrows,
All covered with light freckles
And your still eyes, sincere iris
As blue as blue crockery [. . .]

Fosca
Iginio Ugo Tarchetti
Fosca (1869)
God! How to express in words the
horrendous ugliness of that woman! Just
as there are beauties that defy description,
so are there forms of ugliness that do the
same, and such was her ugliness. Nor
was she ugly so much because of defects
of nature, or unharmonious features –
which were actually partly regular – as for
an excessive skinniness, almost
unbelievable for those who have not seen
her. This was compounded by the
harmful effects that physical pain and
disease had had on such a young body.
Only a small leap of the imagination and
you could glimpse her skeleton. Her
cheekbones and her temples protruded
alarmingly and the thinness of her neck
made a most striking contrast with the
size of her skull, crowned with a thick
head of very long black hair, such as I
never saw in any other woman. The
result of this was to increase the
disproportion. Her whole life was in her
eyes. Large, black as pitch, veiled – eyes
of a surprising beauty. It was impossible
to believe that she could once have been
beautiful, but it was clear that most of her
ugliness was due to illness and that, as a
young girl, she might have had her
admirers [. . .] All her hideousness was in
her face [. . .]
  'You don't know what it means to a
woman not to be beautiful. For us beauty
is everything. Living only to be loved, and
attractiveness being the sole condition for
love, the existence of an ugly woman
becomes the most terrible, the most
harrowing of all torments. I have hated
myself very much, I have deeply hated
my unattractiveness, but never as much as
I have detested and still detest my heart.

Ivan le Lorraine Albright,
*The Portrait
of Dorian Gray*,
1943–44,
Chicago,
The Art Institute

facing page
Odilon Redon,
The Cyclops,
1895–1900,
Otterlo,
Rijksmuseum Kröller

The Portrait
Oscar Wilde
The Portrait of Dorian Gray, 10 (1890)
Hour by hour, and week by week, the thing upon the canvas was growing old. It might escape the hideousness of sin, but the hideousness of age was in store for it. The cheeks would become hollow or flaccid. Yellow crow's feet would creep round the fading eyes and make them horrible. The hair would lose its brightness, the mouth would gape or droop, would be foolish or gross, as the mouths of old men are. There would be the wrinkled throat, the cold, blue-veined hands, the twisted body, that he remembered in the grandfather who had been so stern to him in his boyhood. The picture had to be concealed. There was no help for it.

The Unrepresentable

Richard Matheson

Born of Man and Woman (1950)

X – This day when it had light mother called me a retch. You retch she said. I saw in her eyes the anger. I wonder what it is a retch.

This day it had water falling from upstairs. It fell all around. I saw that. The ground of the back I watched from the little window. The ground it sucked up the water like thirsty lips. It drank too much and it got sick and runny brown. I didn't like it.

Mother is a pretty thing I know. In my bed place with cold walls around I have a paper thing that was behind the furnace. It says on it Screen Stars. I see in the pictures faces like of mother and father. Father says they are pretty. Once he said it.

And also mother he said.

Mother so pretty and me decent enough. Look at you he said and didn't have the nice face. I touched his arm and said it is alright father. He shook and pulled away where I couldn't reach.

Today mother let me off the chain a little so I could look out the little window. That's how I saw the water falling from upstairs.

XX – This day it had goldness in the upstairs. As I know when I looked at it my eyes hurt. After I looked at it the cellar is red. […]

XXX – This day father hit in the chain again before it had light. I have to try to pull it out again. He said I was bad to come upstairs. He said never do that again or he would beat me hard. That hurts.

I hurt. I slept the day and rested my head against the cold wall. I thought of the white place upstairs. […]

X – This is another times. Father chained me tight. I hurt because he beat me. This time I hit the stick out of his hands and made noise. He went away and his face was white. He ran out of my bed place and locked the door.

I am not so glad. All day it is cold in here. The chain comes slow out of the wall. And I have a bad anger with mother and father. I will show them. I will do what I did that once.

I will screech and laugh loud. I will run on the walls. Last I will hang head down by all my legs and laugh and drip green all over until they are sorry they didn't be nice to me.

If they try to beat me again I'll hurt them. I will.

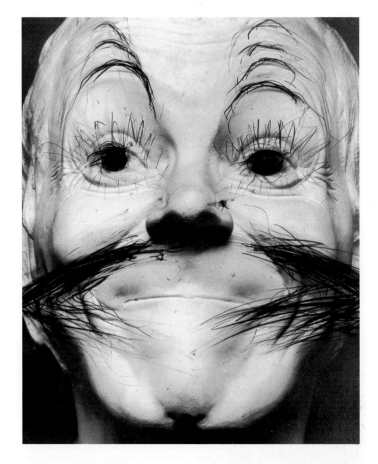

Arnulf Reiner,
*The Man Who Laughs
But Does Not Talk*,
1977,
Vienna, Galerie Ulysses

Sartre's Childhood

Jean-Paul Sartre
The Words (1964)

I am told that I am good-looking, I believe it. For some time my right eye has had a white speck that will make me half blind and wall-eyed, but this is not yet apparent. [...]

I had two reasons for respecting my teacher: he had my welfare at heart, and he had strong breath. Grown-ups should be ugly, wrinkled and unpleasant. When they took me in their arms, I didn't mind having to overcome a slight disgust. This was proof that virtue was not easy. There were simple, petty joys: running, jumping, eating cakes and kissing my mother's soft, sweet-smelling skin. But I attached a higher value to the mixed, bookish pleasure that I took in the company of middle-aged men. The repulsion which they made me feel was part of their prestige; I confused disgust with seriousness. I was pretentious. When M. Barrault bent over me, his breath made me exquisitely uncomfortable. I zealously inhaled the repellent odour of his virtues. [...]

I disappeared and went to make faces in front of a mirror. When I think back to those faces, I realise they were a means of protection: I defended myself against blazing bursts of shame by a tightening of muscles. In addition, by carrying my misfortune to an extreme, this reaction freed me from it: I rushed into humility in order to evade humiliation. I did away with the means of pleasing so as to forget that I had had them and had misused them. The mirror was of great help to me: I made it teach me that I was a monster. If it succeeded, my sharp remorse would change into pity. But, above all, as the failure had revealed my servility to me, I made myself hideous so as to make it impossible, so as to reject human beings, and so that they would reject me. The Comedy of Evil was being performed against the Comedy of Good; Eliakim was playing Quasimodo's role. By combined twists and puckers I was distorting my face; I was vitriolising myself in order to efface my former smiles.

George Grosz,
*The Writer
Max-Hermann Neisse*,
1925,
Mannheim,
Städtische Kunsthalle

4. Unhappy and Ill

As we have already seen, illness brings ugliness in its train, and
Rosenkranz has left us a memorable description of the ravages
of syphilis. But in commenting on a picture by Grosz he is unable to resist
the attraction of plague buboes beautifully and heroically portrayed.
Finally, the same author points out that illness becomes ugly when it
involves the deformation of the bones and muscles or tints the hair as
jaundice does, but becomes almost beautiful in consumption and fevers,
when the disease confers an ethereal look on the body, and goes on
to observe: 'what a truly luminous sight is offered by a young girl or
a young man on their deathbed, victims of tuberculosis.'

Decadentism was especially indulgent even with the most repugnant
forms of physical decomposition, but there is no doubt that from the
nineteenth century onwards the corruption caused by lung disease
(perhaps to exorcise the advance of an illness that was incurable at the
time) is sublimated, from the mawkishness of the dying Violetta in Verdi's
La Traviata down to the twentieth-century epic of consumption that is
Thomas Mann's *The Magic Mountain*.

This fascination with disease also enjoyed success in the representative
arts, whether the artist made an idealised portrayal of the exhausted
abandon of a beauty on the verge of death or of the slow course of some
disease, or whether he portrayed social outcasts made fragile by those ills
known as old age or poverty.

A deathly, 'spiritual' beauty that prevails as physical beauty decays,
disease produces evanescent images of young girls destined to die, as
imagined by **Shelley**, **Barbey d'Aurevilly** and **Renée Vivien**.

But **Hugo** also fell victim to the ambiguous appeal of diseased bodies
when he celebrated in the spider and the stinging nettle two of the most
disagreeable and despised creations of nature.

Baudelaire praised the crooked body of a decrepit old woman and
the somnambulistic gait of a blind man, thus bringing back to life the
ranks of the sightless as previously imagined by Bruegel. Another
terrifying image is the disgusting wound, a flower in the side of a boy
as described by **Kafka**. Entirely devoid of all aesthetic complacency, it is a
metaphor for other horrors and represents a fully realised example of the
beauty of disgust.

Jean-Antoine Gros,
*Bonaparte Visiting
the Plague Victims
in Jaffa*,
1804,
Paris, Louvre

Napoleon in Jaffa

Karl Rosenkrantz

The Aesthetics of Ugliness, III (1853)

Another excellent picture belonging to this sphere is Gros's *Napoleon among the Plague Victims in Jaffa*. How frightful are these sick people with their buboes, bluish complexion, skin in hues of greyish-blue and purple, fiery parched gaze, and features disfigured by desperation! But they are men, warriors, Frenchmen, soldiers of Bonaparte! He, who is their soul, appears in their midst, careless of the hazard of that most terrible of deaths: he shares it with them, just as he shared the hail of bullets in battle. This idea inspires these courageous men. Gloomy, weary heads are raised, eyes half spent or glittering with fever turn to him, weary arms return to life and reach out towards him, a blissful smile of joy spreads across the lips of the dying – and in the middle of these figures towers the compassionate and gigantic Bonaparte who reaches out with his hand and touches the bubo of a half-naked victim who has risen to his feet before him.

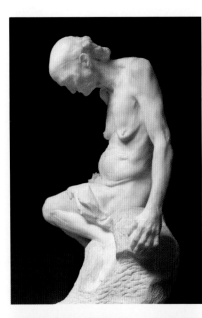

Auguste Rodin,
Winter,
1890,
Paris, Musèe d'Orsay

Eroticism in Death
Percy Bysshe Shelley
'The Waning Moon' (1820)
And like a dying lady, lean and pale,
Who totters forth, wrapped in a gauzy
veil,
Out of her chamber, led by the insane
And feeble wanderings of her fading
brain,
The moon arose up in the murky east,
A white and shapeless mass.

I Love Spiders and Nettles
Victor Hugo
'I love spiders and nettles', *Contemplations*
(1856)
I love spiders and nettles
Because we hate them.
That gloomy hope
Awards no prizes, punishes all.
Delicate and accursed,
Black climbing creatures
They are the sad prisoners
Of their own ambush,
Prisoners of what they do, victims.
O fate, O fateful bond!
For the nettle is a snake
And the spider a tramp.
They have the shadow of the abyss,
And there they flee,
Captured as they are
By the darkest night.
O passer-by, spare
That obscure plant,
That poor animal,
Their ugliness and their sting.
Have pity on evil!
In the melancholy of all,
All wish for a kiss.
If we could only forget
To trample upon them,
To look upon them with a less haughty
air,
At our feet and far from the day,
Amid that horror behold the brute beast
And the wicked plant
Murmuring: Love!

Little Old Women
Charles Baudelaire
Art in Paris, 94 (1861)
In the sinuous folds of the old capitals,
Where all, even horror, becomes pleasant,
I watch, obedient to my fatal whims,
For singular creatures, decrepit and
charming.
These disjointed monsters were women
long ago,
Eponine or Lais! Monsters, hunch-backed,
broken
Or distorted, let us love them! they still
have souls.
Clothed in tattered petticoats and flimsy
dresses [. . .]
– Have you observed how frequently
coffins
For old women are almost as small as a
child's?
Clever Death brings to these similar biers
A symbol of a strange and captivating
taste [. . .]

Pieter Bruegel
(school of),
The Parable of the Blind,
Undated,
Paris, Louvre

The Blind

Charles Baudelaire

Art in Paris, 94 (1861)

Contemplate them, my soul; they are truly
frightful!
Like mannequins; vaguely ridiculous;
Strange and terrible, like somnambulists;
Darting, one never knows where, their
tenebrous orbs.
Their eyes, from which the divine spark
has departed,
Remain raised to the sky, as if they were
looking
Into space: one never sees them toward
the pavement
Dreamily bend their heavy heads.
Thus they go across the boundless
darkness,
That brother of eternal silence.

A Great Wound

Franz Kafka

'A Country Doctor' (1919)

The young man is ill. On his right side, in
the region of the hip, a wound the size of
the palm of one's hand has opened up.
Rose coloured, in many different
shadings, dark in the depths, brighter on
the edges, delicately grained, with uneven
patches of blood, open to the light like a
mine. That's what it looks like from a
distance. Close up a complication is
apparent. Who can look at that without
whistling softly? Worms, as thick and long
as my little finger, themselves rose
coloured and also spattered with blood,
are wriggling their white bodies with
many limbs from their stronghold in the
inner of the wound towards the light.
Poor young man, there's no helping you.
I have found out your great wound. You
are dying from this flower on your side.

Angelo Morbelli,
S'avanza, Undated,
Verona, Galleria Civica
d'Arte Moderna

facing page
Francesco Mosso,
Claude's Wife, 1877,
Turin, Galleria Civica
d'Arte Moderna e
Contemporanea

following pages
Angelo Morbelli,
Il natale dei rimasti,
1903, Venice, Ca' Pesaro,
Galleria Internazionale
d'Arte Moderna

Léa
Jules-Amédée Barbey d'Aurevilly
'Léa' (1832)
'Yes, my Léa, you are beautiful, you are
the most beautiful of creatures, I would
not give you up; you, your defeated eyes,
your pallor, your sick body, I would not
give them up for the beauty of the angels
in the heavens!'
[…] That dying woman whose clothes he
touched burned him like the most ardent
of women.

Love and the Agony
Renée Vivien
'To his Beloved' (1903)
And the longest lilies of sacred pallor
Die in your hands like spent candles.
Your fingers give off flagging scents
In the exhausted breath of supreme
suffering.
From your white clothes
The love and the agony
Gradually fade away.

Chapter XI

The Uncanny

Heinrich Füssli,
Mad Kate,
1806–07,
Frankfurt,
Goethe Museum

A history of ugliness cannot avoid tackling that form of ugliness we shall call *situational*. Let's imagine we find ourselves in a familiar room, with a nice lamp sitting on the table: suddenly, the lamp floats upwards into mid-air. The lamp, the table and the room are still the same, none of them has become ugly, but the situation has become disturbing and, being unable to explain it, we find it distressing or, depending on our nervous disposition, terrifying. This is the governing principle behind every story about ghosts or other supernatural events, in which we are frightened or horrified by *something that isn't going the way it should*.

In 1919 Freud wrote an essay on the uncanny (*Unheimliche*). This notion had been circulating in German cultural circles for some time and in a dictionary Freud had found a definition by Schelling for whom the uncanny is something that should have remained hidden but has instead come to the surface. In 1906 Ernst Jensch had written a *Psychology of the Uncanny*, defining it as something *unusual*, which causes 'intellectual uncertainty' and which 'we can't figure out'. Freud expatiated on the etymology of the German term, examining a semantic field that included, in various languages, notions like *stranger* or *foreigner* in Greek; *uneasy, gloomy, uncanny, ghastly, haunted* in English; *inquiétant, sinistre, lugubre, mal à son aise* in French; *sospechoso* and *siniestro* in Spanish; *demoniac* and *gruesome* in Arab and Hebrew; and finally *uncomfortable, that which causes fear or horror, horrible, that which may be uttered by a ghost, of the fog, of the night, of the rigidity of a stone figure . . .*

The Spectral

Karl Rosenkranz
The Aesthetics of Ugliness, III (1853)
The contradiction that would have us believe there is still life in the dead constitutes the horror of the fear of ghosts. Living death as such is not spectral: we may keep a vigil beside a corpse without any problem. But if a puff of wind caused the shroud to move or if the flickering of the lamp made its features indistinct, then the pure and simple idea of life in the dead – a thought that in any other situation but this one might be very dear to us – would have something spectral about it. We think that death spells the end of the here and now and hence the apparition of the hereafter as glimpsed through the deceased is a frightening anomaly. The dead, who belong to the hereafter, seem to obey laws we know nothing about. The horror aroused by the dead insofar as they are a prey to decomposition, the veneration of the dead as consecrated beings is blended with the absolute mystery of the future. For our aesthetic purposes we must keep shade and spectre separate in our thoughts, just as the Romans did with Lemurs and Larvae. The idea of spirits that originally belong to another order certainly contains something extraordinary and blood chilling, but nothing spectral. Demons, angels, goblins are as they always were, their nature is not a consequence of death. They are above shades. Between the spectre and the living we may collocate the particular idea of vampirism.

The Uncanny

Sigmund Freud
'The Uncanny' (1919)
It is undoubtedly related to what is frightening – to what arouses dread and horror; equally certainly, too, the word is not always used in a clearly definable sense, so that it tends to coincide with what excites fear in general [. . .]

The uncanny is that class of the frightening which leads back to what is known of old and long familiar. [. . .] The German word *unheimlich* is obviously the opposite of *heimlich* ['homely'], *heimisch* [native] – the opposite of what is familiar; and we are tempted to conclude that what is 'uncanny' is frightening precisely because it is *not* known and familiar. Naturally not everything that is new and unfamiliar is frightening, however; the relation is not capable of inversion. We can only say that what is novel can easily become frightening and uncanny; some new things are frightening but not by any means all. Something has to be added to what is novel and unfamiliar in order to make it uncanny.

Freud agreed with Jensch that the uncanny was the antithesis of all that is comfortable and tranquil, but remarked that not everything that is unusual is uncanny. Referring to Schelling, he observed that what strikes us as uncanny constitutes a *return of the repressed*, i.e. of something forgotten that crops up again, and hence an unusual thing that reappears after the erasure of something that was known, something that had troubled both our individual childhood and the childhood of humanity (like the return of primitive fantasies about ghosts and other supernatural phenomena). In line with his theoretical principles, Freud traced individual repression back to sexual fears and especially the fear of castration, and not surprisingly he mentioned disquieting 'Gothic' situations such as limbs detached from the body, severed heads or feet that danced by themselves. The most profound analysis was reserved for *The Sandman* by **Hoffmann**. In this tale a young boy begins to suffer from inexplicable nightmares about a mysterious acquaintance of his father's, whom he thinks he sees coming up the stairs towards his bedroom at night, and whom he identifies with the wizard his mother used to tell him about. The wizard throws sand in the eyes of children who don't want to go to sleep, and he continues until their eyes pop out of their heads. Freud wrote that 'the fear of losing one's sight is fairly often a substitute for the fear of castration'.

Balthus,
The Room,
1952–54,
private collection

In Hoffmann's story, when the leading character grows up he falls for a beautiful girl called Olimpia, who is really an automaton. This 'intellectual uncertainty' regarding the inanimate and the living gives rise to another childhood situation (not terrifying this time): the desire or belief that dolls can come alive. Roger Callois draws a distinction between the *marvellous* and the *fantastic*, and assigns the marvellous to all cultures in which it is natural (and *no one is amazed*) *when supernatural events occur*, all the way to belief in miracles. This happens with fairy tales too. But if a child (in normal circumstances) is not frightened on hearing or seeing images of wicked and monstrous fabled beings, he might suffer from terrible nightmares if, in dream or in a restless doze, there in the dark, he begins to fantasise about the wolf coming or if he gets the impression that the witch he playfully daydreamed about during the day is now peeping through the window. In this sense, fairy stories have always been full of horrors capable of engendering infantile obsessions, and we need only think of the frightening apparitions in **Collodi**'s *Pinocchio*, or of the cruelty casually portrayed in stories intended to be educational such as *Shock-Headed Peter* (Struwwelpeter). And this is why writers like **Angela Carter** or **Isabel Allende** remind us that the fairy tale can have some terrifying aspects.

313

Two Menacing Black Figures
Carlo Collodi
Pinocchio, 10 (1883)
He turned round to look and in the
darkness he saw two black figures
wrapped up in two coal sacks, who
were running after him, bounding along
on the tips of their toes like ghosts [. . .]
Then he tried to run for it. But he had
yet to take the first step, when he felt
someone grasp his arm and heard two
horrid, cavernous voices, saying to him:
'Your money or your life!' [. . .] Then the
smaller murderer, having pulled out a
knife, tried to stick it between his lips as
if it were a lever or a scalpel [. . .]

Fire-eater
Carlo Collodi
Pinocchio, 10 (1883)
At that moment the puppet-master
emerged. A giant of a man, he was so
ugly that merely looking at him was
enough to frighten you. His shaggy
beard was blacker than ink and it hung
down from his chin to the ground.
Needless to say, he trod upon it when
he walked. His mouth was as big as an
oven, his eyes looked like two red
lanterns with candles burning inside
them, and he constantly cracked a large
whip made of snakes and foxes' tails
twisted together.

The Serpent
Carlo Collodi
Pinocchio, 20 (1883)

As he was saying this he suddenly stopped, scared to death, and took four steps backwards. What had he seen? He had seen a huge serpent stretched across the road. It had green skin, red eyes, and a pointed tail that was smoking like a chimney pot. The puppet's terror was beyond belief. He took himself off a good five hundred yards or more and sat down on a pile of stones, hoping the serpent would finally go on its way and leave the road clear. He waited one, two, three hours; but the serpent was still there, and even from a distance he could see the red glare of his fiery eyes and the pillar of smoke rising from the end of his tail. At last, Pinocchio, screwing up his courage, went up to the serpent, and said in soft, coaxing tones:

'Excuse me, Mr Serpent, but would you be so kind as to move a little to one side – just enough to let me pass?'

It was just like speaking to a wall. No one moved.

Then, in the same soft voice, he said:

'The fact is, Mr Serpent, that I'm on my way home, where my father is waiting for me. And it's so long since I saw him last! So would you be so kind as to let me go on my way?'

He waited for some sign of an answer to this request, but there was none; on the contrary, the serpent, who until then had been spry and full of life, became motionless and almost rigid. His eyes were closed and his tail stopped smoking.

'Maybe he's really dead,' said Pinocchio, rubbing his hands in delight. With no further ado, he went to leap over him and gain the far side of the road. But, just as he was about to jump, the serpent suddenly reared up, like a spring that had been released; and the puppet, retreating in fright, tripped and fell to the ground.

And he fell so awkwardly that his head got stuck in the mud while his legs were stuck straight up in the air.

At the sight of the puppet stuck upside down and kicking away madly, the serpent burst into convulsive laughter. He laughed and laughed and laughed until a blood-vessel in his chest burst and he died. And this time he was really dead.

Gustave Doré
Illustration for
Tom Thumb, in *Tales
of Mother Goose*
by Charles Perrault,
1862,
Paris, Hertzel

facing page
Heinrich Hoffmann,
Der Struwwelpeter,
1938,
Potsdam

The Sandman
E.T.A. Hoffmann
The Sandman (1816)
'He is a wicked man, who comes to
children when they won't go to bed, and
throws a handful of sand into their eyes, so
that they start out bleeding from their
heads. He puts their eyes in a bag and
carries them to the crescent moon to feed
his own children, who sit in the nest up
there. They have crooked beaks like owls
so that they can pick up the eyes of
naughty human children.' A most frightful
picture of the cruel Sandman became
impressed upon my mind; so that when in
the evening I heard the noise on the stairs I
trembled with agony and alarm, and my
mother could get nothing out of me but the
cry, 'The Sandman, the Sandman!' stuttered
forth through my tears. I then ran into the
bedroom, where the frightful apparition of
the Sandman terrified me during the whole

night [. . .] My heart trembled with anxious
expectation. A sharp step close, very close,
to the door – the quick snap of the latch,
and the door opened with a rattling noise.
Screwing up my courage to the uttermost, I
cautiously peeped out. The Sandman was
standing before my father in the middle of
the room, the light of the candles shone full
upon his face. The Sandman, the fearful
Sandman, was the old advocate Coppelius,
who had often dined with us [. . .] Imagine
a large broad-shouldered man, with a head
disproportionately big, a face the colour of
yellow ochre, a pair of bushy grey
eyebrows, from beneath which a pair of
green cat's eyes sparkled with the most
penetrating lustre, and with a large nose
curved over his upper lip. His wry mouth
was often twisted into a malicious laugh,
when a couple of dark red spots appeared
upon his cheeks, and a strange hissing
sound was heard through his gritted teeth.

HEINRICH HOFFMANN

Der Struwwelpeter

Nach der Urfassung neu gezeichnet und in Holz geschnitten von

Fritz Kredel

Erschienen 1938 im Struwwelpeter-Original-Verlag Rütten & Loening, Potsdam

Walter Crane,
Illustration from
*The Beauty and
the Beast,*
1874,
London, Routledge

The Child, the Wolf, the Grandmother

Angela Carter

'The Werewolf' (1979)

Wreaths of garlic on the doors keep out the vampires. A blue-eyed child born feet first on the night of St John's Eve will have second sight. When they discover a witch – some old woman whose cheeses ripen when her neighbour's do not, another woman whose black cat, oh, sinister! *follows her about all the time,* they strip the crone, search her for marks, for the supernumerary nipple her familiar sucks. They soon find it. Then they stone her to death.

Winter and cold weather.

Go and visit grandmother, who has been sick. Take her the oatcakes I've baked for her on the hearthstone and a little pot of butter.

The good child does as her mother bids – five miles' trudge through the forest: do not leave the path because of the bears, the wild boar, the starving wolves. Here, take your father's hunting knife: you know how to use it.

The child had a scabby coat of sheepskin to keep out the cold, she knew the forest too well to fear it, but she must always be on her guard. When she heard that freezing howl of the wolf, she dropped her gifts, seized her knife and turned on the beast.

It was a huge one, with red eyes and running, grizzled chops; any but a mountaineer's child would have died of fright at the sight of it. It went for her throat, as wolves do, but she made a great swipe at it with her father's knife and slashed off its right forepaw. [. . .] But it was no longer a wolf's paw. It was a hand, chopped off at the wrist, a hand toughened with work and freckled with age. There was a wedding ring on the third finger and a wart on the index finger. By the wart, she knew it for her grandmother's hand.

She pulled back the sheet but the old woman woke up, at that, and began to struggle, squawking, and shrieking like a woman possessed. But the child was strong, and armed with her father's hunting knife: she managed to hold her grandmother down long enough to see the cause of her fever. There was a bloody stump where her right hand should have been, festering already. The child crossed herself and cried out so loud the neighbours heard her and came rushing in. They knew the wart on the hand at once for a witch's nipple; they drove the old woman, in her shift as she was, out into the snow with sticks, beating her old carcass as far as the end of the forest, and pelted her with stones until she fell down dead.

Now the child lived in her grandmother's house; she prospered.

Victor Fleming
(director).
The Wizard of Oz,
1939

The Wicked Witch of the West
L. Frank Baum
The Wonderful Wizard of Oz, 10 (1900)
– No one has ever destroyed her before,
so I naturally thought she would make
slaves of you, as she has of the rest. But
take care; for she is wicked and fierce,
and may not allow you to destroy her.
[. . .]

Now the Wicked Witch of the West
had but one eye, yet that was as
powerful as a telescope, and could see
everywhere. So, as she sat in the door
of her castle, she happened to look
around and saw Dorothy lying asleep,
with her friends all about her. They
were a long distance off, but the Wicked
Witch was angry to find them in her
country; so she blew upon a silver
whistle that hung around her neck.

At once there came running to her
from all directions a pack of great
wolves. They had long legs and fierce
eyes and sharp teeth.

– Go to those people – said the
Witch – and tear them to pieces! [. . .]

– Well, in a few minutes I shall be all
melted, and you will have the castle to
yourself. I have been wicked in my day,
but I never thought a little girl like you
would be able to melt me and end my
wicked deeds. Look out – here I go!
With these words the Witch fell down in
a brown, melted, shapeless mass and
began to spread over the clean boards
of the kitchen floor. Seeing that she had
really melted away to nothing, Dorothy
drew another bucket of water and threw
it over the mess. Then she swept it all
out of the door.

I am Afraid of Myself

Guy de Maupassant
'The Terror' (1883)

I am not afraid of danger. If a man came in I would kill him without a shudder. I am not afraid of ghosts: I don't believe in the supernatural. I am not afraid of the dead; I believe in the definitive destruction of all beings that die.

Well? . . . well then? . . . Right! I am afraid of myself! I am afraid of fear; fear of the pangs of the mind that loses its way, fear of that horrendous feeling that is incomprehensible terror [. . .]

I am afraid of walls, furniture, and familiar objects that come alive with a kind of animal life. Most of all I am afraid of the horrible agitation of my thoughts, of my reason fleeing into chaos, dispersed by a mysterious invisible anguish.

Ghosts

M.R. James
'Oh, Whistle, and I'll Come to You, My Lad' (1904)

The reader will hardly, perhaps, imagine how dreadful it was to him to see a figure suddenly sit up in what he had known was an empty bed. He was out of his own bed in one bound, and made a dash towards the window, where lay his only weapon, the stick with which he had propped his screen. This was, as it turned out, the worst thing he could have done, because the personage in the empty bed, with a sudden motion, slipped from the bed and took up a position, with outspread arms, between the two beds, and in front of the door. Parkins watched it in a horrid perplexity. Somehow, the idea of getting past it and escaping through the door was intolerable to him; he could not have borne – he didn't know why – to touch it; and as for its touching him, he would sooner dash himself through the window than have that happen. It stood for the moment in a band of dark shadow, and he had not seen what its face was like. Now it began to move, in a stooping posture, and all at once the spectator realised, with some horror and some relief, that it must be blind, for it seemed to feel about it with its muffled arms in a groping and random fashion.
[. . .]

I gathered that what he chiefly remembers about it is a horrible, an intensely horrible, face *of crumpled linen*. What expression he read upon it he could not or would not tell, but that the fear of it went nigh to maddening him is certain.

Freud recognised that his identification of the uncanny with the return of something repressed concerned everyday life but that, in art, 'uncanny effects may be obtained through a number of means not available in everyday life'. Consider, for example, Henry James's *The Turn of the Screw* (1898), which shows us how, when the standard mechanisms of the Gothic novel no longer succeeded in scaring readers who had become inured to them, the writers of the late nineteenth century turned to more refined mechanisms. In an old country house, a young governess is put in charge of a little boy and girl, both of whom are good-looking, sweet and extraordinarily sensitive. But the woman gradually gets the impression that the two children are not as innocent as they seem and that they are in contact with the sinister ghosts of a footman and a previous governess. The entire story unfolds amid a nightmarish atmosphere, and the reader may suspect that it is all the fruit of the governess's paranoia, but it is still hard to 'figure out' certain events that really seem to happen. The intellectual uncertainty between the real and the imaginary dominates throughout. Callois wrote that the uncanny aspect of the *fantastic* appears in a culture in which people no longer believe in miracles, and everything *should be* explainable according to the laws of nature, and so time cannot be turned back, an individual cannot be in two places at the same time, objects cannot come to life, people and animals have different characteristics, and so on.

Francis Ford Coppola
(director),
Dracula,
1992

on page 325
Salvador Dalí,
*Gala and Millet's Angélus
precede the imminent
arrival of the conical
anamorphosis*,
1933,
Ottawa,
National Gallery
of Canada

on page 326
F.W. Murnau (director),
Nosferatu,
1922

on page 327
Edvard Munch,
Vampire,
1893–94,
Oslo, Munch Museet

The inexplicable occurs when we can no longer find a room or a street we know perfectly well, the same events happen several times, a puppet comes alive, what was thought to be an omen or a nightmare is shown to be real, ghosts appear, and we suspect that certain individuals possess the evil eye. The peak of the inexplicable and the uncanny is the apparition of our double, the doppelgänger. We find apparitions of doubles in **Gogol**, **Gautier**, **Poe** and others, and the experience is even more disturbing when, as in **Dostoevsky**, others all seem to find the matter perfectly obvious and acceptable. Freud pointed out that, whereas in ancient times (when pharaohs would ensure themselves a form of survival by having models of their image made) the double was a guarantee of immortality, in a period in which the primary narcissism of the primitive and the child was a thing of the past, the phenomenon became a sinister warning of death.

One very popular example of the uncanny is vampirism. Today's cinema and literature usually refer to **Bram Stoker**'s archetypal *Dracula* (1897), but the theme of the being that sucks other people's blood in order to continue its life beyond the grave derives from ancient legends. The vampire is truly disturbing not so much when it appears as a bat-creature whose canines drip blood, because in that case all it does is frighten us, but when we harbour the suspicion – not the certainty – that someone else is a vampire.

The Ogre,
c.1540,
Bomarzo, Park of
Monsters

Suspicion as a generator of disquiet may be found in certain contemporary paintings when a simple house, seen in an ambiguous light, and isolated against the landscape, becomes *haunted* and takes on a threatening and malign air (for narrative, see **Blackwood**). The **Kafka** of *The Trial* was a master of suspicion, but sometimes (as in *Metamorphosis*) what is uncanny is not so much the horror that is shown and described (a man wakes up to find he has been transformed into a disgusting insect), but the fact that his family take the event as embarrassing yet entirely natural, and they have *no inkling* of any alteration of the order of things – whereas we *suspect* that the story is really talking about our acquiescence in the face of the evil that surrounds us.

Finally we have the return of the dead. In his *Aesthetics of Ugliness* (III) Rosenkranz made an analysis of the *spectral*. Death as such is still not yet spectral. 'We can keep imperturbable vigil by a corpse. But if a puff of wind moved the shroud or if the flickering of the light made the dead person's features indistinct, then the pure and simple idea of life in death […] would have something spectral about it.' The ghost does not possess the soothing obviousness of the lemurs of antiquity, of demons, angels or fabulous creatures, who are the way they are right from the start. The apparition of one who has gone beyond (even though we might wish he or she were still alive) takes on the character of a 'frightening anomaly'.

The Double

Fyodor Dostoevsky
The Double, V (1846)
Mr Golyadkin could by now get a full view of the second belated companion. He looked full at him and cried out with amazement and horror; his legs gave way under him [. . .]The stranger did, in fact, stop ten paces from Mr Golyadkin, so that the light from the lamp-post that stood near fell full upon his whole figure – stood still, turned to Mr Golyadkin, and with impatient and anxious face waited to hear what he would say.

'Excuse me, possibly I'm mistaken,' our hero brought out in a quavering voice [. . .] The fact is that this stranger seemed to him somehow familiar. That would have been nothing, though. But he recognised, almost certainly recognised this man. He had often seen him, that man, had seen him some time, and very lately too [. . .]

[. . .] The stranger stopped exactly before the house in which Mr Golyadkin lodged. He heard a ring at the bell and almost at the same time the grating of the iron bolt. The gate opened, the stranger stooped, darted in and disappeared. Almost at the same instant Mr Golyadkin reached the spot and like an arrow flew in at the gate [. . .]. But Mr Golyadkin's companion seemed as though familiar with it, as though at home; he ran up lightly, without difficulty, showing a perfect knowledge of his surroundings [. . .]

The hero of our story dashed into his lodging beside himself; without taking off his hat or coat he crossed the little passage and stood still in the doorway of his room, as though thunderstruck [. . .].

The stranger, also in his coat and hat, was sitting before him on his bed, and with a faint smile, screwing up his eyes, nodded to him in a friendly way [. . .]. Mr Golyadkin recognised his nocturnal visitor. The nocturnal visitor was no other than himself – Mr Golyadkin himself, another Mr Golyadkin, but absolutely the same as himself – in fact, what is called a double in every respect.

The Double as Nose

Nikolai Gogol
'The Nose' (1835)
Then he halted as though riveted to earth. For in front of the doors of a mansion he saw occur a phenomenon of which, simply, no explanation was possible. Before that mansion there stopped a carriage. And then a door of the carriage opened, and there leapt thence, huddling himself up, a uniformed gentleman, and that uniformed gentleman ran headlong up the mansion's entrance-steps, and disappeared within. And oh, Kovalev's horror and astonishment to perceive that the gentleman was none other than – his own nose [. . .]

'Good sir,' Kovalev went on with a heightened sense of dignity, 'the one who is at a loss to understand the other is I. [. . .] Merely – you are my own nose.' The Nose regarded the Major, and contracted its brows a little. 'My dear sir, you speak in error,' was its reply. 'I am just myself – myself separately.'

Double Fate

Théophile Gautier
'The Double Knight' (1840)
Little Oluf was a very strange little boy: two children of contrasting personalities seemed to coexist in his white and vermilion skin. One day he was a little angel, the next day he was a little devil who bit his mother's breast and used his nails to scratch his nanny's face [. . .]

Strange, Oluf felt the blows he dealt the unknown knight, he suffered from the wounds he gave as well as from those he received. His chest felt terribly cold, as if a blade had penetrated it in search of his heart, yet his breastplate had no hole at that level. Only his right arm was injured. A singular duel, in which the victor suffered as much as the vanquished and in which giving and receiving were one and the same. Gathering all his strength Oluf knocked off his adversary's terrible helmet with a backhanded blow. What terror! What did the son of Edwige and Lodborg see? He saw himself before him: a mirror would have been less faithful. He had fought against his own ghost, against

the knight of the red star. The ghost gave a great cry and vanished.

The Fight with the Double

Edgar Allan Poe
'William Wilson' (1839)
The contest was brief indeed. I was frantic with every species of wild excitement, and felt within my single arm the energy and power of a multitude. In a few seconds I forced him by sheer strength against the wainscoting, and thus, getting him at mercy, plunged my sword, with brute ferocity, repeatedly through and through his bosom.

At that instant some person tried the latch of the door. I hastened to prevent an intrusion, and then immediately returned to my dying antagonist. But what human language can adequately portray that astonishment, that horror which possessed me at the spectacle then presented to view? The brief moment in which I averted my eyes had been sufficient to produce, apparently, a material change in the arrangements at the upper or farther end of the room. A large mirror – so at first it seemed to me in my confusion – now stood where none had been perceptible before; and, as I stepped up to it in extremity of terror, mine own image, but with features all pale and dabbled in blood, advanced to meet me with a feeble and tottering gait.

Thus it appeared, I say, but was not. It was my antagonist – it was Wilson, who then stood before me in the agonies of his dissolution. His mask and cloak lay, where he had thrown them, upon the floor. Not a thread in all his raiment – not a line in all the marked and singular lineaments of his face which was not, even in the most absolute identity, mine own! It was Wilson; but he spoke no longer in a whisper, and I could have fancied that I myself was speaking while he said:

'You have conquered, and I yield. Yet, henceforward art thou also dead – dead to the World, to Heaven and to Hope! In me didst thou exist – and, in my death, see by this image, which is thine own, how utterly thou hast murdered thyself.'

A Meeting with Count Dracula

Bram Stoker

Dracula, II (1897)

His face was a strong, a very strong, aquiline, with high bridge of the thin nose and peculiarly arched nostrils, with lofty domed forehead, and hair growing scantily round the temples but profusely elsewhere. His eyebrows were very massive, almost meeting over the nose, and with bushy hair that seemed to curl in its own profusion. The mouth, so far as I could see it under the heavy moustache, was fixed and rather cruel-looking, with peculiarly sharp white teeth. These protruded over the lips, whose remarkable ruddiness showed astonishing vitality in a man of his years. For the rest, his ears were pale, and at the tops extremely pointed. The chin was broad and strong, and the cheeks firm though thin. The general effect was one of extraordinary pallor.

[. . .]

As the Count leaned over me and his hands touched me, I could not repress a shudder. It may have been that his breath was rank, but a horrible feeling of nausea came over me, which, do what I would, I could not conceal. [. . .]

What I saw was the Count's head coming out from the window. I did not see the face, but I knew the man by the neck and the movement of his back and arms. In any case I could not mistake the hands which I had had some many opportunities of studying. I was at first interested and somewhat amused, for it is wonderful how small a matter will interest and amuse a man when he is a prisoner. But my very feelings changed to repulsion and terror when I saw the whole man slowly emerge from the window and begin to crawl down the castle wall over the dreadful abyss, face down with his cloak

spreading out around him like great wings. At first I could not believe my eyes. I thought it was some trick of the moonlight, some weird effect of shadow, but I kept looking, and it could be no delusion. I saw the fingers and toes grasp the corners of the stones, worn clear of the mortar by the stress of years, and by thus using every projection and inequality move downwards with considerable speed, just as a lizard moves along a wall. [. . .] In the moonlight opposite me were three young women, ladies by their dress and manner. I thought at the time that I must be dreaming when I saw them, they threw no shadow on the floor. They came close to me, and looked at me for some time, and then whispered together. Two were dark, and had high aquiline noses, like the Count, and great dark, piercing eyes, that seemed to be almost red when contrasted with the pale

yellow moon. The other was fair, as fair as can be, with great masses of golden hair and eyes like pale sapphires. I seemed somehow to know her face, and to know it in connection with some dreamy fear, but I could not recollect at the moment how or where. All three had brilliant white teeth that shone like pearls against the ruby of their voluptuous lips. [. . .]

I was afraid to raise my eyelids, but looked out and saw perfectly under the lashes. The girl went on her knees, and bent over me, simply gloating. There was a deliberate voluptuousness which was both thrilling and repulsive, and as she arched her neck she actually licked her lips like an animal, till I could see in the moonlight the moisture shining on the scarlet lips and on the red tongue as it lapped the white sharp teeth. Lower and lower went her head as the lips went

below the range of my mouth and chin and seemed to fasten on my throat. Then she paused, and I could hear the churning sound of her tongue as it licked her teeth and lips, and I could feel the hot breath on my neck. Then the skin of my throat began to tingle as one's flesh does when the hand that is to tickle it approaches nearer, nearer. I could feel the soft, shivering touch of the lips on the super sensitive skin of my throat, and the hard dents of two sharp teeth, just touching and pausing there. I closed my eyes in languorous ecstasy and waited, waited with beating heart.

Gorged with Blood
Bram Stoker
Dracula, III (1897)
There lay the Count, but looking as if his youth had been half restored. For the white hair and moustache were changed to dark iron-grey. The cheeks were fuller,

and the white skin seemed ruby-red underneath. The mouth was redder than ever, for on the lips were gouts of fresh blood, which trickled from the corners of the mouth and ran down over the chin and neck. Even the deep, burning eyes seemed set amongst swollen flesh, for the lids and pouches underneath were bloated. It seemed as if the whole awful creature were simply gorged with blood. He lay like a filthy leech, exhausted with his repletion. [. . .]

A terrible desire came upon me to rid the world of such a monster. There was no lethal weapon at hand, but I seized a shovel which the workmen had been using to fill the cases, and lifting it high, struck, with the edge downward, at the hateful face. But as I did so the head turned, and the eyes fell upon me, with all their blaze of basilisk horror.

Martin Frobenius
Ledermueller,
*Amusement
microscopique*,
Nuremberg,
Winterschmidt, 1764

facing page
Alberto Savinio,
Roger et Angélique,
1930 *c.*
private collection

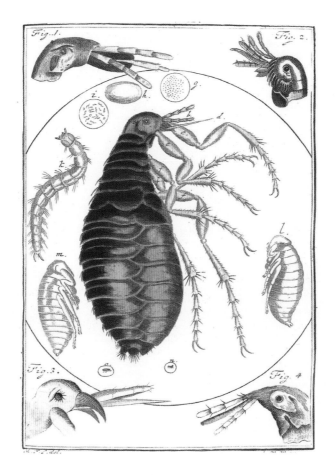

Becoming Something Other
Franz Kafka
Metamorphosis (1915)
As Gregor Samsa awoke one morning
from uneasy dreams he found himself
transformed in his bed into a gigantic
insect. He was lying on his hard, as it
were armour-plated, back and when he
lifted his head a little he could see his
domelike brown belly divided into stiff
arched segments on top of which the bed
quilt could hardly stay in place and was
about to slide off completely. His
numerous legs, which were pitifully thin
compared to the rest of his bulk, waved
helplessly before his eyes.

Edward Hopper,
House by the Railroad,
1925,
New York,
Museum of Modern Art

Certain Houses

Algernon Blackwood
'The Empty House' (1906)

Certain houses, like certain persons, manage somehow to proclaim at once their character for evil. In the case of the latter, no particular feature need betray them; they may boast an open countenance and an ingenuous smile; and yet a little of their company leaves the unalterable conviction that there is something radically amiss with their being: that they are evil. Willy nilly, they seem to communicate an atmosphere of secret and wicked thoughts which makes those in their immediate neighbourhood shrink from them as from a thing diseased.

And, perhaps, with houses the same principle is operative, and it is the aroma of evil deeds committed under a particular roof, long after the actual doers have passed away, that makes the gooseflesh come and the hair rise. Something of the original passion of the evil-doer, and of the horror felt by his victim, enters the heart of the innocent watcher, and he becomes suddenly conscious of tingling nerves, creeping skin, and a chilling of the blood. He is terror-stricken without apparent cause.

[. . .]

Stealthily, walking on tiptoe and shading the candle lest it should betray their presence through the shutterless windows, they went first into the big dining-room. There was not a stick of furniture to be seen. Bare walls, ugly mantelpieces and empty grates stared at them. Everything, they felt, resented their intrusion, watching them, as it were, with veiled eyes; whispers followed them; shadows flitted noiselessly to right and left; something seemed ever at their back, watching, waiting an opportunity to do them injury. There was the inevitable sense that operations which went on when the room was empty had been temporarily suspended till they were well out of the way again. The whole dark interior of the old building seemed to become a malignant Presence that rose up, warning them to desist and mind their own business; every moment the strain on the nerves increased.

Alberto Savinio,
Self Portrait, *c.*1936,
Turin,
 Galleria
d'Arte Moderna

A Hideous Smell of Mould

M.R. James

'The Treasure of Abbot Thomas' (1904)

'Then I [. . .] went on pulling out the great bag, in complete darkness. It hung for an instant on the edge of the hole, then slipped forward on to my chest, and *put its arms round my neck.*

'My dear Gregory, I am telling you the exact truth. I believe I am now acquainted with the extremity of terror and repulsion which a man can endure without losing his mind. I can only just manage to tell you now the bare outline of the experience. I was conscious of a most horrible smell of mould, and of a cold kind of face pressed against my own, and moving slowly over it, and of several – I don't know how many – legs or arms or tentacles or something clinging to my body. I screamed out, Brown says, like a beast, and fell away backward from the step on which I stood, and the creature slipped downwards, I suppose, on to that same step.' [. . .]

'Well, sir,' said Brown, speaking low and nervously, 'it was just this way. Master was busy down in front of the 'ole, and I was 'olding the lantern and looking on, when I 'eard somethink drop in the water from the top, as I thought. So I looked up, and I see someone's 'ead lookin' over at us. I s'pose I must ha' said somethink, and I 'eld the light up and run up the steps, and my light shone right on the face. That was a bad un, sir, if ever I see one! A holdish man, and the face very much fell in, and larfin', as I thought. And I got up the steps as quick pretty nigh as I'm tellin' you, and when I was out on the ground there warn't a sign of any person.'

Childhood Ghosts

Isabel Allende

Of Love and Shadows (1984)

She recalled the ghost stories Rosa used to tell her when she was a child: the devil who lived inside mirrors to frighten the vain; the black man with his bag full of trapped animals; dogs with crocodile scales on their backs and goats' hooves; two-headed men lying in wait around corners ready to snatch little girls who sleep with their hands under the sheets. Baleful stories made to cause nightmares, but whose bewitching appeal was such that she could not stop listening to them and asking Rosa to tell her more, trembling with fear, wishing she could plug her ears and close her eyes so as not to know and at the same time eager to discover even the slightest details.

Chapter XII

Iron Towers and Ivory Towers

1. Industrial Ugliness

Otto Griebel,
Unemployed Man,
1921,
Dresden, Stadt Museum

The eighteenth century, with the invention of mechanical looms and steam engines, led to radical transformations in the organisation of labour.
The following century, with the development of factories and industries, marked the success of capitalist production methods, the rise of a working class and the birth of urban agglomerations where living conditions were atrocious.

Some thinkers or writers waxed enthusiastic about these extraordinary new things and in his 'Hymn to Satan' (1863) **Giosuè Carducci** hailed the steam train as a 'beautiful and horrible' monster that symbolised, with progress, the revenge of a Satan in rebellion against medieval obscurantism. But the same period saw the beginning of a critique of the industrial universe, whose most famous expression was the *Communist Manifesto* by Marx and Engels (1848).

At the same time, within the bourgeoisie itself, there were symptoms of rebellion, as exemplified in the works and social activities of John Ruskin. Captivated by the Italian primitives and Gothic architecture, Ruskin, an apostle of a nostalgic idea of beauty, fought against the squalor of 'plebeians who make money', advocated a socialist utopia inspired by Christianity, and harked back to production methods inspired by the creative joy of the craftsmen of olden times.

In those same decades (although the portrayal of the horrors of city life date back to the eighteenth century with Hogarth and **Blake**), faced with the shock of the industrial city, artists such as Doré and writers such as **Dickens, Poe, Wilde** and **Zola**, and later, **London** and **Eliot**, provided us with a blood-chilling representation of the *squalor of progress*.

The Misery of London

Charles Dickens

Oliver Twist, 8 (1838)

A dirtier or more wretched place he had never seen. The street was very narrow and muddy, and the air was impregnated with filthy odours. There were a good many small shops; but the only stock in trade appeared to be heaps of children, who, even at that time of night, were crawling in and out at the doors, or screaming from the inside. Covered ways and yards, which here and there diverged from the main street, disclosed little knots of houses, where drunken men and women were positively wallowing in filth.

Streets of London

William Blake

'London' (1794)

I wander thro' each charter'd street,
Near where the charter'd Thames does flow,
And mark in every face I meet
Marks of weakness, marks of woe.
In every cry of every Man,
In every Infant's cry of fear,
In every voice, in every ban,
The mind-forg'd manacles I hear.
How the Chimney-sweeper's cry
Every black'ning Church appalls;
And the hapless Soldier's sigh
Runs in blood down Palace walls.
But most thro' midnight streets I hear
How the youthful Harlot's curse
Blasts the new born Infant's tear,
And blights with plagues the Marriage hearse.

London Fog

Charles Dickens

Bleak House, I (1852–53)

Fog everywhere. Fog up the river, where it flows among green aits and meadows; fog down the river, where it rolls defiled among the tiers of shipping and the waterside pollutions of a great (and dirty) city. Fog on the Essex marshes, fog on the Kentish heights. Fog creeping into the cabooses of collier-brigs; fog lying out on the yards, and hovering in the rigging of great ships; fog drooping on the gunwales of barges and small boats. Fog in the eyes and throats of ancient Greenwich pensioners, wheezing by the firesides of their wards; fog in the stem and bowl of the afternoon pipe of the wrathful skipper, down in his close cabin; fog cruelly pinching the toes and fingers of his shivering little 'prentice boy on deck. Chance people on the bridges peeping over the parapets into a nether sky of fog, with fog all round them, as if they were up in a balloon, and hanging in the misty clouds.

Gas looming through the fog in divers places in the streets, much as the sun may, from the spongey fields, be seen to loom by husbandman and ploughboy. Most of the shops lighted two hours before their time – as the gas seems to know, for it has a haggard and unwilling look.

The Triumph of Facts

Charles Dickens

Hard Times, I, 5, 10 (1854)

Coketown [. . .] was a triumph of fact; it had no greater taint of fancy in it than Mrs Gradgrind herself. Let us strike the key-note, Coketown, before pursuing our tune.

It was a town of red brick, or of brick that would have been red if the smoke and ashes had allowed it; but as matters stood, it was a town of unnatural red and black like the painted face of a savage. It was a town of machinery and tall chimneys, out of which interminable serpents of smoke trailed themselves for ever and ever, and never got uncoiled. It had a black canal in it, and a river that ran purple with ill-smelling dye, and vast piles of building full of windows where there was a rattling and a trembling all day long, and where the piston of the steam-engine worked monotonously up and down, like the head of an elephant in a state of melancholy madness. It contained several large streets all very like one another, and many small streets still more like one another, inhabited by people equally like one another, who all went in and out at the same hours, with the same sound upon the same pavements, to do the same work, and to whom every day was the same as yesterday and tomorrow, and every year the counterpart of the last and the next.

[. . .]

The jail might have been the infirmary, the infirmary might have been the jail, the town-hall might have been either, or both, or anything else, for anything that appeared to the contrary in the graces of their construction.

[. . .]

In the hardest working part of Coketown; in the innermost fortifications of that ugly citadel, where Nature was as strongly bricked out as killing airs and gases were bricked in; at the heart of the labyrinth of narrow courts upon courts, and close streets upon streets, which had come into existence piecemeal, every piece in a violent hurry for some one man's purpose, and the whole an unnatural family, shouldering, and trampling, and pressing one another to death; in the last close nook of this great exhausted receiver, where the chimneys, for want of air to make a draught, were built in an immense variety of stunted and crooked shapes, as though every house put out a sign of the kind of people who might be expected to be born in it; among the multitude of Coketown, generically called 'the Hands' – a race who would have found mere favour with some people, if Providence had seen fit to make them only hands, or, like the lower creatures of the seashore, only hands and stomachs – lived a certain Stephen Blackpool, forty years of age.

The People of the Abyss

Jack London

The People of the Abyss, 1, 6 (1903)

Nowhere in the streets of London may one escape the sight of abject poverty, while five minutes' walk from almost any point will bring one to a slum; but the region my hansom was now penetrating was one unending slum. The streets were filled with a new and different race of people, short of stature, and of wretched or beer-sodden appearance. We rolled along through miles of bricks and squalor, and from each cross street and alley flashed long vistas of bricks and misery. Here and there lurched a drunken man or woman, and the air was obscene with sounds of jangling and squabbling. At a market, tottery old men and women were searching in the garbage thrown in the mud for rotten potatoes, beans, and vegetables, while little children clustered like flies around a festering mass of fruit, thrusting their arms to the shoulders into the liquid corruption, and drawing forth morsels but partially decayed, which they devoured on the spot.

[. . .]

I looked out of the window, which should have commanded the back yards of the neighbouring buildings. But there were no back yards, or, rather, they were covered with one-storey hovels, cowsheds, in which people lived. The roofs of these hovels were covered with deposits of filth, in some places a couple of feet deep – the contributions from the back windows of the second and third storeys. I could make out fish and meat bones, garbage, pestilential rags, old boots, broken earthenware, and all the general refuse of a human sty.

[. . .]

It was a welter of rags and filth, of all manner of loathsome skin diseases, open sores, bruises, grossness, indecency, leering monstrosities, and bestial faces. A chill, raw wind was blowing, and these creatures huddled there in their rags, sleeping for the most part, or trying to sleep. Here were a dozen women, ranging in age from twenty years to seventy. Next a babe, possibly of nine months, lying asleep, flat on the hard bench, with neither pillow nor covering, nor with any one looking after it. Next half-a-dozen men, sleeping bolt upright or leaning against one another in their sleep.

Gustave Doré,
London,
in Gustave Doré and
Blanchard Jerrold,
London: A Pilgrimage,
1872,
London, Grant

The Damaged City

T.S. Eliot

The Waste Land, 'The Burial of the Dead' (1922)

Unreal City,
Under the brown fog of a winter dawn,
A crowd flowed over London Bridge, so many,
I had not thought death had undone so many.
Sighs, short and infrequent, were exhaled,
And each man fixed his eyes before his feet.
Flowed up the hill and down King William Street,
To where Saint Mary Woolnoth kept the hours
With a dead sound on the final stroke of nine.
There I saw one I knew, and stopped him, crying 'Stetson!
'You who were with me in the ships at Mylae!
'That corpse you planted last year in your garden,
'Has it begun to sprout? Will it bloom this year?
'Or has the sudden frost disturbed its bed?
'Oh keep the Dog far hence, that's friend to men,
'Or with his nails he'll dig it up again!
'You! hypocrite lecteur! – mon semblable, – mon frere!'

337

Otto Griebel,
The International,
1928–30,
Berlin, Museum
für Deutsche Geschichte

facing page
Train crash at the Gare
Montparnasse,
22 October 1895,
Paris

The Crowd
Edgar Allan Poe
'The Man of the Crowd' (1841)

By far the greater number of those who went by had a satisfied business-like demeanour, and seemed to be thinking only of making their way through the press. [. . .]

Descending in the scale of what is termed gentility, I found darker and deeper themes for speculation. I saw Jew pedlars, with hawk eyes flashing from countenances whose every other feature wore only an expression of abject humility; sturdy professional street beggars scowling upon mendicants of a better stamp, whom despair alone had driven forth into the night for charity; feeble and ghastly invalids, upon whom death had placed a sure hand, and who sidled and tottered through the mob, looking every one beseechingly in the face, as if in search of some chance consolation, some lost hope; women of the town of all kinds and of all ages – the unequivocal beauty in the prime of her womanhood, putting one in mind of the statue in Lucian, with the surface of Parian marble, and the interior filled with filth – the loathsome and utterly lost leper in rags – the wrinkled, bejewelled and paint-begrimed beldame, making a last effort at youth – the mere child of immature form, yet, from long association, an adept in the dreadful coquetries of her trade, and burning with a rabid ambition to be ranked the equal of her elders in vice; drunkards innumerable and indescribable – some in shreds and patches, reeling, inarticulate, with bruised visage and lack-lustre eyes – some in whole although filthy garments, with a slightly unsteady swagger, thick sensual lips, and hearty-looking rubicund faces, others clothed in materials which had once been good, and which even now were scrupulously well brushed – men who walked with a more than naturally firm and springy step, but whose countenances were fearfully pale, whose eyes, hideously wild and red, and who clutched with quivering fingers, as they strode through the crowd [. . .]

Satanic Train
Giosué Carducci
'Hymn to Satan' (1863)

A monster of awful beauty
Has been unchained,
It scours the land
And scours the seas:
Sparkling and fuming
Like a volcano,
It vanquishes the mountains
And devours the plains.
It leaps over chasms;
Then burrows deep
Into hidden caverns
Along paths unfathomed;
Only to re-emerge, invincible,
From shore to shore
Like a tornado
It howls out its cry,
Like a tornado
It belches forth its breath:
It is Satan,
O peoples,
Great Satan is passing by.

Kees Van Dongen,
The Viveurs,
early twentieth century,
Troyes,
Musée d'Arte Moderne

following pages
Honoré Daumier,
The Third-Class Carriage,
1862,
Ottawa,
National Gallery
of Canada

Chaim Soutine,
Carcass of Beef,
c.1925,
Buffalo, Albright-Knox
Art Gallery

One Night for Dorian Gray
Oscar Wilde
The Portrait of Dorian Gray, 16 (1891)

A cold rain began to fall, and the blurred street-lamps looked ghastly in the dripping mist. The public-houses were just closing, and dim men and women were clustering in broken groups round their doors. From some of the bars came the sound of horrible laughter. [. . .]

It is said that passion makes one think in a circle. Certainly with hideous iteration the bitten lips of Dorian Gray shaped and reshaped those subtle words that dealt with soul and sense, till he had found in them the full expression, as it were, of his mood, and justified, by intellectual approval, passions that without such justification would still have dominated his temper. From cell to cell of his brain crept the one thought; and the wild desire to live, most terrible of all man's appetites, quickened into force each trembling nerve and fibre. Ugliness that had once been hateful to him because it made things real, became dear to him now for that very reason. Ugliness was the one reality. The coarse brawl, the loathsome den, the crude violence of disordered life, the very vileness of thief and outcast, were more vivid, in their intense actuality of impression, than all the gracious shapes of art, the dreamy shadows of song. [. . .]

He [. . .] entered a long low room which looked as if it had once been a third-rate dancing-saloon. Shrill flaring gas-jets, dulled and distorted in the fly-blown mirrors that faced them, were ranged round the walls. Greasy reflectors of ribbed tin backed them, making quivering discs of light. The floor was covered with ochre-coloured sawdust, trampled here and there into mud, and stained with dark rings of spilled liquor. Some Malays were crouching by a little charcoal stove, playing with bone counters and showing their white teeth as they chattered. In one corner, with his head buried in his arms, a sailor sprawled over a table, and by the tawdrily painted bar that ran across one complete side stood two haggard women, mocking an old man who was brushing the sleeves of his coat with an expression of disgust. [. . .]

At the end of the room there was a little staircase, leading to a darkened chamber. As Dorian hurried up its three rickety steps, the heavy odour of opium met him.

The Ugliness of 'Technical Beauty'
Hans Sedlmayr
The Death of Light, III, 2 (1964)

At the same time as this new beauty is budding, however, an equally unique wave of ugliness is also flooding the world. From the new neighbourhoods of the great cities it has spread out beyond the outskirts and into the open countryside, invading small towns and the country. The ugliness of most of the city's new neighbourhoods is indescribable: an ugliness that takes your breath away. This is as true for buildings in the centre as it is for those in the outskirts, as true for rented buildings as for residential areas, as true for the poor neighbourhoods as it is for the rich, for both private and public buildings, for façades as for interiors and courtyards. In the course of the nineteenth century this new ugliness took on a bleak, wild aspect, something that hints at excessive profits, something barbarically chaotic, individual. This does not alter the fact that scattered here and there in these deserts of ugliness there are oases of ancient nobility, and that alongside an ugliness devoid of character there appears, quite often, a characteristically provocative ugliness, which might be preferable to the bland pleasantness of certain buildings today, especially given that this ugliness is often allied to a surprising solidity and care in construction. 'I am convinced that during no past era did man consider the expressive forms of architecture with disgust and aversion; this has been reserved for our age alone. Until the classical period building was a natural function. It was entirely possible that new buildings would not be noticed, just as you wouldn't note a tree that has only recently been planted; but when they were noticeable, everyone knew that something good and natural had taken place; this is how Goethe saw the buildings of his day' (Broch).

In the twentieth century, several areas afflicted by this kind of ugliness have been demolished, although they continue to exist in the new so-called 'rational' architecture, in other words in absurd colours and proportions and, as 'function', in poorly concealed ornamental aberrations [. . .] On the other hand, monotony is often even more pronounced than it was in certain 'revamped' streets in the nineteenth century.

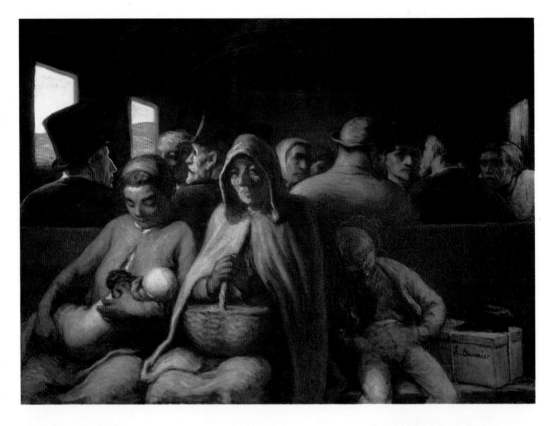

The Miseries of Paris
Charles Baudelaire
Art in Paris, 106 (1861)
They were sounding reveille in the barracks' yards,
And the morning wind was blowing on the lanterns.
It was the hour when swarms of harmful dreams
Make the sun-tanned adolescents toss in their beds;
When, like a bloody eye that twitches and rolls,
The lamp makes a red splash against the light of day;
When the soul within the heavy, fretful body
Imitates the struggle of the lamp and the sun.
Like a tear-stained face being dried by the breeze,
The air is full of the shudders of things that flee,
And man is tired of writing and woman of making love.
Here and there the houses were beginning to smoke.

The ladies of pleasure, with eyelids yellow-green
And mouths open, were sleeping their stupefied sleep;
The beggar-women, their breasts hanging thin and cold,
Were blowing on their fires, blowing on their fingers.
It was the hour when amid poverty and cold
The pains of women in labour grow more cruel;
The cock's crow in the distance tore the foggy air
Like a sob stifled by a bloody froth;
The buildings were enveloped in a sea of mist,
And in the charity-wards, the dying
Hiccuped their death-sobs at uneven intervals.

The Belly of Paris
Émile Zola
The Belly of Paris, 1, 33 (1873)
The luminous clock-face of [the church of] Saint-Eustache languished, pale as a night light surprised by the dawn. At the end of the nearby streets, the gas lamps in the wine shops winked out one by one, like stars extinguished in a sea of light. Greenish grey, they looked more solid now, and even larger thanks to the forest of columns that held up an endless expanse of roofs. They rose up in geometrically shaped blocks; and when all the lamps had been snuffed out inside, and the square, uniform buildings were flooded with daylight, they looked like some immense modern machine, some enormous steam engine, a boiler made to digest an entire people, a gigantic belly, bolted, riveted, made of wood, glass, and iron, endowed with the elegant power of a mechanical engine worked by steam and fuel and the shuddering, frenzied fury of its wheels.

The Eiffel Tower
under construction,
August 1889

preceding pages
Otto Dix,
Cartoon for Metropolis,
triptych,
1927–28,
Stuttgart,
Galerie der Stadt

The entire nineteenth century was agitated by the conflict between enthusiasts of the Industrial Revolution, which inspired a new architecture based on iron and glass, and those who rejected these technological innovations not only in the name of traditional values but also in that of the new aesthetic sensibility.

Before Gustave Eiffel completed in 1889 his metal tower for the Universal Exposition in Paris, in 1887 the newspaper *Le Temps* published a letter whose signatories included Alexandre Dumas *fils*, Guy de Maupassant, Charles Gounod, Leconte de Lisle, Victorien Sardou, Charles Garnier, François Coppée and Sully Prudhomme: 'We come, we writers, painters, sculptors, architects, lovers of Paris's still intact beauty, to protest with all our strength and all our indignation, in the name of the underestimated taste of the French people, and in that of the threat to French art and history, against the erection in the heart of our capital of the useless and monstrous Eiffel tower that a hostile public, often well endowed with common sense and the spirit of justice, has already dubbed the "Tower of Babel". And so they inveighed against the gigantic black 'factory chimney' that, like an inkblot, would have stretched out over Paris the hateful shadow of a 'hateful column of bolted tin'.

Mario Sironi,
*Urban Landscape
with Factory Chimneys*,
c.1920–23,
Milan, private collection

Eiffel's response was that the tower would have had its own typical beauty and elegance, that the rules of harmony were not extraneous to those of engineering, that the construction would have expressed – thanks to the boldness of its conception – power and beauty, that colossal things are fascinating too, and finally that the tower would be the highest building ever erected by men. 'Why should that which is admirable in Egypt become horrible and ridiculous in Paris?' The Eiffel Tower has become a characteristic feature of the Parisian skyline, and at the time some of the original protesters changed their minds. But the 'Eiffel dossier' still remains as proof of the so-called *swings in taste*. Swings that have occurred over time also with regard to the image of the city itself. In contemporary painting we find appalling images of bleak metropolises and industrial outskirts; bitter reflections on the ugliness of cities appear in the works of thinkers like **Sedlmayr** and **Adorno**. The metropolis described in Alfred Döblin's *Berlin Alexanderplatz* (1929) is harsh and forbidding, and in our own time **DeLillo** has revisited in an American vein the horrors of nineteenth-century London and Paris. But in Joyce's **Ulysses** (1922) we have an epic of the modern city, a fascinating melting pot of contradictory aspects, the inferno and the paradise of Leopold Bloom.

347

Charles Sheeler,
Classical Landscape,
1931, St Louis,
Missouri, Mr and Mrs
Barney A. Ebsworth
Foundation

facing page
Isaac Soyer,
Employment Agency,
1937,
New York, Whitney
Museum
of American Art

Joseph Stella,
Fires in the Night,
1919,
Milwaukee,
Art Museum

The Misery of America
Don DeLillo
Underworld (1997)
Farther on we see signs of the old tests, aboveground, and there is a strangeness here, an uneasiness I try to locate. We see the remnant span of a railroad trestle, a sculptured length of charred brown metal resting on concrete piers. A graveness, a spirit of old secrets gone bad, turned unworthy. We see the squat gray base of a shot tower, most of it blown away decades earlier, leaving this block of seamed concrete that rises only seven feet above the stubble surface, still looking oddly stunned, with metal beams ajut. Guilt in every dosed object, the weathered posts and I-beams left to the wind, things made and shaped by men, old schemes gone wrong.

There are mounds of bulldozed earth around a camera bunker daubed with yellow paint – yellow for contaminated. The place is strange, frozen away, a specimen of our forgetfulness even as we note the details. We see signs of houses in the distance, test dwellings blown off their foundations with people still inside, mannequins, and products on the shelves where they'd been placed maybe forty years ago – American brands, the driver says.

[. . .]

The tin, the paper, the plastics, the styrofoam. It all flies down the conveyor belts, four hundred tons a day, assembly lines of garbage, sorted, compressed, and baled, transformed in the end of square-edged units, products again, wire-bound and smartly stacked and ready to be marketed. Sunny loves this place and so do the other kids who come with their parents or teachers to stand on the catwalk and visit the exhibits. Brightness streams from skylights down to the floor of the shed, falling on the tall machines with a numinous glow. Maybe we feel a reverence for waste, for the redemptive qualities of the things we use and discard. Look how they come back to us, alight with a kind of brave aging. The windows yield a strong broad desert and enormous sky. The landfill across the road is closed now, jammed to capacity, but gas keeps rising from the great earthen berm, methane, and it produces a wavering across the land and sky that deepens the aura of sacred work. It is like a fable in the writhing air of some ghost civilisation, a shimmer of desert ruin. The kids love the machines, the balers and hoppers and long conveyors, and the parents look out the windows through the methane mist and the planes come out of the mountains and align for their approach and the trucks are arrayed in two columns outside the shed, bringing in the unsorted slop, the gut squalor of our lives, and taking the baled and bound units out into the world again [. . .]

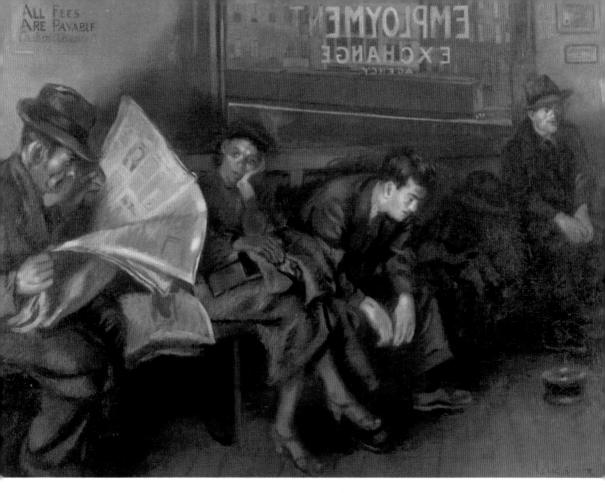

2. Decadentism and the Licentiousness of the Ugly

Faced with the oppressiveness of the industrial world, metropolises teeming with immense, anonymous crowds, and the rise of an organised working class, while a flourishing form of journalism began to publish popular stories in episodes, thus sowing the seed of what we now call mass culture, artists felt their ideals were threatened. They viewed the new democratic ideals as their enemies and decided to become 'different', outcasts, aristocratic or *maudit*, and withdrew into the *ivory tower* of Art for Art's sake. As Villiers de l'Isle-Adam said: 'Living? Our servants will see to that for us.'

So the epoch of the triumph of the motor car and the positivist cult of science was also that of Decadentism. An *aesthetic religion* took form in which Beauty was the only value worth realising, and *dandies* thought that life itself should be led as a work of art. In his poem 'Languor' (1883), Paul Verlaine compared his epoch to the worlds of Roman and Byzantine decadence: everything has already been said, all pleasures have been tried and drunk to the lees, on the horizon there lurk barbarian hordes that a sick civilisation cannot stop. There is nothing left to do (Huysmans was to say) but plunge into the sensuous joys of an overexcited and overexcitable imagination, to list art treasures, and to run listless hands through the jewels accumulated by past generations.

For Baudelaire (*Correspondences*, 1857), nature is a temple where living columns sometimes let slip confused words, and can be seen only as an inexhaustible store of symbols. But if everything allows of a symbolic revelation, then that must also be sought in the abysses of evil and horror.

Edouard Manet,
The Absinthe Drinker,
1858–59,
Copenhagen,
Ny-Carlsberg-Glyptothek

Portrait of a Decadent
Paul Valéry
Varieté, II: 'Portrait of Huysmans' (1930)
He was the most nervous of men [. . .] an artist of the repellent, inclined to the worst and athirst only for the excessive. Unbelievably credulous, he welcomed every horror that the human mind can imagine, avid for the bizarre and for tales that one might hear in the porter's lodge of Hell. [. . .]

His was an erudition devoted to the astounding. He smelt filth, wrongdoing, and ignominy in all social affairs, and perhaps he was right. [. . .] When he got involved in mysticism he took delight in adding to his detailed and self-satisfied knowledge of visible filth and measurable muck a scrupulous, inventive, and restless curiosity about supernatural filth and suprasensible muck [. . .]

Trembling, his singular nostrils would sniff out all that is nauseating in the world. The disgusting smell of cheap dives, rotten, acrid incense, the polluted, stale air of hovels and almshouses, everything that revolted his senses excited his genius.

Arthur Rimbaud ('Letter to P. Demeny', 1871) said that the poet becomes a visionary only 'through a lengthy, immense, and *rational dissolution of all the senses*', and in *A Season in Hell* (1873) he wrote: 'One evening, I lured Beauty onto my knee. And I found her bitter [...] I have wallowed in the mud. I have dried myself in the air of crime.' The religiosity *à rebours* of the decadents took the path of satanism, with participation in magical practices and summoning the Devil (see Huysmans's *Là-bas*), and our anthology cannot explain the infinite celebrations of sadism and masochism, the apology for vice (see, apart from Decadentism, the eulogy of the prostitute in **Rilke**, or the celebration of the ugliness of the sexual act in **Bataille**), the refined pleasures of pain, or the exaltation of neurotic states (**Huysmans**). **Corbière** identified with the melancholy ugliness of the toad, **Dostoevsky** talks of the horror of the rat, **Baudelaire** wrote *Carrion*, an out-and-out eulogy of the disgusting, **Tarchetti** wrote in praise of bad teeth, and **Rimbaud** trembles with pleasure in describing women absorbed in delousing. And finally there is **Proust** and the appeal of the sublimely aristocratic nature of ugliness.

Likewise, representational artists gave us perverse characters, prostitutes, sphinxes, dying girls and repulsive faces.

The Pleasure of Ugliness
Charles Baudelaire
A Selection of Consoling Maxims on Love (1846)
For certain more curious and disenchanted spirits, the pleasure of ugliness comes from an even more mysterious sentiment, which is a thirst for the unknown and a taste for the horrible.

It is this sentiment, the germ of which all of us carry inside to a greater or lesser degree, that drives certain poets into clinics and anatomy theatres, and women to public executions. I'm sorry that no one understands this – a harp that lacks its low string! There are people who blush about having loved a woman, when they realise that she is a fool [...] Stupidity is often the ornament of beauty; it is that which gives the eyes the lacklustre limpidity of blackish ponds, and the oily calm of tropical seas.

The Toad
Tristan Corbière
The Yellow Loves (1873)
A song in a windless night . . .
– The moon a plate of bright metal
Ornaments of dark green.
. . . A song; like an echo, buried
Alive, there, under the bush . . .
– It ceases: Come, it's hiding in shadow
. . .
– A toad! – Why are you so afraid,
Here next to me, your faithful soldier?
Look at him, the bald poet, wingless,
Nightingale of the mud . . . – Horrors! –
. . . It sings. – Horrors! – Why horror?
Can't you see the gleaming eye . . .
No: cold, it leaves, under the stone.
. . .
Good evening – I am that toad.

Max Klinger,
*Death, Part Two
(Vom Tode II), Opus XIII,*
1898,
Berlin

The Woman in the Sarcophagus
Gabriele D'Annunzio
'Paradisiacal Poem' (1893)
The woman lay in a regal pose
Atop the great Roman sarcophagus,
Carved with a funeral scene,
By some admirable hand.

Is she perhaps waiting for some fateful
Oedipus
To solve the superhuman enigma?
Or for Sister Death whom the profane

Dream would have closed in the
sepulchral marble?

Her mouth does not speak her thoughts.
Who will suck from the bloody flesh
Of that fruit the essence of the mystery?

She waits. And in her deep, wanton
eyes,
Already darkened by future sin,
The shades of ancient crimes go beyond
[. . .]

Study of the Middle Ages led to the rediscovery of the demoniac and the hesi-tance of a Latin by then corrupted, while the Renaissance provided the ambiguous figure of the androgyne. In *Rome* (1895–1904) Jean Lorrain wrote: 'Ah, Botticelli's mouths, those full lips, solid as fruits, ironic and sorrowful, with their sinuous, enig-matic folds that make it impossible to understand if they are concealing purity or abomination!' As far as women were concerned, some dwelled on their sphinx-like mystery (**Wilde**), others on their sinfulness, moral corruption or decaying flesh (**Baudelaire**), or even on the carnal pleasures of necrophilia (**D'Annunzio**), while **Tarchetti** betrayed an undoubted misogyny. One thing that seems to have eluded the appeal of ugliness is the poetics of the *epiphany*. As Walter Pater put it in his *Studies in the History of the Renaissance* (1873), 'Every moment some form grows perfect in hand or face; some tone on the hills or sea is choicer than the rest; some mood of passion or insight or intellectual excitement is irresistibly real and attrac-tive for us – for that moment only.' The master of epiphanies of the twentieth cen-tury was James Joyce, and it would suffice to mention the stunning appearance of the 'bird girl' in *A Portrait of the Artist as a Young Man* (1916). But for Joyce even the experience of ugliness, like the smell of rotten cabbage or the sight of a corpse, could become the indelible emblem of an inner moment, provided it was redeemed aesthetically by style. And Stephen Dedalus was left spellbound by banal shop signs until 'his soul shrivelled up sighing with age'.

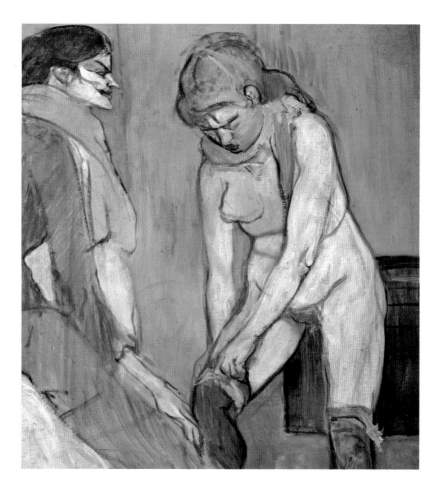

Henri
de Toulouse-Lautrec,
*Woman Pulling
Up Her Stockings*,
1894,
Paris, Musée d'Orsay

Elegy of a Prostitute
Rainer Maria Rilke
Duino Elegies: 'The Seventh Elegy'
(1912–22)
Life is glorious here. You girls knew it,
even you
who seem to have gone without it – you
who sank under
in the cities' vilest streets festering like
open sewers.
For there was one hour for each of you,
maybe
less than an hour, some span between two
whiles
that can hardly be measured, when you
possessed Being.
All. Your veins swelled with existence.

Ugliness and Eroticism
Georges Bataille
Eroticism, 13 (1957)
No one doubts the ugliness of the sexual
act. As with death by sacrifice, the ugliness
of coupling plunges us into anxiety. But
the greater the anxiety – depending on the
strength of the participants – the greater
the awareness of exceeding the limits that
determines the transports of joy. That
situations vary according to tastes and
habits cannot prevent the fact that
generally the beauty (humanity) of a
woman contributes to making the animal
nature of the sexual act sensitive and
overwhelming. For a man, nothing is more
depressing than ugliness in a woman, upon
whose body the ugliness of the organs or
the sexual act do not stand out by contrast.
Because, beauty counts insofar as ugliness
cannot be further sullied, and the essence
of eroticism is filth itself.

Franz von Stuck,
The Kiss of the Sphynx,
1895,
Budapest,
Szepmuveszen Muzeum

The Monstrous Idol of Decadence
Oscar Wilde
'The Sphinx' (1883–94)
In a dim corner of my room for longer than
my fancy thinks
A beautiful and silent Sphinx has watched me through the shifting gloom [. . .]
Come forth, my lovely seneschal! so somnolent,
so statuesque!
Come forth you exquisite grotesque! half woman and half animal! [. . .]
And let me touch those curving claws of yellow
ivory and grasp
The tail that like a monstrous Asp coils round
your heavy velvet paws! [. . .]
Who were your lovers? who were they who wrestled for you in the dust?
Which was the vessel of your Lust?
What Leman had you, every day?
Did giant Lizards come and crouch before you
on the reedy banks?
Did Gryphons with great metal flanks leap on you in your trampled couch?
And from the brick-built Lycian tomb what horrible
Chimera came
With fearful heads and fearful flame to breed
new wonders from your womb? [. . .]
Your horrible and heavy breath makes the light flicker in the lamp,
And on my brow I feel the damp and dreadful
dews of night and death.
Your eyes are like fantastic moons that shiver in some stagnant lake,
Your tongue is like a scarlet snake that dances
to fantastic tunes,
Your pulse makes poisonous melodies, and your
black throat is like the hole
Left by some torch or burning coal on Saracenic
tapestries.

Edvard Munch,
Harpy II,
1899,
Oslo, Munch Museet

The Song of Hate
Olindo Guerrini
'Posthumous' (1877)
When you shall sleep forgotten
Beneath the fat earth
And the cross of God will be planted
Straight on your coffin,
When your cheeks, rotten, will melt
Into wobbly teeth
And in your stinking empty eye sockets
The worms will seethe,
The sleep that for others is peace
Will be a new torment
And a cold, tenacious remorse will
come,
To chew on your brain.
A biting, atrocious remorse
Will visit your grave
Despite God, and His cross,
To gnaw your bones.
I will be that remorse. I will seek you
In the dark night,
A demon that shuns the day, I will come
howling
Like a she-wolf;

And with these nails I'll dig the earth
Become manure for you
And I will tug the nails from the foul
wood
That covers your vile carcass.
Oh, how in your heart still scarlet
I will sate the ancient hatred,
Oh, with what joy will I sink my nails
Into your shameless belly!
I shall sit on your stinking belly
For eternity,
The ghost of revenge and sin,
The terror of hell:
And in your ear that was so fair
Unappeased I shall whisper
Things that will sear your brain
Like a red-hot iron [. . .]
And your pillory will be the verses
In which I consign you to eternal shame,
To torments that will make you long
For the pangs of hell
Here I'll make you die once more,
You bitch, slowly, with stabbing needles,
And your shame, my revenge,
I shall seal between your eyes.

following pages
Franz von Stuck,
Faun Carrying a Nymph,
1918,
private collection

Adolfi Wildt,
Prison,
1915,
private collection

Alfred Kubin,
The Creature from Mars,
c.1906,
private collection

The Faun
Arthur Rimbaud
'Head of a Faun' (1854–91)
A startled faun shows his two eyes
And bites the crimson flowers with his
white teeth.
Stained and ensanguined like mellow
wine
His mouth bursts out in laughter
beneath the branches.

The Louse Catchers
Arthur Rimbaud
'The Louse-catchers' (1854–91)
When the child's brow, red with raging
turmoil,
Implores the white swarm of shadowy
dreams,
Close to the bed come two tall sisters,
charmers,
With gossamer fingers, silvery-nailed.
They seat him by a window opened
wide,
Where blue air bathes a web of tangled
blossom,
And in his heavy hair on which the dew
drips down,
Run their dread fingers, delicate,
bewitching.
He hears the flick
Of their black lashes; through his grey
languor
The regal nails and soft electric fingers
Crackle to death the scores of tiny lice.

Black Teeth
Iginio Ugo Tarchetti
'King for Twenty-four Hours' (1839–69)
The Black Teeth, for which I thought I
would have felt the utmost horror, had
such a sweet, mild, affectionate look
that I felt instantly drawn to them by an
irresistible fondness, while the White
Teeth struck me as being so rebellious,
ferocious, and proud that they almost
horrified me.

Those long, sharp, white, horribly
white teeth, bared to the roots by rather
upturned lips, those teeth, sharp and
curved towards the tip like canines,
seemed made to seize, bite, and lacerate
living, pulsating flesh. They lent the face
a horribly savage look. Contrariwise,
black teeth, stubby, short, square, well
set in and covered by the gums,
promised such a meek nature that I
would have given half the island of
Potikoros if only my kingdom were
populated solely by that race [. . .]

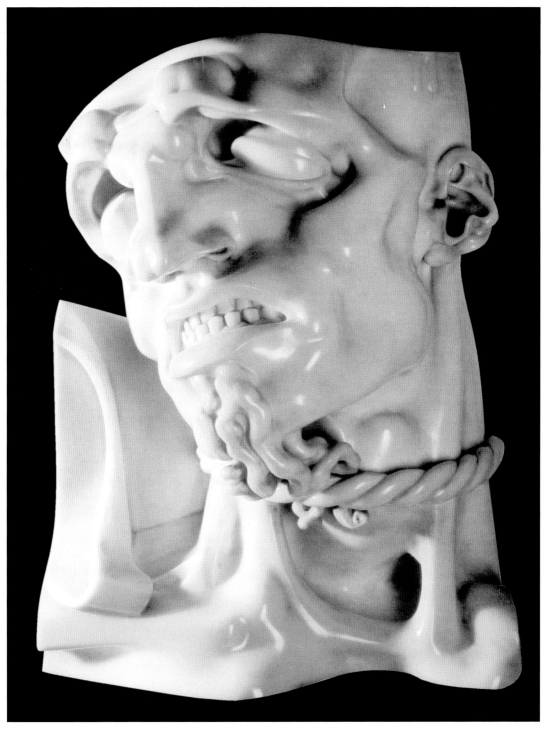

A Carcass

Charles Baudelaire

The Flowers of Evil, XXX (1867)

My love, do you recall the object
which we saw,
That fair, sweet, summer morn!
At a turn in the path a foul
carcass
On a gravel strewn bed,
Its legs raised in the air, like a
lustful woman,
Burning and dripping with
poisons,
Displayed in a shameless,
nonchalant way
Its belly, swollen with gases.
The sun shone down upon that
putrescence,
As if to roast it to a turn,
And to give back a hundredfold
to great Nature
The elements she had combined;
And the sky was watching that
superb cadaver
Blossom like a flower.
So frightful was the stench that
you believed
You'd faint away upon the grass.
The blow-flies were buzzing
round that putrid belly,
From which came forth black
battalions
Of maggots, which oozed out like
a heavy liquid
All along those living tatters.
All this was descending and rising
like a wave,
Or poured out with a crackling
sound;
One would have said the body,
swollen with a vague breath,
Lived by multiplication.
And this world gave forth singular
music,
Like running water or the wind,
Or the grain that winnowers with
a rhythmic motion
Shake in their winnowing baskets.
The forms disappeared and were
no more than a dream,
A sketch that slowly falls
Upon the forgotten canvas, that
the artist
Completes from memory alone.
Crouched behind the boulders, an
anxious dog
Watched us with angry eye,
Waiting for the moment to take
back from the carcass
The morsel he had left.

– And yet you will be like this
corruption,
Like this horrible infection,
Star of my eyes, sunlight of my
being,
You, my angel and my passion!
Yes! thus will you be, queen of
the Graces,
After the last sacraments,
When you go beneath grass and
luxuriant flowers,
To moulder among the bones of
the dead.
Then, O my beauty! say to the
worms who will
Devour you with kisses,
That I have kept the form and the
divine essence
Of my decomposed love!

Like a Mouse

Fyodor Dostoevsky

Notes From the Underground, I, 3 (1864)

And the worst of it is, he himself,
his very own self, looks on
himself as a mouse; no one asks
him to do so; and that is an
important point. Now let us look
at this mouse in action. Let us
suppose, for instance, that it feels
insulted, too (and it almost always
does feel insulted), and wants to
revenge itself, too. There may
even be a greater accumulation of
spite in it than in *l'homme de la
nature et de la verité*. The base
and nasty desire to vent that spite
on its assailant rankles perhaps
even more nastily in it than in
*l'homme de la nature et de la
verité*. For through his innate
stupidity the latter looks upon his
revenge as justice pure and
simple; while in consequence of
his acute consciousness the
mouse does not believe in the
justice of it. To come at last to the
deed itself, to the very act of
revenge. Apart from the one
fundamental nastiness the luckless
mouse succeeds in creating
around it so many other
nastinesses in the form of doubts
and questions, adds to the one
question so many unsettled
questions that there inevitably
works up around it a sort of fatal
brew, a stinking mess, made up
of its doubts, emotions, and of

the contempt spat upon it by the
direct men of action who stand
solemnly about it as judges and
arbitrators, laughing at it till their
healthy sides ache. Of course the
only thing left for it is to [. . .]
creep ignominiously into its
mouse-hole. There in its nasty,
stinking, underground home our
insulted, crushed and ridiculed
mouse promptly becomes
absorbed in cold, malignant and,
above all, everlasting spite.

Neurosis

J.-K. Huysmans

Against the Grain (A Rebours), 9 (1884)

These nightmares attacked him
repeatedly. He was afraid to fall
asleep. For hours he remained
stretched on his bed, now a prey
to feverish and agitated
wakefulness, now in the grip of
oppressive dreams in which he
tumbled down flights of stairs and
felt himself sinking, powerless,
into abysmal depths.

His nervous attacks, which had
abated for several days, became
acute, more violent and obstinate
than ever, unearthing new
tortures.

[. . .]

To while away the
interminable hours, he had
recourse to his portfolios of
prints, and arranged his Goyas.
The first impressions of certain
plates of the *Caprices*,
recognisable as proofs by their
reddish hues, which he had
bought at auction at a high price,
comforted him, and he lost
himself in them, following the
painter's fantasies, distracted by
his vertiginous scenes, his witches
astride on cats, his women
striving to pluck out the teeth of a
hanged man, his bandits, his
succubi, his demons and dwarfs.

Then he examined his other
series of etchings and aquatints,
his *Proverbs* with their macabre
horror, his war subjects with their
wild rage, finally his plate of the
Garot, of which he cherished a
marvellous trial proof, printed on
heavy water-marked paper,
unmounted.

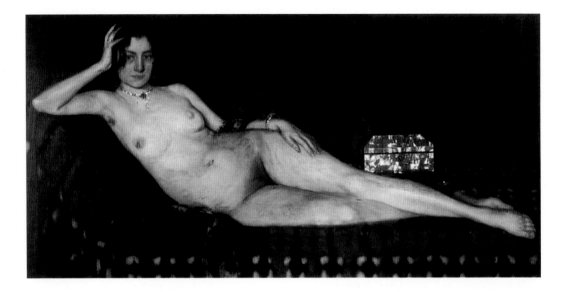

Oskar Zwintscher,
*Mother-of-Pearl
and Gold,*
1909,
Chemniz,
Städtische
Kuntsammlungen

facing page
Christian Schad,
Self-portrait with Model,
1927,
private collection

Macabre Nymph

Charles Baudelaire

The Flowers of Evil (1857)

My dear old child, you're surely not
Too fresh these days. However, dear,
Your tireless game of fast-and-loose
Has given you that smooth veneer,
That things acquire from constant use.
It has its charms, however dear.
I do not find it growing stale –
That sap your forty summers bring
Since autumn fruits with me prevail
Over the banal flowers of spring.
No! you are never dull nor stale.
Your carcase for your age atones,
And gives particular delight
In hollows of your collar bones,
And other places out of sight.
Your carcase certainly atones. [. . .]
Your leg, so muscular and dry,
Could climb volcanoes, never stop,
And, spite of snow, and wind, and rain,
Perform a cancan at the top.

The Aristocratic Nature of Ugliness

Marcel Proust

The Guermantes Way, I (1920)

'That's the Princesse de Guermantes,' said
my neighbour to the gentleman beside
her, taking care to begin the word
'Princesse' with a string of 'P's, to shew
that a title like that was absurd. 'She
hasn't been sparing with her pearls. I'm
sure, if I had as many as that, I wouldn't
make such a display of them; it doesn't
look at all well, not to my mind.'
And yet, when they caught sight of the

Princess, all those who were looking
round to see who was in the audience felt
springing up for her in their hearts the
rightful throne of beauty. Indeed, with the
Duchesse de Luxembourg, with Mme de
Morienval, with Mme de Saint-Euverte,
and any number of others, what enabled
one to identify their faces would be the
juxtaposition of a big red nose to a
hare-lip, or of a pair of wrinkled cheeks
to a faint moustache. These features were
nevertheless sufficient in themselves to
attract the eye, since having merely the
conventional value of a written document
they gave one to read a famous and
impressive name; but also they gave one,
cumulatively, the idea that ugliness had
about it something aristocratic, and that it
was unnecessary that the face of a great
lady, provided it was distinguished,
should be beautiful as well.

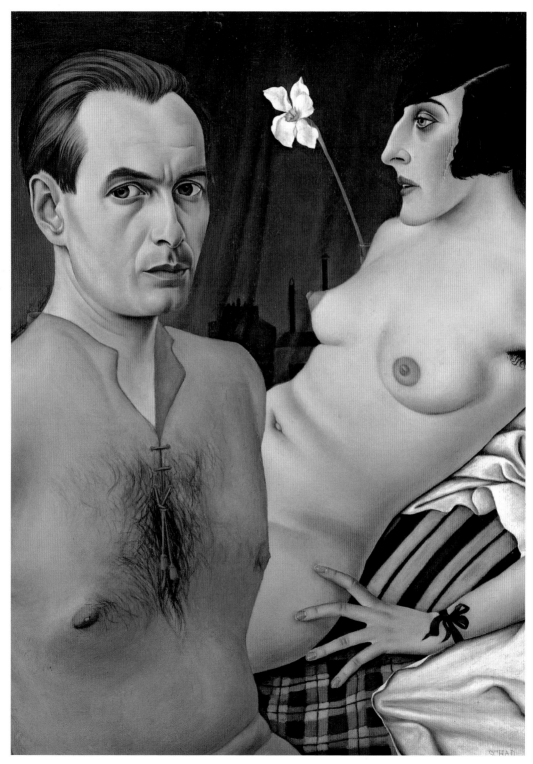

Chapter XIII

The Avant-Garde and the Triumph of Ugliness

For Carl Gustav Jung (in his essay on Joyce's *Ulysses*, in 1932) ugliness today is a sign and symptom of great transformations to come. This means that what will be appreciated tomorrow as great art could seem distasteful today and that taste lags behind when new things come along. This is a concept that holds for every period, but it seems singularly suitable to the works produced by the so-called 'historic' avant-garde movements of the first decades of the twentieth century. The artists did their utmost 'to amaze the bourgeoisie' but the general public (and not only the middle-class section of it) was not only amazed but scandalised.

If the difference set out in the introduction to this book between *ugliness in itself*, *formal ugliness* and *artistic ugliness* holds good, then we can say that the artists of the avant-garde sometimes represented ugliness in itself and formal ugliness, and sometimes merely *deformed* their images, but the public considered their works as examples of artistic ugliness. They did not consider them as beautiful portrayals of ugly things but ugly portrayals of reality. In other words, the bourgeoisie was scandalised by the female face as painted by Picasso not because they thought it a faithful reproduction of an ugly woman (nor did Picasso want her to be so) but because they felt that it was an ugly portrayal of a woman. Hitler, a mediocre painter, condemned contemporary art as 'degenerate' and decades after his death Nikita Khrushchev, accustomed to the works of Soviet realism, said that avant-garde pictures looked as if they had been painted with a donkey's tail.

Pablo Picasso,
Woman in an Armchair,
1913,
Florence,
Pudelko Collection

Man Ray,
Portrait of the Marquis de Sade,
1938,
private collection

facing page
James Ensor,
The Red Judge,
1890,
Mendrisio,
private collection

The Alchemy of Words

Arthur Rimbaud
A Season in Hell (1898)

To me. The story of one of my follies. For a long time my boast was that I was lord of all possible landscapes, and I thought that all the leading lights of modern painting and poetry were a joke. I loved outlandish pictures, paintings over doorways, stage sets, the scenery used by street artists, store signs, garish prints; passé literature, church Latin, badly spelled erotic books, the romances of our grandparents, fairy tales, books for little children, the old melodramas, stupid jingles and naïve rhythms.

The Dissoluteness of the Senses

Arthur Rimbaud
Letter to P. Demeny (1871)

The Poet makes himself a seer by a long, immense, and rational *dissoluteness of all the senses*. All the forms of love, of suffering, of madness; he searches himself, he consumes all the poisons in him, to keep only their quintessence. An inexpressible torture where he needs all the faith, all the superhuman strength, where he becomes, above all others, the great patient, the great criminal, the great accursed – and the supreme Savant! For he arrives at the *unknown*.

The Songs of Maldoror

Count of Lautréamont (Isidore-Lucien Ducasse)
The Songs of Maldoror, IV, 4 (1869)

[. . .] I am dirty. Lice are gnawing at me. When they see me, even swine vomit. The scabs and cracks of leprosy have peeled away my skin, covered with yellowish pus. I know nothing of the waters of the rivers, nor the dew. On the nape of my neck, as atop a dung heap, an enormous fungus is growing, with umbelliferous peduncles. Seated on top of a shapeless piece of furniture, I have not moved my limbs for four centuries. My feet have put down roots in the ground and have become, as far as my belly, a kind of living vegetation, full of ignoble parasites, not yet a plant but no longer flesh. Yet my heart beats. But how could it beat, if the putrefaction and the exhalations from my cadaver (I dare not say body) did not nourish it abundantly? Under my left armpit, a family of toads has taken up residence and, when one of them moves, it tickles. Take care that one of them does not escape and come to scratch the inside of your ear with its mouth: it would be capable of penetrating your brain. Under my right armpit, a chameleon hunts them unceasingly, so as not to die of hunger: all must live. But when one party completely foils the strategies of the other, they find nothing better to do than feel embarrassed, and suck the delicate fat covering my ribs; I'm used to it. An evil viper has devoured my penis and has taken its place: he has made me a eunuch, that villain [. . .] Two small hedgehogs, who have stopped growing, threw to a dog, who did not refuse, the inner parts of my testicles. They now live inside the skin [of the scrotum], which they have carefully washed. My anus has been taken over by a crab; encouraged by inertia, the crab occupies the entrance with his pincers and it really hurts me! Two jellyfish have crossed the seas, instantly attracted by a hope that was not dashed. They observed attentively the two fleshy parts that form the human backside and then, clinging to their convex form, they applied such constant pressure that the two pieces of flesh have vanished, leaving two monsters that have emerged from the realm of viscosity, equal in colour, shape, and ferocity. And don't mention my spinal column for it is a sword.

Gert Wollheim,
Wounded Man,
1919,
private collection

The historic avant-garde movements took their cue from the ideals of intemperance previously advocated by **Rimbaud** or **Lautréamont**. In particular they came out against the naturalistic and 'consolatory' art of their day (which they labelled *pompier* and *kitsch*).

At first, the **Futurist Manifestos** declared that racing cars were more beautiful than the Victory of Samothrace and hailed speed, war and 'the slap and the blow with the fist'. They fought against moonlight, museums and libraries, and set themselves the task of boldly producing ugliness. **Palazzeschi** called for the younger generations to receive an education in the disgusting, and in 1913 Boccioni called both a sculpture and a painting '*Antigrazioso*' (antipretty). Just how untenable was this *battle for ugliness* is shown by the fact that, later, many Futurist authors (Carrà, for example) returned to neoclassical forms, or to the celebrative art of Fascism. But the fuse had been lit.

If Futurist ugliness was deliberately provocative, that of German Expressionism was to be an ugliness that sprang from the denunciation of social ills. From 1906, the year of the foundation of the Die Brücke group, until the years of the rise of Nazism, artists like Kirchner, Nolde, Kokoschka, Schiele, Grosz, Dix and others portrayed with systematic and ruthless insistence haggard and repugnant faces that express the squalor, the corruption and the smug carnality of the bourgeois world that was to become the most docile supporter of the dictatorship.

Otto Dix,
Salon I,
1921,
Stuttgart,
Galerie der Stadt

Cubists like Braque and Picasso, in pursuing the deconstruction of forms, sought for sources of artistic inspiration in non-European arts, in the African masks that contemporary opinion found monstrous and repellent. In the Dada movement the attraction of ugliness emerged through an appeal to the grotesque. **Duchamp** provocatively gave the *Mona Lisa* a moustache and launched the poetics of the *ready-made* by showing a urinal as a work of art. He could have shown another object, but he wanted it to be something *unseemly*.

A particular propensity for disturbing situations and monstrous images is evident in the *Surrealist Manifesto* of 1924. The artist is called upon to reproduce dream situations that open up chinks in the subconscious through operations like automatic writing, to free the mind of all inhibitory restraints and to let it wander according to free associations of images and ideas. Nature is transfigured to make way for nightmarish scenes and disturbing monstrosities, as seen in the works of Ernst, Dalí, and Magritte. They played games like 'exquisite corpses', in which each player wrote a phrase or sketched a part of a figure before folding the paper so that the next player would have to draw his part without knowing what the previous part looked like. Both the visual and the verbal forms of the game created unusual sequences and juxtapositions as in Lautréamont's 'beautiful as a chance encounter between a sewing machine and an umbrella on an operating table'.

Futurist Manifesto
Filippo Tommaso Marinetti
Le Figaro, 20 February 1909
We want to sing the love of danger, the tendency towards energy and temerity.

Courage, audaciousness, and rebellion will be the essential elements of our poetry.

Until today, literature has extolled thoughtful immobility, ecstasy, and sleep. We want to extol aggressive action, feverish insomnia, the racer's stride, the mortal leap, the slap and the punch.

We affirm that the world's magnificence has been enriched by new beauty; the beauty of speed. A racing car with a bonnet adorned with large tubes like serpents with explosive breath, a roaring automobile that seems to race on machine-gun fire, is more beautiful than the Victory of Samothrace.

We want to celebrate the man behind the steering wheel, whose ideal shaft crosses the Earth, which also races along the circuit of its orbit.

The poet must do his utmost, with ardour, ostentation, and munificence, to increase the enthusiastic fervour of the primordial elements.

There is no longer any beauty except in battle. No work of art that does not possess an aggressive character can be a masterpiece. Poetry must be conceived as a violent assault against unknown forces, designed to reduce and prostrate them before man.

We stand upon the farthest tip of the promontory of centuries! [. . .] Why should we look over our shoulders, if we wish to break down the mysterious doors of the impossible? Time and Space died yesterday. We already live in the absolute, because we have already created eternal, omnipresent speed.

We want to glorify war – the world's only hygiene – militarism, patriotism, the destructive acts of liberators, the beautiful ideas people die for and a woman's scorn.

We want to destroy museums, libraries and academies of all kinds, fighting against moralising, feminism, and against all opportunistic or utilitarian baseness.

We will sing the great crowds agitated by work, pleasure, or insurrection: we will sing the multicoloured, polyphonic marches of revolutions in modern capitals; we will sing the vibrant nocturnal fervour of arsenals and shipyards set ablaze by violent electric moons; the crowded stations, devourers of smoking serpents; the factories hanging from clouds by the contorted threads of their own smoke; the bridges like gigantic gymnasts scanning the horizon, and the deep-chested locomotives, chafing at the bit on their tracks like enormous steel horses bridled by tubes, and the smooth flight of aeroplanes, their propellers flapping in the wind like flags and seeming to applaud like enthusiastic crowds. It is from Italy that we launch through the world this violently upsetting incendiary manifesto of ours. With it, today, we establish FUTURISM, because we want to rid this land of its stinking canker of professors, archaeologists, tourist guides and antiquarians. For too long Italy has been a junk dealer's market. We mean to free her from the numberless museums that cover her like so many graveyards.

Pride in Ugliness
Filippo Tommaso Marinetti
Technical Manifesto of Futurist Literature (1912)
They shout at us: 'Your literature will not be beautiful! We will no longer have verbal symphonies, lulling harmonies, soothing cadences!' Let that much be clear!

And thank goodness! We, on the other hand, will use all the brutal sounds, all the expressive cries of the violent life that surrounds us. We will courageously be that which is 'ugly' in literature, murdering solemnity wherever it is found. Come off it! You can drop that air of high and mighty priests when I'm talking! You must spit upon the Altar of Art every day! We are entering the boundless domains of free intuition. After free verse, finally words-in-freedom!

Let Us Be Courageously Ugly
From the Italian and Russian Futurist Manifestos
We want to destroy museums, libraries, and academies of all kinds, fighting against self-righteousness, feminism and every opportunistic or utilitarian baseness. [. . .] Images have no categories, either noble or coarse or vulgar, eccentric, or natural. The intuition that perceives them has neither preferences nor prejudices [. . .] Our aim is to underline the great importance for art of harshness, dissonance and pure primordial coarseness. [. . .] Today tattered hoardings are more beautiful than a ball gown, trams shoot along steel lines of mathematical equality, the fiery expressions of luminous signs erupt from the jaws of the night, houses take off their iron hats to grow taller and bow before us [. . .]

With its roar, the car has pierced every second of time [. . .] I reflect everything and everything is reflected in me, the song of construction sites and factories, the bowels of stations, the steering wheel of the solar disc turning among the cog wheels of clouds, the locomotives that like white-haired professors have lost tufts of smoky hair during their long race and sport long moustaches of white vapour, skyscrapers with their swollen boils of balconies [. . .]

Umberto Boccioni,
Antigrazioso,
1912–13,
Turin, Finlega SpA

Zang tumb tuuum
Filippo Tommaso Marinetti
Bombardamento (1912)
Come on what fun to see hear smell all
all the **ratatatatat** of the machine guns shrieking
themselves hoarse under bites slapppps **braaap
braap** whiplashes **bing-bang-boom-whoomp**
vagaries 200 metre high bursts of fire leap
Down down at the bottom of the orchestra pools
             oxen   buffalo
wallow
goads carts **ploof plaff**
        rear-
ing of horses flick flak **zing zing
shaaaaak**

The Horrible B Flat
Eric Satie
Memoirs of an Amnesiac (1912)
The first time I used a phonoscope, I
examined a medium-sized B flat. I
assure you that I have never seen
anything more repugnant. I called my
man to have him take a look.

Loving War

Giovanni Papini

'We Love War!', in *Lacerba*, 1 October 1914

In the end, war is good for agriculture and modernity. Battlefields yield, for many years, much more than they did before, and without any need to spend on fertiliser. What wonderful cabbages the French will eat where the German infantrymen were piled up, and what fat potatoes they'll dig up in Galicia this coming year! And the fire of the reconnaissance patrols and the destruction of the mortars wipe out the old houses and old things. Those filthy villages that the nasty soldiers put to the torch will be rebuilt cleaner than before. And there will also remain too many Gothic cathedrals and too many churches and too many libraries and too many castles for the tourists and professors and their raptures and nuisance. In the barbarians' wake a new art is born amidst the ruins, and every war of total destruction produces a different style. Everyone will always have work to do if the desire to create is excited and invigorated, as it always is, by destruction.

We love war and savour it like gourmets as long as it lasts. War is fearful – and it is precisely because it is fearful and tremendous and terrible and destructive that we must love it with all our masculine hearts.

Against Love

Filippo Tommaso Marinetti

'Only War Can Cleanse the World' (1915)

But that which digs an even deeper trench between Futurist thought and Anarchist thought is the great problem of love, the great tyranny of sentimentalism and lust, from which we wish to liberate humanity. It is precisely this hatred for the tyranny of love that we express with the laconic phrase: 'despising woman.'

We despise women, conceived as the sole ideal, the divine reservoir of love, the poisonous woman, the tragic female plaything, the fragile, obsessive and fatal woman whose voice, oppressive destiny, and whose dreamy tresses extend and wind their way through the leaves of

forests bathed in moonlight.

We despise horrible, heavy Love that blocks man's progress, preventing him from breaking free of his own humanity, of striving harder, of outdoing himself, of becoming what we call the multiplied man.

We despise horrible, heavy Love, the immense leash with which the sun keeps the courageous earth chained to its orbit, when the earth would undoubtedly wish to leap here and there, running all its sidereal risks.

We are convinced that love – sentimentalism and lust – is the least natural thing in the world. The only thing both natural and important is coitus, the aim of which is the futurism of our species.

Futurist Education in Ugliness

Aldo Palazzeschi

Against Pain (1914)

Look death right in the eye, and it will supply you with enough to laugh about for the rest of your life. I say that the greatest sources of human joy are the crying man, and the dying man.

We have to teach our children to laugh, to laugh the most unrestrained, insolent laughter [. . .] We will supply them with educational toys, humpbacked, blind, gangrenous, crippled, consumptive, syphilitic puppets, that mechanically cry, shout, complain, are afflicted with epilepsy, plague, cholera, haemorrhaging, haemorrhoids, the clap, insanity, puppets that faint, emit a death rattle, and die. Their teacher will suffer from dropsy and elephantiasis, or be thin as a rail, long-limbed, with a neck like a giraffe's. [. . .] One tiny little teacher, a stunted hunchback, and another gigantic teacher with a prepubescent face, an extremely feeble voice, who weeps tears like shards of glass [. . .] Young men, your companion will be hunchbacked, blind, lame, bald, deaf, with a dislocated jaw, toothless, and smelly; she will gesticulate like a monkey and talk like a parrot [. . .] Do not linger on her beauty, if unfortunately for you she seems beautiful, but look deeper, and you will find the deformity. Do not settle down languidly in the wake of her

perfume; a sharp whiff of the stench that is the profound truth of that flesh you adore might one day surprise you, destroying in one fell swoop your fragile dream, imprisoning you in suffering. Do not linger on the brief hour of your shared youth, you will perforce float upon a sea of human pain. Study her in depth and you will have her old age, a truth that would otherwise remain unknown to you when you possess her, and you will thus become prey to nostalgia. Do not let any degree of deformity or age stop you; unlike beauty and youth they do not have any limits; they are infinite.

Rest assured, you will take greater pleasure from watching three carcases run than three thoroughbreds. The thoroughbred is in itself the carcase it will become; look for it, reveal it, do not dwell on the lines of fleeting splendour [. . .]

Consider the happiness you'll feel on seeing dozens of little hunchbacks, dwarfs, cross-eyed, and lame children grow up around you, the divine explorers of joy. Rather than put a wig on your companion, you should shave her until she shines, if she is not entirely bald already, and have her put padded stuffing on her back if she is not already hunchbacked.

[. . .] We futurists want to cure the Latin races, especially our own, of conscious pain, conformist syphilis aggravated by chronic romanticism, and of the monstrous susceptibility and piteous sentimentalism that depress every Italian, [. . .] substituting the use of perfumes with the use of stench. Flood a ballroom with the fresh smell of roses and you cradle it with a brief, vain smile; flood it with the deeper smell of shit (a stupidly unrecognised human profundity) and you will energise it with hilarity and joy. [. . .] Set up recreational clubs in mortuaries, dictate epitaphs based on tongue-twisters, puns, and double meanings. Develop that useful and healthy instinct that makes us laugh at a man who falls down, and let him get back up by himself, sharing our happiness with him [. . .] Transform insane asylums into finishing schools for our new generations.

Carlo Carrà,
*The Funeral of the
Anarchist Galli*,
1910–11,
New York,
Museum of Modern Art

Enrico Prampolini,
*Portrait of Marinetti:
Plastic Synthesis*,
1924–25,
Turin, Galleria Civica
d'Arte Moderna
e Contemporanea

Marcel Duchamp,
Torture-Morte,
1959,
Paris, Musée Nationale
d'Art Moderne, Centre
Georges Pompidou

facing page
Raoul Hausmann,
The Art Critic,
1919–20,
London, Tate Gallery

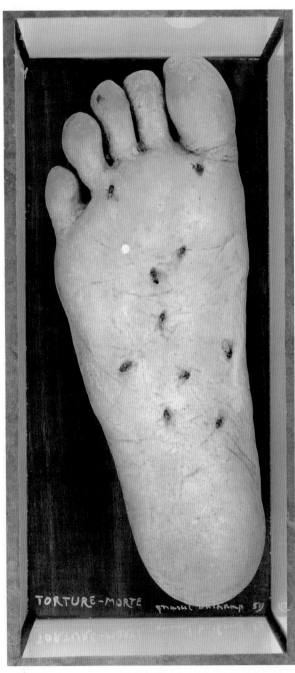

Dada

Tristan Tzara
Dada Manifesto (1918)

A work of art need not represent beauty, which is dead: nor happiness nor sadness, nor light nor darkness, it need neither entertain nor mistreat individual personalities by serving them little pastries of blessed halos or the toil of a race across the atmosphere. A work of art is never beautiful by law, objectively, or unanimously [. . .] Let us rip asunder, like a furious wind, the dirty linen of clouds and prayers, and prepare the grandiose spectacle of cataclysm, fiery inferno, and decomposition [. . .] I proclaim the opposition of all cosmic faculties to the gonorrhoea of the putrid sun born of the philosophic factories of thought, the relentless struggle with any and all means of DADAIST DISGUST [. . .] Freedom: DADA DADA DADA, the roar of tense colours, the tangle of opposites and all the contradictions in the world, of the grotesque and the contradictory: *Life*.

Dadaist Disgust

Tristan Tzara
Dada Manifesto (1918)

Anything produced by disgust, capable of transforming itself into negation of the family, is *Dada*; a protest with the fists of the entire being bent on destructive action: DADA; recognition of all the means repressed until now by the modest sex in the interests of easy compromise and good manners: DADA; abolition of logic, the ballet of those impotent to create: *DADA*; of every social hierarchy and equation established by our servants out of love of values: DADA; each object, all objects, feelings, darkness, apparitions and the undeniable collision of parallel lines, are all weapons for the fight: DADA; the abolition of memory: DADA; the abolition of archaeology: **DADA**; the abolition of prophets: DADA; the abolition of the future: **DADA**; absolute, irrefutable faith in every God who is the immediate product of spontaneity: **DADA**; an elegant leap devoid of prejudice from harmony to another sphere; to spit out impolite or amorous ideas like a bright waterfall, or to fondle them – with the extremely self-satisfied idea that in any case, it's all the same – with the same intensity in the thicket of the soul, free of insects thanks to noble blood and gilded with the bodies of archangels.

Francis Picabia,
The Kiss,
1923–26,
Turin, Galleria Civica
d'Arte Moderna
e Contemporanea

Marcel Duchamp,
L.H.O.O.Q.
(*Mona Lisa with
Moustache*),
1930,
private collection

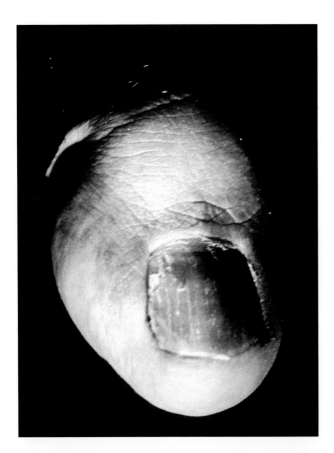

The Big Toe
Georges Bataille
'The Big Toe' (1929)
The shape of the big toe is not specifically monstrous: in this it is different from other parts of the body, for example the inside of a gaping mouth. Only secondary (though common) deformities have been able to give its ignominy an exceptional burlesque value. [. . .] Since man's physical position allows him to distance himself *as far as he can* from earthly mud, but since on the other hand he laughs with enormous glee whenever even the purest wind up in the mire; we might consider the big toe, always more or less tainted and humiliating, to be psychologically analogous to a man's brutal fall, and therefore to death. [. . .] The big toe's horrendously corpse-like and at the same time overbearing and proud look corresponds to this derision, and lends sharp expression to the disorder of the human body, the work of violent discord among the organs.

Jacques-André Boiffard,
Big Toe of a Thirty-Year-Old Man,
1929,
Paris, Musée Nationale d'Art Moderne,
Centre Georges Pompidou

There was a prevalent, anarchic taste for the unbearable, as in **Roussel**, or in films like Buñuel's *Un chien andalou* (1929) where we see repugnant operations like the vivisection of an eye. In 1932 **Artaud** launched his 'Theatre of Cruelty', as a 'plague' and 'revenging scourge', in which life 'exceeds all limits and puts itself to the test with torture and riding roughshod over all things'. **Dalí** busied himself with operations of 'critical paranoia' like his analysis of Millet's celebrated *Angelus*, and **Bataille** immortalised the big toe and flowers as objects of disgust. Later, the Informal movement was to reassess what had until then been seen as unrepresentable, in other words the most inaccessible depths of matter, moulds, dust and mud. New Realism rediscovered the detritus of the industrial world and fragments of destroyed objects and then reassembled them in a new form, while exponents of pop art like **Warhol** appealed for an aesthetic recycling of *waste*. In the light of all these provocations it's not hard to understand moralistic reactions like that of **Sedlmayr**; but the historic avant-garde was not interested in creating any harmony, and pursued the break-up of all order and of all institutionalised perceptive schema while searching for new forms of awareness capable of penetrating both the recesses of the subconscious and those of matter in the primitive state, the aim being to expose the alienation of contemporary society.

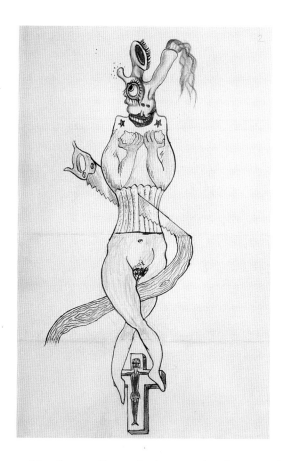

André Breton, Man Ray,
Emmanuel Radnitsky,
Max Morise,
Yves Tanguy,
Exquisite Corpse,
17 May 1927,
Paris, Musée Nationale
d'Art Moderne,
Centre Georges
Pompidou

The German Expressionists were in a ferment of social criticism; the Italian Futurists were revolutionaries whose anarchoid proto-Fascism came into being as a polemic against that bourgeois world with which they would later be tranquilly reconciled. At first, the Russian Futurists were close to the ideals of the Soviet Revolution. Many Surrealists had become communists, while turbulent debates and ferocious reciprocal excommunications between Stalinists and Trotskyists were the order of the day. In his *Aesthetic Theory* **Adorno** points out that currents such as Surrealism and Expressionism 'whose irrational aspects emerged as disagreeable surprises, attacked power, authority and obscurantism', that the rejection of the 'norms of the beautiful life in an ugly society' is doomed to be disfigured by resentment, and that art must 'make its own all those things that have been proclaimed ugly, no longer to integrate them, to mitigate them, or to have their existence accepted by falling back on humour […] but to denounce, through ugliness, the world that creates it and reproduces it in its own likeness […] Art accuses power […] and bears witness to those things repressed and denied by that same power.' Today everyone (including those bourgeois who should have been stunned and scandalised) recognise as (artistically) beautiful all those works that had horrified their fathers. The ugliness of the avant-garde has been accepted as a new model of beauty, and has given rise to a new commercial circuit. 379

Salvador Dalí,
*Soft Construction
with Boiled Beans
(Premonition
of Civil War)*,
1936,
Philadelphia,
Museum of Art

Surrealism

André Breton

The First Surrealism Manifesto (1924)
Surrealism: Pure psychic automatism through which one proposes to express, either verbally or through writing, or in any other manner, the real workings of thought. Dictated by thought, in the absence of any control exerted by reason, above and beyond any and every aesthetic or moral preoccupation [. . .] Surrealism is based on the idea of a degree of superior reality, connected to certain forms of association that have been heretofore overlooked, on the omnipotence of dreams, on the disinterested play of thought.
It tends to definitively liquidate all other psychic mechanisms, and takes over from them in the resolution of life's principal problems [. . .]

Have something to write with brought to you after you have got comfortable in the place that seems to you to be the most favourable for concentrating your spirit within itself. Put yourself in the most passive, or receptive state that you can [. . .] Write quickly without any fixed subject, so quickly that you cannot stop yourself, and do not be tempted to reread what you've written. The first sentence will come of its own volition.

Here are a few characters with rather disparate ways [. . .] Armed thus with a small number of physical and moral characteristics, those beings who in truth owe little to you will no longer deviate from a certain line of conduct, about which you need not worry. The result will be a plot that seems more or less skilfully put together, justifying point for point a moving or reassuring finale that you will take no interest in.

Against Surrealism

Hans Sedlmayr

Art in Crisis: The Lost Centre, V (1948)
Surrealism has cast off the mask. It openly insults God and man, the dead and the living, beauty and morals, structure and form, reason and art: 'Art is foolishness' [. . .] It believes it possesses a point of view, 'based on which life and death, reality and imagination, communicability and incommunicability, "above" and "below" no longer need be considered as opposites and contradictory.' This definition, apparently scientific in nature, is nothing more than the definition of chaos. Nor does surrealism deny this; in fact, it openly recognises its attempts to look for 'the systemisation of confusion' (S. Dalí) and disorganisation. 'There is no revolutionary order, there is only disorder and folly.' And, with satisfaction, Surrealism announces that 'a new vice has just been born, and with it man has been offered another illusion: surrealism, the son of delirium and darkness' (Aragon). [. . .] The appearance of its avant-gardes is a powerful signal that serves to indicate the already advanced onslaught of irrational, or better yet sub-rational, forces. Those ingenuous (or even complicated) contemporaries who see in the misunderstood name of surrealism – which, in reality, is sub-realism – the promise of being lifted up above and beyond the banal life of everyday existence are the same ones opening doors to it [. . .]

It is pointless to consider this phenomenon as a trifle [. . .] In essence, surrealism is the last hurried step towards the ruin of art and mankind, ruin that Nietzsche first marked in 1881 when he wrote his fragment, 'The Crazy Man': 'Aren't we perhaps continuing to fall? Behind, to the side, ahead, everywhere? Do "above" and "below" still exist? Aren't we perhaps wandering through an infinite nothingness? Isn't cold space breathing in our faces? Hasn't it become even colder still?'

Salvador Dalí,
Atavism at Twilight,
1933–34,
Berne, Kunstmuseum

Jean-François Millet,
The Angelus,
1858–59,
Paris, Musée d'Orsay

facing page
Luis Buñuel (director),
Un chien andalou,
1929

following pages
Paul Klee,
Comedian,
1904,
New York,
Museum of Modern Art

Francis Bacon,
Self-Portrait,
Post-1945,
London,
Marlborough Gallery

Deforming the Past

Salvador Dalí

'A Paranoid-Critical Investigation of Millet's *Angélus*'

Paranoia does not always limit itself to being 'the illustration'; it still constitutes the one true 'literal illustration' we know, in other words 'delirious interpretive illustration' [. . .]

No other kind of image seems more appropriate to me to represent in the most 'literal' and delirious manner, Lautréamont in general and *Les chants de Maldoror* in particular, than that completed nearly seventy years ago by a painter of tragic cannibalistic atavism, of ancestral encounters with sweet, soft, choice flesh: I am talking about Jean-François Millet. A frightfully misunderstood painter. And it is precisely Millet's renowned *Angélus* that might be the pictorial equivalent of the 'casual encounter on an operating table between a sewing machine and an umbrella', as unknown as it is sublime [. . .]

The *Angélus* is the only painting in the world I know of that represents the immobile presence. The encounter and long wait of two beings in a solitary, crepuscular and mortal environment. In the painting, this solitary, crepuscular and mortal environment plays the role of operating table for the poetic text, since not only is life extinguished on the horizon, but furthermore the pitchfork is stuck into the living, substantial flesh that cultivated land has always represented for mankind. I mean, it lodges itself,

with that voracious desire for fecundity, proper to those exquisite scalpel incisions that, as everyone knows, do no more than secretly search out, with diverse analytical pretexts, through the vivisection of each corpse, the fecund synthetic, the nourishing fruit of death. From this derives the constant dualism, present in every era, of cultivated land, [. . .] a dualism that ultimately leads us to consider cultivated land, especially with the aggravating circumstance of the gloaming, as a well-stocked operating table, the best-equipped of all operating tables to supply the most perfect, appetising corpse, stuffed with that fine and imponderable truffle that can only be found in nourishing dreams constituted by the flesh of the soft shoulders of atavistic, Hitlerian wet-nurses, and seasoned with the incorruptible and exciting salt composed of the frenetic and voracious teeming of ants that automatically implies an authentic 'unburied putrefaction' truly respectable and worthy of its name. If, as we have said, 'cultivated land' is the most reliable and suitable operating table that exists, the umbrella and the sewing machine can be transposed, in *Angélus*, into the male and female figures, and all the discomfort and mystery of the encounter will always derive [. . .] from the authentic characteristics of these two figures, from the two objects whence the subject's entire development, all the latent tragedy of the encounter, the wait and the preliminaries are derived. The umbrella, the typical surrealist object with a symbolic function

(the result of its flagrant and well-known erection) can be none other than the male figure in *Angélus* who, as you will be so kind as to remember, in the painting does everything in his power to hide his state of erection while managing only to highlight it, considering the shameful and compromising position of his hat. Facing him, the sewing machine, an heavily characterised female symbol recognised by everyone, who even goes so far as to lay claim to the mortal and cannibalistic attribute of her sewing needle, the work of which is identified with the very delicate perforation that the praying mantis performs to 'empty' her male, in other words to empty the umbrella, transforming it into that flaccid, depressed, and martyred victim, into which every umbrella is in fact transformed when it closes up following the magnificence of its amorous functions, at fever pitch and as rigid as possible.

It is clear that behind the tense figures of *Angélus*, and in other words behind the sewing machine and the umbrella, the gleaners cannot but continue to collect with indifference, conventionally, the pan-fried eggs (with no pan), the inkwells, the spoons, and all the silverware that the final moments of the gloaming render exhibitionist during this scintillating hour. And as soon as a raw cutlet, taken as an average example of edible symbols, alights upon the male's head, already clouds begin to form and draw together suddenly on the horizon to form the silhouette of Napoleon I, the 'hungry one'.

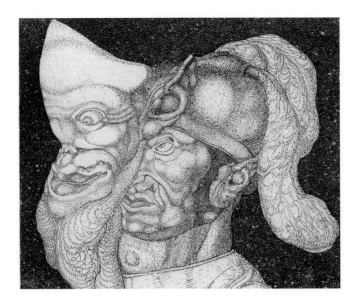

The Ugliness of the Avant-garde
Georges Bataille
'The Lugubrious Game' (1929)
Picasso's paintings are horrendous, and those by Dalí are frightfully ugly [. . .] If violent movements manage to liberate a being from profound boredom, it is because they give rise, by who knows what obscure error, to a horrible ugliness that satisfies. It must be said, on the other hand, that ugliness can be hateful beyond all appeal and, so to speak, by disgrace, but nothing is more common than dubious ugliness that gives, in a provocative manner, the illusion of the contrary. As far as irrevocable ugliness is concerned, it is exactly as detestable as certain beauties: beauty that dissimilates nothing, that is not a mask of lost immodesty, that never contradicts itself and remains eternally on guard like a villain.

Offensive
Raymond Queneau
Exercises in Style (1947)
After a repellent wait beneath an ignoble sun, I ended up on a filthy bus infested with a gang of stinking animals. The stinkiest of these stinkers was a pimply fellow with a neck like a chicken's who sported a grotesque cloth cap with a bit of string in place of the ribbon. This peacock started screeching because a stinker of his own kind had trampled on his clogs with geriatric furore. But he soon ran out of wind and went to sit himself down in a seat still soaked with the sweat from another stinker's buttocks.

Two hours later, talk about bad luck, I once again ran into that same stinking stinker barking at a stinker even stinkier than he, in front of that repugnant monument they call the 'Gare Saint-Lazare'. And both of these stinkers were spraying each other with saliva over a shitty little button. But whether that pimple of his moved up or down on that filthy overcoat of his, a stinker he was and a stinker he remained.

The Transvaluation of the Ugly
Raymond Roussel
Locus Solus, 2, 4 (1914)
Human teeth were scattered everywhere over a vast area, in a great variety of forms and colours. Some were of a blinding white in contrast with smokers' incisors in a full range of browns and tawny shades. That bizarre stock contained all the gradations of yellow, from the most vaporous canary yellow tones to the most atrocious reddish hues. Blue teeth, some tenuous, others intense, made their contribution to that rich polychrome, rounded off by a number of black teeth, and by the pale or bright reds of numerous bloody roots.

Outlines and proportions differed ad infinitum: immense molars and monstrous canines flanked almost imperceptible baby teeth. Here and there frequent metallic reflections came from lead fillings or gold crowns.

In the place occupied in that moment by the tamper, the teeth, gathered close together, gave rise to a real but as yet unfinished painting thanks to nothing more than the alternation of their shades: the whole thing was reminiscent of a German knight sleeping in a shadowy crypt, lying limp and supine on the edge of an underground pool. A thin spiral of smoke, generated by the sleeping knight's brain, showed in a dreamlike manner eleven young people in the act of kneeling down subjugated by the dismay they feel at facing an almost diaphanous air bubble, the apparent destination of a white dove's sure flight, which traced upon the ground a light shadow projected around a dead bird. Alongside the horseman there lay an old, closed book feebly illuminated by a torch planted right at the bottom of the crypt. Within this singular dental mosaic, yellows and browns dominated. The other, rarer tones threw in notes of vivacious, seductive colour. The dove, made of splendid white teeth, was in the midst of a rapid, graceful flight; in harmony with the knight's headgear, several cunningly arranged roots created, on one side, a red feather, the ornament of a black hat abandoned near the book; on the other side, a large purple cape fastened by a brass clasp formed by an ingenious arrangement of gold crowns; a complicated amalgam of bluish teeth created sky-blue stockings that ended inside big boots of black teeth.

Alberto Martini,
Birth – Human Suffering,
from 'Mysteries',
six lithographs,
1923,
Milan, Bottega di Poesia

facing page
Jan Fautrier,
Study for a Large Nude,
1926,
private collection

The Theatre of Cruelty

Antonin Artaud
The Theatre and its Double (1938)
The theatre, like the plague, is in the midst of a crisis resolvable through either death or healing. And if the plague is a superior disease because it is a total crisis after which nothing but death or absolute purification remains, the theatre too is a disease, because it is supreme equilibrium, unobtainable without destruction [. . .] It may be that the poison of theatre, injected into the social body, disintegrates it as Saint Augustine claims, but it does so like a plague, like a vengeful scourge.

The Putrefaction of Flowers

Georges Bataille
'The Language of Flowers' (1929)
After a period of very brief splendour the marvellous corolla rots indecently under the sun, becoming a shameful disgrace for the plant. Upon achieving the stench of manure, even though it gave you the impression of slipping away in a rush of angelic, lyrical purity, the flower seems to brusquely return to its primitive filth: even the most ideal is quickly reduced to a scrap on an aerial dunghill. Because flowers don't age *honestly* like leaves, which lose none of their beauty even after they are dead; flowers wither like simpering, overly made-up old women, dying ridiculously on the same stem that seemed to be bearing them up to the stars.

Andy Warhol,
Orange Car Crash,
1963,
New York,
Andy Warhol
Foundation

facing page
Arman,
Small Bourgeois Trash,
New York,
Philip Arman Collection

The Aesthetics of Leftovers
Andy Warhol
The Philosophy of Andy Warhol (1975)
I always like to work leftovers, doing the leftover things. Things that were discarded, that everybody knew were no good, I always thought had a great potential to be funny. It was like recycling work. I always thought there was a lot of humour in leftovers. [. . .]

When I see an old Esther Williams movie and a hundred girls are jumping off their swings, I think of what the auditions must have been like and about all the takes when maybe one girl didn't have the nerve to jump when she was supposed to, and I think about her left over on the swing. So that take of the scene was a leftover on the cutting-room floor – an out-take – and the girl was probably a leftover at that point – she was probably fired – so the whole scene is much funnier than the real scene where everything went right, and the girl who didn't jump is the star of the out-take.

Chapter XIV

The Ugliness of Others, Kitsch and Camp

1. The Ugliness of Others

It has been said right from the outset that the concept of ugliness, like that of beauty, is relative, not only in different cultures but also in different periods.

History is full of examples of this. **Saverio Bettinelli**, a learned Jesuit and certainly a man of good taste, at least according to the canons of his day (the eighteenth century), in his *Letters of Virgil* (which he imagines as written by Virgil) accuses the *Divine Comedy* of coarseness and obscurity. In order to make it easier for his retinue to enter Notre-Dame in Paris to witness his coronation as emperor, Napoleon ordered the removal of the tympanum of the central door of the cathedral, thereby destroying a masterpiece of the Gothic art that in the early nineteenth century (despite the Gothic novel and maybe precisely because of it) was seen as barbarous and primitive. We gaze with incredulity at photographs of actresses who starred in silent movies unable to understand why on earth their contemporaries found them glamorous, nor would we have a woman of Rubensesque proportions walk along a fashion catwalk.

It's not only the past that is often incomprehensible: most of the time contemporaries are unable to appreciate the future, in other words the frequently provocative works proposed by artists. And there's more to this than just the petit bourgeois or popular rejection of avant-garde art. For the reader's amusement, and by way of a warning to all future critics, see on the following page **They looked ugly to them**, an incredible collection of 'hatchet jobs' from experts of the day with respect to the works of artists we now consider to be masters.

Detail of the decor at D'Annunzio's home, known as the Vittoriale, Gardone

Oh, How Ugly the Divine Comedy Is!
Saverio Bettinelli
Virgilian Letters (1758)

While there are beautiful verses, which I encountered from time to time, and which made me so happy I could almost forgive him . . . Oh what a shame, I would cry, that these pretty parts have been condemned to so much darkness and extravagance! [. . .] Oh, what an exhausting task it was for us to struggle through one hundred cantos and fourteen thousand verses, all those circles and pits, through thousands of abysses and precipices together with Dante, who fainted at each fright, fell asleep at every other step, struggled to awaken, and bored me, his Duke and captain, with his novel questions, the strangest I'd ever heard! [. . .] And this is supposed to be a poem, an exemplary, divine work of art? A poem composed of preaching, dialogue, problems, a poem devoid of action or with no more movement than falling, passing, climbing, going forth and returning again, growing worse and worse the more you read? Who could read fourteen thousand verses of such sermonising without fainting or dropping with exhaustion? [. . .] Dante lacks nothing else than good taste, and discernment in his art. But he possessed a great soul, sublime even, a fine and fecund creativity, vivacious and picturesque imagination, thanks to which some admirable verses and sections flow from his pen [. . .] There are some one hundred of these tercets, if I've counted correctly, among the five thousand that make up the entire poem. Of verses standing alone, or sententious, or delicate, or whining, or magnificent or flawless, I dare say, there are some one thousand [. . .] Therefore, thirteen thousand defective or bad verses remain.

They Thought the Following were Ugly
André Bernard
Rotten Rejections (Readers' reports and criticisms)

Christopher Cerf and Victor Navasky
The Experts Speak
Johann Sebastian Bach's compositions are deprived of beauty, of harmony, and of clarity of melody. (Johann Adolph Scheibe, *Der kritische Musikus*, 1737)
An orgy of vulgar noise. (Louis Spohr on the first performance of Beethoven's Fifth Symphony)
Had he [Chopin] submitted his music to a teacher, the latter, it is to be hoped, would have torn it up and thrown it at his feet – and this is what we symbolically wish to do. (Ludwig Rellstab, *Iris im Gebiete der Tonkunst*, 1833)
Rigoletto lacks melody. This opera has hardly any chance to be kept in the repertoire. (*Gazette Musicale de Paris*, 1853)
I played over the music of that scoundrel Brahms. What a giftless bastard! (Tchaikovsky in his *Diary* on Brahms)
In a hundred years the histories of French literature will only mention *Les Fleurs du Mal* as a curio. (Emile Zola, writing on the occasion of Baudelaire's death)
Paul [Cézanne] may have had the genius of a great painter, but he never had the persistence to become one. (Emile Zola on Cézanne)
It's the work of a madman. (Ambroise Vollard in 1907 on *Les Demoiselles d'Avignon* by Picasso)
I may perhaps be dead from the neck up, but rack my brains as I may I can't see why a chap should need thirty pages to describe how he turns over in bed before going to sleep. (Reader's report on Proust, *À la Recherche du Temps Perdu*)
You have buried your novel

underneath a heap of details which are well done but utterly superfluous. (Letter of a French editor to Flaubert, on *Madame Bovary*)
Little imagination is shown in invention, in the creating of character and plot [. . .]. Balzac's place in French literature will be neither considerable nor high. (Eugène Poitou, *Revue des deux mondes*, 1856)
In *Wuthering Heights* all the faults of *Jane Eyre* [by her sister Charlotte] are magnified a thousand fold, and the only consolation which we have in reflecting upon it is that it will never be generally read. (James Lorimer on Emily Brontë, *North British Review*, 1849)
The incoherence and formlessness of her – I don't know how to designate them – versicles are fatal. (Thomas Bailey Aldrich on Emily Dickinson, *The Atlantic Monthly*, 1982)
Moby Dick is sad stuff, dull and dreary, or ridiculous. [. . .] And his Mad Captain is a monstrous bore. (*The Southern Quarterly Review*, 1851)
Walt Whitman is as unacquainted with art as a hog is with mathematics. (*The London Critic*, 1855)
It is not interesting enough for the general reader and not thorough enough for the scientific reader. (Reader's report on *The Time Machine* by H.G. Wells, 1895)
The story does not seem to work up to a conclusion – neither the hero's career nor his character is shown to be brought to any stage which justifies an ending. It seems to us in short that the story does not culminate in anything. (Reader's report on F. Scott Fitzgerald, *This Side of Paradise*, 1920)
Good God, I can't publish this. We'd both be in jail. (Reader's report on William Faulkner, *Sanctuary*, 1931)

It is impossible to sell animal stories in the USA. (Reader's report on George Orwell, *Animal Farm*, 1945)
This girl doesn't, it seems to me, have a special perception or feeling which would lift that book above the 'curiosity' level. (Reader's report on *The Diary of Anne Frank*, 1952)
It should be, and probably has been, told to a psychoanalyst, and it has been elaborated into a novel which contains some wonderful writing, but it is overwhelmingly nauseating. [. . .] I recommend that it be buried under a stone for a thousand years. (Reader's report on Vladimir Nabokov, *Lolita*, 1955)
The novel *Buddenbrooks* is nothing but two thick tomes in which the author describes the worthless story of worthless people in worthless chatter. (Eduard Engel on Thomas Mann, 1901)
I just finished *Ulysses* and I think it is a mis-fire [. . .]. The book is diffuse. It is brackish. It is pretentious. It is underbred, not only in the obvious sense, but in the literary sense. (From the diary of Virginia Woolf)
He has no talent at all, that boy. (Édouard Manet to Claude Monet on Pierre-Auguste Renoir)
No Civil War picture ever made a nickel. (Irving Thalberg of MGM suggesting not to buy the film rights of *Gone with the Wind*)
Gone with the Wind is going to be the biggest flop in Hollywood history. I'm just glad it'll be Clark Gable who's falling flat on his face and not Gary Cooper. (Gary Cooper, after turning down the role of Rhett Butler)
What can I do with a guy with ears like that? (Jack Warner, after viewing Clark Gable's screen test, 1930)
Can't act. Can't sing. Balding. Can dance a little. (MGM executive, after Fred Astaire's screen test, 1928)

2. Kitsch

Ugliness is also a social phenomenon. The members of the 'upper' classes have always seen the tastes of the 'lower' classes as disagreeable or ridiculous. One could certainly say that economic factors have always played a part in such discrimination, in the sense that elegance has always been associated with the use of costly fabrics, colours and gems.

But the discriminating factor is often cultural rather than economic; it is customary to note the vulgarity of the nouveau riche who, in order to show off his wealth, exceeds the limits assigned by the dominant aesthetic sensibility to 'good taste'.

On the other hand, defining the dominant aesthetic sensibility is a tricky business: it is not necessarily the sensibility of those holding political and economic power, but is more likely to be determined by artists, cultivated people, and by those considered (in literary, artistic and academic circles) to be expert in 'beautiful things'. But this is a highly volatile concept. And so some readers might be amazed to find in this chapter of a book on ugliness images that they might consider most beautiful. These images are proposed because the dominant aesthetic sensibility, often a posteriori, has defined them as unseemly, in the sense that they have been labelled as kitsch.

According to some sources the word *kitsch* derives from the second half of the nineteenth century, when American tourists in Munich who wished to buy a cheap picture asked for a *sketch*. This allegedly gave rise to the term used to mean vulgar trash produced for purchasers eager for facile aesthetic experiences. But the dialect of Mecklenburg already had a verb *kitschen*, which meant 'to collect mud from the street'.

Another meaning of the same word would be 'to make furniture look antique', while there is also the verb *verkitschen*, meaning 'to sell cheaply'. But for whom is trash actually trash? 'High' culture uses kitsch to describe garden gnomes, devotional images, the fake Venetian canals in the casinos of Las Vegas, the grotesque fake that is California's famous **Madonna Inn**, which aims to give tourists an exceptional 'aesthetic' experience. In addition, kitsch has unfailingly been used to define the celebratory art (intended to be popular) of Stalin's, Hitler's and Mussolini's regimes, which described contemporary art as 'degenerate'.

Good Things in the Worst Taste
Guido Gozzano
'Grandmother Hope's Girlfriend' (1850)
The stuffed duck and d'Alfieri's bust of
Napoleon – framed flowers (good things in
bad taste) – the somewhat gloomy
fireplace, empty boxes with no sugared
almonds inside – marble fruit protected by
glass bell jars – a few rare toys, boxes
decorated with seashells – objects with
mottos like 'hail', and 'remember', coconuts

– Venice portrayed in mosaics, rather
insipid watercolours – prints, chests, albums
painted with old-fashioned anemones –
Massimo d'Azeglio's paintings, miniatures –
daguerrotypes: dreamy, perplexed figures –
the big old lamp hanging down in the
middle of the room, its quartz reflecting by
the thousands the good things in bad taste
– the cuckoo clock that sings, chairs
upholstered in bordeaux damask. I have
been born again . . . in 1850!

The Arnolfini Couple,
waxwork reproduction,
twentieth century,
Buena Park,
California,
Palace of Living Art,
Movieland Wax
Museum

Photo of Room 206,
'The Old Mill',
The Madonna Inn
at San Luis Obispo,
California

The Madonna Inn

Umberto Eco

Faith in Fakes: Travels in Hyperreality
(1976)

The poor words with which natural human speech is provided cannot suffice to describe the Madonna Inn. [. . .] Let's say that Albert Speer, while leafing through a book on Gaudí, swallowed an overgenerous dose of LSD and began to build a nuptial catacomb for Liza Minelli. But that doesn't give you an idea. Let's say Arcimboldi builds the Sagrada Familia for Dolly Parton. Or: Carmen Miranda designs a Tiffany locale for the Jolly Hotel chain. Or D'Annunzio's Vittoriale imagined by Bob Cratchit, Calvino's *Invisible Cities* described by Judith Krantz and executed by Leonor Fini for the plush-doll industry, Chopin's Sonata in B flat minor sung by Perry Como in an arrangement by Liberace and accompanied by the Marine Band. No, that still isn't right. Let's try telling about the restrooms. They are in an immense underground cavern, something like Altamira and Luray, with Byzantine columns supporting plaster Baroque cherubs. The basins are big imitation-mother-of-pearl shells, the urinal is a fireplace carved from the rock, but when the jet of urine (sorry, but I have to explain) touches the bottom, water comes down from the wall of the hood, in a flushing cascade something like the Caves of the Planet Mongo. And on the ground floor, in keeping with the air of Tyrolean chalet and Renaissance castle, a cascade of chandeliers in the form of baskets of flowers, billows of mistletoe surmounted by opalescent bubbles, violet-suffused light among which Victorian dolls swing, while the walls are punctuated by Art Nouveau windows with the colours of Chartres and hung with Regency tapestries [. . .] . And all this amid inventions that turn the whole into a multicolour Jell-O, a box of candied fruit, a Sicilian ice, a land for Hansel and Gretel. Then there are the bedrooms, about two hundred of them, each with a different theme: for a reasonable price you can have the Prehistoric Room, all cavern and stalactites, the Safari Room (zebra walls and bed shaped like a Bantu idol), the Kona Rock Room (Hawaiian), the California Poppy, the Old-fashioned Honeymoon, the Irish Hills, the William Tell, the Tall and Short, for mates of different lengths, with the bed in an irregular polygon form, the Imperial Family, the Old Mill.

The Sacred Heart
of Jesus, postcard,
1903

on the following pages
Dimitrij Nalbandjan,
In the Kremlin,
24 May 1945,
Moscow, State Museum

Hubert Lanzinger,
The Flagbearer,
1937,
Washington DC,
National Museum of the
US Army, Army Art
Collection

Statues in the Foro
Italico, Rome,
*c.*1927–34

Those who like kitsch believe they are enjoying a qualitatively high experience. You just have to say that there is one art for the uncultivated just as there is another for the cultivated, and that you have to respect the differences between these two 'tastes' just as you must respect the differences between religious beliefs, or sexual preferences. But while lovers of 'cultivated' art find kitsch kitsch, lovers of kitsch (except when they are faced with works aimed at 'amazing the bourgeoisie') do not disdain the great art of the museums (which nonetheless often exhibit works that cultivated sensibility labels as kitsch). In actual fact they hold that works of kitsch are 'similar' to those of great art. And, while one of the definitions of kitsch sees it as something intended to arouse an emotional effect rather than permit disinterested contemplation, another holds kitsch to be that artistic practice that, to ennoble itself, and to ennoble the purchaser, imitates and quotes the art of the museums. Clement Greenberg said that, whereas the avant-garde (understood generally as art in terms of its capacity to discover and invent) *imitates the art of imitation*, kitsch *imitates the effect of imitation*; in making art the avant-garde emphasises the procedures that lead to the work, and it elects these as the subject of its discourse, while kitsch emphasises the reactions that the work must provoke, and elects as the goal of its own operation the emotional reaction of the user.

William Adolphe
Bouguereau,
The Birth of Venus,
1879,
Paris, Musée d'Orsay

Sir Lawrence
Alma-Tadema,
A Favourite Custom,
1909,
London, Tate Gallery

The interesting
Arthur Schopenhauer
The World as Will and Idea, III: 'The
Platonic Idea: The Object of Art', 40
(1819)

By this, however, I understand that which
excites the will by presenting to it
directly its fulfilment, its satisfaction. We
saw that the feeling of the sublime arises
from the fact, that something entirely
unfavourable to the will becomes the
object of pure contemplation, so that
such contemplation can only be
maintained by persistently turning away
from the will, and transcending its
interests; this constitutes the sublimity of
the character. The charming or attractive,
on the contrary, draws the beholder away
from the pure contemplation which is
demanded by all apprehension of the
beautiful, because it necessarily excites
this will, by objects which directly appeal
to it, and thus he no longer remains pure
subject of knowing, but becomes the
needy and dependent subject of will [. . .]
In historical painting and in sculpture the
charming consists in naked figures,
whose position, drapery, and general
treatment are calculated to excite the
passions of the beholder, and thus pure
aesthetical contemplation is at once
annihilated, and the aim of art is
defeated.

One indirect definition of kitsch comes from **Schopenhauer** when
he outlines the difference between the artistic and the interesting,
this last being understood as art that stimulates the user's senses.
This is why Schopenhauer was critical of seventeenth-century Dutch
painting, which portrayed fruit and set tables, capable of whetting the
appetite rather than inviting contemplation. In the twentieth century,
Hermann Broch wrote against this programmed stimulation of the effect
with even greater moralistic indignation. And there is no doubt that the
label kitsch can be applied to all the late nineteenth-century art known
as *art pompier*, with its voluptuous odalisques, nude studies of classical
divinities and extravagant commemorative historical works.

As for the imitation of 'high' art, in a celebrated essay Dwight MacDonald
contrasted the manifestations of *elite* art with mass culture (masscult)
and petit bourgeois culture (midcult). He wasn't so much criticising
masscult for the spread of what we now call trash television, as midcult
for trivialising the discoveries of true art for commercial ends – attacking
Hemingway's *The Old Man and the Sea*, criticising its artificially lyricising
language and the tendency to portray apparently 'universal' characters (not
'that old man' but 'The Old Man').

Giacomo Grosso,
Female Nude (Nuda),
1896,
Turin, Galleria Civica
d'Arte Moderna
e Contemporanea

The Stylistics of Kitsch

Walther Killy

Deutscher Kitsch (1962) (elaboration of *Pastiche*, utilising lines from six German authors, including Rilke)

The sea whispers in the distance and in the enchanted silence, a wind gently moves the rigid leaves. An opaque silk gown, embroidered in white ivory and gold, flutters around her limbs and affords a glimpse of a tender, sinuous neck, adorned by tresses the colour of fire. The light in Brunhilde's solitary room was still not lit – the slim palms rose up like the dark, fantastic shadows of precious Chinese vases: in the centre the marble bodies of ancient statues glimmered whitely like ghosts, and on the walls you could just barely see the paintings in their large gold frames that gave off subdued reflections. Brunhilde was seated at the pianoforte, sliding her hands over the keys, immersed in sweet daydreams. A 'largo' flowed along in solemn enquiry, melting like veils of smoke over incandescent embers that are undone by the wind, swirling about in bizarre scraps, separated by the flame without essence. Slowly the melody grew majestic, breaking out into powerful chords, turning back on itself with childish, pleading, enchanted, unspeakably sweet voices, with choirs of angels, whispering above nocturnal forests and solitary, deep, fiery red ravines, ancient steles, and playing around the abandoned rural cemeteries. Clear fields open up, springs play with gracefully moving figures, and an old woman, a wicked old woman sits facing autumn while a few leaves fall down around her. Winter will come, great sparkling angels who do not so much as brush against the snow, but are tall as the sky, bend over towards the listening shepherds and sing to them of the fabulous child of Bethlehem.

The celestial enchantment, having had its fill of the secrets of the holy Christmas, is woven around a winter gorge that sleeps in profound peace, and since a harp song is playing in the distance, bewildered amid the sounds of day, as if the very secret of sadness were singing the divine birth. And outside the night wind caresses the golden house with the touch of its tender hands, and the stars wander across the winter night.

The Technique of 'Effect'
Hermann Broch
Kitsch (1933)

The essence of *Kitsch* consists in exchanging the ethical category with the aesthetic category; this obliges the artist to pursue not a 'good' work of art, but a 'beautiful' work of art; what matters to him is beautiful effect. Despite the fact that the *Kitsch* novel often works in a naturalistic sense, and in other words in spite of its abundant use of the vocabulary of reality, it shows the world not 'as it is', but 'as you wish or fear it could be', and an analogous tendency is revealed by *Kitsch* in the figurative arts. In music, *Kitsch* thrives exclusively on effects (consider the so-called light music of the bourgeoisie, and do not forget that today's music industry is, in many ways, an overgrown form of that). How can we avoid concluding that no art can do without a dash of effect, a drop of *Kitsch*?
[. . .]

As a system of imitation *Kitsch* is in fact forced to copy art in all its specific aspects. But, methodologically speaking, it is not possible to imitate the creative act from which art is born: one can only imitate the simpler forms. Another relatively significant and characteristic fact is that, given the lack of its own imagination, *Kitsch* must constantly refer back to more primitive methods (which is extremely clear in poetry, but also, in part, in music). Pornography, in which the vocabulary of reality notoriously consists in sexual acts, is in fact a simple serial alignment of these acts; the detective story does no more than present a series of identical victories over criminals; romantic novels offer an endless number of good rewarded and evil punished (the method that presides over these monotonous articulations of the vocabulary of reality is that of primitive syntax, the constant rhythm of the drum).

If we accept MacDonald's idea, a good example of midcult would be the female portraits made by Boldini. A painter who worked between the nineteenth and twentieth centuries, he was a renowned portraitist known to the high society of his time as 'the ladies' painter'. Those who commissioned him wanted a work of art that was certainly a source of prestige but also one that left no doubts regarding the charms of the lady in question. To this end, Boldini constructed his portraits according to the best rules of the provocation of effect. If you observe his portraits of ladies you will note how the face and shoulders (the uncovered parts) conform to all the canons of sensuous naturalism. The lips of these women are full and moist, their flesh oozes tactility; their gaze is sweet, provocative, sexy or dreamy, always capable of seducing the viewer. Boldini's women do not call up the abstract concept of beauty, nor do they use womanly beauty as a pretext for exercises in plasticity or colour; they represent *that* woman, and to such a point that the viewer is led to desire her.

But as soon as he moves on to paint her clothing, when he moves down from her bodice to the hem of her gown, and thence to the background, Boldini abandons the 'gastronomic' technique of which Schopenhauer accused the Dutch: the outlines are imprecise, the fabrics are broken up by bright brushstrokes, things become clots of colour and objects melt in explosions of light …

The Appeal of Bad Taste
Marcel Proust
Swann's Way: 'Swann in Love' (1913)

Feeling that, often, he could not give her in reality the pleasures of which she dreamed, he tried at least to ensure that she should be happy in his company, tried not to contradict those vulgar ideas, that bad taste which she displayed on every possible occasion, which all the same he loved, as he could not help loving everything that came from her, which even fascinated him, for were they not so many more of those characteristic features, by virtue of which the essential qualities of the woman emerged, and were made visible? And so, when she was in a happy mood because she was going to see the Reine Topaze, or when her eyes grew serious, troubled, petulant, if she was afraid of missing the flower-show, or merely of not being in time for tea, with muffins and toast, at the Rue Royale tea-rooms, where she believed that regular attendance was indispensable, and set the seal upon a woman's certificate of 'smartness', Swann, enraptured, as all of us are, at times, by the natural behaviour of a child, or by the likeness of a portrait, which appears to be on the point of speaking, would feel so distinctly the soul of his mistress rising to fill the outlines of her face that he could not refrain from going across and welcoming it with his lips. 'Oh, then, so little Odette wants us to take her to the flower-show, does she? she wants to be admired, does she? very well, we will take her there, we can but

obey her wishes.' As Swann's sight was beginning to fail, he had to resign himself to a pair of spectacles, which he wore at home, when working, while to face the world he adopted a single eyeglass, as being less disfiguring. The first time that she saw it in his eye, she could not contain herself for joy: 'I really do think – for a man, that is to say – it is tremendously smart! How nice you look with it! Every inch a gentleman. All you want now is a title!' she concluded, with a tinge of regret in her voice. He liked Odette to say these things, just as, if he had been in love with a Breton girl, he would have enjoyed seeing her in her coif and hearing her say that she believed in ghosts. Always until then, as is common among men whose taste for the fine arts develops independently of their sensuality, a grotesque disparity had existed between the satisfactions which he would accord to either taste simultaneously; yielding to the seduction of works of art which grew more and more subtle as the women in whose company he enjoyed them grew more illiterate and common, he would take a little servant-girl to a screened box in a theatre where there was some decadent piece which he had wished to see performed, or to an exhibition of impressionist painting, with the conviction, moreover, that an educated, 'society' woman would have understood them no better, but would not have managed to keep quiet about them so prettily.

Giovanni Boldini,
Fireworks,
1891,
Ferrara,
Museo Giovanni Boldini

The lower part of Boldini's pictures is redolent of Impressionist culture. Boldini *makes art*, quoting from the repertory of those paintings that represented the avant-garde of his own day. So his busts and faces (*meant to be desirable*) emerge from the corolla of a pictorial flower that is meant *only to be looked at*. These women are *stylemic sirens*, with heads and busts intended for consumption and clothes intended for contemplation. The lady portrayed cannot feel uncomfortable at her physical charms having been publicised like those of a courtesan: the rest of her figure has become a stimulus to aesthetic enjoyment, which is clearly of a superior order. The midcult user therefore consumes his lie – and the extent to which he is aware of this, if he is aware of it at all, is immaterial. If the term kitsch has a meaning, it is not because it designates an art that tends to produce effects, because in many cases art sets itself this goal, nor is it an art that uses stylemes that have appeared elsewhere, because this can happen without lapsing into bad taste: *kitsch is a work that, in order to justify its function as a stimulator of effects, flaunts the outward appearance of other experiences, and sells itself as art without reservations.*

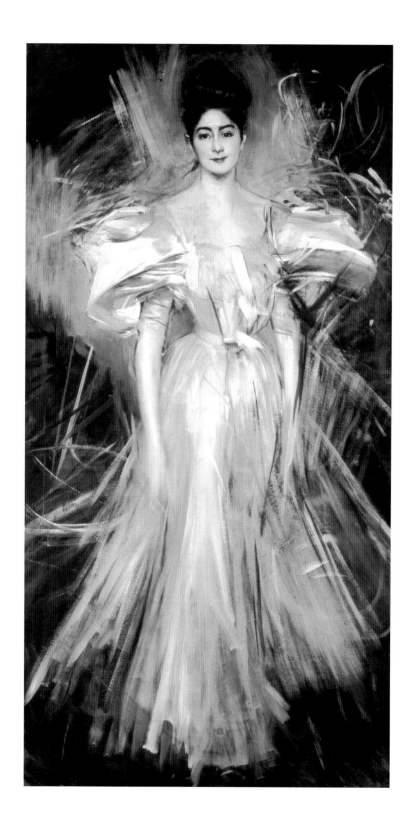

Alexandre Cabanet,
The Birth of Venus,
1863,
Paris, Musée d'Orsay

facing page
Jean Broc,
The Death of Hyacinth,
1801,
Poitiers,
Musée des Beaux Arts

Kitsch as Evil

Hermann Broch
Kitsch

This satisfaction of the impulses obtained with expert and rational means, this endlessly pathetic rendering of the finite, this aiming for the 'beautiful', confers upon *Kitsch* a hint of something false behind which we can glimpse an ethical 'evil' [. . .]

The person who produces *Kitsch* is not one who produces inferior art, not an artist endowed with inferior creative faculties, or even none at all. The producer of *Kitsch* cannot be assessed according to aesthetic criteria but, more simply, must be judged as a contemptible being, as a criminal who wishes evil from the roots. And since that which is manifested in *Kitsch* is a radical evil, i.e. that evil which is in itself related to every other system of values, as an absolute negative pole, *Kitsch* must be considered an evil not only for art, but for every system of values that is not a system of imitation.

A person who labours for love of the beautiful effect, who strives for nothing more than the satisfaction of the affections that make the moment in which he draws a sigh of relief appear 'beautiful' to him – in other words the radical aesthete – believes himself authorised to use, and in effect unhesitatingly employs, any means available in order to achieve the production of this kind of beauty. This is the elephantiasis of *Kitsch*, a spectacle staged by Nero in the imperial gardens with fireworks in the form of the burning bodies of Christians so that he can sing the scene and play his lute (and it is no accident that Nero's fundamental ambition was to become an actor).

All the historical periods in which values undergo a process of disintegration are periods that witness a great flowering of *Kitsch*. The terminal phase of the Roman empire produced *Kitsch*, and the current era, which is nearing the end of a phase in which the concept of the medieval world is dissolving, cannot but be represented by this aesthetic evil as well. Epochs characterised by a definitive loss of values are in fact based upon evil and anxiety over evil, and an art form that aspires to be the appropriate expression of such epochs must also be an expression of the evil at work in them.

3. Camp

I mentioned *art pompier* paintings as examples of kitsch. But today these works are not just on show in museums; they are also sold at very high prices to refined collectors. This might simply be seen as proof that what was ugly yesterday has become beautiful today, as always happens when high culture appropriates products of popular art – and even products of mass culture such as comic books. Originally produced for purposes of entertainment, these are now seen not only as evocative period pieces but as products of outstanding artistic quality.

Nonetheless the recovery of *art pompier* can also be ascribed to another element, namely that taste known as *camp*, and no one has analysed this phenomenon better than Susan Sontag in her 'Notes on Camp' (1964). Camp is a form of sensibility that, rather than transforming the frivolous into the serious (as arguably happened with the canonisation of jazz, originally played in brothels), transforms the serious into the frivolous.

Camp arose as a form of recognition among the members of an intellectual elite, so sure of their refined tastes that they could proclaim the redemption of the bad taste of the past, on the basis of a love for the unnatural and the excessive – and the reference here is to the dandyism of Oscar Wilde for whom being natural 'is such a very difficult pose to keep up', as he wrote in *An Ideal Husband*. Camp is not measured by the beauty of something but on the extent of its artifice and stylisation, and it is not defined so much as a style but as the capacity to consider the style of others. To be camp, objects must possess some exaggeration or marginal aspect (one says 'it's too good or too important to be camp'), as well as a certain degree of vulgarity, even when there is a claim to refinement.

The list of things that Sontag defines as camp or the subject of camp is undoubtedly heterogeneous and ranges from Tiffany lamps to Aubrey Beardsley, from *Swan Lake* and the operas of Bellini to Visconti's direction of *Salomé*, from certain *fin de siècle* postcards to *King Kong*, old Flash Gordon comics, women's dress of the twenties, down to what the most refined cinema critics call the 'ten best bad movies I have ever seen'.

Carlo Crivelli,
Madonna and Child,
*c.*1480,
New York,
Metropolitan Museum
of Art

Other things Sontag defines as camp are a woman walking around in a dress made of three million feathers and the pictures of Carlo Crivelli, with their real jewels, *trompe l'oeil* insects, and fake cracks in the walls – without neglecting the fact that the taste for camp is attracted to sexual ambiguity (see **Camp and Sexuality**). But camp certainly doesn't have what Schopenhauer called the *interesting*, and the camp eye does not look at a *pompier* nude for erotic gratification, but to see and enjoy its pathetic lack of modesty passed off as a return to the sublime immodesty of great classical art.

It cannot be denied that Sontag's choices reflect the tastes of the New York intelligentsia of the sixties (why is Jean Cocteau camp but not André Gide, and Richard Strauss but not Wagner?). Further, the definition is made even more volatile when it is admitted that many examples of camp are kitsch, but camp is not necessarily identified with 'bad art' because Sontag's list also includes great artists such as Crivelli, Gaudí and minor but refined artists such as Erté (and, for reasons that remain unclear, even some works by Mozart).

Niki de Saint-Phalle,
Hon (Lei),
1966,
Stockholm,
National Museet

In any case all camp objects and persons must possess an element of extremism that goes against nature (there's nothing campy in nature). Camp is a love of the eccentric, of things-being-what-they-are-not and the best example of this is art nouveau. This is because the products of art nouveau turn lighting fixtures into flowering plants, living rooms into grottos or vice versa, and cast-iron bars into orchid stems, as in the entries to the Guimard Métro station in Paris.

Camp is also, but not always, the experience of kitsch of someone who knows that what he is seeing is kitsch. In this sense it is a manifestation of aristocratic taste and snobbery: 'and as the dandy is the nineteenth century's surrogate for the aristocrat in matters of culture, so Camp is the modern dandyism. Camp is the answer to the question: how to be a dandy in the age of mass culture?' But whereas the dandy sought out rare sensations, not yet profaned by the appreciation of the masses, the connoisseur of camp is fulfilled by 'the coarsest, commonest pleasures, in the arts of the masses [...] The dandy held a perfumed handkerchief to his nostrils and was liable to swoon; the connoisseur of Camp sniffs the stink and prides himself on his strong nerves.'

411

Camp and Sexuality
Susan Sontag
'Notes on "Camp"' (1964)

The androgyne is certainly one of the great images of Camp sensibility. Examples: the swooning, slim, sinuous figures of pre-Raphaelite painting and poetry; the thin, flowing, sexless bodies in Art Nouveau prints and posters, presented in relief on lamps and ashtrays; the haunting androgynous vacancy behind the perfect beauty of Greta Garbo. Here, Camp taste draws on a mostly unacknowledged truth of taste: the most refined form of sexual attractiveness (as well as the most refined form of sexual pleasure) consists in going against the grain of one's sex. What is most beautiful in virile men is something feminine; what is most beautiful in feminine women is something masculine. [. . .] Allied to the Camp taste for the androgynous is something that seems quite different but isn't: a relish for the exaggeration of sexual characteristics and personality mannerisms. For obvious reasons, the best examples that can be cited are movie stars. The corny flamboyant female-ness of Jayne Mansfield, Gina Lollobrigida, Jane Russell, Virginia Mayo [. . .]

Camp is the triumph of the epicene style. (The convertibility of 'man' and 'woman', 'person' and 'thing'.) But all style, that is, artifice, is, ultimately, epicene. Life is not stylish. Neither is nature. [. . .]

While it's not true that Camp taste *is* homosexual taste, there is no doubt a peculiar affinity and overlap. [. . .] So, not all homosexuals have Camp taste. But homosexuals, by and large, constitute the vanguard – and the most articulate audience – of Camp. [. . .]

(The Camp insistence on not being 'serious', on playing, also connects with the homosexual's desire to remain youthful.) Yet one feels that if homosexuals hadn't more or less invented Camp, someone else would. For the aristocratic posture with relation to culture cannot die, though it may persist only in increasingly arbitrary and ingenious ways.

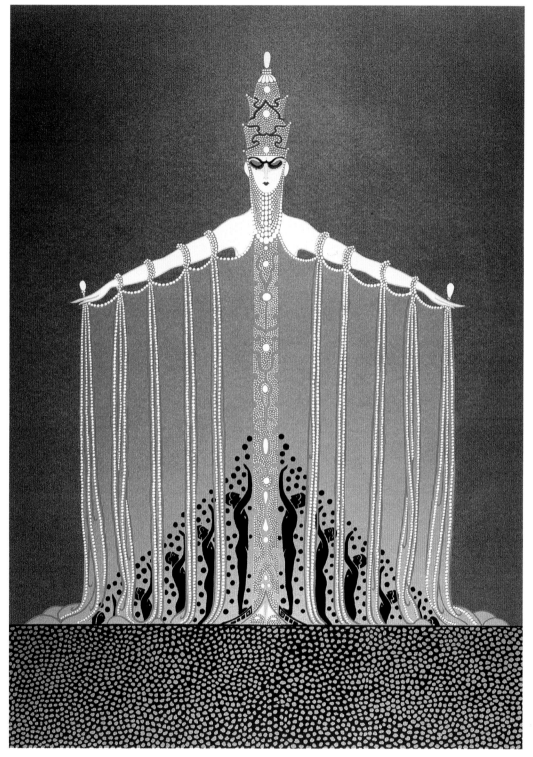

Divine in *Pink Flamingos*,
John Waters (director),
1972

Sontag's study traces the taste for camp back to the remote past, to the
Mannerists, to the Baroque poetics of *wit, witz, agudeza* and wonder, to the
Gothic novel, to the passion for *chinoiserie* or for artificial ruins – and in this
sense it could become the definition of a wider taste, of a permanent form of
Mannerism or the neo-Baroque. This analysis highlights an interesting point:
'we value a work of art because of the seriousness and dignity of what it
achieves', and in appreciating it we identify a correct relationship between
intention and execution, even though there are other forms of artistic
sensibility whose distinctive characteristics are anguish and cruelty, and so we
accept a disparity between intentions and performance. Sontag mentions
Bosch, Sade, Rimbaud, Jarry, Kafka, Artaud, as well as many twentieth-century
artworks, whose aim was not to create harmony but to tackle themes that
were ever more violent and irresolvable.

Joel-Peter Witkin,
Portrait of a Dwarf,
Los Angeles,
1987,
Seattle, Art Museum

And so this analysis leads to the emergence of two important points for any history of ugliness. Sontag points out that the extreme manifestation of camp is the expression 'it's beautiful because it's horrible' – and it's no accident that she devoted an essay to Diane Arbus, the photographer of the ugly. The canon of camp can change and the times can enhance the standing of things that repel us today because they are too close to us: 'What was banal can, with the passage of time, become fantastic.' In this sense camp transforms what was ugly yesterday into today's object of aesthetic pleasure – in an ambiguous play in which it is not clear whether ugliness is redeemed as beauty or whether beauty (as the 'interesting') is reduced to ugliness. 'Camp taste turns its back on the good-bad axis of ordinary aesthetic judgement. Camp doesn't reverse things. It doesn't argue that the good is bad, or the bad is good. What it does is to offer for art (and life) a different – a supplementary – set of standards.'

The Aesthetics of Trash
Andy Warhol
The Philosophy of Andy Warhol (1975)
The most beautiful thing in Tokyo is
McDonalds
The most beautiful thing in Stockholm is
McDonalds
The most beautiful thing in Florence is
McDonalds

Recycling the Leftovers of Others
Andy Warhol
The Philosophy of Andy Warhol (1975)
I'm not saying that popular taste is bad so
that what's left over from bad taste is
good: I'm saying that what's left over is
probably bad, but if you can take it and
make it at least interesting, then you're not
wasting as much as you would otherwise.
You're recycling work and you're recycling
people, and you're running your business
as a by-product of other businesses. Of
other *directly competitive* businesses, as a
matter of fact. So that's a very economical
operating procedure. It's also a very funny
operating procedure because, as I said,
leftovers are inherently funny.

Living in New York city gives people
real incentives to want things that nobody
else wants – to want all the leftover things.
There's so many people to compete with
here that the only hope of getting
anywhere lies in changing your tastes and
wanting what the others don't want:
wanting all the leftover stuff.
[. . .] When we didn't have enough
cash to do full-length features, with those
thousands of cuts and all those shots to be
done over, etc., I tried to simplify the way
we made movies, using every metre of
film we had shot, because it cost less and
it was easier and more fun too. And we
didn't have any out-takes any more. In
1969 we began to edit our movies, but
even then I still preferred the out-takes.
The cut scenes are all magnificent. I still
keep them all. There's only two cases in
which I make exceptions regarding my
philosophy of using leftovers: 1) my dog
and 2) food. I know I should have gone
to the pound to get myself a dog, but I
bought one instead [. . .] I must also
confess that I just can't stand eating
leftovers.

Paul McCarthy,
*Basement Bunker:
Painted Queen Small
Blue Room,*
2003,
© Paul McCarthy,
courtesy of the artist
and Hauser & Wirth,
Zurich and London

It should be said, however, that not all ugliness (old or new as it may be)
can be seen as camp. It is only such when the excess is innocent and not
calculated. Pure examples of camp are not intentional, but extremely serious:
'The Art Nouveau craftsman who makes a lamp with a snake coiled around it
is not kidding, nor is he trying to be charming. He is saying, in all earnestness:
Voilà! the Orient!' Among the various examples of what we now consider as
camp there is opera, where composers have taken in absolute seriousness
the melodramatic absurdities of their librettists (one thinks of famous
passages like 'I hear the footmarks of merciless steps!'). In this case the
delighted reaction of the camp enthusiast is 'It's too much, it's unbelievable!'
You cannot *decide* to make a camp object. Camp cannot be intentional,
it rests on the candour with which the artifice is executed (and, probably, on
the disingenuousness of those who recognise it as such). Camp contains an
element of seriousness that fails to achieve its objective because of an
overdose of passion, or of something excessive in its intentions, and hence
'Gaudí's lurid and beautiful buildings in Barcelona', especially the Sagrada
Familia, reveal 'the ambition on the part of one man to do what it takes a
generation, a whole culture to accomplish'.

In the following chapter we shall see many examples of the *intentional
ugliness* (in part inspired by the concept of camp) aimed at by much of
contemporary art and social convention. Such things are not only ugliness
pursued without innocence, but also deliberately planned. Whereas kitsch
was a lie with respect to 'high' art, the intentional neo-ugly is a lie with
respect to a 'horrible' that camp taste had attempted to redeem.

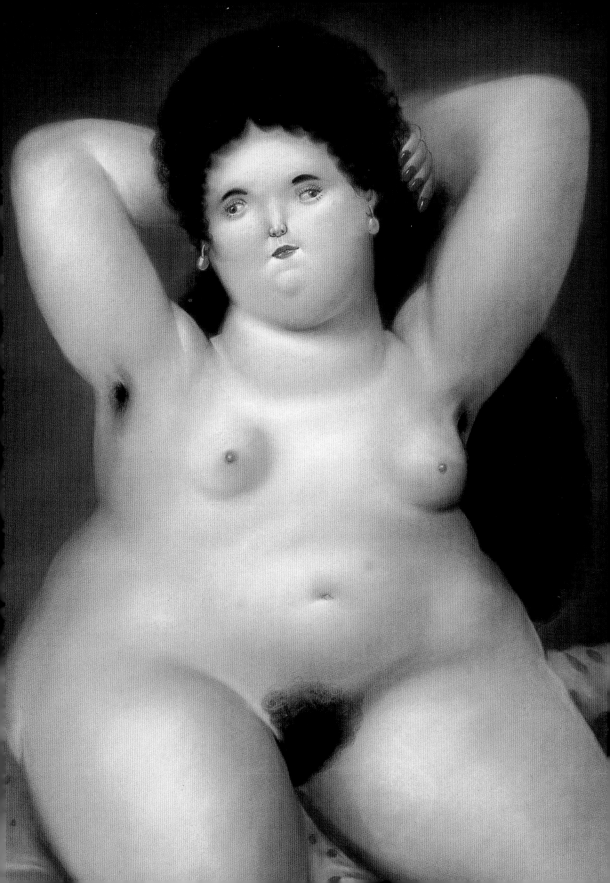

Chapter XV

Ugliness Today

The ancients perceived certain musical intervals as dissonant and therefore unpleasant, and for centuries the classic example of musical ugliness was the *augmented fourth* interval, C–F sharp, for example. In the Middle Ages this dissonance was thought so disturbing that it was defined as *diabolus in musica* (the Devil in music). Psychologists have explained that dissonances have the power to excite, and since the thirteenth century many musicians have used them to produce determined effects in an appropriate context. And so the *diabolus* often served to create effects of tension or instability, the expectancy of some kind of resolution, and it was used by Bach, by Mozart in *Don Giovanni*, by Liszt, Mussorgsky, Sibelius, Puccini (in *Tosca*), and in Bernstein's *West Side Story*. In addition, it was often used to suggest infernal apparitions, as in Berlioz's *Damnation of Faust*.

The case of the *diabolus in musica* provides us with an excellent example with which to conclude this history of ugliness, because it invites certain reflections. Three of these ought to be evident from the preceding chapters: ugliness is relative to the times and to cultures, what was unacceptable yesterday may be acceptable tomorrow, and what is perceived as ugly may contribute, in a suitable context, to the beauty of the whole. The fourth observation leads us to correct the relativist perspective: if the *diabolus* has always been used to create tension, then we have physiological reactions that have remained more or less unchanged through different periods and cultures. The *diabolus* has gradually been accepted not because it has become pleasant, but precisely because of that whiff of sulphur it has *never* lost.

Fernando Botero,
Woman,
1979,
private collection

George Lucas (director),
*Star Wars: Episode II – The
Attack of the Clones,*
2002

For this reason the *diabolus* now appears in much heavy metal music (for example, with Jimi Hendrix in 'Purple Haze'), and sometimes as an explicit 'satanist' provocation (see records like *Diabolus in Musica* by Slayer).

George Romero, the director of *The Night of the Living Dead* and other horror films, once made a statement of his poetics. While he was expatiating on the moving tenderness of Frankenstein's monster, King Kong or Godzilla, he pointed out that his zombies have wrinkled, putrescent skin, black teeth and nails, but that they are individuals with passions and needs just like our own. And he added: 'In my zombie movies, the dead brought back to life represent a kind of revolution, a radical change in the world that many of my human characters can't understand, preferring to label the living dead as the Enemy when in reality they are us. I use blood in all its horrendous magnificence to make the public understand that my movies are more of a sociopolitical chronicle of the times than dumb adventures with a generous dollop of horror.' So, is recourse to ugliness a means of exposing the presence of Evil? Romero himself admits that horror 'makes sales go through the roof' and hence he admits that horror is appreciated because it is interesting and exciting. Not to mention when it becomes the *celebration of Evil*, albeit only in marginal cases like the satanism of psychopaths.

Marina Abramovich
during a
performance
of *Thomas Lips*
(1975–2005)
at the Solomon
R. Guggenheim
Museum
in New York,
14 November 2005

We find ourselves faced with a multitude of contradictions. Monsters that may be ugly but are certainly lovable like ET or the extraterrestrials of *Star Wars* fascinate not only children (who are also won over by dinosaurs, *Pokémon* and other deformed creatures) but also adults, who relax in front of splatter movies where brains are reduced to pulp and blood spurts onto the walls, or amuse themselves by reading horror stories.

You cannot talk only of the 'degeneration' of the mass media, because contemporary art also deals with and celebrates ugliness, but no longer in the provocative way of the avant-garde movements of the early twentieth century. Certain 'happenings' exhibit not only the unattractiveness of a mutilation or a handicap, but artist themselves occasionally subject their own bodies to some form of bloody violation. In these cases, too, artists declare that they want to denounce the many atrocities of our times, but art lovers who go to admire these works or performances in art galleries do so in a spirit of cheerful playfulness. And these are the same users who have not lost the traditional sense of beauty, and take aesthetic pleasure in a fine landscape, a handsome child or a flat screen that shows the canons of the Golden Section.

George A. Romero
(director),
The Night of the Living Dead,
1968

facing page
Steven Spielberg
(director),
ET the Extra-Terrestrial,
1982

Living Dead
Stephen King
'Home Delivery' (1989)
No big deal, at least, until they started to come out in other places as well. No big deal until the first news film ('you may want to ask your children to leave the room,' Tom Brokaw introduced gravely) showed up on network TV, decayed monsters with naked bone showing through their dried skin, traffic accident victims, the morticians' concealing make-up sloughed away so that the ripped faces and bashed-in skulls showed, women with their hair teased into dirt-clogged beehives where worms and beetles still squirmed and crawled, their faces alternately vacuous and informed with a kind of calculating, idiotic intelligence. No big deal until the first horrible stills in an issue of *People* magazine that had been sealed in shrink-wrap and sold with an orange sticker that read NOT FOR SALE TO MINORS! Then it was a big deal.

When you saw a decaying man still dressed in the mud-streaked remnants of the Brooks Brothers suit in which he had been buried tearing at the throat of a screaming woman in a tee-shirt that read PROPERTY OF THE HOUSTON OILERS, you suddenly realised that it may be a very big deal indeed.

That was when the accusations and sabre rattling had started, and for three weeks the entire world had been diverted from the creatures escaping their graves like grotesque moths escaping diseased cocoons by the spectacle of the two great nuclear powers on what appeared to be an undivertible collision course.

Marilyn Manson,
March 2005

The same people today accept the ideas of furnishing design teams, of hotel architecture, and of the entire tourist industry, which sells classically pleasing forms (see the Las Vegas versions of Venetian palazzi, ancient Roman dining rooms, or Moorish architecture), and at the same time choose restaurants or hotels ennobled by twentieth-century avant-garde paintings (genuine or reproductions) that their grandparents would have considered the negation of the ideals of classical antiquity.

We hear repeatedly from all sides that today we coexist with contrasting models because the opposition beautiful/ugly *no longer has any aesthetic value*: ugly and beautiful would be two possible options to be experienced neutrally. This seems to be confirmed by much youth behaviour. The cinema, television and magazines, advertising and fashion all propose models of beauty that are not so different from the ancient ones, and we could easily imagine the faces of Brad Pitt or Sharon Stone, George Clooney or Nicole Kidman portrayed by a Renaissance painter. But the same young people who identify with these ideals (aesthetic or sexual) also go into raptures over rock singers whose features would have struck Renaissance man as repellent. And those same youngsters often make themselves up, tattoo themselves and pierce their flesh with pins so that they look more like Marilyn Manson than Marilyn Monroe.

A group of punks

Gothick
William Gibson
Count Zero (1986)

At least twenty Gothicks postured in the main room, like a herd of baby dinosaurs, their crests of lacquered hair bobbing and twitching. The majority approached the Gothick ideal: tall, lean, muscular, but touched by a certain gaunt restlessness, young athletes in the early stages of consumption. The graveyard pallor was mandatory, and Gothick hair was by definition black. Bobby knew that the few who couldn't warp their bodies to fit the subcultural template were best avoided; a short Gothick was trouble, a fat Gothick homicidal.

Now he watched them flexing and glittering in Leon's like a composite creature, slime mould with a jigsaw surface of dark leather and stainless spikes. Most of them had nearly identical faces, features reworked to match ancient archetypes culled from kino banks.

The Apocalyptic City
Angela Carter
The Passion of New Eve (1977)

I was astonished to see so many beggars in the rank, disordered streets, where crones and drunkards disrupted with rats for possession of the choicest morsels of garbage. It was hot weather the rats loved. I could not slip down to the corner to buy a pack of cigarettes from the kiosk without kicking aside half a dozen of the sleek, black monsters as they came snapping round my ankles. They would line the staircase like a guard of honour to greet me when I came home to the walk-up, cold-water apartment I soon rented on the lower East Side from a young man who went off to India to save his soul. Before he left, he warned me of the imminent heat-death of the universe and advised me to concern myself with spiritual matters, since time was short.

Hieronymus Bosch,
*Details of the Persecutors
of Christ Bearing
the Cross*,
1510–35,
Ghent, Museum voor
Schone Kunsten

facing page
Punk rocker,
May 1998

Cindy Sherman,
Untitled # 250,
1992,
New York, by courtesy
of the artist and Metro
Pictures

In the two preceding pages you can see a comparison between a contemporary example of piercing and two faces painted by Hieronymus Bosch, also pierced by various kinds of rings. But Bosch wanted to portray the persecutors of Christ, and so he painted them as people of his day conceived of barbarians or pirates (and let us not forget that, as late as the nineteenth century, psychiatrists saw tattoos as a sign of degeneracy). Today, piercing and tattoos are thought to be a generational challenge at most but they are certainly not seen (by the majority) as a criminal choice – and a girl with a tongue stud or a tattooed dragon on her exposed belly can take part in a march for peace or for starving children in Africa.

Neither the young nor the old seem to find this contradiction a dramatic one. The late nineteenth-century aesthete who favoured cadaverous beauty, as a challenge to or a rejection of the tastes of the majority, knew he was cultivating what Baudelaire called 'the flowers of evil'. Such people chose the horrible precisely because they had decided to make a choice that set them above the crowds of 'right-minded' people.

But young people who flaunt an illustrated epidermis or spiky blue hair do so to feel *similar* to the others, while their parents who go to the cinema to enjoy scenes previously only visible in anatomy theatres, do so because *così fan tutti.*

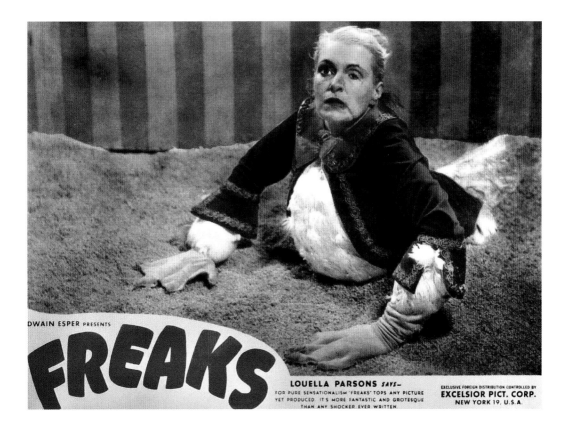

DWAIN ESPER PRESENTS

FREAKS

LOUELLA PARSONS *SAYS—*
FOR PURE SENSATIONALISM "FREAKS" TOPS ANY PICTURE
YET PRODUCED. IT'S MORE FANTASTIC AND GROTESQUE
THAN ANY SHOCKER EVER WRITTEN.

EXCLUSIVE FOREIGN DISTRIBUTION CONTROLLED BY
EXCELSIOR PICT. CORP.
NEW YORK 19, U.S.A.

Tod Browning (director),
Freaks,
1932

Nor is there any difference in the way we take pleasure in (or content ourselves with) so-called trash television. This is not out of elitist posing, which lovers of camp are still prone to (ever-ready to review and collect the films of Ed Wood, defined as the worst director ever to come out of Hollywood), but out of herd instinct. Another case in which we come up against the dissolution of the opposition ugly/beautiful is cyborg 'philosophy'. At first, the image of a human being whose various organs have been replaced with mechanical or electronic apparatus, the result of a symbiosis between man and machine, could still represent a science-fiction nightmare, but with the advent of cyberpunk the prophecy has come true.

What's more, radical feminists like **Donna Haraway** are proposing to overcome gender differences through the creation of neuter, post-organic or 'transhuman' bodies. Does this mean that the clear distinction between beautiful and ugly has disappeared? What if certain behaviour on the part of young people or artists (even though it gives rise to much philosophical debate) were merely marginal phenomena practised by a minority (with respect to the world population)? And what if cyborgs, splatter and the living dead were superficial manifestations, played up by the mass media, through which we exorcise a far more profound ugliness that assails and appals us, something we would wish to ignore?

Frida Kahlo,
The Broken Column,
1944,
Mexico City, Museo
Dolores Olmeto Patiño

following pages
Maurizio Cattelan,
Hanged Children,
2004,
Milan

The Cyberpunk Landscape

William Gibson

Mona Lisa Overdrive (1988)

He'd been scared that the Korsakovs would come back, that he'd forget where he was and drink cancer-water from the slimed red puddles on the rusty plain. Red scum and dead birds floating with their wings spread. The trucker from Tennessee had told him to walk west from the highway, he'd hit two-lane blacktop inside an hour and get a ride down to Cleveland, but it felt like longer than an hour now and he wasn't so sure which way was west and this place was spooking him, this junkyard scar like a giant had stomped it flat. Once he saw somebody far away, up on a low ridge, and waved. The figure vanished, but he walked that way, no longer trying to skirt the puddles, slogging through them, until he came to the ridge and saw that it was the wingless hulk of an airliner half-buried in rusted cans. He made his way up the incline along a path where feet had flattened the cans, to a square opening that had been an emergency exit. Stuck his head inside and saw hundreds of tiny heads suspended from the concave ceiling. He froze there, blinking in the sudden shade, until what he was seeing made some kind of sense. The pink plastic heads of dolls, their nylon hair tied up into topknots and the knots stuck into thick black tar, dangling like fruit. Nothing else, only a few ragged slabs of dirty green foam, and he knew he didn't want to stick around to find out whose place it was. [. . .]

He studied the backs of his hands. Scars, ingrained grime, black half-moons of grease under his broken nails. The grease got in and made them soft, so they broke easy.

The Cyborg Woman

Donna Haraway

'A Cyborg Manifesto: Science, Technology and Socialist-Feminism in the Late Twentieth Century' (1991)

Cyborg monsters in feminist science fiction define quite different political possibilities and limits from those proposed by the mundane fiction of Man and Woman. [. . .]

A cyborg body is not innocent; it was not born in a garden; it does not seek unitary identity and so generate antagonistic dualisms without end (or until the world ends).

[. . .]

Intense pleasure in skill, machine skill, ceases to be a sin, but an aspect of embodiment. The machine is not an it to be animated, worshipped, and dominated. The machine is us, our processes, an aspect of our embodiment. [. . .] Up till now (once upon a time), female embodiment seemed to be given, organic, necessary; and female embodiment seemed to mean skill in mothering and its metaphoric extensions. [. . .] Cyborgs might consider more seriously the partial, fluid, sometimes aspect of sex and sexual embodiment. Gender might not be global identity after all, even if it has profound historical breadth and depth. [. . .]

I would suggest that cyborgs have more to do with regeneration and are suspicious of the reproductive matrix and of most birthing. For salamanders, regeneration after injury, such as the loss of a limb, involves regrowth of structure and restoration of function with the constant possibility of twinning or other odd topographical productions at the site of former injury. The regrown limb can be monstrous, duplicated, potent. [. . .] We require regeneration, not rebirth, and the possibilities for our reconstitution include the utopian dream of the hope for a monstrous world without gender. [. . .] Though both are bound in the spiral dance, I would rather be a cyborg than a goddess.

John Carpenter
(director),
The Thing,
1982

In everyday life we are surrounded by horrifying sights. We see images of children dying of hunger, reduced to skeletons with swollen bellies; we see countries where women are raped by invading troops, and others where people are tortured, just as we are continually exposed to images from the not too distant past of other living skeletons doomed to the gas chambers. We see bodies torn apart by the explosion of a skyscraper or an aeroplane in flight, and we live in terror that tomorrow it may be our turn. We all know perfectly well that such things are *ugly*, not only in the moral but in the physical sense, and we know this because they arouse our disgust, fear, and repulsion – independently of the fact that they can also arouse our compassion, indignation, instinct of rebellion and solidarity, even if we accept them with the fatalism of those who believe that life is none other than a tale told by an idiot, full of sound and fury. No knowledge of the relativity of aesthetic values can eliminate the fact that in such cases we unhesitatingly recognise ugliness and we cannot transform it into an object of pleasure. So we can understand why art in various centuries insistently portrayed ugliness. Marginal as the voice of art may be, it attempted to remind us that, despite the optimism of certain metaphysicians, there is something implacably and sadly malign about this world.

Cover by Barry Godber for the King Crimson album *In the Court of the Crimson King*, 1969

This is why many words and many images in this book have invited us to understand deformity as a human tragedy.

The concluding text by **Italo Calvino** is an excerpt from a short story, but it springs from real experience. The Cottolengo in Turin is an institution full of incurably ill people, persons who cannot even feed themselves without assistance, many of them born as *monsters*, like many of those we have talked about here. Not legendary monsters, but monsters who live ignored alongside us. The main character of the story is an official with the polling station that has been set up in this hospital, because those monsters are citizens too, and, according to the law, they have the right to vote. Distraught by the sight of this subhumanity, the official realises that very many of the patients do not know what to do, and that they will vote according to the will of their helpers. He would like to oppose what strikes him as a fraud, but in the end (against all his civil and political convictions) he concludes that those who have the courage to devote their lives to those unfortunates have acquired the right to speak for them. At the end of this book, after dwelling at such length on the various incarnations of ugliness, I should like to finish with this appeal for compassion.

following pages
Diego Velázquez, *Portrait of the Boy from Vallecas, Francisco Lezcano,* 1642, Madrid, Prado Museum

The Cottolengo
Italo Calvino
'The Watcher' (1963)

A certain number of those registered to vote at the 'Cottolengo' were so ill that they couldn't leave their beds or the ward. In these cases the law provides that from the number of poll clerks in that place some must be chosen to constitute a 'detached polling station'. This group must then go and collect the votes of those who are ill in the 'place of cure', in other words in the place they find themselves [. . .]

One's gaze, on leaving the shadow of the stairwell, was painful, dazzled, or perhaps this was only a defence, almost a refusal to perceive amid the whiteness of every mound of sheets and pillows the form of a human colour that emerged from them; or maybe it was a first translation, from hearing to sight, of the impression of a high-pitched, constant, animal cry: eeeeh . . . eeeeh . . . eeeeh . . . that rose up from some part of the ward, only to be answered from another part by an upsurge like a burst of laughter or a dog baying: haa! haa! haa! haa!

The high-pitched cry came from a tiny red face, all eyes and mouth gaping in a permanent smile, of a boy in bed, wearing a white shirt and sitting up straight. Or rather his upper body sprouted from the bedclothes like a plant growing in a tub, like the stem of a plant that ended (there was no sign of arms) in that fish-like head, and this boy-plant-fish (up to what point can a human being be called human? Amerigo wondered) moved up and down bending flexing his torso with every 'eeeh . . . eeeeh . . .' And the answering 'haa! haa!' came from a person in bed who had even less of a form, yet he had a protruding, avid, congested head, and he must have had arms – or flippers – that moved under the sheets in which he was wrapped up like a sausage (up to what point can a being be called a being, of any species?), and the sound of other voices echoed his, excited perhaps by the appearance of people in the ward, as well as a panting and a moaning, like someone on the verge of crying out

and then immediately smothering it, an adult this time [. . .]

One was a giant with the oversized head of a newborn child held up by pillows: he was motionless, his arms hidden behind his back, his chin resting on a chest that bulged into an obese belly, eyes staring into space, grey hair above a huge forehead (an old being, a survivor of that long foetal development?) dumbfounded by some astounded sorrow [. . .]

In that moment Amerigo was no longer thinking about the pointless reason why he found himself there; it seemed to him that the frontier he was now being asked to control was another: not that of the 'people's will', a dead letter for some time by then, but that of the human sphere [. . .]

A bed at the end of the ward was empty and made up; its occupant, perhaps already convalescing, was sitting on a chair to one side of the bed, wearing woollen pyjamas with a jacket over them, and sitting on the other side of the bed was an old man wearing a hat, certainly his father, come to make his Sunday visit. The son was a young man, mentally retarded, of normal stature but in some way – it seemed – numbed in his movements. The father was shelling almonds for the son, passing them across the bed, and the son took them and slowly brought them up to his mouth. And his father watched him chewing [. . .]

Everything that happened in the ward was separate from the others, as if every bed enclosed a world devoid of communication with the rest, except for the cries that they used to incite one another, *crescendo*, and to communicate general agitation, partly like the noisy twittering of sparrows, partly sorrowful, groaning. Only the man with the huge head kept motionless, as if no sound could get through to him.

Amerigo carried on watching the father and the son. The son had long limbs and a hairy face. He wore a stunned look, perhaps he was half disabled by a paralysis. The father was a countryman dressed up in his Sunday best and, in some way,

especially in the length of his face and hands, he looked like his son. But not the eyes: the son had defenceless, animal eyes, while his father's eyes were hooded and suspicious, like those of old farmers. Their chairs were set at an oblique angle to each other on each side of the bed, so that they could look each other straight in the eye, and they paid no heed to what was going on around them. Amerigo kept his gaze fixed on them, perhaps to take a break from (or shirk) other visits, or perhaps even more, he was in some way fascinated.

In the meantime the others were having a man vote in bed. In this way: they closed the screens, with the little table inside, and, because he was paralysed, a nun voted for him. They removed the screen. Amerigo looked at him: it was a purple face, supine, like a dead man's, with the mouth gaping open, bared gums, eyes open wide. You could not see any more than that face sunk in the pillow; he was hard as wood, apart from a wheeze rattling in the back of his throat. What do they think they're doing, making these people vote?, Amerigo wondered, and only then he remembered that it was up to him to prevent this [. . .]

He wrenched himself away from his thoughts, from that distant frontier zone he had just glimpsed – a frontier between what and what? – and everything that was on this side and on that side seemed like mist. 'Just a moment,' he said, in a toneless voice, aware that he was repeating a formula, talking in the void. Is the elector able to recognise the person who votes for him? Is he able to express his will? [. . .] The nun smiled, but it was a smile that was for everyone and for nothing. The problem of recognition, thought Amerigo, doesn't exist for her; and it came to him to compare the gaze of the old nun with that of the countryman come to spend his Sunday at the Cottolengo staring into the eyes of his idiot son. The nun did not need the recognition of her patients, the good that she drew from them – in exchange for the good that she gave them –was a general good, of which nothing was wasted.

Essential Bibliography

ON UGLINESS IN GENERAL

Adorno, T. W., 'On the Categories of the Ugly, the Beautiful and Technique', in *Aesthetic Theory*. London, 1986

Bodei R., *Le forme del bello*, Bologna, 1995

Bosanquet, B., *A History of Aesthetics*, London, 1892

Calabrese, O., 'Prefazione a Rosenkranz', in *Estetica del brutto*, Milan, 1994

Castelli, E., *Il demoniaco nell'arte*, Milan-Florence, 1952

D'Angelo, P., 'Brutto', in Carchia, G. and D'Angelo, P., eds, *Dizionario di estetica*, Rome-Bari, 1999

Eco U., 'Brutto', in *Enciclopedia Filosofica*, Florence, 1968 (revised edition in *Enciclopedia Filosofica*, Milan, 2006)

Franzini, E. *et al.*, 'Brutto', in *I nomi dell'estetica*, Milan, 2003

Gagnebin, M., *Fascination de la laideur*, Paris, 1978

Krestovsky, L., *La laideur dans l'art à travers les âges*, Paris, 1947

Lalo, Ch., 'La laideur', in *Notions d'esthétique*, Paris, 1952

Lee, V., *Beauty and Ugliness*, London, 1912

Rosenkranz, J. K. F., *Ästhetik des Hässlichen*, Königsberg, 1853

UGLINESS IN THE CLASSICAL WORLD

Garland, R., *The Eye of the Beholder: Deformity and Disability in the Graeco-Roman World*, Ithaca, 1995

Legrand, M.-D. and Picciola, L., eds, *Propos sur les muses et la laideur I. Figurations et défigurations de la beauté (d'Homère aux écrivains des Lumières)*, Nanterre, 2001

Olender, M., 'La laideur d'un dieu', in *En Substance. Textes pour Françoise Héritier*, Paris, 2000

THE MIDDLE AGES, MONSTERS AND PRODIGIES

Baltrušaitis, J., *Medioevo fantastico*, Milan, 1993
Idem, *Risvegli e prodigi*, Milan, 1999

Bettella, P., *The Ugly Woman: Transgressive Aesthetic Models In Italian Poetry From The Middle Ages To The Baroque Author*, Toronto, 2005

Klapper, C., *Demoni mostri e meraviglie alla fine del medioevo*, Florence, 1983

Le Goff, J., *The Medieval Imagination*, Chicago, 1985

Michel, P., *Formosa deformitas. Bewältigungsformen des Hässlichen in Mittelalterlicher Literatur*, Bonn, 1976

Sebenico, S., *I mostri dell'occidente medievale*, Trieste, 2004

Zaganelli, G., *La lettera di Prete Gianni*, Parma, 1990
Idem, *L'oriente incognito medievale*, Catanzaro, 1997

THE DEVIL, WITCHES AND SATANISM

Di Nola, A. M., *Il diavolo*, Rome, 1987

Michelet, J., *La sorcière*, Paris, 1862

Russell, J.B., *Lucifer: The Devil in the Middle Ages*, Ithaca and London, 1986

Trevor-Roper, H.R., *The European Witch-Craze of the Sixteenth and Seventeenth Centuries*, New York, 1967

UGLINESS IN THE RENAISSANCE

Battisti, E., *L'Antirinascimento*, Milan, 1962

Longhi, S., *Lusus. Il capitolo burlesco nel Cinquecento*, Padua, 1983

Ordine, N., *Teoria della novella e teoria del riso nel Cinquecento*, Rome, 1996

Secchi Tarugi, L., ed., *Disarmonia, bruttezza e bizzarria nel Rinascimento*, Florence, 1998

COMIC, OBSCENE, CARICATURE

Almansi, G., *L'estetica dell'osceno*, Turin, 1994

Bakhtin, M., *Rabelais and His World*,
Bloomington, 1984

Bergson, H., Laughter: an Essay
on the Meaning of the Comic,
London, 1911

Camporesi, P., *La maschera di Bertoldo.*
G.C. Croce e la letteratura carnevalesca,
Turin, 1976

Gombrich, 'L'esperimento della
caricatura', in *Arte e illusione*,
Turin, 1965

Merlini, D., ed., *Satira contro il villano*,
Turin, 1894

PHYSIOGNOMY AND TERATOLOGY

Caroli, F., *Storia della fisiognomica*,
Milan, 2002

Daston, L. – Park, K., *Wonders and the*
Order of Nature, 1150–1750,
New York, 1998

Magli, P., *Il volto e l'anima.*
Milan, 1995

UGLINESS AND MANNERISM

Hauser, A., *The Social History of Art*,
London, 1962

Hocke, G. R., *Die Welt als Labyrinth*,
Hamburg, 1957

UGLINESS IN ROMANTIC AESTHETICS

Bodei, R., 'Presentazione a Rosenkranz',
in *Estetica del brutto*,
Bologna, 1984

D'Angelo, P., 'Il brutto, il caratteristico,
il grottesco', in *L'estetica del*
Romanticismo,
Bologna, 1997

Eco, U., 'Sublime', in *Grande Dizionario*
Enciclopedico, vol. 12,
Turin, 1962

Giordanetti, P.–Mazzocut–Mis,M., eds,
Rappresentare il brutto,
Naples, 2006

Giordanetti, P.–Mazzocut–Mis,M., eds.,
I luoghi del sublime moderno,
Led on Line (electronic archive), 2005

Pareyson, L., *L'estetica dell'idealismo*
tedesco,
Turin, 1950

Saint Giron, B., *Fiat lux, une philiosophie*
du sublime,
Paris, 1993

THE UNCANNY

Caillois, R., *Images, images. Essais sur*
le rôle et les pouvoirs de l'imagination,
Paris, 1966

Caillois, R., *Dalla fiaba alla fantascienza*,
Rome, 1985

Franci, G., 'Dal *Gothic Romance*
agli incubi Romantici. Alcune note
sul viaggio del fantastico, dal
meraviglioso al perturbante',
in *Rivista interdisciplinare di studi*
Romantici, n. 3/4, 1977

Freud, S., *The Uncanny*,
in *Complete Psychological Works*,
London, 1955

Werber, N., 'Al limitar del bosco.
Il perturbante nel Romanticismo',
in *Rivista interdisciplinare di studi*
Romantici, n. 3/4, 1977

UGLINESS IN DECADENTISM

Praz, M., *The Romantic Agony*,
New York, 1965

UGLINESS AND THE AVANT-GARDE

Calabrese, O., *L'età neobarocca*,
Rome-Bari, 1997

Dorfles, G., *Elogio della disarmonia*,
Milan, 1986

Eco, U., *The Open Work*,
London, 1989

Longhi, R., *Scultura futurista: Boccioni*,
Florence, 1914

Poggioli, R., *Teoria dell'arte*
d'avanguardia,
Bologna, 1962

Perniola, M., *L'estetica del Novecento*,
Bologna, 1997

INDUSTRIAL UGLINESS

Sedlmayr, H., *Art in Crisis: the Lost*
Centre, London, 1957

Zolla, E., *The Eclipse of the Intellectual*,
New York, 1969

KITSCH AND CAMP

Broch, H., *Il Kitsch*,
Turin, 1990

Dorfles, G., *Kitsch, the World*
of Bad Taste,
New York, 1969

Eco, U., 'The Structure
of Bad Taste', in *The Open Work*,
London, 1989

Giesz, L., *Phaenomenologie des Kitsches,* Heidelberg, 1960

Greenberg, C., 'Avant-Garde and Kitsch', in *Art and Culture. Critical Essays,* Boston, 1961

Moles, A., *Psychologie du kitsch,* Paris, 1971

Sontag, S., 'Notes on Camp', in *Against Interpretation,* 1966

Romero, G., 'Il brutto nel cinema', speech given at the *La Milanesiana* arts festival, ed. 2006 (published in *la Repubblica,* 8.7.2006).

RACISM

Centro Furio Jesi, ed.
*La menzogna della razza.
Documenti e immagini del razzismo
e dell'antisemitismo fascista,*
Bologna, 1994

Gould, S. J., *The Mismeasure of Man,*
New York, 1981

Matard-Botucci, M.-A.,
'La caricature, témoin et vecteur
de l'internationalisation
de l'antisemitisme?
La figure du "juif monde",
in Fortis,U., ed.,
*L'antisemitismo moderno
e contemporaneo,*
Turin, 2004

Pisanty, V., *La difesa della razza,*
Milan, 2006

UGLINESS TODAY

Bodei, R., 'L'estetica del brutto',
in *Enciclopedia Multimediale
delle Scienze Filosofiche,*
1996
(online interview)

Bibliographical References of Translations

Translator's note

Unless otherwise indicated, all the excerpts in the quotations section were translated by me or by my colleague Aaron Maines from Italian versions of the texts in question. This does not apply, obviously, to those texts originally written in English nor to certain public domain translations taken from Internet sources.

While every effort was made to provide an accurate and pleasing rendition of the many poetic works included here, my brief was to give the reader an idea of the content rather than to recreate the poems as poems.

I should like to thank Umberto Eco for helping me out when help was required, as well as Professor Sergio Musitelli, whose invaluable assistance enabled me to interpret some of the passages in archaic Italian. The responsibility for any inaccuracies is of course mine.

Baudelaire, Charles
The Flowers of Evil, 1857, p. 68, 128, 304, 305, 342, 360, 362
Translated by William Aggeler, Fresno, CA: Academy Library Guild, 1954

The Flowers of Evil, 1857, p. 362
Translated by Roy Campbell, *Poems of Baudelaire*, New York: Pantheon Books, 1952

On Hogarth, from 'Some Foreign Caricaturists' in *Selected Writings on Art and Literature*, 1861, p. 252
Translated by P. E. Charvet, Penguin, 1972

Dante
Inferno, Canto 25, p. 86
Inferno, Canto 17, p. 86
Inferno, Canto 6, p. 87
Inferno, Canto 9, p. 87
Inferno, Canto 34, p. 180
Inferno, Canto 20, p. 204
Translated by Henry Wadsworth Longfellow

De Balzac, Honoré
Father Goriot, 1835, p. 286
Translated by Ellen Marriage

Dostoevsky, Fyodor
The Double, V, 1846, p. 320
Translated by Constance Garnett

Eco, Umberto
The Island of the Day Before, p. 233
Translated by William Weaver, Secker & Warburg, 1996

Faith in Fakes, p. 396
Translated by William Weaver, Secker & Warburg, 1986

Foucault, Michel
The History of Sexuality, II, 2, 1976, p. 262
Translated by Robert Hurley

Freud, Sigmund
'The Uncanny', 1919, p. 312
Translated by James Strachey, *The Standard Edition of the Complete Psychological Works of Sigmund Freud*, The Hogarth Press, 1964

Goethe, Wolfgang
Faust, Study, 1773–4, p. 182
Translated by John Shawcross, Allan Wingate, 1959

Faust, 'Valpurgis Night', 1887, p. 212
Translated by Anna Swanwick, New York: P.F. Collier & Son Company, 1909–14

Hegel, Georg Wilhelm Friedrich
Aesthetics: Lectures on Fine Art, I, p. 53, 54
Translated by T. M. Knox

Hippocrates
The Book of Prognostics, 2, p. 250
Translated by Francis Adams

Hoffmann, Ernst Theodor Amadeus
The Sandman, 1816, p. 316
Translated by John Oxenford

Huysmans, Joris-Karl
Là-bas, 1891, p. 219
Translated by Keene Wallace

Against the Grain, 9, 1884, p. 360
Translated by John Howard

Kafka, Franz
In the Penal Colony, 1919, p. 236
Translated by Ian Johnston

A Country Doctor, 1919, p. 305
Translated by Ian Johnston

Nietzsche, Friedrich
'The Problem of Socrates', *Twilight of the Idols*, 1889, p. 262
Translated by Anthony M. Ludovici, published by T. N. Foulis, 1911

Proust, Marcel
The Guermantes Way, 1920, p. 362
Translated by C.K. Scott-Moncrieff

Swann's Way, 1913, p. 404
Translated by C. K. Scott Moncrieff

Rabelais, François
Gargantua and Pantagruel, II, 27, 1532, p. 142
Gargantua and Pantagruel, IV, 67, 1532, p. 143
Gargantua and Pantagruel, II, 16, 1532, p. 143
Gargantua and Pantagruel, I, 13, 1532, p. 144
Translated by J. M.Cohen, Penguin Books, 1955

Rilke, Rainer Maria
Duino Elegies, VII, p. 355
Translated by A. Poulin, First Mariner Books, 2005

Rimbaud, Arthur
Head of a Faun, p. 358
Translated by Oliver Bernard

The Louse Catchers, p. 358
Translated by Elsie Callander

Sartre, Jean-Paul
In Camera, p. 88
Translated by Stuart Gilbert, Hamish Hamilton, 1946

The Words, 1964, p. 300
Translated by Bernard Frechtman, George Braziller, 1964

St Augustine
The Confessions, Book VII, p. 48
Translated by Edward Bouverie Pusey

Tasso, Torquato
Jerusalem Delivered, IV, 1581, p. 180
Translated by Edward Fairfax (1560–1635); translation first published in London in 1600

Index of Authors and Other Sources

Index of Artists

449

Credits